D1564769

THE FATHERS
OF THE CHURCH

A NEW TRANSLATION

VOLUME 121

THE FATHERS OF THE CHURCH

A NEW TRANSLATION

ST. JEROME

COMMENTARY ON GALATIANS

Translated by

ANDREW CAIN

THE CATHOLIC UNIVERSITY OF AMERICA PRESS
Washington, D.C.

LIBRARY OF CONGRESS CATALOGING-IN-PUBLICATION DATA
Jerome, Saint, d. 419 or 20.
[Commentarius in Ep. ad Galatas. English]
Commentary on Galatians / St. Jerome ; translated by Andrew Cain.
p. cm. — (The fathers of the church ; v. 121)
Includes bibliographical references and indexes.
ISBN 978-0-8132-0121-4 (cloth : alk. paper)
1. Bible. N.T. Galatians—Commentaries.   I. Cain, Andrew.   II. Title.
BR65.J473C6413 2011
227'.4077—dc22
2010021325

CONTENTS

ABBREVIATIONS

AAAD	*Antichità altoadriatiche*
AClass	*Acta Classica: Proceedings of the Classical Association of South Africa*
AEHE V	*Annuaire de l'École pratique des hautes études, Ve sec., sciences religieuses*
AnnSE	*Annali di storia dell'esegesi*
AS	*Anatolian Studies*
AugStud	*Augustinian Studies*
Bib	*Biblica*
BSAF	*Bulletin de la société nationale des antiquaires de France*
CCSL	Corpus Christianorum, Series Latina
CQ	*Classical Quarterly*
CSQ	*Cistercian Studies Quarterly*
CSEL	Corpus Scriptorum Ecclesiasticorum Latinorum
FOTC	Fathers of the Church, Washington, DC: The Catholic University of America Press, 1947–
FZPhTh	*Freiburger Zeitschrift für Philosophie und Theologie*
GB	*Grazer Beiträge*
GCS	Die griechischen christlichen Schriftsteller der ersten drei Jahrhunderte
GIF	*Giornale italiano di filologia*
HSCP	*Harvard Studies in Classical Philology*
HThR	*Harvard Theological Review*
JAOS	*Journal of the American Oriental Society*
JbAC	*Jahrbuch für Antike und Christentum*
JBL	*Journal of Biblical Literature*
JECS	*Journal of Early Christian Studies*
JJP	*Journal of Juristic Papyrology*
JR	*Journal of Religion*
JThS	*Journal of Theological Studies*
MedSec	*Medicina nei Secoli*

MP	*Medieval Prosopography*
NICNT	New International Commentary on the New Testament
NIGTC	New International Greek Testament Commentary
NovTest	*Novum Testamentum*
NT	New Testament
NTA	*New Testament Apocrypha*, ed. W. Schneemelcher, 2 vols.
OCP	*Orientalia christiana periodica*
OCT	Oxford Classical Texts
OT	Old Testament
PAAJR	*Proceedings of the American Academy for Jewish Research*
PG	Patrologia Graeca, ed. J.-P. Migne, Paris, 1857–66
PL	Patrologia Latina, ed. J.-P. Migne, Paris, 1878–90
RBén	*Revue bénédictine*
REA	*Revue des études anciennes*
REAug	*Revue des études augustiniennes*
RHE	*Revue d'histoire ecclésiastique*
RhM	*Rheinisches Museum für Philologie*
RHPhR	*Revue d'histoire et de philosophie religieuses*
RicSRel	*Ricerche di storia religiosa*
RSCr	*Rivista di storia del cristianesimo*
RSR	*Revue des sciences religieuses*
RThPh	*Revue de théologie et de philosophie*
SC	Sources chrétiennes, Paris: Éditions du Cerf, 1942–
SCO	*Studi Classici e Orientali*
SecCent	*Second Century*
SicGymn	*Siculorum gymnasium*
SJOT	*Scandinavian Journal of the Old Testament*
StudPatr	*Studia patristica*
ThTo	*Theology Today*
ThZ	*Theologische Zeitschrift*
TRE	*Theologische Realenzyklopädie*, Berlin: Walter de Gruyter, 1976–
TZ	*Trierer Zeitschrift für Geschichte und Kunst des Trierer Landes und seiner Nachbargebiete*
VChr	*Vigiliae christianae*
VetChr	*Vetera christianorum*
ZAC	*Zeitschrift für Antikes Christentum*
ZNTW	*Zeitschrit für Neutestamentliche Wissenschaft*

SELECT BIBLIOGRAPHY

Texts and Translations
Jerome

Antin, P., ed. *Sancti Hieronymi Presbyteri Opera: Hebraicae quaestiones in libro Geneseos, Liber interpretationis hebraicorum nominum.* CCSL 78. Turnhout: Brepols, 1959.

Bareille, L'Abbé. *Œuvres complètes de saint Jérôme*, vol. 10. Paris: Vivès, 1884. Pp. 225–373.

Ceresa-Gastaldo, A., ed. and trans. *Gerolamo, Gli Uomini Illustri (De viris illustribus).* Florence: Nardini, 1988.

Halton, T., trans. *St. Jerome, On Illustrious Men.* FOTC 100. Washington, DC: The Catholic University of America Press, 2000.

Hayward, C. T. R., trans. *Jerome's Hebrew Questions on Genesis.* Oxford: Oxford University Press, 1995.

Heine, R., trans. *The Commentaries of Origen and Jerome on St. Paul's Epistle to the Ephesians.* Oxford: Oxford University Press, 2002.

Hilberg, I., ed. *Sancti Hieronymi Epistulae.* CSEL 54–56. Vienna: F. Tempsky, 1910–18.

Hritzu, J. N. *St. Jerome, Dogmatic and Polemical Works.* FOTC 53. Washington, DC: The Catholic University of America Press, 1965.

Hurst, D., and M. Adriaen, eds. *Sancti Hieronymi Presbyteri Commentariorum in Mathaeum libri IV.* CCSL 77. Turnhout: Brepols, 1969.

Morin, G., ed. *Sancti Hieronymi Presbyteri Tractatus sive homiliae in Psalmos, in Marci Evangelium aliaque varia argumenta.* CCSL 78. Turnhout: Brepols, 1959.

Raspanti, G., ed. *Sancti Hieronymi Presbyteri Commentarii in Epistulam Pauli Apostoli ad Galatas.* CCSL 77A. Turnhout: Brepols, 2006.

Schneemelcher, W., ed. *New Testament Apocrypha.* 2 vols. Louisville: John Knox Press, 1989.

Other Patristic Writers

Amacker, R., and É. Junod, eds. and trans. *Pamphile et Eusèbe de Césarée, Apologie pour Origène. Texte critique, traduction et notes.* Vol. 1. SC 464. Paris: Éditions du Cerf, 2002.

Bruyn, T. de, trans. *Pelagius' Commentary on St. Paul's Epistle to the Romans.* Oxford: Oxford University Press, 1993.

Chadwick, H., trans. *Origen: Contra Celsum.* Cambridge: Cambridge University Press, 1965.

Cooper, S. A., trans. *Marius Victorinus' Commentary on Galatians: Introduction, Translation, and Notes.* Oxford: Oxford University Press, 2005.

Devreesse, R., ed. *Les anciens commentateurs grecs de l'Octateuque et des Rois (fragments tirés des chaînes).* Vatican City: Biblioteca Apostolica Vaticana, 1959.

Doutreleau, L., ed. and trans. *Didyme l'Aveugle: Traité du Saint-Esprit. Introduction, texte critique, traduction, notes et index.* SC 386. Paris: Éditions du Cerf, 1992.

Edwards, M., ed. *Ancient Christian Commentary on Scripture: Galatians, Ephesians, Philippians.* Downers Grove: InterVarsity Press, 1999.

Frede, H. J., ed. *Ein neuer Paulustext und Kommentar,* 1. *Untersuchungen;* 2. *Die Texte.* Freiburg: Herder, 1973–74.

Goltz, E. F. von der, ed. *Eine textkritische Arbeit des zehnten bezw. sechsten Jahrhunderts herausgegeben nach einem Kodex des Athlosklosters Lawra.* Leipzig: Hinrichs, 1899.

Heine, R., trans. *Origen, Homilies on Genesis and Exodus.* FOTC 71. Washington, DC: The Catholic University of America Press, 1982.

Hill, R. C. *Didymus the Blind, Commentary on Zechariah.* FOTC 111. Washington, DC: The Catholic University of America Press, 2006.

Plumer, E., trans. *Augustine's Commentary on Galatians: Introduction, Text, Translation, and Notes.* Oxford: Oxford University Press, 2003.

Scheck, T., trans. *Origen, Commentary on the Epistle to the Romans, Books 1–5.* FOTC 103. Washington, DC: The Catholic University of America Press, 2001.

———. *Origen, Commentary on the Epistle to the Romans, Books 6–10.* FOTC 104. Washington, DC: The Catholic University of America Press, 2002.

Simbeck, K., and O. Plasberg, eds. *M. Tulli Ciceronis scripta quae manserunt omnia, fasc. 47: Cato maior, Laelius, De gloria.* Berlin: Teubner, repr. 1997.

Simonetti, M., trans. *Origene: Omelie sul Cantico dei Cantici.* Milan: Città Nuova, 1998.

Staab, K., ed. *Pauluskommentare aus der griechischen Kirche aus Katenenhandschriften gesammelt und herausgegeben.* Münster: Aschendorff, 1933.

Tappert, T. G., trans. *Luther's Works,* vol. 54: *Table Talk.* Philadelphia: Fortress Press, 1967.

Secondary Works

Modern Studies on Jerome

Adkin, N. "Gregory of Nazianzus and Jerome: Some Remarks." In M. Flower and M. Toher, eds. *Georgica. Greek Studies in Honour of George Cawkwell.* London: Institute of Classical Studies, University of London, 1991. Pp. 13–24.

———. "The Date of the Dream of Saint Jerome." *SCO* 43 (1993): 263–73.

———. "Terence's *Eunuchus* and Jerome." *RhM* 137 (1994): 187–95.

———. "'Heri catechumenus, hodie pontifex' (Jerome, *Epist.* 69.9.4)." *AClass* 36 (1993): 113–17.

———. "Hieronymus Sallustianus." *GB* 24 (2005): 93–110.

———. "Hieronymus Eunuchinus." *GIF* 58 (2006): 327–34.

Antin, P. "*Hilarius latinae eloquentiae Rhodanus* (Jérôme, *In Gal.* prol. 2)." *Orpheus* 13 (1966): 3–25.

Arns, P. E. *La technique du livre d'après saint Jérôme.* Paris: Boccard, 1953.

Bammel, C. P. "Die Pauluskommentare des Hieronymus: die ersten wissenschaftlichen lateinischen Bibelkommentare?" In *Cristianesimo Latino e cultura Greca sino al sec. IV, XXI Incontro di studiosi dell'antichità cristiana, Rome 7–9 maggio 1992.* Rome: Institutum Patristicum Augustinianum, 1993. Pp. 187–207.

Bardy, G. "Saint Jérôme et ses maîtres hébreux." *RBén* 46 (1934): 145–64.

Brown, D. *Vir Trilinguis. A Study in the Biblical Exegesis of Saint Jerome.* Kampen: Kok Pharos Publishing, 1992.

Bulic, F. "Stridone luogo natale di S. Girolamo." In *Miscellanea Geronimiana. Scritti varii pubblicati nel XV centenario dalla morte di San Girolamo.* Rome: Tipografia Poliglotta Vaticana, 1920. Pp. 253–330.

Cain, A. "Defending Hedibia and Detecting Eusebius: Jerome's Correspondence with Two Gallic Women (*Epp.* 120–121)." *MP* 24 (2003): 15–34.

———. "Miracles, Martyrs, and Arians: Gregory of Tours' Sources for his Account of the Vandal Kingdom." *VChr* 59 (2005): 412–37.

———. "In Ambrosiaster's Shadow: A Critical Re-evaluation of the Last Surviving Letter-exchange between Pope Damasus and Jerome." *REAug* 51 (2005): 257–77.

———. "*Vox clamantis in deserto:* Rhetoric, Reproach, and the Forging of Ascetic Authority in Jerome's Letters from the Syrian Desert." *JThS,* n.s., 57 (2006): 500–25.

———. "Origen, Jerome, and the *Senatus Pharisaeorum.*" *Latomus* 65 (2006): 727–34.

———. "*Liber manet:* Pliny, *Epist.* 9.27.2 and Jerome, *Epist.* 130.19.5." *CQ,* n.s., 58 (2008): 708–10.

———. *The Letters of Jerome: Asceticism, Biblical Exegesis, and the Construction of Christian Authority in Late Antiquity.* Oxford: Oxford University Press, 2009.

———. "Jerome's *epistula* 117 on the *subintroductae:* Satire, Apology, and Ascetic Propaganda in Gaul." *Augustinianum* 49 (2009): 119–43.

———. "Rethinking Jerome's Portraits of Holy Women." In Cain and Lössl, eds. *Jerome of Stridon.* Pp. 47–57.

———. "Tertullian, Cyprian, and Lactantius in Jerome's *Commentary on Galatians.*" *REAug* 55 (2009): 23–51.

————. "Jerome's *Epitaphium Paulae*: Hagiography, Pilgrimage, and the Cult of Saint Paula." *JECS* 19 (2010): 105–39.

————. "An Unidentified Patristic Quotation in Jerome's *Commentary on Galatians* (3.6.11)." *JThS*, n.s., 61 (2010): 216–25.

————. "Gregory of Elvira, Lactantius, and the Reception of the *De ira Dei*." *VChr* 64 (2010): 109–14.

————. "Three Further Echoes of Lactantius in Jerome." *Philologus* 154 (2010): 88–96.

————. "Aelred of Rievaulx and Jerome's *Commentary on Galatians*." *CSQ* 45 (2010): 3–6.

————. "Terence in Late Antiquity." In *A Companion to Terence*. Edited by A. Agoustakis and J. Thorburn. Malden, MA: Wiley-Blackwell, 2012. Forthcoming.

————. "Jerome's Pauline Commentaries between East and West: Tradition and Innovation in the *Commentary on Galatians*." In *Interpreting the Bible and Aristotle: The Alexandrian Commentary Tradition between Rome and Baghdad*. Edited by J. Watt and J. Lössl. Aldershot: Ashgate Publishing, 2012. Forthcoming.

Cain, A., and N. Lenski, eds. *The Power of Religion in Late Antiquity*. Aldershot: Ashgate Publishing, 2009.

Cain, A., and J. Lössl, eds. *Jerome of Stridon: His Life, Writings and Legacy*. Aldershot: Ashgate Publishing, 2009.

Canellis, A. "Saint Jérôme et les passions: Sur les *quattuor perturbationes* des Tusculanes." *REAug* 54 (2000): 178–203.

————. "Le livre III de l'*In Zachariam* de Saint Jérôme et la tradition alexandrine." *Adamantius* 13 (2007): 66–81.

————. "L'*In Zachariam* de Jérôme et la Tradition Alexandrine." In Cain and Lössl, eds. *Jerome of Stridon*. Pp. 153–62.

Cavallera, F. *Saint Jérôme: Sa vie et son oeuvre*. 2 vols. Paris: E. Champion, 1922.

Ceresa-Gastaldo, A. "La tecnica biografica del *De viris illustribus* di Girolamo." *Renovatio* 14 (1979): 221–36.

Clark, E. "The Place of Jerome's Commentary on Ephesians in the Origenist Controversy: The *Apokatastasis* and Ascetic Ideals." *VChr* 41 (1987): 154–71.

Curran, J. *Pagan City and Christian Capital. Rome in the Fourth Century*. Oxford: Oxford University Press, 2000.

Deniau, F. "Le commentaire de Jérôme sur Ephésiens nous permet-il de connaître celui d'Origène?" In H. Crouzel, G. Lomiento, and J. Ruis-Camps, eds. *Origeniana: Premier colloque international des études origéniennes (Montserrat, 18–21 septembre 1973)*. Bari: Università di Bari, 1975. Pp. 163–79.

Duval, Y.-M., ed. *Jérôme entre l'Occident et l'Orient: XVIe centenaire du départ de saint Jérôme de Rome et de son installation à Bethléem. Actes du colloque de Chantilly, septembre 1986*. Paris: Institut d'Études Augustiniennes, 1988.

————. *La décrétale* Ad Gallos Episcopos: *son texte et son auteur. Texte critique, traduction française et commentaire.* Leiden: E. J. Brill, 2005.

Feichtinger, B. *Apostolae apostolorum. Frauenaskese als Befreiung und Zwang bei Hieronymus.* Frankfurt am Main: P. Lang, 1995.

Fodor, I. "Le lieu d'origine de S. Jérôme: reconsidération d'une vieille controverse." *RHE* 81 (1986): 498–500.

Fontaine, J. "Un sobriquet perfide de Damase, *matronarum auriscalpius.*" In D. Porte and J.-P. Néraudau, eds. *Hommages à Henri le Bonniec. Res sacrae.* Brussels: Latomus, 1988. Pp. 177–92.

Friedmann, H. *A Bestiary for Saint Jerome: Animal Symbolism in European Religious Art.* Washington, DC: Smithsonian Institution Press, 1980.

Fürst, A. *Augustins Briefwechsel mit Hieronymus.* Münster: Aschendorff, 1999.

————. *Hieronymus: Askese und Wissenschaft in der Spätantike.* Freiburg: Herder, 2003.

————. "Jerome Keeping Silent: Origen and His Exegesis of Isaiah." In Cain and Lössl, eds. *Jerome of Stridon.* Pp. 141–52.

Graves, M. *Jerome's Hebrew Philology: A Study based on his Commentary on Jeremiah.* Leiden: E. J. Brill, 2007.

Grützmacher, G. *Hieronymus: Eine biographische Studie zur alten Kirchengeschichte.* 3 vols. Berlin: Dieterich, 1901–8.

Hagendahl, H. *The Latin Fathers and the Classics: A Study on the Apologists, Jerome, and Other Christian Writers.* Göteborg: Elanders Boktryckeri Aktiebolag, 1958.

————. "Die Bedeutung der Stenographie für die spätlateinische christliche Literatur." *JbAC* 14 (1971): 24–38.

Hamblenne, P. "L'apprentissage du grec par Jérôme: quelques ajustements." *REAug* 40 (1994): 353–64.

Helm, R. "Hieronymus und Eutrop." *RhM* 76 (1927): 138–70 and 254–306.

Hinson, E. G. "Women Biblical Scholars in the Late Fourth Century: The Aventine Circle." *StudPatr* 23 (1997): 319–24.

Hunter, D. G. "The Raven Replies: Ambrose's *Letter to the Church at Vercelli* (*Ep. ex. coll.* 14) and the Criticisms of Jerome." In Cain and Lössl, eds. *Jerome of Stridon.* Pp. 175–89.

Jay, P. "Jérôme auditeur d'Apollinaire de Laodicée à Antioche." *REAug* 20 (1974): 36–41.

————. "La datation des premières traductions de l'Ancien Testament sur l'hébreu par saint Jérôme." *REAug* 28 (1982): 208–12.

————. *L'exégèse de saint Jérôme d'après son Commentaire sur Isaïe.* Paris: Institut d'Études Augustiniennes, 1985.

————. "Combien Jérôme a-t-il traduit d'homélies d'Origène?" *StudPatr* 23 (1989): 133–37.

Jeanjean, B. *Saint Jérôme et l'hérésie.* Paris: Institut d'Études Augustiniennes, 1999.

————. "Le *Dialogus Attici et Critobuli* de Jérôme en Palestine entre 411 and 415." In Cain and Lössl, eds. *Jerome of Stridon.* Pp. 59–71.

Kamesar, A. *Jerome, Greek Scholarship, and the Hebrew Bible: A Study of the Quaestiones Hebraicae in Genesim*. Oxford: Oxford University Press, 1993.

Kelly, J. N. D. *Jerome: His Life, Writings, and Controversies*. London: Harper & Row, 1975.

King, D. "*Vir Quadrilinguis?* Syriac in Jerome and Jerome in Syriac." In Cain and Lössl, eds. *Jerome of Stridon*. Pp. 209–23.

Krumeich, C. *Hieronymus und die christlichen feminae clarissimae*. Bonn: Habelt, 1993.

———. *Paula von Rom. Christliche Mittlerin zwischen Okzident und Orient*. Bonn: Habelt, 2002.

Lançon, B. "Maladie et médecine dans la correspondance de Jérôme." In Duval, ed. *Jérôme entre l'Occident et l'Orient*. Pp. 355–66.

Laurence, P. *Jérôme et le nouveau modèle féminin. La conversion à la vie parfaite*. Paris: Institut d'Études Augustiniennes, 1997.

Letsch-Brunner, S. *Marcella—Discipula et Magistra. Auf den Spuren einer römischen Christin des 4. Jahrhunderts*. Berlin: Walter de Gruyter, 1998.

Lössl, J. "Who attacked the Monasteries of Jerome and Paula in 416 AD?" *Augustinianum* 44 (2004): 91–112.

———. "Martin Luther's Jerome: New Evidence for a Changing Attitude." In Cain and Lössl, eds. *Jerome of Stridon*. Pp. 237–51.

Lübeck, E. *Hieronymus quos noverit scriptores et ex quibus hauserit*. Leipzig, 1872.

Mathisen, R. "The Use and Misuse of Jerome in Gaul during Late Antiquity." In Cain and Lössl, eds. *Jerome of Stridon*. Pp. 191–208.

Moreschini, C. "L'utilizzazione di Porfirio in Gerolamo." In C. Moreschini and G. Menestrina, eds. *Motivi letterari ed esegetici in Gerolamo: Atti del convegno tenuto a Trento il 5–7 dicembre 1995*. Brescia: Morcelliana, 1997. Pp. 175–95.

Murphy, F. X., ed. *A Monument to Saint Jerome: Essays on Some Aspects of his Life, Works and Influence*. New York: Sheed & Ward, 1952.

Nautin, P. "L'excommunication de saint Jérôme." *AEHE V* 80/81 (1972–73): 7–37.

———. *Origène: Sa vie et son œuvre* (Paris: Beauchesne, 1977).

———. "La date des commentaires de Jérôme sur les épîtres pauliniennes." *RHE* 74 (1979): 5–12.

———. "L'activité littéraire de Jérôme de 387 à 392." *RThPh* 115 (1983): 247–59.

Newman, H. I. "Jerome's Judaizers." *JECS* 9 (2001): 421–52.

———. "How Should We Measure Jerome's Hebrew Competence?" In Cain and Lössl, eds. *Jerome of Stridon*. Pp. 131–40.

Niedermann, M. "Le lieu de naissance de saint Jérôme." In M. Niedermann, *Recueil Max Niedermann*. Neuchâtel: Secrétariat de l'Université, 1954. Pp. 248–51.

O'Connell, J. P. *The Eschatology of Saint Jerome*. Mundelein, IL: St. Mary of the Lake Seminary Press, 1948.

Opelt, I. "Hieronymus' Leistung als Literarhistoriker in der Schrift *De viris illustribus.*" *Orpheus,* n.s., 1 (1980): 52–75.

———. "S. Girolamo ed i suoi maestri ebrei." *Augustinianum* 28 (1988): 327–38.

Pabel, H. M. *Herculean Labours: Erasmus and the Editing of St. Jerome's Letters in the Renaissance.* Leiden: E. J. Brill, 2008.

Pricoco, S. "Motivi polemici e prospettive classicistiche nel *De viris illustribus* di Girolamo." *SicGymn* 32 (1979): 69–99.

Raspanti, G. "San Girolamo e l'interpretazione occidentale di *Gal* 2,11–14." *REAug* 49 (2003): 297–321.

———. "*Adgrediar opus intemptatum.* L'*Ad Galatas* di Girolamo e gli sviluppi del commentario biblico latino." *Adamantius* 10 (2004): 194–216.

———. "L'esegesi della lettera ai Galati nel IV secolo d.C. Dal commentario dottrinale di Mario Vittorino ed Ambrosiaster a quello filologico di Girolamo." *Ho Theològos* 25 (2007): 109–28.

———. "The Significance of Jerome's *Commentary on Galatians* in his Exegetical Production." In Cain and Lössl, eds. *Jerome of Stridon.* Pp. 163–71.

Rebenich, S. *Hieronymus und sein Kreis: Prosopographische und sozialgeschichtliche Untersuchungen.* Stuttgart: Steiner, 1992.

———. "Jerome: the *vir trilinguis* and the *Hebraica veritas.*" *VChr* 47 (1993): 50–77.

———. "Asceticism, Orthodoxy and Patronage: Jerome in Constantinople." *StudPatr* 33 (1997): 358–77.

———. *Jerome.* London: Routledge, 2002.

———. "Inventing an Ascetic Hero: Jerome's *Life of Paul the First Hermit.*" In Cain and Lössl, eds. *Jerome of Stridon.* Pp. 13–27.

Rice, E. F. *Saint Jerome in the Renaissance.* Baltimore: Johns Hopkins University Press, 1985.

Ridderbos, B. *Saint and Symbol: Images of Saint Jerome in Early Italian Art.* Groningen: Bouma, 1984.

Rocca, G. *L'Adversus Helvidium di san Girolamo nel contesto della letteratura ascetico-mariana del secolo IV.* Bern: Peter Lang, 1998.

Roswell, H. T. "A Quotation from Marcus Caelius Rufus in St. Jerome, *In Galatas* III 5, 509." *Eranos* 57 (1959): 59–61.

Rousseau, P. "Jerome on Jeremiah: Exegesis and Survival." In Cain and Lössl, eds. *Jerome of Stridon.* Pp. 73–83.

Russo, D. *Saint Jérôme en Italie: Étude d'iconographie et de spiritualité (XIIIe–XVe siècle).* Rome: École Française de Rome, 1987.

Schatkin, M. "The Influence of Origen upon St. Jerome's Commentary on Galatians." *VChr* 24 (1970): 49–58.

Steinhausen, J. "Hieronymus und Laktanz in Trier." *TZ* 20 (1951): 126–54.

Testard, M. "Les dames de l'Aventin, disciples de saint Jérôme." *BSAF* (1996): 39–63.

Vessey, M. "Conference and Confession: Literary Pragmatics in Augustine's '*Apologia contra Hieronymum*.'" *JECS* 1 (1993): 175–213.

Vogels, H. "Ambrosiaster und Hieronymus," *RBén* 66 (1956): 14–19.

Wiesen, D. S. *St. Jerome as a Satirist: A Study in Christian Latin Thought and Letters.* Ithaca: Cornell University Press, 1964.

Williams, M. H. *The Monk and the Book: Jerome and the Making of Christian Scholarship.* Chicago: University of Chicago Press, 2006.

Patristic History, Literature, and Biblical Interpretation

Adkin, N. "Pride or Envy? Some Notes on the Reason the Fathers Give for the Devil's Fall." *Augustiniana* 34 (1984): 349–51.

———. "The Shadow and the Truth: An Unidentified Antithesis in the Fathers." *GIF* 36 (1984): 245–52.

———. "The Fathers on Laughter." *Orpheus,* n.s., 6 (1985): 149–52.

Bardy, G. "*Tractare, Tractatus.*" *RSR* 33 (1946): 211–35.

Barnes, T. D. *Tertullian: A Historical and Literary Study.* Oxford: Oxford University Press, 1971.

Borzì, S. "Sull'attribuzione della Disputa fra Giasone e Papisco ad Aristone di Pella." *VetChr* 41 (2004): 347–54.

Brakke, D. *Athanasius and Asceticism.* Baltimore: Johns Hopkins University Press, 1998.

Brown, P. *The Body and Society: Men, Women and Sexual Renunciation in Early Christianity.* London: Columbia University Press, 1989.

Bruyn, T. de. "Constantius the *Tractator*: Author of an Anonymous Commentary on the Pauline Epistles?" *JThS,* n.s., 43 (1992): 38–54.

Buytaert, É. M. *L'héritage littéraire d'Eusèbe d'Emèse: Étude critique et historique.* Louvain: Bureaux du Muséon, 1949.

Carriker, A. J. *The Library of Eusebius of Caesarea.* Leiden: E. J. Brill, 2003.

Clark, E. "Interpretive Fate amid the Church Fathers." In *Hagar, Sarah, and their Children.* Edited by P. Trible and L. Russell. Louisville: John Knox Press, 2006. Pp. 127–47.

Cocchini, F. *Il Paolo di Origene: Contributo alla storia della recezione delle epistole paoline nel III secolo.* Rome: Edizioni Studium, 1992.

———. "Da Origene a Teodoreto." In *Origeniana Septima: Origenes in den Auseinandersetzungen des 4. Jahrhunderts.* Edited by W. A. Bienert and U. Kühneweg. Leuven: Leuven University Press, 1999. Pp. 292–309.

Courcelle, P. *Les lettres grecques en Occident de Macrobe à Cassiodore.* Paris: Boccard, 1948 = *Late Latin Writers and their Greek Sources.* Trans. H. E. Wedeck. Cambridge: Harvard University Press, 1969.

Crouzel, H. "L'apocatastase chez Origène." In L. Lothar, ed. *Origeniana quarta. Die Referate des 4. Internationalen Origeneskongresses (Innsbruck, 2.–6. September 1985).* Innsbruck: Tyrolia-Verlag, 1987. Pp. 282–90.

Dassmann, E. *Der Stachel im Fleisch: Paulus in der frühchristlichen Literatur bis Irenäus.* Münster: Aschendorff, 1979.

Derda, T., and E. Wipszycka. "L'emploi des titres *abba, apa* et *papas* dans l'Église byzantine." *JJP* 24 (1994): 23–56.

Duval, Y.-M. "Pélage en son temps: Données chronologiques nouvelles pour une présentation nouvelle." *StudPatr* 38 (2001): 95–118.

———. *L'affaire Jovinien. D'une crise de la société romaine à une crise de la pensée chrétienne à la fin du IVe et au début du Ve siècle.* Rome: Institutum Patristicum Augustinianum, 2003.

Fladerer, L. *Augustinus als Exeget: zu einen Kommentaren des Galaterbriefes und der Genesis.* Vienna: Österreichischen Akademie der Wissenschaften, 2010.

Fredriksen Landes, P. *Augustine on Romans: Propositions from the Epistle to the Romans, Unfinished Commentary on the Epistle to the Romans.* Chico: Scholars Press, 1982.

Froehlich, K. *Biblical Interpretation in the Early Church.* Philadelphia: Fortress Press, 1984.

———. "Which Paul? Observations on the Image of the Apostle in the History of Biblical Exegesis." In B. Nassif, ed. *New Perspectives on Historical Theology.* Grand Rapids: W. B. Eerdmans, 1996. Pp. 279–99.

Grant, R. "The *Stromateis* of Origen." In *Epektasis: Mélanges patristiques offerts au Cardinal Jean Daniélou.* Edited by J. Fontaine and C. Kannengiesser. Paris: Beauchesne, 1972. Pp. 285–92.

Haar Romeny, R. B. ter. *A Syrian in Greek Dress: The Use of Greek, Hebrew and Syriac Biblical Texts in Eusebius of Emesa's Commentary on Genesis.* Leiden: E. J. Brill, 1997.

Hagen, K. *Luther's Approach to Scripture as seen in his "Commentaries" on Galatians 1519–1538.* Tübingen: Mohr Siebeck, 1993.

Hunter, D. G. "*On the Sin of Adam and Eve*: A Little-Known Defense of Marriage and Childbearing by Ambrosiaster." *HThR* 82 (1989): 283–99.

——— and S. A. Cooper. "Ambrosiaster *Redactor sui*: The Commentaries on the Pauline Epistles (Excluding Romans)." *REAug.* Forthcoming.

Kieffer, R. *Foi et justification à Antioche: interprétation d'un conflit (Ga 2, 14–21).* Paris: Éditions du Cerf, 1982.

Laurence, P. "La faiblesse féminine chez les Pères de l'Église." In V. Boudon-Millot and B. Pouderon, eds. *Les Pères de l'Église face à la science médicale de leur temps.* Paris: Beauchesne, 2005. Pp. 351–77.

Layton, R. "Recovering Origen's Pauline Exegesis: Exegesis and Eschatology in the *Commentary on Ephesians.*" *JECS* 8 (2000): 373–411.

———. *Didymus the Blind and his Circle in Late-Antique Alexandria: Virtue and Narrative in Biblical Scholarship.* Urbana: University of Illinois Press, 2004.

Leyerle, B. *Theatrical Shows and Ascetic Lives: John Chrysostom's Attack on Spiritual Marriage.* Berkeley: University of California Press, 2001.

Lindemann, A. *Paulus im ältesten Christentum: Das Bild des Apostels und die Rezeption der paulinischen Theologie in der frühchristlichen Literatur bis Marcion.* Tübingen: Mohr Siebeck, 1979.

Loewe, R. "The Medieval History of the Latin Vulgate." In G. W. H. Lampe, ed. *The Cambridge History of the Bible*, vol. 2. *The West from the Fathers to the Reformation.* Cambridge: Cambridge University Press, 1975. Pp. 102–54.

Lössl, J. "A Shift in Patristic Exegesis: Hebrew Verity in Augustine, Jerome, Julian of Aeclanum and Theodore of Mopsuestia." *AugStud* 32 (2001): 157–75.

Lubac, H. de. *Histoire et esprit: L'intelligence de l'Écriture d'après Origène*. Paris: Éditions Montaigne, 1950 = *History and Spirit: The Understanding of Scripture according to Origen*. Trans. A. Englund Nash. San Francisco: Ignatius Press, 2007.

Luck, G. "Lucifer, Fallen Angel." *Euphrosyne* 29 (2001): 297–318.

Lunn-Rockliffe, S. *Ambrosiaster's Political Theology*. Oxford: Oxford University Press, 2007.

Maier, H. O. "The topography of heresy and dissent in late-fourth-century Rome." *Historia* 44 (1995): 232–49.

Mara, M. G. "Ricerche storico-esegetiche sulla presenza del corpus paolino nella storia del cristianesimo dal II al V secolo." In M. G. Mara, *Paolo di Tarso e il suo epistolario*. Aquila: Japadre, 1983. Pp. 6–64.

Margerie, B. de. *An Introduction to the History of Exegesis, vol. 2: The Latin Fathers*. Petersham, MA: St. Bede, 1995.

Martini, C. "De ordinatione duarum Collectionum quibus Ambrosiastri *Quaestiones* traduntur." *Antonianum* 21 (1947): 23–48.

———. "Le recensioni delle *Quaestiones Veteris et Novi Testamenti* dell'Ambrosiaster." *RicSRel* 1 (1954): 40–62.

Marx, A. "La chute de Lucifer (Ésaïe 14, 12–15; Luc 10, 18): préhistoire d'un mythe." *RHPhR* 80 (2000): 171–85.

Mayer, W. *The Homilies of St John Chrysostom—Provenance. Reshaping the Foundations*. Rome: Pontificium Institutum, 2005.

McGinn, B. "Ocean and Desert as Symbols of Mystical Absorption in the Christian Tradition." *JR* 74 (1994): 155–81.

McGuckin, J. A., ed. *The Westminster Handbook to Origen*. Louisville: John Knox Press, 2004.

Mühlenberg, E. "Zur exegetischen Methode des Apollinaris von Laodicea." In *Christliche exegese zwischen Nicaea und Chalcedon*. Edited by J. van Oort and U. Wickert. Kampen: Kok Pharos, 1992. Pp. 132–47.

Neuschäfer, B. *Origenes als Philologe*, 2 vols. Basel: Reinhardt, 1987.

Novotný, J. A. "Eusebius of Emesa as interpreter of St. Paul." In *Studiorum Paulinorum Congressus internationalis catholicus 1961*. Rome: Pontificium Institutum Biblicum, 1963. Vol. 2. Pp. 471–79.

———. "Les fragments exégétiques sur les livres de l'Ancien Testament d'Eusèbe d'Émèse." *OCP* 57 (1991): 27–67.

Orbán, Á. *Les dénominations du monde chez les premiers auteurs chrétiens*. Nijmegen: Dekker & Van de Vegt, 1970.

Pettis, J. "Number symbolism." In *The Westminster Handbook to Origen*. Edited by J. A. McGuckin. Louisville: John Knox Press, 2004. Pp. 158–59.

Plumpe, J. *Mater Ecclesia: An Inquiry into the Concept of the Church as Mother in Early Christianity*. Washington, DC: The Catholic University of America Press, 1943.

Raspanti, G. *Mario Vittorino esegeta di S. Paolo*. Palermo: L'Epos, 1996.

————. "Aspetti formali dell'esegesi paolina dell'Ambrosiaster." *AnnSE* 16 (1999): 507–36.

Regnault, L. *Abba, dis-moi une parole.* Solesmes: Abbaye St-Pierre, 1984.

Rondet, H. "Le symbolisme de la mer chez saint Augustin." In *Augustinus Magister: Congrès International Augustinien, Paris, 21–24 Septembre 1954*, 2 vols. Paris: Institut d'Études Augustiniennes, 1954. Vol. 2. Pp. 691–711.

Simonetti, M. *Biblical Interpretation in the Early Church: An Historical Introduction to Patristic Exegesis.* Trans. J. A. Hughes. Edinburgh: T & T Clark, 1994.

Souter, A. *The Earliest Latin Commentaries on the Epistles of St. Paul.* Oxford: Oxford University Press, 1927.

Spinelli, G. "Ascetismo, monachesimo e cenobitismo ad Aquileia nel IV secolo." *AAAD* 22 (1982): 273–300.

Trigg, J. W. *Origen: The Bible and Philosophy in the Third-Century Church.* Atlanta: John Knox Press, 1983.

Turner, C. H. "Greek Patristic Commentaries on the Pauline Epistles." In J. Hastings, ed. *A Dictionary of the Bible, Supplement.* Edinburgh: T & T Clark, 1898. Pp. 484–531.

Ulfgard, H. *The Story of Sukkot: The Setting, Shaping and Sequel of the Biblical Feast of Tabernacles.* Tübingen: Mohr Siebeck, 1998.

Vercruysse, J.-M. "Les Pères de l'Église et la chute de l'ange: Lucifer d'après Is 14 et Ez 28." *RSR* 75 (2001): 147–74.

Wiles, M. F. *The Divine Apostle: The Interpretation of St Paul's Epistles in the Early Church.* Cambridge: Cambridge University Press, 1967.

Wright, J. "Origen in the Scholar's Den: A Rationale for the Hexapla." In *Origen of Alexandria: His World and His Legacy.* Edited by C. Kannengiesser and W. L. Petersen. Notre Dame: University of Notre Dame Press, 1988. Pp. 48–62.

Early Christian Heresy and Heresiology

Clark, E. *The Origenist Controversy: The Cultural Construction of an Early Christian Debate.* Princeton: Princeton University Press, 1992.

Drijvers, H. J. W. "Marcionism in Syria: Principles, Problems, Polemics." *SecCent* 6 (1987–88): 153–72.

————. "Marcion's Reading of Gal. 4,8: Philosophical Background and Influence on Manichaeism." In *A Green Leaf: Papers in Honour of Jes P. Asmussen.* Leiden: E. J. Brill, 1988. Pp. 339–48.

Ehrman, B. D. *The Orthodox Corruption of Scripture: The Effect of Early Christological Controversies on the Text of the New Testament.* Oxford: Oxford University Press, 1993.

Greschat, K. *Apelles und Hermogenes: zwei theologische Lehrer des zweiten Jahrhunderts.* Leiden: E. J. Brill, 2000.

Häkkinen, S. "Ebionites." In *A Companion to Second-Century Christian "Heretics."* Edited by A. Marjanen and P. Luomanen. Leiden: E. J. Brill, 2005. Pp. 247–78.

Harnack, A. von. *Porphyrius, Gegen die Christen, 15 Bücher: Zeugnisse, Fragmente und Referate*. Berlin: Verlag der Königliche Akademie der Wissenschaften, 1916.

————. *Marcion: Das Evangelium vom fremden Gott: Eine Monographie zur Geschichte der Grundlegung der katholischen Kirche*. Leipzig: Hinrichs, 1924.

Hoffmann, R. J. *Marcion: On the Restitution of Christianity. An Essay on the Development of Radical Paulinist Theology in the Second Century*. Chico: Scholars Press, 1984.

Hunter, D. G. *Marriage, Celibacy, and Heresy in Ancient Christianity: The Jovinianist Controversy*. Oxford: Oxford University Press, 2007.

Jensen, A. *God's Self-Confident Daughters: Early Christianity and the Liberation of Women*. Trans. O. C. Dean. Louisville: John Knox Press, 1996.

Junod, É. "Les attitudes d'Apelles, disciple de Marcion, à l'égard de l'Ancien Testament." *Augustinianum* 22 (1982): 113–33.

Kelly, J. N. D. *Early Christian Doctrines*. London: Harper & Row, 1978.

Knox, J. *Marcion and the New Testament: An Essay in the Early History of the Canon*. Chicago: University of Chicago Press, 1942.

Lampe, P. *From Paul to Valentinus: Christians at Rome in the First Two Centuries*. Translated by M. G. Steinhauser. Minneapolis: Fortress Press, 2003.

Layton, B., ed. *The Rediscovery of Gnosticism, Volume 1: The School of Valentinus*. Leiden: E. J. Brill, 1980.

Lieu, S. *Manichaeism in the Later Roman Empire and Medieval China: A Historical Survey*. Manchester: Manchester University Press, 1985.

Lössl, J. "Augustine, 'Pelagianism,' Julian of Aeclanum, and Modern Scholarship." *ZAC* 10 (2007): 129–50.

Lüdemann, G. *Heretics: The Other Side of Early Christianity*. Translated by J. Bowden. Louisville: John Knox Press, 1996.

McGowan, A. "Marcion's Love of Creation." *JECS* 9 (2001): 295–311.

Quispel, G. "Marcion and the Test of the New Testament." *VChr* 52 (1998): 349–60.

Rasimus, T. "Ophite Gnosticism, Sethianism and the Nag Hammadi Library." *VChr* 59 (2005): 235–63.

Regul, J. *Die antimarcionitischen Evangelienprologe*. Freiburg: Herder, 1969.

Rinaldi, G. "Studi Porfiriani I. Porphyrius Bataneotes." *KOINΩNIA* 4 (1980): 25–37.

Steward-Sykes, A. "Bread and fish, water and wine: The Marcionite Menu and the Maintenance of Purity." In *Marcion und seine Kirchengeschichtliche Wirkung: Marcion and His Impact on Church History*. Edited by G. May and K. Greschat. Berlin: Walter de Gruyter, 2002. Pp. 207–20.

Thomassen, E. *The Spiritual Seed: The Church of the "Valentinians."* Leiden: E. J. Brill, 2006.

Trevett, C. "Fingers up Noses and Pricking with Needles: Possible Reminiscences of Revelation in Later Montanism." *VChr* 49 (1995): 258–69.

————. *Montanism: Gender, Authority and the New Prophecy*. Cambridge: Cambridge University Press, 1996.

Tyson, J. B. *Marcion and Luke-Acts: A Defining Struggle.* Columbia: University of South Carolina Press, 2006.

Williams, D. "Monarchianism and Photinus of Sirmium as the Persistent Heretical Face of the Fourth Century." *HThR* 99 (2006): 187–206.

Williams, R. *Arius: Heresy and Tradition.* Grand Rapids: W. B. Eerdmans, 2002.

Modern Scholarship on the Bible

Allison, D. C. "Peter and Cephas: One and the Same." *JBL* 111 (1992): 489–95.

Alstrup Dahl, N., and D. Hellholm. "Garment-Metaphors: the Old and New Human Being." In *Antiquity and Humanity: Essays on Ancient Religion and Philosophy.* Edited by A. Yarbro Collins and M. M. Mitchell. Tübingen: Mohr Siebeck, 2001. Pp. 139–58.

Anderson, R. D. *Ancient Rhetorical Theory and Paul.* Leuven: Peeters, 1999.

Arnold, C. E. "Returning to the Domain of the Powers: *Stoicheia* as Evil Spirits in Galatians 4:3, 9." *NovTest* 38 (1996): 55–76.

Barclay, J. M. G. *Obeying the Truth: A Study of Paul's Ethics in Galatians.* Edinburgh: T & T Clark, 1988.

Barr, J. "'*Abba*, Father' and the Familiarity of Jesus' Speech." *ThTo* 91 (1988): 173–79.

———. "*Abba* Isn't Daddy." *JThS*, n.s., 39 (1988): 28–47.

Barrett, C. K. "*Shaliaḥ* and Apostle." In *Donum Gentilicium, New Testament Studies in Honour of David Daube.* Edited by E. Bammel, C. K. Barrett, and W. D. Davies. Oxford: Oxford University Press, 1978. Pp. 88–102.

Barton, J. *Holy Writings, Sacred Text: The Canon in Early Christianity.* Louisville: John Knox Press, 1997.

Beale, G. K. *The Book of Revelation.* Grand Rapids: W. B. Eerdmans, 1999.

Betz, H. D. *Galatians.* Philadelphia: Fortress Press, 1979.

Blinzler, J. "Lexikalisches zu dem Terminus *ta stoicheia tou kosmou* bei Paulus." In *Studiorum Paulinorum Congressus internationalis catholicus 1961.* Rome: Pontificium Institutum Biblicum, 1963. Vol. 2. Pp. 429–43.

Borgen, P. "Crucified for his own Sins—Crucified for our Sins: Observations on a Pauline Perspective." In *The New Testament and Early Christian Literature in Greco-Roman Context: Studies in Honor of David E. Aune.* Edited by J. Fotopoulos. Leiden: E. J. Brill, 2006. Pp. 17–35.

Breytenbach, C. "Probable Reasons for Paul's Unfruitful Missionary Attempts in Asia Minor (A Note on Acts 16:6–7)." In *Die Apostelgeschichte und die hellenistische Geschichtsschreibung: Festschrift für Eckhard Plümacher zu seinem 65. Geburtstag.* Edited by C. Breytenbach and J. Schröter. Leiden: E. J. Brill, 2004. Pp. 157–69.

Bruce, F. F. *Commentary on Galatians.* NIGTC. Grand Rapids: W. B. Eerdmans, 1982.

Burton, P. *The Old Latin Gospels: A Study of their Texts and Language.* Oxford: Oxford University Press, 2000.

D'Angelo, M. R. "*Abba* and 'Father': Imperial Theology and the Jesus Traditions." *JBL* 111 (1992): 611–30.

Darbyshire, G., S. Mitchell, and L. Vardar. "The Galatian Settlement in Asia Minor." *AS* 50 (2000): 75–97.

Davies, W. D. *Jewish and Pauline Studies*. Philadelphia: Fortress Press, 1984.

Dines, J. M. *The Septuagint*. Edinburgh: T & T Clark, 2004.

Dölger, F. J. *Sphragis: Eine altchristliche Taufbezeichnung in ihrer Beziehung zur profanen und religiösen Kultur des Altertums*. Paderborn: Schöningh, 1911.

Ehrman, B. D. "Cephas and Peter." *JBL* 109 (1990): 463–74.

Ellingworth, P. *The Epistle to the Hebrews. A Commentary on the Greek Text*. NIGTC. Grand Rapids: W. B. Eerdmans, 1993.

Fee, G. *Pauline Christology: An Exegetical-Theological Study*. Peabody: Hendrickson Publishers, 2007.

Fenner, F. *Die Krankheit im Neuen Testament: Eine religionsgeschichtliche und medizingeschichtliche Untersuchung*. Leipzig: Hinrichs, 1930.

Fredriksen Landes, P. "Judaism, the Circumcision of Gentiles, and Apocalyptic Hope: Another Look at Galatians 1 and 2." *JThS*, n.s., 42 (1991): 532–58.

Freeman, P. *The Galatian Language: A Comprehensive Survey of the Language of the Ancient Celts in Greco-Roman Asia Minor*. Lewiston: Edwin Mellen Press, 2001.

Gaventa, B. "The Maternity of Paul: An Exegetical Study of Galatians 4:19." In *The Conversation Continues: Studies in Paul and John in Honor of J. Louis Martyn*. Edited by R. Fortna and B. Gaventa. Nashville: Abingdon Press, 1990. Pp. 189–201.

Gnadt, M. "*Abba* isn't Daddy—Aspekte einer feministische-befreiungstheologische Revision des *Abba* Jesu." In *Von der Wurzel getragen: christlich-feministische Exegese in Auseinandersetzung mit Antijudaismus*. Edited by L. Schottroff and M.-T. Wacker. Leiden: E. J. Brill, 1996. Pp. 115–31.

Greer, R. A. *The Captain of our Salvation: A Study in the Patristic Exegesis of Hebrews*. Tübingen: Mohr Siebeck, 1973.

Güting, E. "Amen, Eulogie, Doxologie: eine textkritische Untersuchung." In *Begegnungen zwischen Christentum und Judentum in Antike und Mittelalter: Festschrift für Heinz Schreckenberg*. Edited by D.-A. Koch and H. Lichtenberger. Göttingen: Vandenhoeck & Ruprecht, 1993. Pp. 133–62.

Hartin, P. J. *James of Jerusalem: Heir to Jesus of Nazareth*. Collegeville: Liturgical Press, 2004.

Hartog, P. *Polycarp and the New Testament: The Occasion, Rhetoric, Theme, and Unity of the Epistle to the Philippians and Its Allusions to New Testament Literature*. Tübingen: Mohr Siebeck, 2002.

Hirsch, E. "Zwei Fragen zu Galater 6." *ZNTW* 29 (1930): 192–97.

Hultgren, A. "The Scriptural Foundations for Paul's Mission to the Gentiles." In *Paul and His Theology*. Edited by S. Porter. Leiden: E. J. Brill, 2006. Pp. 21–44.

Hurowitz, V. "'His Master shall Pierce his Ear with an Awl' (Exodus 21.6):

Marking Slaves in the Bible in Light of Akkadian Sources." *PAAJR* 58 (1993): 47–77.

Jeremias, J. *Abba: Studien zur neutestamentlichen Theologie und Zeitgeschichte*. Göttingen: Vandenhoeck & Ruprecht, 1966.

Keck, L. E. "The Jewish Paul among the Gentiles: Two Portrayals." In *Early Christianity and Classical Culture: Comparative Studies in Honor of Abraham J. Malherbe*. Edited by J. T. Fitzgerald, T. H. Olbricht, and L. M. White. Leiden: E. J. Brill, 2003. Pp. 461–81.

Kremendahl, D. *Die Botschaft der Form: Zum Verhältnis von antiker Epistolographie und Rhetorik im Galaterbrief*. Göttingen: Vandenhoeck & Ruprecht, 2000.

Lehmann, H. J. "The Syriac translation of the Old Testament—as evidenced around the middle of the fourth century (in Eusebius of Emesa)." *SJOT* 1 (1987): 66–86.

Leschhorn, W. "Die Anfänge der Provinz Galatia." *Chiron* 22 (1992): 315–36.

Lightfoot, J. B. *The Epistle of St. Paul to the Galatians*. Grand Rapids: W. B. Eerdmans; repr., 1967.

Longenecker, R. N. *Galatians*. Dallas: Word Books, 1990.

MacDonald, D. "Apocryphal and Canonical Narratives about Paul." In *Paul and the Legacies of Paul*. Edited by W. S. Babcock. Dallas: Southern Methodist University Press, 1990. Pp. 55–70.

Matera, F. J. *Galatians*. Sacra Pagina 9. Collegeville: Liturgical Press, 1992.

McHugh, J. *The Mother of Jesus in the New Testament*. London: Darton, Longman & Todd, 1975.

Meeks, W. *The Origins of Christian Morality*. New Haven: Yale University Press, 1993.

Metzger, B. *Manuscripts of the Greek Bible: An Introduction to Palaeography*. Oxford: Oxford University Press, 1981.

———. *A Textual Commentary on the Greek New Testament*. 2d ed. Stuttgart: Deutsche Bibelgesellschaft, 2005.

Mussner, F. *Theologie der Freiheit nach Paulus*. Freiburg: Herder, 1976.

Painter, J. *Just James: The Brother of Jesus in History and Tradition*. Columbia: University of South Carolina Press, 2004.

Roetzel, C. J. *The Letters of Paul: Conversations in Context*. Louisville: John Knox Press, 1991.

———. *Paul: The Man and the Myth*. Columbia: University of South Carolina Press, 1998.

Segal, A. F. *Paul the Convert: The Apostolate and the Apostasy of Saul the Pharisee*. New Haven: Yale University Press, 1990.

Seland, T. "Saul of Tarsus and Early Zealotism: Reading Gal 1,13–14 in Light of Philo's Writings." *Bib* 83 (2002): 449–71.

Seybold, K. "Zur Vorgeschichte der liturgischen Formel Amen." *ThZ* 48 (1992): 109–17.

Stralan, J. "Burden-bearing and the Law of Christ: A Re-examination of Galatians 6:2." *JBL* 94 (1975): 266–76.

Strobel, K. "State formation by the Galatians of Asia Minor: politico-historical and cultural processes in Hellenistic central Anatolia." *Anatolica* 28 (2002): 1–46.

———. "Galatien, die Galater und die Poleis der Galater: historische Identität und ethnische Tradition." *Eirene* 42 (2006): 89–123.

Tolmie, D. F. *Persuading the Galatians: A Text-centred Rhetorical Analysis of a Pauline Letter.* Tübingen: Mohr Siebeck, 2005.

Towner, P. H. *The Letters to Timothy and Titus.* NIGNT. Grand Rapids: W. B. Eerdmans, 2006.

Willmington, H. L. *Willmington's Guide to the Bible.* Wheaton: Tyndale House Publishers, 1982.

Witherington, B. *Grace in Galatia: A Commentary on St. Paul's Letter to the Galatians.* Grand Rapids: W. B. Eerdmans, 1998.

Wright, N. T. *What Saint Paul Really Said.* Grand Rapids: W. B. Eerdmans, 1997.

Miscellaneous

Blumenthal, H. J. *Aristotle and Neoplatonism in Late Antiquity: Interpretations of the* De Anima. Ithaca: Cornell University Press, 1996.

Bonner, S. F. *Education in Ancient Rome. From the Elder Cato to the Younger Pliny.* Berkeley: University of California Press, 1977.

Casson, L. *Ships and Seamanship in the Ancient World.* Princeton: Princeton University Press, 1971.

Drijvers, H. J. W. *Cults and Beliefs at Edessa.* Leiden: E. J. Brill, 1980.

Faraone, C. *Ancient Greek Love Magic.* Cambridge: Cambridge University Press, 1999.

Grant, M. *The Jews in the Roman World.* London: Orion Books; repr., 1999.

Grendler, P. F. *Schooling in Renaissance Italy.* Baltimore: Johns Hopkins University Press, 1989.

Hall, E. *Inventing the Barbarian: Greek Self-Definition through Tragedy.* Oxford: Oxford University Press, 1989.

Halliwell, S. *Greek Laughter: A Study of Cultural Psychology from Homer to Early Christianity.* Cambridge: Cambridge University Press, 2008.

Herman, G. *Ritualised Friendship and the Greek City.* Cambridge: Cambridge University Press, 1987.

Horstmanshoff, H. F. J. "La castration dans les textes latins médicaux." In *Maladie et maladies dans les textes latins antiques et médiévaux.* Edited by C. Deroux. Brussels: Société d'Études Latines de Bruxelles, 1998. Pp. 85–94.

Janson, T. *Latin Prose Prefaces: Studies in Literary Conventions.* Stockholm: Almqvist & Wiksell, 1964.

Katz, J. "How the Mole and Mongoose Got Their Names: Sanskrit Ākhú- and nakulá-." *JAOS* 122 (2002): 296–310.

Leeman, A. D. *Gloria. Cicero's waardering van de roem en haar achtergrond in de hellenistische wijsbegeerte en de romeinse samenleving.* Rotterdam: Wyt & Zonen, 1949.

Leinkauf, T., and C. Steel, eds. *Plato's* Timaeus *and the Foundations of Cosmology in Late Antiquity, the Middle Ages and the Renaissance*. Ithaca: Cornell University Press, 2005.

Matijasic, R. "Oil and Wine Production in Istria and Dalmatia in Classical Antiquity and the Early Middle Ages." In *La production du vin et de l'huile*. Edited by M.-C. Amouretti and J.-P. Brun. Paris: École Francaise d'Athènes, 1993. Pp. 247–61.

Nelson, M. *The Barbarian's Beverage: A History of Beer in Ancient Europe*. London: Routledge, 2005.

Nussbaum, M. "The Stoics on the Extirpation of the Passions." *Apeiron* 20 (1987): 129–77.

Powell, J. "Cicero's translations from Greek." In *Cicero the Philosopher: Twelve Papers*. Edited by J. Powell. Oxford: Oxford University Press, 1995. Pp. 273–300.

Resnick, I. M. "*Risus Monasticus*: Laughter and Medieval Monastic Culture." *RBén* 97 (1987): 90–100.

Ross, K. *Roman Edessa: Politics and Culture on the Eastern Fringes of the Roman Empire, 114–242 CE*. London: Routledge, 2001.

Rougé, J. "La navigation hivernale sous l'empire romain." *REA* 54 (1952): 316–25.

Scullard, H. H. *The Elephant in the Greek and Roman World*. Ithaca: Cornell University Press, 1974.

Segal, J. B. *Edessa: The Blessed City*. Oxford: Oxford University Press, 1970.

Serarcangeli, C., and G. Rispoli. "La mutilazione crudele: note storiche su castratori e castrati." *MedSec*, n.s., 13 (2001): 441–54.

Striker, G. "Cicero and Greek Philosophy." *HSCP* 97 (1995): 53–61.

Thraede, K. *Grundzüge griechisch-römischer Brieftopik*. Munich: Beck, 1970.

Wilson, S. *Related Strangers: Jews and Christians 70 C.E.–170 C.E.* Minneapolis: Fortress Press, 1995.

Winter, B. W. *Philo and Paul among the Sophists*. Cambridge: Cambridge University Press, 1997.

INTRODUCTION

INTRODUCTION

1. JEROME'S LIFE AND WORKS[1]

The Early Years

Jerome was born around 347 into an affluent Christian household in Stridon, a small and virtually unknown town on the border between the Roman provinces of Dalmatia and Pannonia.[2] When he was around the age of twelve, his land-owning father Eusebius sent him to Rome to receive an aristocratic secondary education in Latin grammar, literature, and rhetoric. As Jerome would boast later in life, he studied under Aelius Donatus, the most famous Latin grammarian in the fourth century AD and the author of commentaries on Virgil and Terence as well as a grammar textbook that became a staple in the medieval and Renaissance classroom.[3] Jerome went on to receive specialized

1. The standard English-language biography of Jerome is J. N. D. Kelly, *Jerome: His Life, Writings, and Controversies* (London: Harper & Row, 1975), but see also the excellent abbreviated biography in S. Rebenich, *Jerome* (London: Routledge, 2002), 3–59. In German, Rebenich's *Hieronymus und sein Kreis: Prosopographische und sozialgeschichtliche Untersuchungen* (Stuttgart: Steiner, 1992) and Alfons Fürst's *Hieronymus: Askese und Wissenschaft in der Spätantike* (Freiburg: Herder, 2003) are indispensable treatments. The older biographies by Georg Grützmacher (*Hieronymus: Eine biographische Studie zur alten Kirchengeschichte*, 3 vols. [Berlin: Dieterich, 1901–8]) and Ferdinand Cavallera (*Saint Jérôme: Sa vie et son oeuvre*, 2 vols. [Paris: E. Champion, 1922]) have been superseded by the abovementioned studies. Finally, I should call attention to the recently published collection of essays in *Jerome of Stridon: His Life, Writings and Legacy*, ed. A. Cain and J. Lössl (Aldershot: Ashgate Publishing, 2009).

2. There has been much debate about Stridon's precise location. See, e.g., M. Niedermann, "Le lieu de naissance de saint Jérôme," in idem, *Recueil Max Niedermann* (Neuchâtel: Secrétariat de l'Université, 1954), 248–51; I. Fodor, "Le lieu d'origine de S. Jérôme: reconsidération d'une vieille controverse," *RHE* 81 (1986): 498–500.

3. For an overview of Donatus's later influence, see P. F. Grendler, *School-*

3

training in Rome in rhetorical theory and declamation, which was supposed to prepare him for a lucrative career in law or government.

The young student had much more on his mind than just academics. He started to become serious about his childhood faith. At some point he was baptized and would spend Sundays visiting martyrs' tombs in the Roman catacombs with friends. Yet for all his deepening religiosity, the small-town boy in him evidently had trouble resisting the allures of big-city life. Cryptic allusions in his later writings suggest that during these years he lost his virginity.[4] This certainly would help to explain why Jerome, as an adult monk, idealized virginity and displayed such contempt for human sexuality.

In the middle or late 360s Jerome completed his studies and moved to the Gallic city of Trier. At that time Trier was a key administrative center and the residence of the emperor Valentinian, and thus it was an obvious stopping-point for an ambitious young careerist looking for employment opportunities in the imperial bureaucracy.[5] The few years Jerome spent there are, regrettably, his "lost years." One of the very few concrete personal events that we can assign to this period is a profound conversion experience and consequent decision to become a monk. Some deeply religious Christians of that age made their dramatic renunciation of the world immediately after baptism. It took Jerome almost a decade to come to the edge of that precipitous cliff. Had the lure of a promising secular career, and perhaps also the hope for marrying and raising a family, kept his monastic impulse in check until then? We will never know. What we *can* know is that Jerome's break with his former life—once he made it—was decisive.

After leaving Trier, Jerome headed for the northeastern Italian city of Aquileia, a stronghold for Christian asceticism in the

---

ing in Renaissance Italy (Baltimore: Johns Hopkins University Press, 1989), 162–202. Jerome was quite proud of having studied under Donatus, and on more than one occasion (see, e.g., *Comm. Eccl.* 1.9) he referred to Donatus affectionately as "my teacher" (*praeceptor meus*).

4. Kelly, *Jerome*, 20–21.

5. J. Steinhausen, "Hieronymus und Laktanz in Trier," *TZ* 20 (1951): 126–54.

late fourth century.[6] Here he joined like-minded Christians such as Chromatius, the future bishop of Aquileia, in an informal monastic community. Around 373, the Aquileian community dissolved because of an internal rift, and Jerome traveled eastward to Antioch in search of new monastic prospects. He remained in the Syrian capital and its environs for the next seven or so years. All the while he enjoyed the patronage of Evagrius, a priest and later the bishop of Antioch, who, shortly before Jerome's arrival, had made a Latin translation of Athanasius of Alexandria's Greek *Life of St. Antony*, which glorifies Antony as the first great desert monk and a mighty champion of Nicene orthodoxy.[7]

For about two years (c. 375–c. 377) Jerome lived in Maronia, a semi-rural hamlet owned by Evagrius. It was located about thirty miles from Antioch, on the outskirts of the town of Chalcis. In contemporary letters and later writings Jerome vividly portrayed himself as the stereotypical Syrian holy man: a chain-wearing, long-haired monk who lived in a cave and wandered the sun-scorched desert alone, weeping incessantly over his sins and fasting nearly to the point of starvation.[8] This literary self-portraiture inspired a rich tradition of late medieval and Renaissance iconography that celebrated Jerome as a penitent monk fighting heroic spiritual battles in the exotic eastern wilderness.[9] Recent scholarship, however, has exposed the gaping disparity between the historical reality of his actual experience and his embellished re-creation of it.[10] It has in fact been demonstrated that his revisionist autobiography was motivated by a desire to promote himself to fellow Latin Christians as an expert on ascetic spirituality.[11]

6. G. Spinelli, "Ascetismo, monachesimo e cenobitismo ad Aquileia nel IV secolo," *AAAD* 22 (1982): 273–300.

7. D. Brakke, *Athanasius and Asceticism* (Baltimore: Johns Hopkins University Press, 1998), 201–65.

8. See, e.g., *Epp.* 17.2; 22.7; 52.1; 125.12.

9. H. Friedmann, *A Bestiary for Saint Jerome: Animal Symbolism in European Religious Art* (Washington, DC: Smithsonian Institution Press, 1980), 48–100; B. Ridderbos, *Saint and Symbol: Images of Saint Jerome in Early Italian Art* (Groningen: Bouma, 1984), 63–88; D. Russo, *Saint Jérôme en Italie: Étude d'iconographie et de spiritualité (XIIIe–XVe siècle)* (Rome: École Française de Rome, 1987), 201–51.

10. Rebenich, *Hieronymus und sein Kreis*, 86–98.

11. A. Cain, "*Vox clamantis in deserto*: Rhetoric, Reproach, and the Forging

6INTRODUCTION

Jerome's aspirations to be a Christian author were manifesting themselves by the middle and late 370s. He tried his hand at Biblical exposition by writing a commentary on Obadiah, which no longer survives. He also composed the *Life of Paul of Thebes*, a hagiographic romance portraying its hero, Paul, instead of Antony the Great, as the real founder and rightful figurehead of solitary desert monasticism. This is a short but incredibly ambitious work in which Jerome communicated his eastern-style monastic ideals to a western audience in a novelistic way and tried to create a spiritual classic that would rival and even supplant the wildly popular *Life of St. Antony*.[12]

By 380, Jerome had moved on to Constantinople, where he would reside for approximately two years. He met Gregory of Nyssa and studied theology under Gregory of Nazianzus, all the while continuing to diversify his literary résumé.[13] In the late summer of 382, Jerome accompanied the bishops Paulinus of Antioch and Epiphanius of Salamis to Rome for an ecclesiastical summit. This was the first time he was to set foot in Rome since his student days.

Rome (382–385)

Jerome spent three fruitful but controversy-ridden years in Rome. He served as the sometime-secretary of the papal chancery, assisting Pope Damasus I in drafting official correspondence to the eastern and western churches.[14] Damasus, who ruled the Roman see from 366 until his death on 11 Decem-

---

of Ascetic Authority in Jerome's Letters from the Syrian Desert," *JThS*, n.s., 57 (2006): 500–525; idem, *The Letters of Jerome: Asceticism, Biblical Exegesis, and the Construction of Christian Authority in Late Antiquity* (Oxford: Oxford University Press, 2009), chaps. 1 and 5.

12. See S. Rebenich, "Inventing an Ascetic Hero: Jerome's *Life of Paul the First Hermit*," in *Jerome of Stridon*, ed. Cain and Lössl, 13–27.

13. S. Rebenich, "Asceticism, Orthodoxy and Patronage: Jerome in Constantinople," *StudPatr* 33 (1997): 358–77. On Jerome's relationship with Gregory, see N. Adkin, "Gregory of Nazianzus and Jerome: Some Remarks," in *Georgica. Greek Studies in Honour of George Cawkwell*, ed. M. Flower and M. Toher (London: Institute of Classical Studies, University of London, 1991), 13–24.

14. For one such piece of official correspondence for which he may have been responsible, see Y.-M. Duval, *La décrétale* Ad Gallos Episcopos: *son texte et son auteur. Texte critique, traduction française et commentaire* (Leiden: E. J. Brill, 2005).

ber 384, was the longest-reigning pope in the fourth century. In terms of his accomplishments, he was the most productive one as well. He initiated important liturgical reforms, undertook expensive building projects, and did more than any predecessor to consolidate papal power under the notion of Petrine primacy. But Damasus also faced a barrage of criticism from contemporary pagans and Christians for his allegedly lavish lifestyle and for pandering to aristocratic Christian women, which earned him the snide nickname "ear-tickler of matrons."[15] The elderly pontiff must have been impressed with Jerome's growing expertise as a Biblical scholar, for he took him as a personal Scriptural adviser[16] and even commissioned him to revise the Gospels of the Old Latin Bible[17] according to the Greek, a monumental work that Jerome completed in 384. Damasus's sponsorship of the project, however, could not shield it from critics who accused Jerome of tampering with the Lord's words when he emended passages "against the authority of the ancients and the opinion of the entire world."[18]

Jerome's talents earned him patronage not only from a powerful pope but also from a group of aristocratic Christian women who practiced an ascetic lifestyle and cultivated interests in Biblical studies.[19] The widow Marcella,[20] the figurehead of this so-called "Aventine circle," would frequently approach him, either in person or through correspondence, with questions about He-

15. J. Fontaine, "Un sobriquet perfide de Damase, *matronarum auriscalpius*," in *Hommages à Henri le Bonniec. Res sacrae*, ed. D. Porte and J.-P. Néraudau (Brussels: Latomus, 1988), 177–92.

16. Cain, *The Letters of Jerome*, Chap. 2.

17. "Old Latin Bible" is an umbrella term used to describe the many pre-Vulgate Latin translations of the Bible. See P. Burton, *The Old Latin Gospels: A Study of their Texts and Language* (Oxford: Oxford University Press, 2000).

18. *Ep.* 27.1.

19. M. Testard, "Les dames de l'Aventin, disciples de saint Jérôme," *BSAF* (1996): 39–63; E. G. Hinson, "Women Biblical Scholars in the Late Fourth Century: The Aventine Circle," *StudPatr* 23 (1997): 319–24. See also C. Krumeich, *Hieronymus und die christlichen feminae clarissimae* (Bonn: Habelt, 1993); B. Feichtinger, Apostolae apostolorum. *Frauenaskese als Befreiung und Zwang bei Hieronymus* (Frankfurt am Main: P. Lang, 1995).

20. S. Letsch-Brunner, *Marcella—Discipula et Magistra. Auf den Spuren einer römischen Christin des 4. Jahrhunderts* (Berlin: Walter de Gruyter, 1998).

brew philology and Biblical exegesis.[21] One of Marcella's friends
was the widow Paula.[22] Paula came under the tutelage of Jerome
as the Scriptural and spiritual mentor not only to herself but also
to her teenage daughter Eustochium, to whom he dedicated in
384 his most famous ascetic treatise, a manual on how the Christian virgin can remain pure (*Ep.* 22). This writing stirred up a
hornet's nest of controversy. Jerome's insinuation that marriage
was a necessary evil reserved for second-class spiritual citizens in-
censed Christians who did not subscribe to his extreme ascetic
ideology. Even more offensive to many secularized lay and clerical Christians in Rome was his satirizing of their "worldly" life-
styles.[23]

Jerome's public relations troubles did not end there. With
Pope Damasus's death on 11 December 384, Jerome lost his
protector and became more vulnerable than ever to attacks
from enemies within the Roman clerical establishment, whom
he had incited with his satire. Earlier that same autumn, Paula's oldest daughter, Blesilla, a recent convert to the ascetic way
of life, died at the age of twenty as a consequence of carrying
her fasting regimen to an extreme. At the funeral Paula's fellow aristocrats whispered among themselves that "those detest-
able monks" should be stoned and driven out of Rome for cor-
rupting the young girl.[24] Jerome had to be especially worried
because he had been Blesilla's spiritual mentor.

Paula turned a deaf ear to the criticisms being hurled at her
spiritual mentor. In fact, her respect for him only deepened, and
in the spring of 385 the two began formal planning for a Holy
Land pilgrimage. Paula's aristocratic friends and family were pro-

21. Of the prolific correspondence they traded in Rome, only sixteen letters
from him survive (*Epp.* 23–29, 32, 34, 37, 38, 40–44).

22. Over the past century and a half, Paula has been the subject of several biographies, the most recent being Christa Krumeich's *Paula von Rom. Christliche
Mittlerin zwischen Okzident und Orient* (Bonn: Habelt, 2002).

23. Jerome continued into the twilight of his career to defend the satiric
method of moral critique he had employed in *Ep.* 22; see *Epp.* 52.17; 117.1;
130.19; Rufinus, *Apol. c. Hier.* 2.5, 43. See also A. Cain, "Jerome's *Epistula* 117
on the *subintroductae:* Satire, Apology, and Ascetic Propaganda in Gaul," *Augustinianum* 49 (2009): 119–43.

24. *Ep.* 39.6.

foundly distressed at this news, especially because there was talk that she might relocate to Palestine permanently. They worried about her emotional and financial well-being. They still nursed a grudge about Blesilla's death, but what trumped all else was their suspicion about the motives of an obscure provincial upstart like Jerome in worming his way into the confidence of an enormously wealthy widow. Over the next few months animosities escalated. Certain members of Paula's family conspired with Jerome's enemies in the Roman church to find a way to be rid of him once and for all. In the late summer of 385, Jerome landed in the local episcopal court to face very grave charges that he had used his profession of monasticism as a cover for seducing Christian noblewomen and gaining access to their fortunes—and bedchambers. The verdict did not go his way, and he was forced by church authorities to leave Rome immediately.[25]

Bethlehem (386–420)

On a windy day in August, almost three years to the day after he had arrived in Rome, Jerome left Italy in utter disgrace, never again to return. The ship ferrying him and a select group of his male Christian friends docked at the Syrian port of Seleukeia. The party made its way to Antioch, where it was joined a few weeks later by Paula and her retinue, which included Eustochium and their domestic servants. Once reunited, the two groups set out for Jerusalem. Following a short stay at the Mount of Olives monastery-hostelry complex run by Melania the Elder and Jerome's old friend Rufinus of Aquileia, they embarked on a tour of many major and minor sites of Biblical history in Palestine, including Bethlehem, the reputed birthplace of Christ. They then made an excursion to Egypt and visited various monasteries in Nitria. By the late spring of 386, Jerome and Paula had returned to the tiny village of Bethlehem. Here they would live as inseparable monastic companions until her death in 404, and here he would remain until his in 420. During their first three years in Bethlehem they completed substantial build-

25. For a recent reappraisal of the circumstances surrounding Jerome's expulsion, see Cain, *The Letters of Jerome*, 99–128.

ing projects financed in full by Paula's fortune: monastic living quarters for men and for women and a hostelry for Christian pilgrims that by the early fifth century was bustling with visitors from all over the world.[26]

During his first several years in Bethlehem, even as he shouldered duties as a host to pilgrims and as a monastic administrator,[27] Jerome managed to churn out an impressive list of literary works.[28] Among these was the *De viris illustribus*.[29] This production, completed in 393, is a catalogue of the great (mostly Christian) authors past and present and their writings. He began the work, in the first chapter, with the Apostle Peter and ended, in Chapter 135, with himself and his own rapidly burgeoning output.[30] The notice Jerome provided for himself is in fact the longest and most detailed one he gave for any living writer. The *De viris illustribus* is remarkable because it represents Jerome's attempt to fix a canon of Christian literature and, more to the point, to write himself into that canon. The fact that he included himself at all is significant enough, but his last-place position is even more so. It was a symbolic way to convey that he was the most eminent then-living successor to the past luminaries of the Christian literary tradition. What began with Peter, the chief of the apostles, ended, or rather found its greatest contemporary expression, with him.

---

26. E.g., in a letter of 403 to Paula's daughter-in-law Laeta (*Ep.* 107.2), Jerome boasted that he daily welcomed crowds of monks from India, Persia, and Ethiopia.

27. He not only oversaw the day-to-day activities of his troupe of monks, but he had pastoral duties, which included preaching to them. About one hundred of his sermons survive. They have been edited by Germain Morin and appear in *S. Hieronymi presbyteri Tractatus sive homiliae in Psalmos, in Marci evangelium aliaque varia argumenta*, CCSL 78 (Turnhout: Brepols, 1958).

28. P. Nautin, "L'activité littéraire de Jérôme de 387 à 392," *RThPh* 115 (1983): 247–59.

29. See T. Halton, *St. Jerome, On Illustrious Men*, FOTC 100 (Washington, DC: The Catholic University of America Press, 2000).

30. A. Ceresa-Gastaldo, "La tecnica biografica del *De viris illustribus* di Girolamo," *Renovatio* 14 (1979): 221–36; S. Pricoco, "Motivi polemici e prospettive classicistiche nel *De viris illustribus* di Girolamo," *SicGymn* 32 (1979): 69–99; I. Opelt, "Hieronymus' Leistung als Literarhistoriker in der Schrift *De viris illustribus*," *Orpheus*, n.s., 1 (1980): 52–75.

Jerome's thirty-five years in Bethlehem were notoriously punctuated by bitter clashes with rival Christian writers over ascetic spirituality, Biblical translation and interpretation, and theology. The best known of these polemical skirmishes was the heated public debate about Origen's theology during the 390s.[31] Throughout the 380s and early 390s, Jerome had often eulogized the third-century Biblical scholar Origen of Alexandria.[32] He saw it as one of his missions to make Origen available to western readers in Latin translation, and by 393 he had translated seventy-eight of Origen's homilies on Ezekiel, Jeremiah, Isaiah, Song of Songs, and Luke.[33] He not only translated Origen, but he also consciously patterned himself after him, and during the nascent stages of his career as a textual critic and interpreter of the Bible he presented himself to western audiences as the Latin Origen.[34]

In 393, Bishop Epiphanius of Salamis launched his campaign to extirpate Origen's controversial teachings from Palestine. Early on he targeted Jerusalem, where Origen's theology was defended by its bishop John and by Rufinus. In a puzzling move, Jerome aligned himself with Epiphanius's faction and began to denounce Origen with the same panache as he formerly had praised him. While he was in Bethlehem, Epiphanius had ordained Jerome's younger brother Paulinian and several others in his monastery without the permission of John, whose ecclesiastical jurisdiction extended over Bethlehem. John was furious and excommunicated Jerome and everyone associated with his community.[35] This sentence lasted three long years,[36] and its stipulations were far-

31. For an excellent narrative of this controversy, see E. Clark, *The Origenist Controversy: The Cultural Construction of an Early Christian Debate* (Princeton: Princeton University Press, 1992).

32. On Origen as a Biblical scholar, see B. Neuschäfer, *Origenes als Philologe*, 2 vols. (Basel: Reinhardt, 1987).

33. P. Jay, "Combien Jérôme a-t-il traduit d'homélies d'Origène?" *StudPatr* 23 (1989): 133–37; A. Fürst, "Jerome Keeping Silent: Origen and his Exegesis of Isaiah," in *Jerome of Stridon*, ed. Cain and Lössl, 141–52.

34. M. Vessey, "Jerome's Origen: The Making of a Christian Literary Persona," *StudPatr* 28 (1993): 135–45.

35. P. Nautin, "L'excommunication de saint Jérôme," *AEHE V* 80/81 (1972–73): 7–37.

36. It was lifted by John on Holy Thursday (April 2) of 397.

reaching. Jerome and his monks were forbidden from entering any of the churches in the diocese of Jerusalem, the priests in his monastery were not allowed to administer the sacraments, and nobody in the community apparently was permitted even to receive the Eucharist.

Things went from bad to worse in the early autumn of 395. John obtained from Flavius Rufinus, the powerful praetorian prefect of the East, an official order banishing Jerome and his monks permanently from Palestine. Flavius Rufinus was assassinated on 27 November 395, before the order could be carried out. The matter was abruptly dropped, but the personal hostilities between Rufinus of Aquileia and Jerome continued to simmer. From the late 390s to the early 400s they engaged in an acrimonious pamphlet war, and their friendship became a casualty of theological politics. Of the many accusations they hurled at each other, the most damning was Rufinus's charge that Jerome was a hypocrite for making such an about-face with respect to Origen. Far more was at stake for Jerome than simply a changed opinion about a long-dead ecclesiastical writer. If Origen was to be regarded as a heretic, as Jerome now advocated, then Jerome's own theological orthodoxy, not to mention his public identity as Origen's successor in the Latin world, was subject to the same anathema. Jerome seems to have recognized that he had backed himself into a corner, and he tried to strike a compromise, now claiming that, while he admired Origen's scholarly achievements, he condemned teachings of his that were heretical. But the damage to his image had already been done.

Even as the flames of the Origenist controversy had died down, Jerome suffered a devastating personal loss. Paula, his friend, patron, and monastic companion of almost twenty years, died on 26 January 404. She was famous among Christians throughout Palestine for her holy life and generous patronage of monks. Her funeral was attended by an untold number of bishops, priests, monks, nuns, and laypeople. It is said that even the solitaries emptied their cells, thinking it would be a sacrilege not to pay their respects properly to a woman of her faith.[37] Paula's passing left a gaping hole in the administration of the monastic complex

37. *Ep.* 108.30.

she co-founded, and her daughter Eustochium stepped in to assume the reins of the convent. A few months after Paula's death, a grieving Jerome composed an elaborate epistolary epitaph in praise of her piety and accomplishments (*Ep.* 108). It was cast ostensibly as a consolation letter to Eustochium, but Jerome nevertheless intended it for a much broader readership. His main aim in composing this tribute was to nudge the institutional church to recognize Paula officially as a saint.[38] His efforts paid off, and she was canonized during the fifth century as the direct result of his campaigning. Ever since then, her feast day has been observed in the western church on January 26.

Jerome was one of the most versatile, prolific, and gifted writers in the first several centuries of the church. Almost every conceivable prose genre employed by Christians in antiquity—from the letter and the Biblical commentary to the historical chronicle and the hagiographical *Life*—is represented in his mammoth literary corpus. But it is his immense body of scholarly work on the Bible as both translator and commentator for which he was best known in his own day and posthumously. Starting in the early 390s, Jerome was regularly inundated with requests for translation and exegesis from Christians in Gaul, Italy, Spain, North Africa, and elsewhere.[39] His final three-and-a-half decades comprised a period of astonishing scholarly productivity in this regard. Between 390 and 405, he translated the canonical OT from the Hebrew.[40] He also produced scores of commentaries on individual Biblical books. For the OT he wrote massive commentaries on Isaiah (408–410)[41] and Ezekiel (410–414), an unfinished commentary on Jeremiah (414–416), and smaller-scale commentaries on Ecclesiastes (388–389), Daniel (407),[42] and the Psalms

38. A. Cain, "Jerome's *Epitaphium Paulae:* Hagiography, Pilgrimage, and the Cult of Saint Paula," *JECS* 18:1 (2010): 105–39. I have nearly completed an exhaustive commentary on this fascinating letter.

39. See Cain, *The Letters of Jerome,* 168–96, for a close examination of several pieces of his exegetical correspondence from the Bethlehem years.

40. P. Jay, "La datation des premières traductions de l'Ancien Testament sur l'hébreu par saint Jérôme," *REAug* 28 (1982): 208–12.

41. P. Jay, *L'exégèse de saint Jérôme d'après son Commentaire sur Isaïe* (Paris: Institut d'Études Augustiniennes, 1985).

42. J. Braverman, *Jerome's Commentary on Daniel: A Study of Comparative Jewish*

(before 393). For over a decade he labored over the first Latin commentary on the Minor Prophets (393–406).[43] For the NT he composed commentaries on Matthew (398) and Paul's epistles to Philemon, the Galatians, the Ephesians, and Titus (386).

The last few years of Jerome's life were filled with hardship. His health, which had never been consistently good,[44] continued on a steep decline. The old lion nevertheless mustered the strength to leap into one last polemical tussle, this time with the Pelagians.[45] In 416, tragedy struck his monastic settlement at Bethlehem. A band of marauders, some of whom may have been supporters of Pelagius looking for revenge, ransacked his monastery and Eustochium's convent.[46] The monks and nuns were terrorized, and one deacon was even killed during the attack. The monastic complex was set on fire, and Jerome and his community fled the premises. A year later, Jerome wrote to a friend, complaining bitterly that his monastery had been left in ruins.[47]

Jerome died on 30 September 420. To this day, the thirtieth of September is commemorated as his feast day in the western church.

---

and Christian Interpretations of the Hebrew Bible (Washington, DC: Catholic Biblical Association of America, 1978).

43. For the importance of the commentaries on the Minor Prophets in the broader scope of his exegetical corpus, see M. H. Williams, The Monk and the Book: Jerome and the Making of Christian Scholarship (Chicago: University of Chicago Press, 2006), 97–131.

44. Jerome's letters and other works are littered with complaints about sickness and his generally poor health. For references, see B. Lançon, "Maladie et médecine dans la correspondance de Jérôme," in Jérôme entre l'Occident et l'Orient: XVIe centenaire du départ de saint Jérôme de Rome et de son installation à Bethléem. Actes du colloque de Chantilly, septembre 1986, ed. Y.-M. Duval (Paris: Institut d'Études Augustiniennes, 1988), 355–66.

45. In 415 he wrote his Dialogue against the Pelagians. See further B. Jeanjean, "Le Dialogus Attici et Critobuli de Jérôme en Palestine entre 411 and 415," in Jerome of Stridon, ed. Cain and Lössl, 59–71.

46. J. Lössl, "Who Attacked the Monasteries of Jerome and Paula in 416 AD?" Augustinianum 44 (2004): 91–112.

47. Ep. 139.

The Legacy of Jerome

In his own lifetime Jerome was an extremely marginalized figure. He was not a bishop but a non-practicing priest[48] who, seemingly more often than not, found himself outlawed by the institutional church. All but a tiny minority of like-minded Christians found his hardline ascetic philosophy even remotely appealing.[49] He was no Augustine; technical scholarship was his strong suit, not theological synthesis.[50] Yet even in this area his impressive accomplishments met with fierce resistance. His Hebrew scholarship was rejected by most of the Biblical authorities of his day as being a dangerous and unnecessary innovation that put the Jews in control of the Christian Scriptures. For this and other reasons Jerome's Vulgate translation of the Bible, in many respects his greatest scholarly achievement, was a colossal failure in its own time.[51] To make matters worse, Jerome's contentiousness, both real and perceived, made even his closest friends and supporters shake their heads in bewilderment. His personality, as it comes through in his writings, continues to have this same polarizing effect on modern readers, who routinely weigh in with epithets like "irascible" and "curmudgeonly."

In the centuries following his death, the historical Jerome faded from sight. In time, he was replaced by "Saint Jerome," an almost mythical icon of ascetic self-renunciation and divinely

48. He was ordained around 377 by Bishop Paulinus of Antioch.

49. Cain, *The Letters of Jerome,* 135–40. Martin Luther famously despised Jerome's personality and ascetic ideology, to the point that he even doubted his salvation: "Unless there is some special forgiveness of sins beyond that which is common and which all of us stand in need of, he is lost": *Luther's Works,* vol. 54: *Table Talk,* trans. T. G. Tappert (Philadelphia: Fortress Press, 1967), 44.

50. This partially explains why Jerome, in stark contrast to Augustine, was so rarely cited as an authority in the theological controversies about grace and free will that rocked the Gallic church during the fifth and sixth centuries. See R. Mathisen, "The Use and Misuse of Jerome in Gaul during Late Antiquity," in *Jerome of Stridon,* ed. Cain and Lössl, 191–208.

51. Even down to the thirteenth century many clerics and monks still continued to read and copy from Old Latin versions of the Bible instead of Jerome's Vulgate. See R. Loewe, "The Medieval History of the Latin Vulgate," in *The Cambridge History of the Bible,* vol. 2: *The West from the Fathers to the Reformation,* ed. G. W. H. Lampe (Cambridge: Cambridge University Press, 1975), 102–54.

inspired scholarship of the Bible. Throughout the Middle Ages and Renaissance an enormously popular cult grew up around this once-obscure son of a Dalmatian landowner.[52] On 20 September 1295, just ten days prior to Jerome's feast day, Pope Boniface VIII officially christened him, along with Ambrose (d. 397), Augustine (d. 430), and Pope Gregory the Great (d. 604), one of the four Doctors of the Latin church. It would take nearly a millennium, but Jerome finally, in death, received the recognition that the vast majority of his contemporaries had denied him.

2. THE *COMMENTARY ON GALATIANS:*
DATE AND OCCASION

In 386 Jerome wrote his commentaries on Philemon, Galatians, Ephesians, and Titus (in this order) inside the space of about four months. They were commenced in June or July and completed in the early autumn.[53] In the preface to Book 2 of the Ephesians commentary Jerome complains about having to write so much in so little time and claims to have dictated as much as a staggering one thousand lines on some days. He was in such a hurry to finish because he needed to send copies of his commentaries to Rome before the rapidly approaching end of the navigation season around October. Seasonal winds and inclement weather conditions restricted long-distance sea-travel between Palestine and Italy to the late spring and summer months.[54] If Jerome had narrowly missed this deadline, he might have had to wait up to half a year before trying again.

Like most of Jerome's Biblical commentaries, the one on Galatians was dedicated to Paula and Eustochium. This was in recognition not only of his shared monastic commitment with them

---

52. E. F. Rice, *Saint Jerome in the Renaissance* (Baltimore: Johns Hopkins University Press, 1985).

53. P. Nautin, "La date des commentaires de Jérôme sur les épîtres pauliniennes," *RHE* 74 (1979): 5–12.

54. J. Rougé, "La navigation hivernale sous l'empire romain," *REA* 54 (1952): 316–25; L. Casson, *Ships and Seamanship in the Ancient World* (Princeton: Princeton University Press, 1971), 270–73.

in Bethlehem but also of Paula's financial generosity in underwriting the often considerable expenses of writing materials, secretaries, and other odds and ends involved in the production of his scholarship.[55] But as we learn from the preface to Book 1, a mandate came from another important patron as well:

It has been only a few days since I finished my commentary on Paul's epistle to Philemon and moved on to his epistle to the Galatians, reversing my course and passing over many things in between. All of a sudden a letter arrived for me from Rome bearing the news that the venerable widow Albina has returned to the Lord and that the holy Marcella, deprived of the companionship of her mother, now more than ever seeks comfort from you, Paula and Eustochium. Since this is impossible at the moment because of the great distance of land and sea that stretches out between us, she desires me at least to treat this suddenly inflicted wound with the medicine of Scripture. I certainly know her zeal and her faith. I know that a fire is always burning in her chest and that she overcomes her gender and is unmindful of her human limitations. And I know that she crosses the Red Sea of this world to the tambourine-sound of the divine books. To be sure, when I was in Rome she never saw me without asking me something about Scripture, even when she was in a hurry.

Jerome's intimate association of Marcella with the *Commentary* from its very inception—indeed, his ostensible framing of it as a piece of consolatory exegesis offered up in her honor—is more than a simple nod to a cherished patron, though it is that as well. By portraying Marcella as an exceptionally committed Christian who also happened to be his intensely loyal Scriptural student and spiritual advisee who turned to him in times of personal crisis, Jerome was validating his own spiritual and exegetical authority in a subtle but powerfully symbolic way. For the more heroic Marcella was made out to be,[56] the more credible he seemed as a teacher able to attract and then retain such a precocious disciple (the same can be said about Paula and Eustochium, who are accentuated as the dedicatees).[57] The cred-

---

55. On the importance of patrons in ensuring that Jerome's scholarly enterprises would see the light of day, see Williams, *The Monk and the Book,* 233–60.

56. Marcella's heroism is elegantly captured by the Old Testament intertext about the crossing of the Red Sea.

57. See further A. Cain, "Rethinking Jerome's Portraits of Holy Women," in *Jerome of Stridon,* ed. Cain and Lössl, 47–57.

ibility of the *Commentary* itself is likewise significantly reinforced inasmuch as it is implied to be the fruit of Jerome's close spiritual and intellectual bond with a circle of exemplary women.

The tying of Marcella to the genesis of the *Commentary* served an even more pragmatic function: to inculcate in her a profound sense of personal responsibility for the fate of this work. Jerome counted on influential literary patrons like her to facilitate the dissemination of his writings and thereby to help him to maintain a forceful and abiding textual presence in the West. This was especially the case now that he was situated in faraway Palestine, cut off from Rome, his former base of operations, by hundreds of miles of open sea. In the prefaces to his two major Pauline commentaries (on Galatians and on Ephesians) Jerome nudges members of his literary circle to be not only conscientious custodians of his writings but also their apologists. Thus he enjoins Paula: "I beseech you . . . not to hand my little works over readily to those who are slanderous and envious . . . and [who] suppose themselves learned and erudite if they detract from others. I beseech you to reply to them: Let them thrust in the pen themselves . . . Let them put themselves to the test and learn from their own labor to be forgiving to those who labor."[58]

After that summer in 386, Jerome never wrote another commentary on a Pauline epistle. It is not that he lost interest in the Apostle. Quite to the contrary, in fact. To take just one example, Paul's teachings on virginity and marriage in 1 Corinthians 7 formed the centerpiece of his debate about ascetic spirituality with the monk Jovinian in the early 390s.[59] By inclination, however, Jerome was overwhelmingly an OT scholar. During his first few years in Bethlehem, he was busy honing his Hebrew reading skills under the guidance of local Palestinian Jews.[60] Af-

58. *Comm. Eph.* 1, preface: quoted from R. Heine, *The Commentaries of Origen and Jerome on St. Paul's Epistle to the Ephesians* (Oxford: Oxford University Press, 2002), 76.

59. See especially Y.-M. Duval, *L'affaire Jovinien. D'une crise de la société romaine à une crise de la pensée chrétienne à la fin du IVe et au début du Ve siècle* (Rome: Institutum Patristicum Augustinianum, 2003), and D. G. Hunter, *Marriage, Celibacy, and Heresy in Ancient Christianity: The Jovinianist Controversy* (Oxford: Oxford University Press, 2007).

60. G. Bardy, "Saint Jérôme et ses maîtres hébreux," *RBén* 46 (1934): 145–

ter completing the four Pauline commentaries, Jerome turned his attention to various projects relating to the Old Testament, such as a commentary on Ecclesiastes and three desk-reference works, *On Hebrew Names, On Hebrew Places,* and *Hebrew Questions on Genesis,*[61] all written between 389 and 393, and by 390 he had begun translating the OT from the Hebrew.

3. LITERARY SOURCES OF
THE *COMMENTARY ON GALATIANS*

Peripheral Influences

Jerome's *Commentary on Galatians* is an extraordinarily learned work that draws from a broad range of sources both Christian and non-Christian, both Greek and Latin. The Latin classics surface at every turn in the form of direct quotations, paraphrases, or allusions. Sometimes Jerome borrows others' phraseology in order to enhance his own prose. For instance, Cicero's remark about the Pythagoreans, according to whom "an opinion already decided was so potent that it made authority not supported by reason prevail" (*tantum opinio praeiudicata poterat, ut etiam sine ratione valeret auctoritas*),[62] is echoed in the compliment Jerome pays to Marcella's intellectual independence: "My authority did not prevail with her if it was not supported by reason" (*nec sine ratione praeiudicata apud eam valebat auctoritas*).[63]

On a few occasions Jerome uses classical literature as a polemical counterpoint to Christian literature. In the preface to Book 3 he says, "If anyone is looking for eloquence or enjoys rhetorical declamations, he has Demosthenes and Polemon in Greek and Cicero and Quintilian in Latin. The church of Christ has drawn its members not from the Academy or the Lycaeum but from the common people." Jerome aims to make a

---

64; I. Opelt, "S. Girolamo ed i suoi maestri ebrei," *Augustinianum* 28 (1988): 327–38.

61. For an English translation of this work with an accompanying commentary, see C. T. R. Hayward, *Jerome's Hebrew Questions on Genesis* (Oxford: Oxford University Press, 1995).

62. *De natura deorum* 1.5.10.

63. *Comm. Gal.* 1, pref.

similar point when he cites Terence's famous line, "Flattery attracts friends, and truth, hatred" (*obsequium amicos, veritas odium parit*),[64] in conjunction with Paul's remark, "Have I now become your enemy by telling you the truth?" He proceeds to show how inferior Terence is to Paul: "The Apostle has tempered his statement to those he had called fools and infants and has personalized it, targeting individual people and the Galatian Christians. The poet, however, went perilously astray by making a generalized pronouncement about universal behavior."[65] In terms of non-Christian sources, Jerome does not confine himself to classical literature. For instance, from the late antique epitomator Eutropius he takes over an anecdote illustrating the emperor Titus's fastidiousness about doing good deeds.[66]

Christian sources not surprisingly are even more integral components of the *Commentary*'s literary matrix. In addition to selected Biblical commentaries (see below), Jerome drew directly from a few miscellaneous Greek patristic texts such as the second-century *Debate between Jason and Papiscus,* Clement of Alexandria's *Hypotyposeis,* Eusebius of Caesarea's *Ecclesiastical History,* and Epiphanius of Salamis's *Panarion.* As for the Latin Fathers, Jerome mentions Tertullian and Cyprian only once by name and Lactantius twice. This may initially give the impression that their influence on the *Commentary* was slight. Numerous surreptitious echoes of their writings, however, show that this North African triad helped to shape the theological, heresiological, and literary contours of the *Commentary* in notable ways.[67] Let us take just one example out of many. In Gal 1.4, Paul speaks of how Christ "gave himself for our sins to redeem us from the present evil age." Jerome tries to show that by "present evil age" Paul does not mean that any period of time is intrinsically evil. He explains:

Forests are brought into ill repute when robberies abound in them, not because the ground or the trees commit sin but because they have

64. *Andr.* 68.   65. *Comm. Gal.* 2.4.15–16.
66. *Comm. Gal.* 3.6.10.
67. A. Cain, "Tertullian, Cyprian, and Lactantius in Jerome's *Commentary on Galatians,*" *REAug* 55 (2009): 23–51. I have indicated each of these echoes in the footnotes to the present translation.

gained a bad reputation as places where murders occur. We also despise the sword by which human blood is poured out as well as the cup in which poison is mixed, not because the sword and cup commit sin but because those who use these things for evil purposes deserve reproach.[68]

Jerome has lifted this sword-and-cup analogy directly from the pages of Tertullian, who had applied it in a different context to illustrate that the flesh is basically a passive vessel that the soul can use for good or evil.[69]

Greek Sources

The classical and patristic sources just surveyed in brief comprise what we might call the peripheral sources of Jerome's *Commentary*—peripheral because they do not provide core exegetical content. Moving from periphery to center, we come to Greek patristic commentaries and other related works on Galatians that Jerome consulted in preparation for his own work. In the preface to Book 1 he lists his sources:

I . . . have followed the commentaries of Origen. He wrote five extraordinary volumes on Paul's epistle to the Galatians and rounded out the tenth book of his *Miscellanies* with a brief section expounding it. He also produced various homilies and scholia that would be sufficient all by themselves. I say nothing of my seeing guide Didymus; [Apollinaris,] who recently left the church at Laodicea; the ancient heretic Alexander; Eusebius of Emesa; and Theodore of Heraclea; all of whom have left behind modest commentaries of their own on the topic at hand.[70]

Didymus the Blind (c. 313–c. 398)   Didymus was the last head of the great catechetical school at Alexandria, which closed its

---

68. *Comm. Gal.* 1.1.4–5.

69. *De res. carn.* 16.4–8 (ANF 3:556): "The soul alone, therefore, will have to be judged at the last day pre-eminently as to how it has employed the vessel of the flesh; the vessel itself, of course, not being amenable to a judicial award: for who condemns the cup if any man has mixed poison in it? or who sentences the sword to the beasts, if a man has perpetrated with it the atrocities of a brigand?"

70. Jerome likely gained access (for copying) to many of these commentaries through his regular trips to the famed ecclesiastical library in Caesarea, about fifty miles to the northwest of Bethlehem: cf. Jay, *L'exégèse de saint Jérôme*, 529–34. For an overview of the history of this illustrious library, see A. J. Carriker, *The Library of Eusebius of Caesarea* (Leiden: E. J. Brill, 2003), 1–36.

doors soon after his death at the ripe age of eighty-five.[71] Despite being blind since the age of four and never learning how to read, he mastered all of the known sciences and had an encyclopedic knowledge of Scripture.[72] Rufinus of Aquileia, a great admirer of his, called him a "prophet" and "apostolic man."[73] Didymus was an extremely prolific author. He composed various theological treatises, including *On the Trinity* and *On the Holy Spirit*; the latter survives in a Latin translation completed by Jerome in 387.[74] Didymus also wrote commentaries on Genesis, Job, Psalms, Proverbs, Isaiah, Zechariah, Hosea, Matthew, John, Acts, 1 and 2 Corinthians, Galatians, and Ephesians. Jerome briefly studied under him while in Alexandria in early 386[75] and later spoke of their friendship.[76] Although his stay lasted under a month,[77] Jerome must have kept his teacher busy. Didymus, he proudly stated, had composed a commentary on Zechariah[78] at his request and had dedicated a commentary on Hosea to him.[79] In posterity, Didymus suffered for his intense admiration for Origen: when Origen's works were condemned at the Second Council of Constantinople in 553, so were his. As a result, Didymus and his writings were largely forgotten during the Middle Ages. Comparatively little remains in the original Greek of his vast literary production. His commentary on Galatians is completely lost.

Apollinaris of Laodicea (c. 315–c. 392)   Apollinaris was the bishop of Laodicea on the Syrian coast in the latter half of the fourth

71. R. Layton, *Didymus the Blind and his Circle in Late-Antique Alexandria: Virtue and Narrative in Biblical Scholarship* (Urbana: University of Illinois Press, 2004).

72. Palladius, *Hist. laus.* 4; Jerome, *Vir. ill.* 109.

73. *Apol. c. Hier.* 2.25.

74. L. Doutreleau, *Didyme l'Aveugle: Traité du Saint-Esprit. Introduction, texte critique, traduction, notes et index*, SC 386 (Paris: Éditions du Cerf, 1992).

75. The evidence is compiled by Cavallera in *Jérôme*, 2.127–30.

76. *Comm. Is.*, pref. (CCSL 73:3): *Didymus, cuius amicitiis nuper usi sumus.*

77. Rufinus (*Apol. c. Hier.* 2.12), who had spent about eight years around Didymus, mocked Jerome for having spent no more than thirty days in Alexandria in his entire life, and Jerome did not deny the charge.

78. For a recent translation of this commentary, see R. C. Hill, trans., *Didymus the Blind, Commentary on Zechariah*, FOTC 111 (Washington, DC: The Catholic University of America Press, 2006).

79. *Vir. ill.* 109.

century. According to Jerome, he wrote "innumerable volumes" on Scripture.[80] These included commentaries on Ecclesiastes, Isaiah, Hosea, Malachi, Matthew, Romans, 1 Corinthians, Galatians, and Ephesians, some of which survive in fragments. Jerome attended his lectures when he was living in Antioch in the late 370s.[81] Nothing is extant of Apollinaris's commentary on Galatians. But if there is truth to Jerome's later comment that his interpretations were little more than outlines,[82] it seems unlikely that his Galatians commentary would have been of much use to Jerome. Be that as it may, Apollinaris's immense treatise *Against Porphyry* in thirty books may have informed Jerome's references to Porphyry in the *Commentary on Galatians*.[83]

Alexander (3d century?)   Alexander is called simply the "ancient heretic" (*veterem haereticum*).[84] Alexander Souter,[85] evidently taking his cue from C. H. Turner,[86] identified him as the Valentinian teacher by the same name whom Tertullian mentions in *De carne Christi* 15.3, 16.1, and 17.1.[87] This theory seems as plausible as any, all the more so because both components of Jerome's epithet could apply to Tertullian's Gnostic: he was a "heretic" and

---

80. *Vir. ill.* 104. E. Mühlenberg, "Zur exegetischen Methode des Apollinaris von Laodicea," in *Christliche exegese zwischen Nicaea und Chalcedon,* ed. J. van Oort and U. Wickert (Kampen: Kok Pharos, 1992), 132–47.

81. P. Jay, "Jérôme auditeur d'Apollinaire de Laodicée à Antioche," *REAug* 20 (1974): 36–41.

82. Jerome said that Apollinaris's commentaries read like "chapter headings": *Apollinaris autem more suo sic exponit omnia, ut universa transcurrat et punctis quibusdam atque intervallis, immo compendiis grandis viae spatia praetervolet, ut non tam commentarios quam indices capitulorum nos legere credamus (Comm. Is.,* pref. [CCSL 73:4]).

83. A. Fürst, *Augustins Briefwechsel mit Hieronymus* (Münster: Aschendorff, 1999), 13.

84. Book 1, pref.

85. *The Earliest Latin Commentaries on the Epistles of St. Paul* (Oxford: Oxford University Press, 1927), 108.

86. "Greek Patristic Commentaries on the Pauline Epistles," in *A Dictionary of the Bible, Supplement,* ed. J. Hastings (Edinburgh: T & T Clark, 1898), 484–531 (at p. 489).

87. Alexander argued that Christ did not possess real human flesh. See E. Thomassen, *The Spiritual Seed: The Church of the "Valentinians"* (Leiden: E. J. Brill, 2006), 496–97.

he was "ancient," which indicates that from Jerome's perspective he lived a long time ago. Alexander is otherwise unattested.[88] His commentaries are altogether lost, and we have no sense of the range of his exegetical production.

Eusebius of Emesa (c. 300–359)   Eusebius was the bishop of Emesa in Phoenicia in the middle of the fourth century.[89] He was born around 300 into a noble family in Edessa, at the time a melting pot of Hellenistic and Syrian culture.[90] Although Syriac was Eusebius's mother-tongue,[91] he received a classical education in Greek, and it was in Greek that he composed his numerous Biblical commentaries. These included a commentary on the Pentateuch[92] and a compendious one in ten books on Galatians, which is lost except for nineteen Greek fragments[93] of varying length preserved in *catenae*, or "chains" of excerpts from patristic Biblical commentaries collected after the sixth century to provide preachers with instructional material for sermons.

88. Cf. T. D. Barnes, *Tertullian: A Historical and Literary Study* (Oxford: Oxford University Press, 1971), 126, who is apparently unaware of the possible connection between Tertullian's and Jerome's Alexanders.

89. For studies of his life and works, see É. M. Buytaert, *L'héritage littéraire d'Eusèbe d'Émèse: Étude critique et historique* (Louvain: Bureaux du Muséon, 1949), and more recently R. B. ter Haar Romeny, *A Syrian in Greek Dress: The Use of Greek, Hebrew and Syriac Biblical Texts in Eusebius of Emesa's Commentary on Genesis* (Leiden: E. J. Brill, 1997).

90. See J. B. Segal, *Edessa: The Blessed City* (Oxford: Oxford University Press, 1970); H. J. W. Drijvers, *Cults and Beliefs at Edessa* (Leiden: E. J. Brill, 1980).

91. H. J. Lehmann, "The Syriac translation of the Old Testament—as evidenced around the middle of the fourth century (in Eusebius of Emesa)," *SJOT* 1 (1987): 66–86 (at p. 73).

92. For the surviving fragments, see R. Devreesse, *Les anciens commentateurs grecs de l'Octateuque et des Rois (fragments tirés des chaînes)* (Vatican City: Biblioteca Apostolica Vaticana, 1959), 55–103. Cf. J. A. Novotný, "Les fragments exégétiques sur les livres de l'Ancien Testament d'Eusèbe d'Émèse," *OCP* 57 (1991): 27–67.

93. These fragments are printed in K. Staab, *Pauluskommentare aus der griechischen Kirche aus Katenenhandschriften gesammelt und herausgegeben* (Münster: Aschendorff, 1933), 46–52. See J. A. Novotný, "Eusebius of Emesa as Interpreter of St. Paul," in *Studiorum Paulinorum Congressus internationalis catholicus 1961*, 2 vols. (Rome: Pontificium Institutum Biblicum, 1963), 2.471–79, with an emphasis on Eusebius's exegesis of Galatians.

Theodore of Heraclea (d. 355) Theodore was the anti-Nicene bishop of Heraclea in Thrace in the middle of the fourth century. He composed commentaries on the Psalter, Matthew, John, and the Pauline epistles. Jerome remarks that as a commentator Theodore wrote "in an elegant and precise style that followed mainly the literal interpretation."[94] His writings have come down to us in fragments, and nothing of his commentary on Galatians has been preserved.

Origen (185–254) Origen wrote commentaries on nearly every book of the Bible, and he was the first systematic interpreter of Paul in the early church.[95] His commentary on Romans, the oldest extant commentary on this Biblical book, survives mostly through Rufinus's Latin translation.[96] He composed commentaries also on Ephesians, Philippians, Colossians, Thessalonians, Hebrews, Titus, and Galatians, the last of which, originally in five books, survives in only seven fragments. Three in Greek are found in the Mount Athos manuscript Laura 184 (B. 64).[97] They are too brief, however, to shed any significant light on the commentary as a whole. The other four are transmitted in Latin through Rufinus's translation (397) of the *Apology for Origen*, which Pamphilus of Caesarea, in collaboration with Eusebius, had composed in Greek between 307 and 310 (the Greek origi-

---

94. *Vir. ill.* 90 (trans. Halton, FOTC 100:123).

95. F. Cocchini, *Il Paolo di Origene: Contributo alla storia della recezione delle epistole paoline nel III secolo* (Rome: Edizioni Studium, 1992). For all matters biographical, see J. W. Trigg, *Origen: The Bible and Philosophy in the Third-Century Church* (Atlanta: John Knox Press, 1983). A more concise overview of Origen's life and literary works can be found in *The Westminster Handbook to Origen*, ed. J. A. McGuckin (Louisville: John Knox Press, 2004), 1–44. See also Pierre Nautin's magisterial study *Origène: Sa vie et son œuvre* (Paris: Beauchesne, 1977).

96. T. Scheck, trans., *Origen, Commentary on the Epistle to the Romans, Books 1–5*, FOTC 103 (Washington, DC: The Catholic University of America Press, 2001), and idem, trans., *Origen, Commentary on the Epistle to the Romans, Books 6–10*, FOTC 104 (Washington, DC: The Catholic University of America Press, 2002).

97. These fragments are printed in E. F. von der Goltz, *Eine textkritische Arbeit des zehnten bezw. sechsten Jahrhunderts herausgegeben nach einem Kodex des Athosklosters Lawra* (Leipzig: Hinrichs, 1899), 72–74. On this manuscript, see further B. Metzger, *Manuscripts of the Greek Bible: An Introduction to Palaeography* (Oxford: Oxford University Press, 1981), 112.

nal has been lost). Origen's lengthy excursus on Galatians at the end of the tenth book of his now-fragmentary *Miscellanies* has been preserved in Latin by Jerome, who translated it word-for-word and inserted it into his treatment of Gal 5.13–14.[98]

The Extent of the Greek Influences: "I dictated either my own or others' ideas"

Jerome, then, accessed a veritable smorgasbord of Greek commentaries on Galatians. But how much material did he take from each of them? In the cases of Didymus, Apollinaris, Alexander, and Theodore, we are completely in the dark since their commentaries have been lost. As for Didymus, we know that Jerome relied heavily on his commentaries on Ephesians and especially Zechariah[99] when composing his own commentaries on these Biblical books. We cannot, however, confidently posit a comparable degree of dependence on his Galatians commentary without so much as a fragment of this work in hand.

We are on somewhat safer ground when it comes to Eusebius of Emesa's commentary on Galatians. Comparison of the nineteen fragments of this with the corresponding parts of Jerome's *Commentary* reveals that Jerome virtually copies Eusebius in two places.[100] On many other occasions his interpretations resemble Eusebius's less in wording than in spirit. Bammel plausibly attributes this to both men's shared stake in the exegetical tradition leading back to Origen.[101] Recently I have argued that an anonymous patristic quotation Jerome includes in *Comm. Gal.* 3.6.11 is a translation of a passage taken from Eusebius's commentary

---

98. *Comm. Gal.* 3.5.13a.

99. A. Canellis, "Le livre III de l'*In Zachariam* de Saint Jérôme et la tradition alexandrine," *Adamantius* 13 (2007): 66–81; eadem, "L'*In Zachariam* de Jérôme et la tradition alexandrine," in *Jerome of Stridon*, ed. Cain and Lössl, 153–62.

100. For a synoptic comparison of these texts, see C. P. Bammel, "Die Pauluskommentare des Hieronymus: die ersten wissenschaftlichen lateinischen Bibelkommentare?" in *Cristianesimo Latino e cultura Greca sino al sec. IV, XXI Incontro di studiosi dell'antichità cristiana, Rome 7–9 maggio 1992* (Rome: Institutum Patristicum Augustinianum, 1993), 187–207 (pp. 194–95 n. 52). I have juxtaposed Jerome's Latin and these two Eusebian fragments in Greek in the footnotes to *Comm. Gal.* 1.1.13–14.

101. "Die Pauluskommentare des Hieronymus," 195.

on Galatians.[102] This means that we now have a twentieth fragment of Eusebius's commentary.

By his own admission, Jerome owed his most substantial debt
in the *Commentary on Galatians* to Origen ("I have followed the
commentaries of Origen").[103] Origen is mentioned by name (or
by his nickname, "Adamantius") on only a small handful of occasions in the *Commentary*.[104] Nevertheless, his presence can be
felt on virtually every page. For instance, whenever Jerome cites
the OT in Hebrew or Greek,[105] he is almost certainly using Origen's Hexapla, which presented the entire OT in six parallel
columns.[106] References to the second-century Marcion and the
Gnostics Basilides and Valentinus likely derive from Origen's
commentary on Galatians.[107] In addition, throughout the *Commentary* Jerome expresses certain ideas and outlooks that are
conspicuously Origenian. They are too numerous and miscellaneous to categorize here, but I have called attention to them
in the footnotes to the translation and have referred to the relevant passages in Origen's surviving writings (including the extant fragments of Origen's commentary on Galatians), in many
cases quoting these passages in full so as to give the reader a
more tangible sense of Jerome's dependency.

102. A. Cain, "An Unidentified Patristic Quotation in Jerome's *Commentary
on Galatians* (3.6.11)," *JThS*, n.s., 61 (2010): 216–25.

103. A. Souter, *The Earliest Latin Commentaries on the Epistles of St. Paul* (Oxford, 1927), 110–25; M. Schatkin, "The Influence of Origen upon St. Jerome's
Commentary on Galatians," *VChr* 24 (1970): 49–58; G. Raspanti, "*Adgrediar opus
intemptatum*. L'*Ad Galatas* di Girolamo e gli sviluppi del commentario biblico latino," *Adamantius* 10 (2004): 194–216 (esp. pp. 199–207).

104. 1.3.1b; 2.4.28; 3.5.13a.

105. 1.1.4–5; 2.3.10; 2.3.11–12; 2.3.13b–14; 2.3.15–18; 2.5.6; 3.6.18.

106. The first two columns contained the Hebrew text and a transliteration
of it into Greek script, and the remaining four contained the Septuagint corrected against the Hebrew and the three second-century translations of the Hebrew OT into Greek by the Jews Aquila, Symmachus, and Theodotion. Why Origen undertook this project in the first place is debated by scholars. John Wright
suggests that he wanted to pave the way for a corrected text of the OT: "Origen
in the Scholar's Den: A Rationale for the Hexapla," in *Origen of Alexandria: His
World and His Legacy*, ed. C. Kannengiesser and W. L. Petersen (Notre Dame:
University of Notre Dame Press, 1988), 48–62.

107. See below, under section 5, "Orthodoxy and Heresy in the *Commentary
on Galatians*."

Even more insight into the nature and extent of Jerome's indebtedness to Origen in the *Commentary* emerges from a synoptic comparison of the few fragments of Origen's commentary with Jerome's. For our purposes here, one representative example (on Gal 3.19–20) will suffice.

Origen: The Law was given to Moses by angels through the hand and power of Christ the mediator, who, although "he was the Word of God in the beginning and was with God and was God" [Jn 1.1], did the Father's bidding in all things. For "all things were made through him" [Jn 1.3], that is to say, not only creatures but also the Law and the prophets, and the Word himself is the "mediator between God and men" [1 Tm 2.5]. At the conclusion of the ages this Word became man, Jesus Christ. But before this coming in the flesh had been made manifest, he was indeed the mediator of everything, though he was not yet a man.[108]

Jerome: Furthermore, after their idolatry, to which they had been so enslaved in Egypt that they forgot the God of their fathers and would say, "These are your Gods, Israel, who brought you out of the land of Egypt" [Ex 32.4], rituals prescribing how properly to worship God and to punish wrongdoers were instituted through the hand of the mediator, Christ Jesus. For "all things were made through him, and without him nothing was made" [Jn 1.3]—this goes not only for heaven, earth, the sea, and everything we see, but also for the provisions of the Law that were imposed as a yoke by Moses on a stiff-necked people. Also, Paul wrote to Timothy, "For there is one God, and one mediator between God and men, the man Christ Jesus" [1 Tm 2.5]. After he deigned to be born from the womb of the Virgin for the sake of our salvation, the man Christ Jesus was called the broker between God and men. But before he took on a human body, when he was with the Father in the beginning as God [cf. Jn 1.1–2] and was the Word to all the holy people (such as Enoch, Noah, Abraham, Isaac, Jacob, Moses, and all the prophets whom Scripture mentions), he served as God's mouthpiece to them and was only called a mediator although he had not yet assumed human nature.

---

108. *Pamphile et Eusèbe de Césarée, Apologie pour Origène. Texte critique, traduction et notes, t. 1,* ed. R. Amacker and É. Junod, SC 464 (Paris: Éditions du Cerf, 2002), 194–96. This English translation of Rufinus's Latin translation of Pamphilus's Origen-fragment is my own. Here we must assume that Rufinus rendered the Greek more or less faithfully, even though as a translator he occasionally took liberties with Origen's text: see R. Heine, *Origen, Homilies on Genesis and Exodus,* FOTC 71 (Washington, DC: The Catholic University of America Press, 1982), 30–39. For a complete English translation of the Pamphilus-Rufinus text, see T. Scheck, trans., FOTC 120 (Washington, DC: The Catholic University of America Press, 2010).

There are obvious similarities between these two passages. Both commentators cite 1 Tm 2.5. Both refer to Christ's Incarnation and quote from the prologue to John's Gospel. In addition, Jerome's "not only for heaven, earth, the sea, and everything we see, but also for the provisions of the Law that were imposed as a yoke by Moses on a stiff-necked people" echoes Origen's less elaborate "not only creatures but also the Law and the prophets." But there are also differences. Jerome mentions several OT figures not named by Origen, and, unlike Origen, he alludes to Mary's central role in salvation history, thus reflecting his profound interest in Mariology in the 380s.

Moreover, in the above passage Jerome retains the essence of Origen but also introduces elements that either are his own or are borrowed from other Greek exegetes—or a combination of the two (we have no way of narrowing it down further than this because we do not have fragments on Gal 3.19–20 from any of Jerome's other Greek sources). Scrutiny of Jerome's Galatians commentary in conjunction with the other Origen-fragments points generally to the same conclusion.[109] Even taken by itself, this relatively tiny pool of evidence is certainly suggestive. But when interpreted in the light of Jerome's statement that he "followed the commentaries of Origen" and of the recognizable Origenian elements throughout the *Commentary*, we may reasonably surmise that Origen's influence was vast. This picture is nevertheless still too incomplete to warrant the verdict that Jerome's Pauline commentaries "are little more than paraphrases of Origen."[110]

These findings square with how Jerome characterizes his compositional technique in the preface to Book 1: "I summoned my secretary and dictated either my own or others' ideas, all the while paying no attention to the method, the words, or the opinions belonging to each." Jerome remains vague and does

---

109. Raspanti, "*Adgrediar opus intemptatum*," 204–7. Cf. F. Deniau, "Le commentaire de Jérôme sur Ephésiens nous permet-il de connaître celui d'Origène?" in *Origeniana: Premier colloque international des études origéniennes (Montserrat, 18–21 septembre 1973)*, ed. H. Crouzel, G. Lomiento, and J. Ruis-Camps (Bari: Università di Bari, 1975), 163–79.

110. M. Simonetti, *Biblical Interpretation in the Early Church: An Historical Introduction to Patristic Exegesis*, trans. J. A. Hughes (Edinburgh: T & T Clark, 1994), 99.

not so much as hint at the proportional make-up of this mixture. This ambiguity and the fact that for individual interpretations he almost never names his Greek sources (virtually none of which survive anyway) make it next to impossible, in most instances, to pinpoint what truly original contributions Jerome may have made to the exegesis of Galatians.

Jerome's Commentary on Galatians *and the Latin Exegetical Tradition*

Prior to the middle of the fourth century, no Latin exegete had tried his hand at a formal commentary on a Pauline epistle. Up until that point, the Apostle had remained the sole property of Greek and Syriac commentators.[111] Then, in the space of half a century (c. 360–c. 409), there appeared no less than fifty-two commentaries by six different Latin commentators. This sudden flurry of exegetical activity has been dubbed the "Renaissance of Paul."[112]

The father of this late-blooming western tradition was Marius Victorinus, a Neoplatonic philosopher and rhetorician in Rome who converted to Christianity in old age.[113] During the 360s, he produced commentaries on Galatians, Philippians, Ephesians, Romans, and 1 and 2 Corinthians, though only the first three of these survive.[114] Between 366 and 384, the mysterious figure

111. For an overview of this very fulsome tradition, see Turner, "Greek Patristic Commentaries on the Pauline Epistles," in J. Hastings, ed., *A Dictionary of the Bible, Supplement* (Edinburgh: T & T Clark, 1898), 484–531.

112. K. Froehlich, "Which Paul? Observations on the Image of the Apostle in the History of Biblical Exegesis," in *New Perspectives on Historical Theology*, ed. B. Nassif (Grand Rapids: W. B. Eerdmans, 1996), 279–99 (p. 285). For more on this Pauline phenomenon, see M. G. Mara, "Ricerche storico-esegetiche sulla presenza del corpus paolino nella storia del cristianesimo dal II al V secolo," in M. G. Mara, *Paolo di Tarso e il suo epistolario* (Aquila: Japadre, 1983), 6–64, and more recently J. Lössl, "Augustine, 'Pelagianism,' Julian of Aeclanum, and Modern Scholarship," *ZAC* 10 (2007): 129–50 (esp. pp. 129–33).

113. Augustine, a fellow professor and convert to Catholic Christianity, expresses deep admiration for Victorinus in his *Confessions* (8.2.3–6).

114. On Victorinus's Pauline exegesis, see G. Raspanti, *Mario Vittorino esegeta di S. Paolo* (Palermo: L'Epos, 1996), and the thorough introduction in S. A. Cooper, *Marius Victorinus' Commentary on Galatians: Introduction, Translation, and Notes* (Oxford: Oxford University Press, 2005).

known to us today by the moniker "Ambrosiaster" (so called because in later centuries he was confused with Bishop Ambrose
of Milan) wrote important commentaries on the thirteen epistles in the New Testament that bear Paul's name.[115] According
to a recently advanced theory, Ambrosiaster released his commentary on Galatians initially around 378–380 (the "alpha version") and then a slightly revised edition (the "gamma version")
in 384.[116] Next in the tradition came Jerome, whose commentaries on Philemon, Galatians, Ephesians, and Titus date to the
summer and early autumn of 386. During the next decade, pri-
or to 396, Augustine worked on three expositions of Paul—
Propositions from Romans, a commentary on Galatians, and an unfinished commentary on Romans.[117] The Galatians commentary
was completed in 394/5.[118] Sometime between 396 and 405,
an anonymous Latin exegete writing in possibly Rome or Aquileia composed commentaries on the thirteen Pauline epistles
plus one on Hebrews, which is the oldest known commentary
on Hebrews written in Latin.[119] The author is known today as

115. Who this man was exactly has been the subject of fierce debate down
to the present day. None of the many suggestions offered about his identity has
garnered anything close to a scholarly consensus. The case is still wide open,
and he remains—for now, and perhaps forever—the Great Anonymous. For a
brief summary of the debate, see S. Lunn-Rockliffe, *Ambrosiaster's Political Theology* (Oxford: Oxford University Press, 2007), 33–44.

116. See S. A. Cooper and D. G. Hunter, "Ambrosiaster *redactor sui:* The
Commentaries on the Pauline Epistles (Excluding Romans)," forthcoming in
REAug. I am grateful to David Hunter for providing me with a draft of this ar-
ticle prior to its publication.

117. On the two works on Romans, see P. Fredriksen Landes, *Augustine on
Romans: Propositions from the Epistle to the Romans, Unfinished Commentary on the
Epistle to the Romans* (Chico: Scholars Press, 1982).

118. For an annotated translation and study, see E. Plumer, *Augustine's Commentary on Galatians: Introduction, Text, Translation, and Notes* (Oxford: Oxford
University Press, 2003). See also L. Fladerer, *Augustinus als Exeget: zu einen Kommentaren des Galaterbriefes und der Genesis* (Vienna: Österreichischen Akademie
der Wissenschaften, 2010).

119. H. J. Frede, *Ein neuer Paulustext und Kommentar,* 1. *Untersuchungen;* 2.
Die Texte (Freiburg: Herder, 1973–74). T. de Bruyn, "Constantius the *Tractator:*
Author of an Anonymous Commentary on the Pauline Epistles?" *JThS,* n.s., 43
(1992): 38–54, assigns authorship to a certain anti-Pelagian bishop by the name
of Constantius, but this hypothesis has been challenged by Y.-M. Duval, "Pélage

the "Budapest Anonymous" because portions of his commentaries have been preserved in a manuscript housed in the Hungarian National Museum in Budapest. Finally, Pelagius composed his commentaries on the complete Pauline corpus in Rome between 406 and 409.[120]

Jerome, then, was not the first Latin Christian to write a commentary on Galatians. His most immediate predecessor, Ambrosiaster, was active in Rome during the pontificate of Damasus. In addition to Pauline commentaries, he authored over ten dozen short treatises known collectively as the *Questions on the Old and New Testament*.[121] Therefore, Jerome and he overlapped in Rome from 382 to 385. It is unknown whether they actually knew each other personally, but even if they were not acquainted, it did not prevent ideological hostilities from simmering between them. Ambrosiaster almost certainly was one of the unnamed critics who assailed Jerome's revision of the Gospels.[122] He also did not take kindly to Jerome's inordinate exaltation of virginity at the expense of marriage, and his *Question* on original sin seems to have been an attack on the articulation of these ascetic ideals in the letter to Eustochium on preserving virginity (*Ep.* 22).[123]

This polemic was a two-way street. In 383 or 384, Pope Damasus sent Jerome a letter asking him to clear up five problematic passages in Genesis. The five questions had been lifted directly (in much the same wording and order) from Ambrosiaster's *Questions*. Damasus, it seems, wanted to get different, or better, answers from his young client. Jerome, who knew Ambrosiaster's work (as the numerous allusive insults that litter his writings at-

en son temps: Données chronologiques nouvelles pour une présentation nouvelle," *StudPatr* 38 (2001): 95–118 (see p. 101).

120. For a translation and study of the Romans commentary, see T. de Bruyn, *Pelagius' Commentary on St. Paul's Epistle to the Romans* (Oxford: Oxford University Press, 1993).

121. The *Questions* evidently circulated anonymously in two different authorial recensions in the late fourth century. See C. Martini, "De ordinatione duarum Collectionum quibus Ambrosiastri *Quaestiones* traduntur," *Antonianum* 21 (1947): 23–48; idem, "Le recensioni delle *Quaestiones Veteris et Novi Testamenti* dell'Ambrosiaster," *RicSRel* 1 (1954): 40–62.

122. Kelly, *Jerome*, 89–90; Lunn-Rockliffe, *Ambrosiaster's Political Theology*, 22–23.

123. D. G. Hunter, "*On the Sin of Adam and Eve*: A Little-Known Defense of Marriage and Childbearing by Ambrosiaster," *HThR* 82 (1989): 283–99.

test),[124] recognized the origin of these questions and crafted his reply in such a way as to level a devastating criticism at Ambrosiaster's exegetical methodology, without actually mentioning his opponent by name.[125] Jerome must have felt threatened by a senior rival who by the middle 380s was a far more accomplished Biblical scholar than he, and whose work had caught the eye of his powerful papal patron; perhaps an intensely personal resentment fanned the flames of this professional rivalry. In any event, Jerome omitted Ambrosiaster from *De viris illustribus*, and this *damnatio memoriae* was the supreme form of de-legitimization. Jerome's documented attempts to suppress the legacy of a key figure of late fourth-century Biblical exegesis could explain why Ambrosiaster's commentary on Galatians, which he probably had come across in Rome,[126] is nowhere mentioned or even alluded to in his own *Commentary*.

Whether by accident or design—presumably the latter—Ambrosiaster is passed over in silence, as if he occupied absolutely no place in the Latin tradition of Pauline exegesis. The progenitor of this tradition, Marius Victorinus, is at least acknowledged, though hardly in a flattering way. In fact, what Jerome had to say about him in the preface to Book 1 is quite scathing:

I shall undertake a work that no Latin writer before me has attempted and that hardly any among the Greeks have executed in a manner worthy of the exalted nature of the subject matter. I am not unaware that Gaius Marius Victorinus, who taught rhetoric at Rome when I was a boy, produced commentaries on the Apostle. Engrossed in secular learning as he was, however, he was completely ignorant of Scripture, and nobody—no matter how eloquent he may be—is able to discuss competently what he does not know. Am I, then, foolish or rash to promise what he was incapable of accomplishing? Not at all. I believe that I am more cautious and timid because I have recognized the scantness of my own abilities and have followed the commentaries of Origen. . . . [and] Didymus; [Apollinaris]; . . . Alexander; Eusebius of Emesa; and Theodore of Heraclea.

124. H. Vogels, "Ambrosiaster und Hieronymus," *RBén* 66 (1956): 14–19.

125. A. Cain, "In Ambrosiaster's Shadow: A Critical Re-Evaluation of the Last Surviving Letter Exchange between Pope Damasus and Jerome," *REAug* 51 (2005): 257–77. For an analysis of Ambrosiaster's exegetical technique, see G. Raspanti, "Aspetti formali dell'esegesi paolina dell'Ambrosiaster," *AnnSE* 16 (1999): 507–36.

126. So Cooper, *Marius Victorinus' Commentary on Galatians*, 186 n. 21.

The revisionist literary historian in Jerome radically redefines the parameters of the Latin strand of the Pauline tradition. He insinuates that this tradition made a false start with Victorinus. He accuses Victorinus of having been "completely ignorant of Scripture"—the worst possible insult one could level at a commentator on Scripture. The basis for this allegation is presumably the fact that Victorinus rarely quotes other parts of the Bible to illuminate passages in Galatians,[127] whereas Jerome constantly references the rest of the Bible and especially the OT.

Jerome recognized that displacing Victorinus and then crowning himself as the real inaugurator of the Pauline commentary in Latin seemed a bold move. ("Am I, then, foolish or rash to promise what he was incapable of accomplishing?") But it was not empty bravado. Jerome's sense of self-assurance must be understood in the broader context of his ambitious program to transmit the wisdom of the Greek exegetical tradition to the Latin-speaking world. He believed that this tradition, which was older and more venerable than its Latin first cousin, must be a frame of reference for any and all Biblical exegesis done in the Latin language, and in the passage quoted above he positions himself as its ambassador to the West.[128]

4. EXEGESIS AND TEXTUAL CRITICISM IN THE *COMMENTARY ON GALATIANS*

Jerome's *Commentary on Galatians* is quite unlike the other five Latin patristic commentaries on Galatians in that it is a variorum commentary that presents alternative interpretations of giv-

127. Cooper, *Marius Victorinus' Commentary on Galatians,* 107, acknowledges Victorinus's "no doubt scanty acquaintance with the Old Testament," but attributes his myopic focus on Paul to a conscious methodological choice: "Victorinus' primary goal—to explain the meaning and import of the Pauline letters for a contemporary audience—could best be accomplished by explicating Paul on the basis of what Paul himself said."

128. Jerome accomplished his goal partly by elbowing Ambrose aside. See A. Cain, "Jerome's Pauline Commentaries between East and West: Tradition and Innovation in the *Commentary on Galatians,*" in *Interpreting the Bible and Aristotle: The Alexandrian Commentary Tradition between Rome and Baghdad,* ed. J. Watt and J. Lössl (Aldershot: Ashgate Publishing, 2012), forthcoming.

en passages rather than the author's alone. It is essential, Jerome believed, to furnish the discriminating reader with the range of available options and to let him then choose for himself which one seems best.[129] By the same token, though, Jerome is often not shy about steering the reader in the direction of the interpretation he personally finds most convincing.

Patristic commentators tended to interpret the Pauline epistles extremely literally.[130] Jerome was no different. In his commentaries on the OT and Matthew he liberally employs "spiritual" readings[131] to illustrate the deeper sense of the Biblical text above and beyond the literal-historical sense; however, examples of spiritual exegesis are few and far between in his *Commentary on Galatians*. The reason for this is that Jerome's chief aim is to explicate Paul's message in a straightforward fashion, or, as he says in the preface to Book 3, "to elucidate obscure points, to touch only briefly on what is already clear, and to linger over things that are difficult to figure out."[132]

Jerome had a number of tools at his disposal that helped him explain to contemporary Christians the literal meaning of Galatians, that is, the meaning of Paul's words in their historical and theological context. The greatest Christian polymath in all of Latin antiquity, Jerome drew from—to name just a few things—his extensive knowledge of the Bible, secular and ecclesiastical history, geography, ethnography, rhetoric, grammar, and textual criticism. His mastery of this last discipline was particularly cru-

---

129. Cf. Jerome, *Apol. c. Ruf.* 1.16 (trans. Hritzu, FOTC 53:79): "What is the function of commentators? They expound the statements of someone else; they express in simple language views that have been expressed in an obscure manner; they quote the opinions of many individuals and they say: 'Some interpret this passage in this sense, others, in another sense'; they attempt to support their own understanding and interpretation with these testimonies in this fashion, so that the prudent reader, after reading the different interpretations and studying which of these many views are to be accepted and which rejected, will judge for himself which is the more correct; and, like the expert banker, will reject the falsely minted coin."

130. M. F. Wiles, *The Divine Apostle: The Interpretation of St Paul's Epistles in the Early Church* (Cambridge: Cambridge University Press, 1967), 10.

131. By "spiritual" readings I mean allegorical, moral, tropological, and anagogical readings.

132. *Comm. Gal.* 3, pref.

cial to his mission as an interpreter of Paul. He operated under the assumption that before one can properly comment on Scripture, one needs a reliable text with which to work. This point deserves further consideration here, because it is in Jerome's *Commentary on Galatians* that we see the most distinguished Biblical textual critic of the early church plying his trade at a pivotal stage in his scholarly career.

Between 382 and 385, during his second stay in Rome, Jerome came to the conclusion that Biblical exegesis is an activity best left to the trained specialist. This specialist must fit a certain profile. Ideally, he should be an ascetic monk, for Scriptural study is "an all-consuming *askesis*, a mortification of the body and a rejection of the world."[133] He must meet certain intellectual qualifications as well, such as possessing reading fluency in the Biblical languages, a literacy which grants him access to the *ipsissima verba* of Scripture in the "original." In terms of the OT, this means the Hebrew rather than the Septuagint (LXX)[134] and the Old Latin translations based on the LXX.

Jerome championed "Hebrew verity" (*Hebraica veritas*), a hermeneutical methodology that privileges the Hebrew as the final arbiter in all textual and interpretive matters relating to the OT. And since the OT is such a pervasive subtext of the NT writings, this concept has obvious applications for NT studies as well. In a letter to Pope Damasus (383) in which he explains the meaning of the phrase "Hosanna to the son of David," Jerome captures the essence of his methodology:

We therefore must pass over the little streams of opinion and rush back to the very source from which the Gospel writers drew. . . . The Hebrew words themselves must be presented and the opinion of all the commentators must be weighed, so that the reader, after considering

133. M. Vessey, "Conference and Confession: Literary Pragmatics in Augustine's *Apologia contra Hieronymum*," *JECS* 1 (1993): 175–213 (p. 184), on how "the *Studium scripturarum* is an all-consuming *askesis*, a mortification of the body and a rejection of the world. Naturally the province of monks, it can be prosecuted by clergy or laypeople only if they are prepared to follow a monastic way of life."

134. This was a translation of the OT into Greek produced between the third and first centuries BC in Alexandria. For an introduction, see J. M. Dines, *The Septuagint* (Edinburgh: T & T Clark, 2004).

all of these, may more readily discover for himself the proper way of thinking about the issue in question.[135]

The dismissive phrase "little streams of opinion" refers to Bishop Hilary of Poitiers and other patristic authorities referred to elsewhere in the letter who, no matter how reputed for personal holiness or learning they may have been, were rank amateurs in the field of Biblical exegesis because they were ignorant of Hebrew. Thus, Jerome's approach represented a paradigm shift in how power was brokered in the world of Latin Biblical exegesis. No longer were ecclesiastical rank and a reputation for piety necessarily reliable markers of a commentator's competence, unless they happened to be paired with a working knowledge of Hebrew. The implications are clear. Since Jerome was (as far as we know) the only Latin commentator in the late fourth century able to read the OT in its original language, he was—by the high bar of excellence he himself set—the one Christian best equipped to explain the Bible to his fellow Latins.

Although this "back to the sources" approach is accepted as a first principle of Biblical scholarship today, Latin Christians in Jerome's day were fiercely opposed to it. For one thing, it challenged the authoritative status of the LXX, which was widely believed to be divinely inspired.[136] It also seemed to put the OT back into the hands of the Jews, for they were the ones who could read Hebrew (even Jerome learned Hebrew from Jewish tutors). In fact, Jerome was accused of selling out to the Jews.[137] He was very well aware of the controversial nature of his cause, and he took steps to legitimize it before a skeptical Christian public. For instance, in the middle 380s in Rome he released both sides of his selected exegetical correspondence with Pope Damasus, in which he displayed his application of Hebrew verity to OT and NT texts, in order to show that his scholarship came

135. *Ep.* 20.2.

136. See, e.g., J. Lössl, "A Shift in Patristic Exegesis: Hebrew Verity in Augustine, Jerome, Julian of Aeclanum, and Theodore of Mopsuestia," *AugStud* 32 (2001): 157–75.

137. Rufinus, *Apol. c. Hier.* 2.32. See H. I. Newman, "Jerome's Judaizers," *JECS* 9 (2001): 421–52 (esp. pp. 444–45).

with a papal sanction.[138] Several years later, Jerome mounted a three-tier defense of his Hebrew scholarship, and specifically of his translation of the Hebrew OT into Latin, in his *Hebrew Questions on Genesis*, which he composed between 391 and 393. As Adam Kamesar has shown, Jerome's bottom-line approach was to support the LXX found in Origen's Hexapla.[139] His second-tier position was to make his own translation based upon the Hebrew original and then to advocate its use as an auxiliary to the LXX. Finally, he put his translation forward as a replacement of the LXX and its Old Latin translations.

Jerome promoted Hebrew verity also in the *Commentary on Galatians*, an especially appropriate venue given this Pauline epistle's frequent invocation of OT texts and themes. A case in point is his treatment of Gal 3.13–14. Here Paul quotes Dt 21.23 ("Cursed is everyone who is hung on a tree") and gives it a Christological interpretation ("He redeemed us in order that the blessing given to Abraham might come to the Gentiles through Christ Jesus, so that by faith we might receive the promise of the Spirit"). Jerome's first order of business is to determine whether Paul took this versicule from the LXX or the Hebrew. He reviews the readings found in each, and for further reference he compares them with readings given in the Greek translations of the Hebrew Bible done in the second century AD by the Jews Aquila, Symmachus, and Theodotion. He concludes:

I cannot ascertain why the Apostle either added to or took away from the statement, "Everyone who hangs on a tree is cursed by God." For if he was exclusively following the authority of the Septuagint translators, he was obligated to insert the phrase "by God," just as they had done. But if, as a Jew among Jews, he thought that what he had read in his own language was the closest to the truth, he had to omit both "everyone" and "on a tree," which are not found in the Hebrew original. This leads me to believe either that the ancient manuscripts of the Jews contained a different reading than they do now, or that the Apostle (as I said above) captured the sense rather than literal meaning of Scripture. It is more plausible that after Christ had suffered on the cross, someone added "by God" to both the Hebrew manuscripts and our

138. Cain, *The Letters of Jerome*, Chap. 2.

139. *Jerome, Greek Scholarship, and the Hebrew Bible: A Study of the* Quaestiones Hebraicae in Genesim (Oxford: Oxford University Press, 1993), 41–72.

own so as to shame us for believing in Christ, who [according to this reading] was cursed by God.[140]

He is careful to acknowledge the "authority of the Septuagint translators," but at the same time he affirms the superiority of the Hebrew original. He appeals to the authority of Paul himself, who he says relied on the Hebrew because he supposedly regarded it as being "the closest to the truth." As to why his rendering of Dt 21.23 differs from the Hebrew text, Jerome suggests that Jewish scribes after Paul tampered with the original manuscripts in an effort to defame Christ and his followers. His point, moreover, is that once Christians know Hebrew, they are in a position to reclaim the Hebrew Bible from the Jews.

Jerome did not produce his own fresh Latin translation of Galatians to accompany his commentary. He instead used the Old Latin Bible, the version already familiar to his target readership.[141] Instead of retranslating Galatians, Jerome corrected the Old Latin version against the Greek, where necessary.[142] For example, in his commentary on Gal 5.8, he replaces one nonsensical reading with his own alternative translation based on the Greek:

In the Latin manuscripts I have found the reading, "That persuasion of yours comes from God (*ex Deo*) who has called you." I suspect that it originally had been "from the one" (*ex eo*), but due to a misunderstanding and a similarity in spelling it was gradually replaced by "from God" (*ex Deo*). This latter meaning makes no sense because he had just reprimanded them for not obeying the truth, thereby showing that obedience or disobedience lies in their power to choose, yet he now asserts that persuasion and obedience were not so much in the power of the called as in the power of the one doing the calling. Therefore, the reading that is preferable and more faithful [to the Greek] is, "That persuasion of yours does not come from the one who has called you."[143]

---

140. *Comm. Gal.* 2.3.13b–14.

141. It is also possible that he wanted to avert the kind of controversy in which his revision of the Old Latin Gospels had become engulfed a mere two years earlier in Rome, as such a controversy might be a distraction to the exegesis itself.

142. *Comm. Gal.* 1.1.16b (Gal 1.16); 1.2.3–5 (Gal 2.5); 2.4.4–5 (Lk 22.37); 2.5.2 (Acts 15.29); 2.5.4 (Gal 5.4); 3.5.7 (Gal 5.7); 3.5.8. (Gal 5.8); 3.5.9 (Gal 5.9); 3.5.24 (Gal 5.24); 3.5.26 (1 Cor 13.3); 3.6.17a (Gal 6.17).

143. *Comm. Gal.* 3.5.8.

Here and in many other places throughout the *Commentary* Jerome emphasizes how unreliable the Old Latin Bible can be. Its orthographical mistakes and the incompetence of translators are just two cogent reasons for taking the Greek as our ultimate guide.

Jerome famously dubbed himself a "trilingual man" (*vir trilinguis*), by which he meant that he had a firm command of Latin, Greek, and Hebrew.[144] Latin was of course his native language, and he was arguably the purest Latin prose stylist of his age. By the late 380s, he had been a fluent reader and perhaps even a speaker of Greek for at least a decade.[145] Since Greek was a living language for a great many eastern Christians and the second language of some western elites, there was not necessarily any cachet attached to Jerome's knowledge of it.[146] His grasp of Hebrew, however, was another story altogether. He was the only noted Biblical commentator in the West who could rightfully boast at least some reading competence in Hebrew. But just how proficient he really was remains a matter of debate among scholars.[147] Most, though, are willing to grant that while his reading knowledge was certainly not fluent by modern standards, it nevertheless was commendable for a Latin Christian in Jerome's historical context.

Jerome's claim to expertise in Greek and especially Hebrew was absolutely vital to his credibility as a Biblical scholar. In his *Commentary on Galatians* he firms up his linguistic credentials through some strategically worded remarks about his hard-won acquisition of Hebrew: "My reading of Hebrew, a harsh and gut-

144. *Apol. c. Ruf.* 3.6.

145. P. Hamblenne, "L'apprentissage du grec par Jérôme: quelques ajustements," *REAug* 40 (1994): 353–64. Hamblenne argues that Jerome was able to read and speak Greek with ease by the time he left Constantinople in 382.

146. On the Greek literacy of well-educated Romans in late antiquity, see Pierre Courcelle's classic study *Les lettres grecques en Occident de Macrobe à Cassiodore* (Paris: Boccard, 1948) = *Late Latin Writers and their Greek Sources,* trans. H. E. Wedeck (Cambridge: Harvard University Press, 1969).

147. Three of the more recent scholarly studies may be mentioned: S. Rebenich, "Jerome: the *vir trilinguis* and the *Hebraica veritas*," *VChr* 47 (1993): 50–77; M. Graves, *Jerome's Hebrew Philology: A Study Based on his Commentary on Jeremiah* (Leiden: E. J. Brill, 2007); H. I. Newman, "How should we Measure Jerome's Hebrew Competence?" in Cain and Lössl, eds., *Jerome of Stridon*, 131–40.

tural language, has ruined all the elegance of my style and the charm of my Latin prose. . . . How far I have advanced in my unceasing study of Hebrew, I leave to others to judge; I know what I have lost in my own language."[148] Jerome's depreciation of his own style, which is not exactly inelegant, was a conventional kind of protest, as any ancient reader would have recognized. He invoked this convention in this particular context in order to reinforce his claim of being steeped in Hebrew learning, just as he had complained to Marcella a couple of years earlier: "As you know, I have spent so much time reading the Hebrew language that I have become rusty in Latin."[149] In other words, Jerome had come to know Hebrew better than his native Latin—a suggestion as poignant as it is exaggerated for the purpose of persuading readers of his trustworthiness as a scholar of the Bible.

5. ORTHODOXY AND HERESY IN THE COMMENTARY ON GALATIANS

Tertullian called Paul "the apostle of the heretics" (*haereticorum apostolus*).[150] This epithet was not meant as an insult to the author of roughly one-third of the canonical NT. Rather, it was an expression of frustration that the second-century heresiarch Marcion and his followers claimed to ground their teachings in Scripture, when, according to Tertullian, they based them on *erroneous* interpretations of Scripture. No wonder, then, that a central feature of early Christian commentaries on the Bible by orthodox or "right-thinking" (ὀρθός, correct; δόξα, opinion) Christian writers was the refutation of teachings and interpretations that seemed to go against those handed down by the primitive apostolic church.

One main goal of these commentators was to save the Bible from becoming a book of heresies. The word "heresy," from the Greek αἵρεσις, means "choice," as in the act of choosing a religious persuasion or set of beliefs. In the hands of ancient orthodox writers like Irenaeus and Tertullian, this term took on very

---

148. Book 3, pref.   149. *Ep.* 29.7.
150. *Adv. Marc.* 3.5.

sinister connotations and was used to denigrate their theological opponents as false teachers, deceivers, and enemies of God
and his church. "Heresy" for these writers was not some harm-
less difference of opinion about non-essentials, but a matter
of grave eternal consequence because the Gospel itself was at
stake. They took Paul's emphatic warning seriously: "But even if
we or an angel from heaven should preach a gospel to you other than the one we preached to you, let him be accursed! Just
as we have said already, so now I say again: If anyone preaches
to you a gospel besides that which you have received, let him be
accursed!"[151]

From the start to the finish of his literary career, Jerome
styled himself as a watchdog of theological orthodoxy.[152] In one
of the last writings to survive from his pen, he summarized the
mindset that had sustained him all those decades: "I have never
spared heretics, and I have done my best to make the enemies
of the Church my own."[153] Jerome's preoccupation with heresy
and its eradication constitutes one of the thematic undercur-
rents of the *Commentary on Galatians*. About two dozen "heretical" sects[154] and teachers,[155] from the well known to the obscure,
are either named explicitly or alluded to.[156] For many of these
references Jerome was undoubtedly dependent on Origen's
commentary on Galatians and other Greek sources, yet his edi-
torial decision to retain them in his own commentary gives us

151. Gal 1.8–9.

152. B. Jeanjean, *Saint Jérôme et l'hérésie* (Paris: Institut d'Études Augustiniennes, 1999).

153. *Dial. adv. Pelag.*, pref. 2 (NPNF, Ser. 2, 6:449).

154. Apollinarianism (1.1.1); Artotyrites (2, pref.); Borborites (2, pref.);
Cataphrygians (2, pref.); Docetics (1.1.1); Encratites (3.6.8); Manichaeans
(1.1.4–5; 2, pref.); Novatianists (2.4.19); Ophites (2, pref.); Passalorynchites
(2, pref.); Tascodrougitae (2, pref.).

155. Apelles and Philumene (1.1.8–9); Arius (3.5.9); Basilides (1.1.4–5;
1.1.11–12; 1.1.15–16a; 2.4.8–9); Ebion (1.1.1; 1.1.11–12; 2.3.13b–14; 2.5.3);
Julius Cassianus (3.6.8); Mani (1.1.1; 1.1.4–5; 2.4.24b–26; 3.6.1); Marcion
(1.1.1; 1.1.6–7; 1.1.8–9; 1.1.11–12; 1.1.13–14; 1.2.16a; 1.3.1a; 1.3.6; 2.3.13a;
2.4.4–5; 2.4.8–9; 2.4.24b–26; 3.5.12; 3.5.15; 3.6.1; 3.6.6); Photinus (1.1.1); Valentinus (1.1.4–5; 1.1.15–16a; 2.4.8–9; 3.5.12).

156. I have indicated in the footnotes to the translation places where plausible identifications can be made.

precious insight into his authorial priorities. One heretical figure in particular, Marcion, is given special prominence in the
Commentary,[157] and so a sketch of his life and doctrine will provide a context for Jerome's numerous criticisms of him.[158]

Marcion's Life and Theology

Marcion (d. 160) was from the city of Sinope in Pontus, in
modern-day Turkey,[159] and purportedly the son of a bishop. He
was quite well-off; Tertullian calls him a shipowner (*naukleros*)[160]
and refers to his successful shipping business.[161] Epiphanius relates that in his youth Marcion seduced a virgin, was excommunicated by his father, and then left Sinope in embarrassment.[162]
This story was probably fabricated to discredit Marcion,[163] who
actually had a reputation later in life for adhering to a strict ascetic lifestyle. Most scholars take the virgin as a metaphor for
the church, the pristine Bride of Christ whom Marcion corrupted with his teaching.[164] Marcion did leave his native Pontus around 139,[165] though his exact reasons for doing so remain

157. We may apply here Maurice Wiles's observation about Marcion's far-
reaching influence on early orthodox Christian Biblical commentators, that he
"is like a figure standing just off-stage but casting his shadow over every player
on it" (*The Divine Apostle*, 49).

158. For an overview of Jerome's polemic against Marcion, see Jeanjean,
Saint Jérôme et l'hérésie, 200–220, *passim*.

159. Epiphanius, *Pan.* 42.1, 4. On his Pontic origin, see also Hippolytus,
Haer. 7.17; Tertullian, *Adv. Marc.* 5.17.14.

160. *De praescr. haer.* 30; *Adv. Marc.* 5.1; 4.9. Tertullian's use of the Greek
term ναύκληρος rather than the Latin *navicularius* indicates that he is probably preserving a tradition of the Greek-speaking Christian community in Rome,
where Marcion was active during the 140s and 150s.

161. *Adv. Marc.* 5.1.

162. *Pan.* 42.2.

163. Orthodox writers routinely accused heretical opponents of loose living
because it implied their infidelity to truth, which was associated with purity of
life and doctrine. See B. D. Ehrman, *The Orthodox Corruption of Scripture: The Effect of Early Christological Controversies on the Text of the New Testament* (Oxford: Oxford University Press, 1993), 15–17.

164. See, e.g., G. Lüdemann, *Heretics: The Other Side of Early Christianity*, trans.
J. Bowden (Louisville: John Knox Press, 1996), 159.

165. Precise dating of specific events and milestones in Marcion's career is
problematic, but see the illuminating reappraisal of the evidence in J. B. Tyson,

unclear. He turned up in Rome, which was home to the most powerful church in the world at that time.[166] In 144, he had a falling-out with local church authorities, who were not receptive to the radical new theology he had been preaching since at least 130. He severed ties with the Roman church and established his own church, which basically was a mirror-image of the orthodox church with a comparable hierarchy (Marcion served as a bishop) and rites. Sometime during the 150s or thereafter Marcion returned to Asia Minor and lived out the rest of his days.

By the end of the second century, the Marcionite church had grown so significantly in size, influence, and geographical spread that it became a serious rival to the orthodox church.[167] Indeed, as Stephen Wilson points out, "for many in the second century, whether Christian believers or outside observers, the word 'Christianity' would have meant 'Marcionite Christianity.'"[168] Marcion's church continued to attract members, especially in the East, centuries after its founder's death.[169]

If Marcion's theology can be boiled down to one central theme, it is the absolute irreconcilability of the Jewish Law and the Gospel of Christ. Marcion was a hyper-Paulinist and centered his theology on the Apostle's advocacy of justification by grace alone, apart from the works of the Law. The Law brings

---

Marcion and Luke-Acts: A Defining Struggle (Columbia, SC: University of South Carolina Press, 2006), 24–31.

166. For early traditions about Marcion's pre-Roman life, see J. Regul, *Die antimarcionitischen Evangelienprologe* (Freiburg: Herder, 1969), 177–95.

167. Around 150, Justin Martyr said that Marcion had attracted disciples from every race on earth (*1 Apol.* 26), and Tertullian, writing about sixty years later, likened the Marcionites to swarms of wasps building combs in imitation of the bees (*Adv. Marc.* 4.5).

168. S. Wilson, *Related Strangers: Jews and Christians 70 C.E.–170 C.E.* (Minneapolis: Fortress Press, 1995), 208.

169. See, e.g., H. J. W. Drijvers, "Marcionism in Syria: Principles, Problems, Polemics," *SecCent* 6 (1987–88): 153–72. By the early third century Marcionism was widespread in Syrian Edessa: see S. K. Ross, *Roman Edessa: Politics and Culture on the Eastern Fringes of the Roman Empire, 114–242 CE* (London: Routledge, 2001), 121, 128. Marcion's dualism notably influenced the Persian prophet Mani: see H. J. W. Drijvers, "Marcion's Reading of Gal. 4,8: Philosophical Background and Influence on Manichaeism," in *A Green Leaf: Papers in Honour of Jes P. Asmussen* (Leiden: E. J. Brill, 1988), 339–48.

punishment, judgment, vengeance, and death, while the Gospel offers redemption, mercy, and life. How could these two apparent polar opposites originate with a single God? Marcion's solution was to resort to a dualistic explanation of the universe. There are two different deities. One is the capricious and often sadistic Yahweh of the OT. He is the Creator (Demiurge) of the universe and humankind. He is a war-monger, an instigator of strife, and a fickle, self-contradictory being.[170] He also is an exacting judge who gave the Law to the Jews and inflicted harsh penalties on them when they failed to obey it perfectly. The supreme deity, the God and Father of Jesus, could not be more different. He represents perfect goodness and mercy, and he sent his Son to redeem all people, Jew and Gentile alike, from the wrath of the Creator and to give them the promise of eternal life.[171] Marcion called him the "Stranger" because he is a transcendent God who was unknown to the human race prior to revealing himself in Christ.[172] This alien God has no connection whatsoever with the material world, which Marcion viewed as evil because it is the product of the Demiurge.[173] Marcion's low view of matter led him to embrace Docetism (from δοκεῖν,

170. Peter Lampe makes the interesting and not entirely unreasonable suggestion that Marcion's concoction of a warlike and overbearing Creator-God may partly be a projection of his experiences as a *naukleros* during the war-torn reign of Trajan (98–117). During times of crisis and war, private shipowners like Marcion were obligated to allow the state to use their ships for transporting foodstuffs and other goods. Lampe speculates that Marcion may have resented this burdensome compulsory service to the state and that he in turn demonized the Roman imperial administration as the Demiurge. See P. Lampe, *From Paul to Valentinus: Christians at Rome in the First Two Centuries*, trans. M. G. Steinhauser (Minneapolis: Fortress Press, 2003), 241–49.

171. Irenaeus (*Adv. haer.* 1.27.1–2) claimed that Marcion took his dualism directly from a Syrian Gnostic teacher named Cerdo, who was active in Rome around the middle of the second century and who also advocated the antithesis of the Jewish God and the God of Christ. For this reason Irenaeus classified Marcion as a Gnostic. While his theology is colored by some Gnostic elements, there are, however, not enough to consider him a Gnostic, and at any rate his doctrine of salvation by grace alone (rather than through secret knowledge for the privileged few) and his rejection of allegory as an interpretative method are fundamentally *anti*-Gnostic.

172. Tertullian, *Adv. Marc.* 1.9.2.

173. Cf. A. McGowan, "Marcion's Love of Creation," *JECS* 9 (2001): 295–311.

"seem"), the belief that Christ did not take on flesh and blood but assumed only the *appearance* of flesh.

Judaism and Christianity, in Marcion's view, are two separate and fundamentally incompatible religions. He saw no continuity between the OT and the revelation of salvation in Christ in the NT. He rejected the entire OT, not because he thought it was full of lies but because its contents are not edifying to Christians from either an ethical or a theological standpoint. As for the NT, Marcion discarded almost everything but the Pauline epistles, but even these had to be pruned of Jewish elements. The Biblical canon Marcion created for his church reflects his theological concerns.[174] It contained a shorter version of the canonical Gospel of Luke (*Euangelion*), though Luke's name was removed along with any mention of Jesus' Nativity because the birth account would associate Jesus with the Demiurge.[175] The rest of Marcion's NT consisted of ten epistles of Paul (*Apostolikon*). He put Galatians first because he regarded it as the quintessential introduction to Pauline theology.[176] Marcion excised from it and the other epistles any and all favorable references to the OT, the Law, and the God of the Jews. *His* Paul could never have written such things. They had to be interpolations by Jewish-Christian pseudo-apostles who conspired to muddle Paul's Gospel.

Marcion's only known original literary production was the *Antitheses* (Ἀντιθέσεις). This work, fragments of which are pre-

174 Adolf von Harnack attempted a reconstruction of the text of this canon from quotations preserved in the writings of the Fathers. See his *Marcion: Das Evangelium vom fremden Gott. Eine Monographie zur Geschichte der Grundlegung der katholischen Kirche*, 2d ed. (Leipzig: Hinrichs, 1924), pp. 67*–127* (*Apostolikon*) and 183*–240* (*Euangelion*). See also G. Quispel, "Marcion and the Test of the New Testament," *VChr* 52 (1998): 349–60. For a discussion of Marcion's role in the development of the (orthodox) Christian canon, see J. Barton, *Holy Writings, Sacred Text: The Canon in Early Christianity* (Louisville: John Knox Press, 1997), chap. 2 ("Marcion Revisited").

175. Marcion's hybrid version of Luke had at least 682 verses in common with the canonical Luke, which in modern editions of the Bible has 1,150 verses. See J. Knox, *Marcion and the New Testament: An Essay in the Early History of the Canon* (Chicago: University of Chicago Press, 1942), 86.

176. R. J. Hoffmann, *Marcion: On the Restitution of Christianity. An Essay on the Development of Radical Paulinist Theology in the Second Century* (Chico: Scholars Press, 1984), 75.

served in the writings of Marcion's orthodox adversaries, jux-taposed seemingly conflicting verses from the OT and NT. Interestingly, some scholars suspect that this work is explicitly referenced in 1 Tm 6.20, where Timothy is told to be on guard against the ἀντιθέσεις τῆς ψευδωνύμου γνώσεως. According to this view, which assumes quite a late date for this epistle and thus non-Pauline authorship,[177] the Greek should be translated as, "*Antitheses* of falsely called knowledge." As Paul Hartog points out, however, this hypothesis fails to convince because the false teachers condemned in this epistle are of a decidedly Jewish bent (1 Tm 1.7; cf. Ti 1.10, 14; 3.9).[178]

Jerome versus Marcion

It is clear that Marcion viewed himself as the restorer of the true Gospel. In his *Commentary on Galatians,* however, Jerome upheld orthodox views in his condemnation of Marcion's teachings. He stated unequivocally that the gospel Marcion had preached was a false one. Simply put, Marcion did not have the Holy Spirit, and without the Holy Spirit, his so-called gospel forfeits its claim to a divine origin.[179] The seriousness of his error is shown by his mangling of the person of Christ. Contrary to what Marcion teaches, Christ is not divine only but human also, and Jerome encapsulates the orthodox position in a simple formula: "He who is God from all eternity deigned to become man in order to save us."[180] Marcion alleged that Christ did not have real human flesh and was not born of a woman, but appeared all of a sudden as a grown man at a synagogue in Capernaum in the fifteenth year of the emperor Tiberius's reign.[181] Paul's passing

177. For a discussion of past and recent scholarly debate about the question of this epistle's authorship, see P. H. Towner, *The Letters to Timothy and Titus,* NICNT (Grand Rapids: W. B. Eerdmans, 2006), 9–27.

178. *Polycarp and the New Testament: The Occasion, Rhetoric, Theme, and Unity of the Epistle to the Philippians and Its Allusions to New Testament Literature* (Tübingen: Mohr Siebeck, 2002), 91. The alleged reference to Marcion's *Antitheses* has been dismissed as implausible more recently by Towner, *The Letters to Timothy and Titus,* 432.

179. *Comm. Gal.* 1.1.11–12.

180. *Comm. Gal.* 1.1.1.

181. Tertullian, *Adv. Marc.* 1.15, 19; 4.6, 7.

remark, however, that Christ was born "of a woman" is enough to topple the edifice of Marcion's Christology.[182]

Marcion's dualism comes under direct fire. In one instance Jerome highlights the self-contradiction in Marcion's contention that Paul and Christ have nothing to do with the Jewish God. Paul, when declaring a curse on anyone who preaches a different gospel, uses a word (ἀνάθεμα, *anathema*) which is found in the OT and employed by the Jews and, by extension, the Creator.[183] Thus, Paul is tied to the Jewish God after all. This means either that Yahweh is the true God or that Paul was the servant of this inferior God, both of which are unthinkable propositions in Marcionite theology. Later in the *Commentary* Jerome advances a similar argument against Marcion, when he tries to explain how Paul could have wished for his Judaizing opponents to be "forcibly castrated" even though at other times he forbade cursing. Marcion "and everyone else who undermines the Old Testament" reach an impasse here. For how can they possibly defame Yahweh, the Law-giver, as a savage and unrelenting judge yet praise Paul as an apostle of the good God when he says something more severe than anything found in the Jewish Law?[184] The Galatian believers may have let themselves be duped into thinking that keeping the Mosaic Law is necessary for salvation, but at least they believed in the one true God. They were at fault for failing to grasp the nuances of the Law-Gospel connection, not for denying an article of faith. The same cannot be said for Marcion, who split the one Creator into two and made Christ the offspring of one of these new deities, and in doing so put himself at odds with the church's unified stance on the nature of God.[185]

Marcion's positions on the personhood of God aside, Jerome was particularly concerned about the soteriological implications of his attitude toward the OT and the Jewish Law. There are many examples, but one will suffice. From Paul's statement in Gal 2.16 that no one is "justified by observing the Law, but by faith in Jesus Christ," Marcion deduced that the patriarchs and prophets of the OT were excluded from salvation on the

182. *Comm. Gal.* 2.4.4–5.   183. *Comm. Gal.* 1.1.8–9.
184. *Comm. Gal.* 3.5.12.   185. *Comm. Gal.* 1.1.6–7.

grounds that they had lived before Christ was revealed to the world. Jerome, however, points out that Paul is not condemning the Law but only those who think that their justification hangs on observance of the Law. The OT saints do not even factor into this equation because they were justified by their faith in the promise of the Messiah who had not yet come.[186] Since the OT announces the coming of this Messiah, the unity between the OT and NT and between the Law and the Gospel remains unbroken. For "we know about the cross not only from the Gospel, which relates the story of his crucifixion, but also [from writings penned] long before he deigned to come down to earth and assume the form of a crucified man," and the Galatian Christians came to their knowledge of Christ "by continually reading the prophets and by knowing all of the ordinances of the old Law."[187]

6. ACHIEVEMENT AND INFLUENCE OF JEROME'S COMMENTARY ON GALATIANS

Jerome was the greatest Biblical scholar of the ancient Latin church. His *Commentary on Galatians* represents his first substantial attempt at systematic Biblical interpretation. Since he articulated in it the hermeneutical methodology that would come to dominate his later exegetical work, it stands as a key witness to a formative stage in his intellectual development.[188] When compared with the other five extant Latin commentaries on Galatians from the fourth and early fifth centuries, Jerome's *Commentary* stands out for the rigor of its Biblical textual criticism, the breadth of its classical and patristic erudition, and its research-intensiveness and expository thoroughness (it is two-thirds longer than any of the other five commentaries).[189] Its

186. *Comm. Gal.* 1.2.16a; cf. 2.3.13a; 3.5.18.
187. *Comm. Gal.* 1.3.1b.
188. See G. Raspanti, "The Significance of Jerome's *Commentary on Galatians* in his Exegetical Production," in *Jerome of Stridon*, ed. Cain and Lössl, 163–71.
189. See G. Raspanti, "L'esegesi della lettera ai Galati nel IV secolo d.C. Dal commentario dottrinale di Mario Vittorino ed Ambrosiaster a quello filologico di Girolamo," *Ho Theològos* 25 (2007): 109–28.

greatest achievement lies in its preservation of a treasure-trove of otherwise lost Greek exegetical wisdom. This point remains valid even despite the unfortunate fact that, due to Jerome's eclectic compositional technique,[190] the vast majority of this content cannot firmly be assigned to any specific Greek author.

It was not long after its release in late 386 that Jerome's *Commentary* began to have an impact on the exegesis of Paul in the West. It influenced the Galatians commentaries of Augustine (394–395),[191] the Budapest Anonymous (between 396 and 405),[192] and Pelagius (between 406 and 409).[193] It was quoted authoritatively by many early medieval commentators on Galatians, including Primasius (d. c. 560), Claudius of Turin (d. c. 827), Sedulius Scottus (fl. 850), Haimo of Auxerre (d. c. 855), and Raban Maur (d. 856). During the Middle Ages, Robert Grosseteste (d. 1253) and Thomas Aquinas (d. 1274) used it as a source for their own commentaries on Galatians, as did several leading Reformation figures such as Martin Luther (d. 1546),[194] John Calvin (d. 1564), and Heinrich Bullinger (d. 1575). But the *Commentary*'s influence was not restricted to exegetical literature. Aelred of Rievaulx quoted from Jerome's discussion of the fruits of the Spirit in his *Mirror of Charity* (1142–1143).[195]

7. ABOUT THIS TRANSLATION

Until now there has been no English translation of Jerome's *Commentary on Galatians*.[196] I have based this one on the excel-

190. See above section, "The Extent of the Greek Influences: 'I dictated either my own or others' thoughts.'"

191. Plumer, *Augustine's Commentary on Galatians*, 47–53.

192. Frede, *Ein neuer Paulustext und Kommentar*, 1.215–17, 252.

193. Souter, *The Earliest Latin Commentaries*, 228.

194. Luther was quite critical of Jerome's *Commentary*, as he was of Jerome in general. See the many references to his criticisms of the *Commentary* in K. Hagen, *Luther's Approach to Scripture as seen in his "Commentaries" on Galatians 1519–1538* (Tübingen: Mohr Siebeck, 1993). See also J. Lössl, "Martin Luther's Jerome: New Evidence for a Changing Attitude," in *Jerome of Stridon*, ed. Cain and Lössl, 237–51.

195. Cf. *Comm. Gal.* 3.5.22–23 and *De spec. car.* 3.18.42. See A. Cain, "Aelred of Rievaulx and Jerome's *Commentary on Galatians*," *CSQ* 45 (2010): 3–6.

196. A French translation was published over a century ago by L'Abbé Ba-

lent critical edition published in 2006 by Giacomo Raspanti in the Latin series of the *Corpus Christianorum* (vol. 77A). This edition supersedes the faulty and outdated text printed in volume 26 of Migne's *Patrologia Latina*. In the footnotes to my translation I have supplemented Raspanti's catalogue of Biblical, classical, and patristic allusions in Jerome's text with numerous new references discovered through my own source-critical studies on the *Commentary*.[197]

Now that it is accessible in translation, Jerome's monumental *Commentary on Galatians* will (I hope) be of use to scholars and students who are interested not only in Jerome and patristic Biblical exegesis but also more generally in the interpretation of the Pauline epistles. I have tried to tailor this edition to the anticipated needs of these various audiences and for this reason have included a great many references to relevant patristic primary sources and modern scholarship on the epistle to the Galatians, and have itemized the Bibliography at the beginning of this volume accordingly.

---

reille in *Œuvres complètes de saint Jérôme* (Paris: Vivès, 1884), 225–373. It is based, however, on Migne's text. Its usefulness is further limited by the fact that it has no patristic or Scriptural apparatus to speak of.

197. "Tertullian, Cyprian, and Lactantius in Jerome's *Commentary on Galatians*," *REAug* 55 (2009): 23–51; "An Unidentified Patristic Quotation in Jerome's *Commentary on Galatians* (3.6.11)," *JThS*, n.s., 60 (2009): 216–25.

COMMENTARY ON
GALATIANS

BOOK ONE (GALATIANS 1.1–3.9)

T HAS BEEN only a few days since I finished my commentary on Paul's epistle to Philemon and moved on to his epistle to the Galatians, reversing my course and passing over many things in between. All of a sudden a letter arrived for me from Rome bearing the news that the venerable widow Albina has returned to the Lord and that the holy Marcella,[1] deprived of the companionship of her mother, now more than ever seeks comfort from you, Paula and Eustochium.[2] Since this is impossible at the moment due to the great distance of land and sea that stretches out between us, she desires me at least to treat this suddenly inflicted wound with the medicine of Scripture. I certainly know her zeal and her faith. I know that a fire is always burning in her chest and that she overcomes her gender[3] and is

---

1. Marcella was born in Rome in the 330s into an extremely wealthy household. She was married at a young age, but her husband died seven months later. The couple had no children. Marcella's mother, Albina, tried to contract a marriage between her and the ex-consul Naeratius Cerealis in order to secure her daughter's financial future. Marcella would not go along with this and vowed to remain a chaste widow. She died in Rome in 410. Jerome commemorated her in an epitaph addressed in 412 to their mutual Roman friend Principia (*Ep.* 127).

2. Paula was born in 347 in Rome. In the early 360s she married the nobleman Iulius Toxotius. The couple had five children, four daughters (Blesilla, Paulina, Rufina, Eustochium) and one son named after his father. When the elder Toxotius died in 381, Paula, like Marcella before her, vowed to remain a chaste widow. In 385 she and her youngest daughter, Eustochium, left Rome to join forces with Jerome, and in 386 the trio settled into Bethlehem to found monastic communities for men and women. Paula died in 404 and Eustochium around 420. Both were buried in Bethlehem. Several months after Paula's death, Jerome composed a lengthy epitaph memorializing her (*Ep.* 108).

3. Jerome is alluding to the ancient (and medieval) Christian stereotype that

unmindful of her human limitations. And I know that she crosses
the Red Sea of this world to the tambourine-sound of the divine
books.[4] To be sure, when I was in Rome she never saw me without asking me something about Scripture, even when she was in
a hurry. Contrary to what the Pythagoreans do, she did not accept as true whatever answer I would give her, and my authority
did not prevail with her if it was not supported by reason.[5] She
probed everything and shrewdly pondered matters in their entirety, such that I felt that she was not as much my student as my
judge.

Therefore, since I think that it will be most pleasing to her
in her absence and also useful to you who are here by my side,
I shall undertake a work that no Latin writer before me has attempted and that hardly any among the Greeks have executed
in a manner worthy of the exalted nature of the subject matter. I am not unaware that Gaius Marius Victorinus, who taught
rhetoric at Rome when I was a boy, produced commentaries on
the Apostle.[6] Engrossed in secular learning as he was, howev-

---

women constitute the "weaker sex": see P. Laurence, "La faiblesse féminine chez
les Pères de l'Église," in *Les Pères de l'Église face à la science médicale de leur temps,*
ed. V. Boudon-Millot and B. Pouderon (Paris: Beauchesne, 2005), 351–77. Jerome's suggestion that Marcella transcends the natural order is, as it is intended
to be, a glowing assessment of the extraordinary quality of her Christian faith.
He is also paying an indirect compliment to himself, as he emphasizes further
down that this remarkable lady was his loyal pupil.

4 This is an allusion to Ex 15.20–21, where it is told how the prophetess
Miriam took up a tambourine and began dancing and singing and praising the
Lord for drowning the Israelites' Egyptian pursuers in the Red Sea.

5. *Nec sine ratione praeiudicata apud eam valebat auctoritas.* This expression was
taken over from what Cicero (*N.D.* 1.5.10) said in reference to the Pythagoreans (*tantum opinio praeiudicata poterat, ut etiam sine ratione valeret auctoritas*).

6. By "the Apostle," Jerome means none other than St. Paul. This epithet,
which was extremely common among Greek and Latin patristic writers, is but one
manifestation of the exalted status Paul enjoyed in later centuries as the first and
greatest of all Christian theologians and as the most recognizable apostolic face
of the Gospel. See M. F. Wiles, *The Divine Apostle: The Interpretation of St Paul's Epistles in the Early Church* (Cambridge: Cambridge University Press, 1967), 14–25;
C. J. Roetzel, *Paul: The Man and the Myth* (Columbia: University of South Carolina Press, 1998), 152–77. On Paul's reception in second-century Christian literature, see E. Dassmann, *Der Stachel im Fleisch: Paulus in der frühchristlichen Literatur
bis Irenäus* (Münster: Aschendorff, 1979); A. Lindemann, *Paulus im ältesten Chris-*

er, he was completely ignorant of Scripture, and nobody—no matter how eloquent he may be—is able to discuss competently what he does not know. Am I, then, foolish or rash to promise what he was incapable of accomplishing? Not at all. I believe that I am more cautious and timid because I have recognized the scantness of my own abilities[7] and have followed the commentaries of Origen. He wrote five extraordinary volumes on Paul's epistle to the Galatians and rounded out the tenth book of his *Miscellanies* with a brief section expounding it. He also produced various homilies[8] and scholia[9] that would be sufficient all by themselves. I say nothing of my seeing guide Didymus;[10] [Apollinaris,] who recently left the church at Laodicea; the ancient heretic Alexander; Eusebius of Emesa; and Theodore of Heraclea; all of whom have left behind modest commentaries of their own on the topic at hand.[11] Even if I were to borrow just a little from these works, the result would be something praiseworthy.[12] So, then, let me frankly admit that I read all of these books and committed to memory a great many in-

---

tentum: Das Bild des Apostels und die Rezeption der paulinischen Theologie in der frühchristlichen Literatur bis Marcion (Tübingen: Mohr Siebeck, 1979).

7. It was commonplace in ancient prefaces for writers to lament their supposed inadequacies: see T. Janson, *Latin Prose Prefaces: Studies in Literary Conventions* (Stockholm: Almqvist & Wiksell, 1964), 124–27.

8. These were sermons Origen preached at Caesarea. The word *tractatus*, which Jerome uses here, is a technical term for a specific type of sermon that incorporated elements of Biblical exegesis, moral exhortation, and theological reflection: see G. Bardy, "*Tractare, Tractatus,*" *RSR* 33 (1946): 211–35.

9. Scholia were collections of explanations of miscellaneous Biblical passages.

10. Despite being blind since the age of four and never learning how to read, Didymus is said to have mastered all of the known sciences and to have had an encyclopedic knowledge of Scripture (Palladius, *Hist. laus.* 4; Jerome, *Vir. ill.* 109). Jerome's epithet for him here ("my seeing guide") is an allusion simultaneously to Didymus's legendary blindness and to the fact that Jerome had studied under Didymus, albeit for less than a month, when he stayed in Alexandria in 386.

11. For biographical sketches of these various exegetes, see the Introduction.

12. In the preface to his *Commentary on Matthew* (written in 398), Jerome gave an inventory of the patristic commentaries on Matthew he had consulted and said similarly, "Had I simply excerpted a few things from these works, a commentary worthy of remembrance could have been written" (trans. Scheck, FOTC 117:57).

sights, and then I summoned my secretary and dictated either my own or others' ideas, all the while paying no attention to the method, the words, or the opinions belonging to each. It is now up to the Lord's mercy to make sure that others' sage sayings are not lost through my incompetence and that they are as commendable somewhere else as they are in their original context.

As I succinctly summarize the argument of this epistle by way of this preface,[13] I urge you to be aware that the epistles to the Romans and to the Galatians share the same subject matter. There is, however, a key difference between them. In the former, Paul employed a loftier discourse and more sophisticated arguments. In the latter, he was writing to those whom he addressed in later passages as "senseless Galatians"[14] and as "foolish,"[15] and he adopted a style more appropriate for censure than instruction.[16] His aim was to make himself comprehensible to the foolish, and he expressed familiar ideas in familiar language so that an authoritative tone might recall those whom reason had failed to convince.[17] In everything that the Apostle wrote or said in person, he tirelessly taught that the burdensome obligations of the old Law have been abolished and that everything that had preceded in types and symbols (the Sabbath rest, injurious circumcision, the recurring cycle of new moons and of the three annual feasts,[18] the dietary laws, and the daily

13. *Argumentum itaque epistulae huius breviter comprehendens hoc praefatione commoneo ut sciatis.* . . . Presumably intended by Raspanti to be the adjectival modifier of *argumentum, hoc* makes no sense here. This is a rare case when Migne's reading and punctuation should be followed: *Argumentum itaque epistolae huius breviter comprehendens, hac praefatione commoneo, ut sciatis.* . . .

14. Gal 3.1.

15. Gal 3.3.

16. Cf. H. L. Willmington, *Willmington's Guide to the Bible* (Wheaton: Tyndale House Publishers, 1982), 397: "Galatians is a rough sketch of which Romans is the finished picture."

17. F. J. Matera, *Galatians,* Sacra Pagina 9 (Collegeville: Liturgical Press, 1992), 11, describes the epistle to the Galatians as "a sustained exercise in deliberative rhetoric" because Paul's aim was to persuade the Galatian Christians to reject his opponents' gospel of circumcision. In the Greco-Roman world, "deliberative" (συμβουλευτικόν; *deliberativum*) was the rhetorical genre used for exhortation or dissuasion.

18. I.e., Passover, Pentecost, and the Feast of Tabernacles.

ablution, after which one would become defiled again) ceased to have validity with the arrival of evangelical grace, which is fulfilled by the faith of the believing soul and not by the blood of animal sacrifices. Elsewhere in his writings, however, this question for its own part is treated on the side and almost passed over—and then only when it suggested itself to Paul as he was in the midst of speaking about something else. But as I have said, it is especially in these two epistles that he treats the cessation of the old Law and the introduction of the new Law.

The epistle to the Galatians is unique in that Paul was not writing to Jewish believers in Christ who thought that their forefathers' rites had to be observed. He was writing instead to Gentile converts who had fallen away from their pristine faith in the Gospel after being intimidated by the authority of certain people who claimed that Peter, James, and all the churches of Judea were conflating the Gospel of Christ with the old Law. These same people alleged that even Paul himself did one thing in Judea while preaching another thing among the Gentiles and that their faith in the Crucified One was in vain if they thought they had to neglect what the leading apostles observed. For this reason Paul proceeds cautiously, steering a middle course between two extremes so as neither to betray the grace of the Gospel because of being pressured by the sheer number and authority of the elders, nor to detract from his [Jewish] forefathers in his preaching of grace. He makes a stealthy approach as if going by a secret passageway. He shows that Peter did what was expedient for the circumcised believers in his charge lest, if they departed straightaway from their ancient manner of living, they be scandalized and not believe in the Cross. He also shows that it was right for him to defend as true that which another pretended was a dispensation, inasmuch as the preaching of the Gospel to the Gentiles had been entrusted to him. That impious man Porphyry from Batanea did not comprehend any of this.[19] In the first book of his treatise against us [Christians],

19. Porphyry (c. 232–303) was a Neoplatonic philosopher who wrote a treatise in fifteen books against Christianity. The fragments of this work, which have been preserved by Porphyry's Christian opponents, were assembled by Adolf von

he alleged that Peter had been rebuked by Paul because he did not walk uprightly as he spread the Gospel. His intention was to charge Peter with error and Paul with impudence and to implicate the entire community [of Christians] in the lie of fabricated teaching on the grounds that the leaders of the churches disagreed amongst themselves.[20]

In accordance with your request, [Paula and Eustochium,] I have touched upon these themes momentarily and shall delve into them in greater depth in their appropriate places. It is time now to set down and elaborate on each and every one of the Apostle's words.[21]

BOOK ONE

1.1. *Paul, an apostle sent not by men nor through human agency, but through Jesus Christ and God the Father who raised him from the dead.*

It is not out of pride (as some suppose) but out of necessity that Paul puts himself forward as an apostle sent not by men nor through human agency but through Jesus Christ and God the Father. He appeals to this authority to confute those who claimed that he was not one of the [original] twelve apostles but sprang up suddenly out of nowhere or was ordained by the elders [of the church].[22] He may also aim his statement indirect-

---

Harnack in *Porphyrius, Gegen die Christen, 15 Bücher: Zeugnisse, Fragmente und Referate* (Berlin: Verlag der Königliche Akademie der Wissenschaften, 1916). For an overview of Porphyry's life and work, see G. Rinaldi, "Studi Porfiriani I. Porphyrius Bataneotes," *KOINΩNIA* 4 (1980): 25–37. On Jerome's polemic against Porphyry, see C. Moreschini, "L'utilizzazione di Porfirio in Gerolamo," in *Motivi letterari ed esegetici in Gerolamo: Atti del convegno tenuto a Trento il 5–7 dicembre 1995*, ed. C. Moreschini and G. Menestrina (Brescia: Morcelliana, 1997), 175–95.

20. In other words, Peter's leadership as chief of the apostles was nullified by his lapse, Paul was a power-hungry opportunist because he chastised his apostolic superior, and the Christian religion is based on a lie because its first leaders could not even reach a consensus on such a fundamental issue.

21. Jerome's announcement about how thorough he intends to be follows from the conviction, which he shared with Origen (e.g., *Comm. Rom.* 2.6.6), that every single one of Paul's words is divinely inspired and thus requires an attentive reading.

22. Like many modern interpreters of Galatians, Jerome assumed that Paul worded his credentials in this way in order to rebuff opponents who claimed

ly at Peter and the rest of the apostles to emphasize that he received the Gospel not from them but from Jesus Christ himself, the one who had chosen them to be apostles.

This all is meant as a pre-emptive response to those who, after being confronted with his preaching of grace against the burdensome Law, might say, "But Peter said this," "But the apostles established this," "But your forefathers decreed otherwise." Here he makes his point by way of an allusive prelude, but later in the epistle he is more explicit when he writes that nothing was conferred on him by men of apparent importance and that he opposed Peter to his face and was under no compulsion to give in to the hypocrisy of the Jews. It might seem to some that Paul is being presumptuous for speaking, albeit cryptically, against the apostles. After all, this is the same man who came to Jerusalem to confer about the Gospel with these very apostles, to make sure that "he was not running or had run his race in vain."[23] But let us think about the issue in different terms. Down to the present day, Jewish leaders send their own apostles to Galatia, and it was at their prodding even back then, I imagine, that the misguided Galatians started observing the Law. At any rate, other Jewish believers in Christ had come to Galatia and asserted that Peter, the chief of the apostles, and James, the brother of the Lord, kept the ceremonies of the Law.

Paul wanted to make a clear distinction between himself, as one sent by Christ, and those sent by men, and so he began his epistle, "Paul, an apostle sent not by men nor through human agency." The word "apostle," which means "one who has been sent," is a word commonly used by the Hebrews. This is also what Silas' name means—a name bestowed upon him because he was to be sent on a mission.[24] The Hebrews say that among the

---

that his apostolic office was human in nature and origin and that he was therefore inferior in rank to the rest of the apostles. Cf. F. Mussner, *Theologie der Freiheit nach Paulus* (Freiburg: Herder, 1976), 46–47.

23. Gal 2.2.

24. Cf. Acts 15.22. In Hellenistic Jewish circles in the first century AD, ἀπόστολος was an established rendering of *shaliaḥ*, a messenger appointed by a congregation to complete a specific mission. See C. K. Barrett, "*Shaliaḥ* and Apostle," in *Donum Gentilicium, New Testament Studies in Honour of David Daube,*

prophets and holy men there are some who are both prophets
and apostles, while others are only apostles. Moses and Isaiah,
for instance, are both apostles and prophets. God said to Moses,
"I shall send you to Pharaoh,"[25] and Moses replied, "Find someone else to send."[26] God asked Isaiah, "Whom shall I send and
who will go to this people?"[27] We can understand why John the
Baptist should be called both a prophet and an apostle, given
that Scripture says, "There was a man sent by God whose name
was John."[28] In the epistle to the Hebrews Paul[29] did not include
his own name nor the word "apostle," as he usually did in his
epistles, because he was about to speak of Christ ("Having therefore Jesus as the high priest and apostle of our confession"),[30]
and it was not fitting that he and Christ be called apostles in the
same breath.

There are four kinds of apostles.[31] The first is the one who is
sent "not by men nor through human agency, but through Jesus Christ and God the Father." The second is sent by God but

ed. E. Bammel, C. K. Barrett, and W. D. Davies (Oxford: Oxford University Press,
1978), 88–102.

25. Ex 3.10.   26. Ex 4.13.
27. Is 6.8.   28. Jn 1.6.

29. The vast majority of scholars today exclude Hebrews from the authentic
Pauline corpus on stylistic and theological grounds: see, e.g., P. Ellingworth, *The
Epistle to the Hebrews. A Commentary on the Greek Text,* NIGTC (Grand Rapids: W. B.
Eerdmans, 1993), 7–12. Many patristic writers tended to reach the opposite conclusion: see R. A. Greer, *The Captain of our Salvation: A Study in the Patristic Exegesis
of Hebrews* (Tübingen: Mohr Siebeck, 1973). Pantaenus (d. c. 200), the first head
of the famous catechetical school in Alexandria, was the first known Christian
Biblical scholar to attribute authorship to Paul (Eusebius, *H.E.* 6.14.4). According to Eusebius (*H.E.* 6.25.11–14), Origen identified the theology as Pauline but
not the writing style. On several occasions, however, he did assume that Paul was
the author (*Peri Archōn* 1.2.5; 3.1.10; 4.1.24, 27; *C. Cels.* 3.53; 7.29). Jerome acknowledged that Hebrews was written in a different style than the rest of Paul's
epistles, but he accounted for this disparity by arguing that Paul originally had
dictated the letter in Hebrew and that an associate of his later translated it into
Greek (*Vir. ill.* 5.59).

30. Heb 3.1.

31. The taxonomy that follows may come from Origen's *Commentary on Galatians.* Cf. a comparable list formulated by Origen in *Comm. Rom.* 1.2.1 (trans.
Scheck, FOTC 103:63–64) concerning those who are called to be apostles,
prophets, martyrs, and teachers and ministers in the church.

through human agency. The third is sent by man but not by God. The fourth kind is sent not by God, not through human agency, nor by man; he sends himself on his own initiative. To the first category belong Isaiah, the rest of the prophets, and the apostle Paul himself, who are sent not by men nor through human agency but by God the Father and Christ. An example of the second kind of apostle is Joshua the son of Nun, who was made an apostle by God but through the man Moses.[32] The third kind is when someone is ordained because of the favor and partisanship of men. Today we see a great many appointed to the episcopate not because God has deemed them worthy but because they have garnered the favor of the common people.[33] The fourth category is comprised of false prophets and false apostles. "False prophets of this kind," the apostle says, "are workers of iniquity and masquerade as apostles of Christ."[34] They claim that the Lord says so-and-so, but the Lord has not sent them. Paul is nothing like them, for he is sent not by men nor through human agency but by God the Father through Jesus Christ. The heresy of Ebion[35] and Photinus[36] must be repelled because our Lord Jesus Christ is God: the Apostle, who was sent by Christ to

32. Cf. Dt 34.9.

33. Jerome was highly critical of clerics ordained under these circumstances: cf. *Ep.* 69.9: "Yesterday a catechumen, today a bishop; yesterday in the amphitheater, today in the church; in the circus in the evening, and in the morning at the altar; once the patron of actors, now the consecrator of virgins": on this passage, see N. Adkin, "'Heri catechumenus, hodie pontifex' (Jerome, *Epist.* 69.9.4)," *AClass* 36 (1993): 113–17. Jerome may have been inspired by Tertullian's satirizing of the disorder rampant in heretical churches in *De praescr. haer.* 41 (ANF 3:263): "Today one man is their bishop, tomorrow another; today one is a deacon who tomorrow is a reader; today he is a presbyter who tomorrow is a layman."

34. 2 Cor 11.13.

35. Ebion was a fictional heresiarch. Tertullian named him this after the Ebionites, a Jewish Christian sect active during the first few centuries of the church. The Ebionites believed that Christians were obligated to keep the Law and that Jesus was a human prophet. See S. Häkkinen's chapter on "Ebionites," in *A Companion to Second-Century Christian "Heretics,"* ed. A. Marjanen and P. Luomanen (Leiden: E. J. Brill, 2005), 247–78.

36. Photinus (d. 376) was bishop of Sirmium in Pannonia. He accepted Jesus' virgin birth and the accounts of his miracles, but he denied his full divin-

preach the Gospel, denies that he was sent by man. Other heresies creep in the door and insinuate that Christ did not have a real body and that he is God but not man.[37] There is also a new heresy that rips apart the incarnate humanity of Christ.[38] The faith of the church, then, is trapped among formidable shipwrecks of false teaching. If it confesses that Christ is [only] man, then Ebion and Photinus gain ground. If it contends that he is [only] God, then Mani,[39] Marcion,[40] and the author of the new teaching all bubble up to the surface. Let each and every one of them hear that Christ is both God and man—not that one is God and the other man, but rather that he who is God from all eternity deigned to become man in order to save us.[41]

---

ity and believed that he was an extraordinary man who represented by his life the glorious presence of God. See D. Williams, "Monarchianism and Photinus of Sirmium as the Persistent Heretical Face of the Fourth Century," *HThR* 99 (2006): 187–206.

37. This is a reference to the Docetics. They believed that matter is evil and that God could never have united himself with any elements in the material world. They consequently concluded that Jesus' body was not a physical entity but an incorporeal spirit that only seemed human. Docetics also regarded Christ's crucifixion and death as an illusion on the grounds that a spirit cannot suffer and die on a cross like a mortal human body. Docetic doctrine is attested already in the NT (1 Jn 4.1–3; 2 Jn 7).

38. I.e., Apollinarianism, a fourth-century Christological heresy named after its originator, Apollinaris of Laodicea. Apollinaris taught that Christ possessed a human body and a divine mind in place of a rational human mind.

39. Mani (216–276) was a Persian prophet and founder of Manichaeism, a major Gnostic religion that incorporated elements of Christianity, Judaism, Buddhism, and Zoroastrianism. He had a devout upbringing in a Jewish-Christian sectarian community in Assyria (modern-day southern Iraq). At the age of twenty-five Mani left home to preach a new religion he claimed to have received by private divine revelation. He taught a radical dualism, according to which there are two co-equal and eternal principles perpetually at odds: Light, which stands for the spiritual realm of goodness, and Darkness, which corresponds to the evil material realm. Salvation comes through special knowledge which teaches one how to be liberated from the material world. Prior to his conversion to Catholic Christianity, St. Augustine was a Manichee, and in the *Confessions* he tells how he came to question and finally reject Mani's teachings because they could not solve the problem of evil. The best English-language introduction to Mani, his religion, and its influence remains Samuel Lieu's *Manichaeism in the Later Roman Empire and Medieval China: A Historical Survey* (Manchester: Manchester University Press, 1985).

40. On Marcion, see Introduction.

41. Cf. Origen, *Comm. Gal.* 1.1, preserved by Pamphilus in *Apol. pro Orig.* 109:

We should be aware that the phrase "and through God the Father" is not found in Marcion's version of the Apostle.[42] Marcion wished to present Christ as having been resurrected not by God the Father but through his own power, just as Christ says, "Tear down this temple and I shall raise it up on the third day,"[43] and elsewhere, "No one takes my life from me, but I lay it down of my own accord. I have the power to lay it down and I have the power to take it up again."[44]

1.2. *And all the brothers who are with me, to the churches of Galatia.*

At the beginning of his other epistles Paul names Sosthenes[45] and Silas,[46] and sometimes Timothy.[47] In this one only, he felt it necessary to appeal to the authority of the majority, and so he implied the names of all the brothers who perhaps belonged to the circumcision party and whom the Galatians did not hold in contempt.[48] Certainly the consensus of a plurality about a mat-

---

"As for what the Apostle said, 'Paul, an apostle sent not by men nor through human agency, but through Jesus Christ,' this clearly means that Jesus Christ was not a man but had a divine nature. For if he was a man, Paul would not have said, 'Paul, an apostle sent not by men nor through human agency.' For if Jesus was a man and Paul was chosen by him to be an apostle, he became an apostle through human agency. But if he was an apostle through human agency, he would never have said 'nor through human agency.' It is clear that with these words Paul separates Jesus from human nature. For he was not content to say simply 'nor through human agency' but he added 'but through Jesus Christ.' Thus, he said that he had not been chosen an apostle through human agency because he knew that Christ is of a more lofty nature" (translated from Rufinus's Latin [SC 464:174–76]).

42. This testimony, undoubtedly taken from Origen's commentary on Galatians, enables us to reconstruct Marcion's revision of Paul's Greek: Παῦλος ἀπόστολος, οὐκ ἀπ᾽ ἀνθρώπων οὐδὲ δι᾽ ἀνθρώπου, ἀλλὰ διὰ Ἰησοῦ Χριστοῦ τοῦ ἐγείραντος αὐτὸν ἐκ νεκρῶν (the phrase καὶ θεοῦ πατρός is omitted). See A. von Harnack, *Marcion: Das Evangelium vom fremden Gott: Eine Monographie zur Geschichte der Grundlegung der katholischen Kirche* (Leipzig: Hinrichs, 1924), p. 67*.

43. Jn 2.19.   44. Jn 10.18.
45. 1 Cor 1.1.   46. 1 Thes 1.1.
47. 2 Cor 1.1; Phil 1.1; 1 Thes 1.1; Phlm 1.
48. Cf. D. F. Tolmie, *Persuading the Galatians: A Text-centred Rhetorical Analysis of a Pauline Letter* (Tübingen: Mohr Siebeck, 2005), p. 34: "The rhetorical function of these words [i.e., οἱ σὺν ἐμοὶ πάντες ἀδελφοί] is to convey the notion of a group of people standing behind him, endorsing and underscoring everything in the letter."

ter or opinion has great effectiveness when it comes to setting the masses on the right course.

It should be noted that Paul's phrase "to the churches of Galatia" is all-encompassing. He addresses not one church in one city but the churches in the entire province, which he rebukes for having gone astray. This implies that the church is made up of two parts. One has neither spot nor wrinkle and is truly the body of Christ, while the other assembles in the name of Christ but is not mature in virtue. Similarly, wise men are divided into two categories: those who are mature in virtue and those who are novices and still in the pursuit of wisdom. Of the advanced it is said, "I shall send wise men among you,"[49] but of beginners it is said, "Rebuke the wise man and he will treasure you."[50] For the one who is mature in virtue does not require correction. The same goes for the rest of the virtues, in that some men display courage, prudence, piety, chastity, justice, and temperance in their fullest forms, while others manifest them in an incomplete form.

1.3. *Grace and peace to you from God the Father and our Lord Jesus Christ.*

Unlike in his other epistles, he does not speak [simply as a matter of course] of the grace and peace of God the Father and our Lord Jesus Christ, through which our former sins have been forgiven, apart from the merit of works, and peace granted after the pardon. Rather, with foresight he is already building his case against those who knew the Law before the Gospel and thought that they could be justified by works. He wants them to recognize that they have been saved by grace and must persevere in what they have begun.[51]

---

49. Lk 2.49.

50. Prv 9.8.

51. As his comments on v. 3 indicate, Jerome, like most modern commentators (e.g., H. D. Betz, F. F. Bruce, F. J. Matera, B. Witherington), recognized that the opening salutation of Galatians is more theologically and rhetorically rich than the ones in any other of Paul's epistles besides Romans.

1.4–5. Who gave himself for our sins to redeem us from the present evil age, according to the will of our God and Father, to whom belongs glory for ever and ever. Amen.

The Son did not give himself for our sins outside the Father's will, nor did the Father hand over the Son without the Son's consent.[52] The will of the Son is to abide by the will of the Father, as he himself says in the Psalm, "I desire to do your will, my God."[53] The Son gave himself to vanquish the unrighteousness within us by his own righteousness, and he handed himself over in wisdom to defeat foolishness. Holiness personified offered itself to erase wickedness; and strength, feebleness. Christ has freed us in the future age, according to the promises and hopes in which we put our trust. He also has freed us from the present age, during which we who have died together with Christ[54] are being transformed by a newness of mind.[55] We are not of this world, and the world has no affection for us, and for good reason.[56]

What does the phrase "present evil age" mean? The heretics[57] usually take advantage of this opportunity to assert that there are two deities, one who governs light and the future age and the other who presides over darkness and the present age. As for us, we do not say that the age itself, which passes in days, nights, years, and months, is evil. Rather, we use the same terminology (ὁμωνύμως) to affirm that the things occurring during the age are evil.[58] Hence, it is said that each day has enough trouble of its own[59] and that Jacob's days were few and difficult.[60] It is not that the space of time within which Jacob lived was evil, but rather that

52. This is a Pauline idea. See Phil 2.5–8 (NRSV): "Let the same mind be in you that was in Christ Jesus, who, though he was in the form of God, did not regard equality with God as something to be exploited, but emptied himself, taking the form of a slave, being born in human likeness. And being found in human form, he humbled himself and became obedient to the point of death—even death on a cross."

53. Ps 40.8.   54. Cf. 2 Tm 2.11.
55. Cf. Rom 12.2.   56. Cf. Jn 15.19.
57. E.g., Valentinus, Basilides, Mani, and their followers.
58. For a study of the patristic notions of the "world" (or "age"), see Á. Orbán, *Les dénominations du monde chez les premiers auteurs chrétiens* (Nijmegen: Dekker & Van de Vegt, 1970).
59. Cf. Mt 6.34.   60. Cf. Gn 47.9.

the various afflictions he endured took a heavy toll on him. Furthermore, while Jacob was busy serving [Laban] to win the hands [of his daughters Rachel and Leah] and was in a state of despair from many hardships, Esau was enjoying respite. Thus, the same span of time was good for the one, but evil for the other.

If there were no distinction between evils, it would not be written in Ecclesiastes, "Do not say that my former days were better than these."[61] This is also why John says, "The whole world lies under the sway of the evil one."[62] He does not imply that the world itself is evil, but that evil things are done in the world by men who say, "Let us eat and drink, for tomorrow we shall die."[63] And the Apostle adds that we are "redeeming the time because the days are evil."[64] Forests are brought into ill repute when robberies abound in them, not because the ground or the trees commit sin but because they have gained a bad reputation as places where murders occur. We also despise the sword by which human blood is poured out as well as the cup in which poison is mixed, not because the sword and cup commit sin but because those who use these things for evil purposes deserve reproach.[65] So also the age, which is a period of time, is not good or evil in itself; it is called good or evil depending on the people who live in it. This is why we should disdain the fairy-tale nonsense of Valentinus.[66] He contrived his thirty Aeons from

61. Eccl 7.11. 62. 1 Jn 5.19.
63. 1 Cor 15.32. 64. Eph 5.16.

65. Jerome has clearly borrowed his analogy from Tertullian's *De resurrectione carnis* 16.4–8 (ANF 3:556): "The soul alone, therefore, will have to be judged at the last day pre-eminently as to how it has employed the vessel of the flesh; the vessel itself, of course, not being amenable to a judicial award: for who condemns the cup if any man has mixed poison in it? or who sentences the sword to the beasts, if a man has perpetrated with it the atrocities of a brigand?" See A. Cain, *REAug* 55 (2009): 32–34.

66. Valentinus (c. 100–c. 160) was a major Gnostic Christian philosopher of the second century. He taught at Alexandria and later at Rome, where he broke with the church reportedly because he was turned down for a bishopric (Tertullian, *Adv. Valent.* 4). He had many influential followers, making the Valentinian "school" a force to be reckoned with in the early centuries AD: see *The Rediscovery of Gnosticism, Volume 1: The School of Valentinus*, ed. B. Layton (Leiden: E. J. Brill, 1980); E. Thomassen, *The Spiritual Seed: The Church of the "Valentinians"* (Leiden:

the "ages" mentioned in Scripture and said that they were living things which, through their Quadrads, Ogdoads, Decads, and Dodecads, had given birth to ages as numerous as the offspring produced by the sow of Aeneas.[67]

What is the difference between "age" (*saeculum*) and "age of age" (*saeculum saeculi*) or "for ever and ever" (*saecula saeculorum*)? In what contexts are they used to refer to a brief space of time as opposed to eternity? When *olam*, the Hebrew equivalent of "age," has the letter *vav* added to it, it signifies eternity. But when it is written without the *vav*, it denotes the fiftieth year, which the Jews call the Jubilee Year.[68] For this reason the Jew who loved his master, and who on account of his wife and children had his ear pierced, was brought under the yoke of slavery and was ordered

---

E. J. Brill, 2006). Valentinus claimed to have received secret knowledge from Theodas, the reputed disciple of the Apostle Paul. He worked out a typically intricate and fantastical-sounding Gnostic cosmogony. J. N. D. Kelly, *Early Christian Doctrines* (London: Harper & Row, 1978), 23–24, summarizes it: "Above and beyond the universe dwells the supreme Father, Bythos, the unbegotten Monad and perfect Aeon, and by His side Sige (Silence), who is His Ennoia (Thought). From these proceed, by successive emanations, three pairs of aeons, Nous (or Monogenes) and Aletheia (Truth), Logos and Zoe (Life), Anthropos (Man) and Ecclesia (Church), thus completing the Ogdoad. From Logos and Zoe proceed five (the Decad), and from Anthropos and Ecclesia six (the Dodecad), further pairs of aeons. These thirty form the Pleroma, or fulness of the Godhead, but the only-begotten Nous alone possesses the possibility of knowing and revealing the Father. The lowest of the thirty aeons, however, Sophia, yielded to an ungovernable desire to apprehend His nature. She travailed with the guilty yearning she had conceived (Enthymesis), and would have been dissolved into the All had not Horos (Limit: also called Stauros, or Cross), appointed as guardian of the Pleroma, convinced her that the Father is incomprehensible. So Sophia cast away her passion and was allowed to remain within the Pleroma. Nous and Aletheia meanwhile, at the Father's behest, produce a new pair of aeons, Christ and the Holy Spirit, to instruct the aeons in their true relation to Him. Order having been thus restored, they sing the praises of the Father and produce the Saviour Jesus as the perfect fruit of the Pleroma."

67. Cf. Tertullian, *Adv. Marc.* 1.5.1 (ANF 3:274): "Valentinus . . . having once imagined two deities, Bythos and Sige, poured forth a swarm of divine essences, a brood of no less than thirty Aeons, like the sow of Aeneas." See A. Cain, *REAug* 55 (2009): 30–32.

68. Jerome took his peculiar explanation here from rabbinic sources. See H. I. Newman, "How should we measure Jerome's Hebrew Competence?" in Cain and Lössl, eds., *Jerome of Stridon*, 139–40.

to serve "for an age" (that is, until the fiftieth year).[69] In addition, the Moabites and Ammonites did not enter the congregation of the Lord until the fifteenth generation, once an "age" had passed, because all hard times would be improved with the advent of Jubilee.[70] Some say that the phrase "for ever and ever" [lit., "ages of ages"] has the same sense as other phrases—Holy of Holies; heavens of heavens; works of works; songs of songs— and that, as with ages, there are the gradations between heavens, holy things, works, and songs.[71] According to these same writers, the present age started at the creation of heaven and earth and runs until the end of the world, when Christ will act as supreme judge of all. They go further and delve into first principles, caviling about past and future ages and whether they were or will be good or evil. They stumble into such profound speculations that they have churned out an infinite number of books and volumes about this topic.

Paul concludes the prologue to his epistle with the Hebrew word *amen*, which the Septuagint translators rendered as γένοιτο, "let it be," and which Aquila translated as πεπιστωμένως, "verily [said]" or "faithfully [said]." The word *amen* also is always used in the Gospel when the Savior wants to strengthen the import of his words.[72]

---

69. Cf. Ex 21.5–6; Dt 15.17. In ancient Israel, the piercing of the ear in the presence of the elders was a symbol of a slave's willingness to render lifelong service to a master. See V. Hurowitz, "'His Master shall Pierce his Ear with an Awl' (Exodus 21.6): Marking Slaves in the Bible in Light of Akkadian Sources," *PAAJR* 58 (1993): 47–77.

70. Cf. Dt 23.3.

71. One of these unnamed interpreters is doubtless Origen. Cf. the beginning of Origen's first homily on the Song of Songs: "We have learned from Moses that there is not only a 'holy' but a 'Holy of Holies' . . . and that there are not only songs but songs of songs" (my translation of M. Simonetti, *Origene: Omelie sul Cantico dei Cantici* [Milan: Città Nuova, 1998], 18). This homily survives only in a Latin translation done by Jerome in Rome in 383.

72. For the various uses of this word, see K. Seybold, "Zur Vorgeschichte der liturgischen Formel Amen," *ThZ* 48 (1992): 109–17; E. Güting, "Amen, Eulogie, Doxologie: eine textkritische Untersuchung," in *Begegnungen zwischen Christentum und Judentum in Antike und Mittelalter: Festschrift für Heinz Schreckenberg*, ed. D.-A. Koch and H. Lichtenberger (Göttingen: Vandenhoeck & Ruprecht, 1993), 133–62.

1.6–7. I am amazed that you are being removed so quickly from him who called you in the grace of Christ Jesus to another gospel, which is no gospel at all. But there are some who are troubling you and want to undermine the Gospel of Christ.[73]

We come across the word "removal" for the first time in Genesis, where God removed Enoch "and he was not found."[74] We find it later in the Books of Kingdoms when Ahab's wife Jezebel "removed" him from the worship of God to the worship of idols, such that he acted like the Amorites, whom the Lord drove from the sight of the sons of Israel.[75] Although each is a kind of "removal," one was done by God and the other by the devil. The person removed by God is not discovered or caught by surprise by his enemies; this is what I take to be the meaning of the phrase "and he was not found." By contrast, the one removed by the devil is taken in a direction that is not what it seems. Wise men of the world who migrate from one teaching to another are said to be "removed." For instance, they call Dionysius "The Transposed" or "The Removed" because he abandoned his first philosophical creed and fell in with its opposite.[76] For he originally maintained that pain is not an evil, but after being overwhelmed by adversities and tortured by pain, he began to proclaim that pain is the chief of all evils.

He is amazed because the Galatian Christians have been removed so quickly from evangelical freedom to slavery to works

---

73. Jerome fails to make note of it, but it nevertheless is worth mentioning that Galatians is the only one of Paul's epistles in which a thanksgiving does not follow the opening salutation: on the thanksgiving, see C. J. Roetzel, *The Letters of Paul: Conversations in Context* (Louisville: John Knox Press, 1991), 59–71. Paul dispenses with this formality and goes straight to his rebuke of the Galatian Christians, presumably to emphasize the urgency of their spiritual plight. Cf. Origen, *Comm. Rom.* 1.1.9 (trans. Scheck, FOTC 103:77): "In Galatians he does not write a thanksgiving at all because he is amazed at them that they are 'so quickly turning away from him who called them unto another gospel.'"

74. Gn 5.24.

75. Cf. 1 Kgs 21.25–26.

76. Dionysius lived around 300 BC. Late in life, after having suffered greatly from some unknown medical problem, he renounced Stoicism and joined the hedonistic philosophical sect of the Cyrenaics. See Cicero, *Tusc.* 2.60; *Fin.* 5.94; Athenaeus, *Deipn.* 7.281; Diogenes Laertius, *V. Dion.*

of the Law. There are differing levels of guilt involved in being removed from something quickly and in being removed with difficulty. Take martyrdom, for instance. The one who does not put up a fight or suffer but immediately leaps at the chance to deny his faith suffers a different punishment than the person who is compelled to deny what he believes only after being subjected to racks, cords, and fires. The Gospel had recently been preached there, and not much time had elapsed since the Apostle had led the Galatians away from idols and to Christ. He is amazed at how quickly they departed from him in whose name they had been made Christians only a short time ago.

Furthermore, the passage contains an example of hyperbaton[77] which may be construed in its own order as follows: "I am amazed that you are being removed so quickly" from Christ Jesus "who called you in grace," saying, "I have come to call not the just but sinners"[78] to repentance. We are indeed saved by grace and not through the Law.[79]

Paul says, "You have been removed to another gospel, which is no gospel at all." For nothing untrue lasts,[80] and that which is contrary to the truth, does not exist, as it is written, "Lord, hand not your scepter over to those that are not."[81] And, "God called those things that are not"[82] so as to cause that which was not, to be. But if people who believed in the same God and possessed the same Scripture are "removed to another gospel, which is no gospel at all," what ought we to think of Marcion and the rest of the heretics who reject the Creator and pretend that Christ originates from another god? They slip and fall, not because of their interpretation of the Law, nor because of a failure to reconcile the letter and the spirit, but because they are at variance with the entire law of the church.

---

77. Hyperbaton is a figure of speech which inverts or interrupts the natural flow of words in a sentence in order to produce a desired rhetorical effect.

78. Mk 2.17.

79. Cf. Eph 2.8.

80. Cf. Jerome's proverbial-sounding remark to Rufinus in an early letter (*Ep.* 3.6): *Amicitia, quae desinere potest, vera numquam fuit.*

81. Est 14.11.

82. 1 Cor 1.28.

Paul puts it elegantly, "But there are some who are troubling you and want to undermine the Gospel of Christ." According to him, they want to change, undermine, and disturb the Gospel of Christ, but they are unable to do so because the truth by its nature cannot be anything but truth. Everyone who interprets the Gospel in a spirit or mentality at odds with what is written in Scripture causes a disturbance to believers and undermines the Gospel of Christ, causing what is in front to appear behind, and vice versa. If anyone follows only the letter, he puts in front what is behind. If anyone agrees with the interpretations of the Jews, he puts in the back the things which by their very nature should be in front.

Finally, the word "removal" is appropriately used for the Galatians, for "Galatia" means "removal" in the Latin language.[83]

1.8–9. But even if we or an angel from heaven should preach a gospel to you other than the one we preached to you, let him be accursed! Just as we have said already, so now I say again: If anyone preaches to you a gospel besides that which you have received, let him be accursed!

This could be understood as hyperbole and not to mean that an apostle or angel could preach otherwise than they had already spoken. But even if this were possible, it would not justify [the Galatians'] straying from what they had received, all the more so because the Apostle demonstrates in another passage that his own faith is stable, "I know that neither death nor life, neither angels nor principalities, neither the present nor the future, nor any power, neither height nor depth, nor any other created thing will be able to separate us from the love of God which is in Christ Jesus our Lord. My conscience bears witness to me that I speak the truth and do not lie."[84] These are not the words of one who can ever deviate from his faith in and love for Christ.

Some take Paul as speaking literally (rather than hypotheti-

83. In his *Book on Hebrew Names* (CCSL 72:18), Jerome renders *Galatia* as *translatio* ("removal") or *transferens* ("removing"). Though he does not explicitly say so above, he derives the Latin *Galatia* from the Hebrew *galath* ("removed" or "carried away"), and so he suggests that Paul's addressees are Galatians in both name and reality.

84. Rom 8.38–9.1.

cally) about the possibility of apostles or angels regressing. As proof, they cite his admission that he was capable of stumbling if he lived in an undisciplined fashion, "But I discipline my body and bring it into subjection, lest in preaching to others I myself be found to fall short of the mark."[85] They also assert that the angels who did not preserve their position of authority are mutable because they left their habitation and are held in darkness in eternal chains for the Last Judgment.[86] They say that God's nature alone is immutable, as it is written, "You indeed are,"[87] and as God says about himself, "I am your God and I do not change."[88] They point out in addition that the morning-star Lucifer fell and was reduced to nothing, even though he used to send light to all the peoples on earth.[89] That very learned man Tertullian speaks elegantly about this when he refutes Apelles and his virgin Philumene,[90] the latter of whom some wicked angel of a di-

85. 1 Cor 9.27. 86. Cf. Jude 6.
87. Cf. Ps 102.27. 88. Mal 3.6.

89. Cf. Is 14.12. Tertullian and Origen were (as far as we know) the first Christian authors to connect this passage with Christ's statement in Lk 10.18: "I saw Satan fall from heaven like lightning." See J.-M. Vercruysse, "Les Pères de l'Église et la chute de l'ange: Lucifer d'après Is 14 et Ez 28," *RSR* 75 (2001): 147–74. The extra-Biblical development of the Lucifer-as-Satan story is traced by A. Marx, "La chute de Lucifer (Ésaïe 14, 12–15; Luc 10, 18): préhistoire d'un mythe," *RHPhR* 80 (2000): 171–85, and G. Luck, "Lucifer, Fallen Angel," *Euphrosyne* 29 (2001): 297–318. As for the specific reasons for Lucifer's fall, some patristic writers suggested pride, others envy: see N. Adkin, "Pride or Envy? Some Notes on the Reason the Fathers Give for the Devil's Fall," *Augustiniana* 34 (1984): 349–51.

90. Apelles was Marcion's disciple in Rome. He had a good Greek education and was philosophically trained. Tertullian (*De praescr. haer.* 30.5–6) insinuates that Apelles became estranged from the Marcionite community after he seduced the prophetess Philumene and made her his whore. It must be remembered, though, that orthodox writers had the habit of circulating sensationalistic stories like this one in order to discredit their theological opponents. Apelles edited a collection of Philumene's revelations (Φανερώσεις) and he also composed *Syllogisms,* a 38-volume work in which he tried to expose the OT as a self-contradictory text. Apelles went a step further than Marcion in his devaluation of the OT by arguing that it is full of fables and lies. For reconstructions of the teachings of Apelles and Philumene, see É. Junod, "Les attitudes d'Apelles, disciple de Marcion, à l'égard de l'Ancien Testament," *Augustinianum* 22 (1982): 113–33; A. Jensen, *God's Self-confident Daughters: Early Christianity and the Liberation of Women,* trans. O. C. Dean (Louisville: John Knox Press, 1996), 194–204;

abolical bent had possessed[91]—this is the angel, he writes, whom the Apostle had proclaimed, by the prophetic foresight of the Holy Spirit, to be accursed, long before Apelles had been born.[92]

Furthermore, "accursed" is a word used originally by the Jews. It is found in the Book of Joshua and in Numbers, when the Lord ordered everyone to despise everything in Jericho or connected with the Midianites and regard them as accursed.[93] Some suppose that Christ and the Apostle Paul were incapable of condemning or cursing anyone since they were the Son and the servant of the good but previously unknown God.[94] But let us ask them: How is it that the Apostle uses a word employed by the Jews, and, by extension, by the Creator himself, and wishes either an angel or an apostle to be damned, although he himself is not in the habit of being vengeful?

By his statement, "Just as we have said already, so now I say again," Paul indicates that he initially threatened to anathematize preachers of a different gospel. Now, after it has been preached, he carries through with the decree he had enunciated beforehand. So as to make the authority of Peter and John seem less weighty, he declared that an anathema would apply to himself, whom critics accused of doing one thing in Judea and teaching another thing among the Gentiles, and also to an angel, who assuredly is greater even than his apostolic predecessors. For it would not be permissible either for an angel or for him, as their teacher, to preach a different message to the Galatian Christians

---

K. Greschat, *Apelles und Hermogenes: zwei theologische Lehrer des zweiten Jahrhunderts* (Leiden: E. J. Brill, 2000).

91. For Jerome's notion that heretics are demon-possessed, see B. Jeanjean, *Saint Jérôme et l'hérésie* (Paris: Institut d'Études Augustiniennes, 1999), 374–76.

92. Jerome was probably thinking of Tertullian, *De praescr. haer.* 6.5–6 (ANF 3:246): "If, therefore, even 'an angel from heaven should preach any other gospel' than [the apostles'], he would be called accursed by us. The Holy Ghost had even then foreseen that there would be in a certain virgin called Philumene an angel of deceit, 'transformed into an angel of light,' by whose miracles and illusions Apelles was led when he introduced his new heresy." See A. Cain, *REAug* 55 (2009): 27–29.

93. Cf. Nm 21.3; Jos 6.17.

94. Marcion and his followers are targeted here. This "previously unknown God" is Marcion's "Stranger" God, the God and Father of Jesus, who had been unknown to humanity prior to his revelation through Christ.

than they already had received. Paul mentions himself and an angel, but he implies others without naming them. He says, "If *anyone* preaches a gospel to you," using a generalizing term so that he can subtly implicate them without openly insulting them.

1.10. *For do I now persuade others or God? Or do I seek to please others? If I were still pleasing others, I would not be a servant of Christ!*

Let us not imagine that the Apostle is telling us to follow his example by dismissing the judgments of others. After all, he says elsewhere, "Knowing therefore the fear of the Lord, we persuade others; but God knows us well."[95] And also, "Do not give offense to the Jews, Gentiles, or to the church of God, just as I please all others in all things, not seeking my own profit but the profit of the many, so that they may be saved."[96] But if we can please both God and others at the same time, let us also please others. If we can please others only by displeasing God, then our priority must be to please God.[97] At any rate, Paul clarifies why he pleases others in all things, saying, "I do not seek my own profit but the profit of the many, so that they may be saved." Motivated by the love which seeks not its own good but that of others, he pleases others so that they may be saved. In doing so he certainly pleases God first because God desires their salvation.

The word "now" is inserted here to show that we should aim to please or not please people according to the circumstances. This means that he who is now not being a people-pleaser for the sake of Gospel truth was at one time a people-pleaser so that he could secure others' salvation. Paul formerly pleased the Jews when he was a zealot for the traditions of his elders and lived faultlessly according to the Law.[98] He had so much confident enthusiasm for the religious ceremonies of his forefathers that he was complicit in the death of Stephen[99] and went to Damascus to restrain those who had dissociated themselves from the Law.[100] But after going from being a persecutor to a chosen vessel and starting to preach the faith he had once attacked,[101] he began to displease the Jews

95. 2 Cor 5.11.   96. 1 Cor 10.32–33.
97. Cf. 1 Thes 2.3.   98. Cf. Phil 3.6.
99. Cf. Acts 7.57–58.   100. Cf. Acts 9.2–3.
101. Cf. Acts 9.15.

as much as he used to please them. This is what Paul is saying: Do I seek to please the Jews, whom I have displeased in order to please God? If I were to do so, I would no longer be a servant of Christ, and by advocating the Law I would be demolishing the grace of the Gospel. But now I am not tempted even to pretend that I keep the Law, for I am unable to please God and the Jews at the same time, and whoever pleases the Jews, displeases God.

The word "persuade" is customarily used when referring to someone who tries to impose his own views on others. In a great many places in Scripture one reads passages like this one: "Persuasion does not come from the one who has called you";[102] and also this one from the Acts of the Apostles: "Many Jews therefore came to the place where he was staying. Up until evening he was explaining and proclaiming the kingdom of God to them and trying to convince them about Jesus from the Law of Moses and from the prophets."[103] Paul went to considerable lengths in his persuasion because he wanted to quash the rumors that he secretly kept the Law and associated himself with the Judaizers at Jerusalem.

1.11–12. *For I want you to know, brothers, that the Gospel I preached is not man-made. Indeed I neither received it nor learned it from man, but through the revelation of Jesus Christ.*

This passage annihilates the teaching of Ebion and Photinus because it affirms that Christ is not just a man but also God. For if the Gospel Paul preaches is not man-made, and if he neither received it nor learned it from man but through the revelation of Jesus Christ, then Christ, who revealed it to him, cannot be a man, and if he is not a man, then he must be God. We do not deny that he assumed human form; we simply reject the notion that he was only a man.[104]

---

102. Gal 5.8.

103. Acts 28.23.

104. Cf. Origen, *Comm. Gal.* 1.11–12, preserved by Pamphilus in *Apol. pro Orig.* 111: "Pay attention to what he writes because by adding these things to what precedes them one will be able competently to show those who deny the deity of Jesus Christ and say that he is only a man, that Jesus Christ, the Son of God, is not a man but God. For when the Apostle says, 'The Gospel I preached to you is not according to man but according to Jesus Christ,' he clearly shows

A twofold question may be asked. Have the churches throughout the world received a divine or a human gospel, and how few
of us came to an understanding of the Gospel through a revelation from Christ but without a human preaching it to us? Those
who can say, "Do you demand proof that Christ is speaking
through me?"[105] and, "I no longer live, but Christ lives in me,"[106]
do not themselves teach so much as God teaches through them
and says to his saints, "I have spoken: You are gods and all of you
are sons of the Most High."[107] Right after this, God addresses sinners, "You shall die as men and you shall fall as one of the princes."[108] Therefore, it is clear that Peter and Paul are gods when
they speak, inasmuch as they do not die as men and do not fall
as one of the princes; and those who are gods deliver a divine
rather than a human gospel. Marcion, Basilides,[109] and the other
heretical plagues do not possess the Gospel of God because they
do not have the Holy Spirit, and without the Spirit the Gospel
that is taught ceases to be divine.[110]

We should not suppose that the essence of the Gospel is in
the words rather than in the actual meaning of Scripture, or on
the surface rather than in the inmost parts,[111] or in the leaves

---

that Christ Jesus is not a man; and if he is not a man, he is without doubt God,
or rather, he will not be anything other than man and God. Moreover, if what
Paul says is true, that 'I did not receive the Gospel from man but through the
revelation of Jesus Christ,' it is undeniable that Jesus Christ, who revealed it, is
not a man, for it is not in man's power to reveal secret and hidden things. Even
if this could ever be accomplished through man, it is not done by man but by
Christ who speaks in man" (translated from Rufinus's Latin [SC 464:176–78]).

105. 2 Cor 13.3.   106. Gal 2.20.
107. Ps 81.6 (LXX).   108. Ps 81.7 (LXX).

109. Basilides was a Syrian Gnostic teacher who was active in Alexandria during the reign of the emperor Hadrian (117–138). Origen (*Hom. 1 in Luc.*) says
that he had the audacity to compose a gospel and name it after himself (κατὰ
Βασιλείδην εὐαγγέλιον): for a skeleton outline of its possible contents, see Schneemelcher, *NTA,* 1.398. Basilides was the first known Christian philosopher.
His account of creation was similar to Valentinus's, and he maintained a dualistic opposition between the supreme good God and the inferior Demiurge who
created the world and mankind.

110. Literally, "becomes human" (*humanum fit*).

111. Jerome's phrase *non in superficie sed in medulla* and the notion that heretics (cf. Marcion, Basilides, and "other heretical plagues" mentioned in the

of mere words rather than in the root of reason.[112] The prophet says of God, "His words are good to him [who walks uprightly]."[113] Scripture is advantageous to its hearers when it is spoken with Christ, when it is proclaimed with the Father, and when the preacher introduces it with the Spirit. The devil also speaks about Scripture, and all the heresies, according to Ezekiel, take material from it and sew together pillows which they place under the elbow of every age.[114] As for me, when I have Christ in me as I speak, I do not have the gospel of man. But if I am a sinner, I hear, "To the sinner God has said, 'Why do you tell of my statutes and take my covenant on your lips? You despise discipline and have cast my words behind you,'"[115] and so on. Great harm is done to the church when by means of some perverse interpretation the Gospel of Christ turns into the gospel of man—or, what is worse, the gospel of the devil.

There is a difference between receiving and learning. The one who receives the Gospel is introduced to it and induced to trust in it and believes what is written to be true. The one who learns understands the messages that are encoded in Scripture in riddles and parables. His understanding comes not by human revelation but from Christ, who revealed these things to Paul, and from his mouthpiece, Paul.

The word ἀποκάλυψις, which means "revelation," is a uniquely Scriptural coinage that none of the worldly sages among the Greeks employed.[116] For this reason it seems to me that here the

---

previous sentence) have a defective hermeneutical system is derived from Tertullian, *De res. carn.* 3.6 (ANF 3:547–48): "Take away, indeed, from the heretics the wisdom they share with the heathen, and let them support their inquiries from the Scriptures alone: they will then be unable to keep their ground. For that which commends men's common sense is its very simplicity, and its participation in the same feelings, and its community of opinions; and it is deemed to be all the more trustworthy, inasmuch as its definitive statements are naked and open, and known to all. Divine reason, on the contrary, lies in the very pith and marrow of things, not on the surface, and very often is at variance with appearances." See A. Cain, *REAug* 55 (2009): 34–35.

112. Cf. Mt 13.6. 113. Mi 2.7.
114. Cf. Ezek 13.18. 115. Ps 50.16–17.

116. Jerome had only a scant firsthand knowledge of classical Greek literature, and so he is probably reporting the observation of another (Christian) writer, perhaps Origen.

translators of the Septuagint tried to capture the peculiarity of a foreign tongue, just as they did with other words they had rendered from Hebrew into Greek, inventing new words for new concepts.[117] In this instance they used a word which means the unveiling or exposing of something that is covered or concealed. Take the following example as an illustration. Moses spoke with God without hiding his face behind a veil, but when speaking to the Israelites he veiled himself because they were unable to look at his shining face.[118] Let us take another example. When a covering that had been spread out in front of the Ark of the Covenant was removed, previously hidden things were disclosed or, to use the word in question, "revealed."[119] Therefore, if those who are well-read in secular literature begin to mock us for using novel and unsophisticated words, let us direct them to Cicero's books on philosophical questions. Let them see how he, too, had to devise strange locutions unfamiliar to the Latin ear[120]—not to mention the fact that he was translating into our language from Greek, which is akin to Latin. Imagine, then, the challenges facing those who attempt to make sense of the peculiarities inherent in matters of Hebrew philology. For all that, there are still many fewer neologisms in the numerous books of Scripture than what Cicero amassed in that small work of his.

At the outset when I expounded the phrase "Paul, an apostle sent not by men nor through human agency,"[121] I showed that Paul was taking an indirect swipe at Peter and the rest of his apostolic predecessors to affirm that he was not intimidated by any advocate of the Law because he had only Christ as his teacher in the Gospel. The present passage can be taken in the same vein. Furthermore, he is referring to the revelation he had

117. The phrase *nova novis rebus verba fingentes* is a near-verbatim borrowing from Cicero, who used it to describe the coinage of Latin words for Greek philosophical concepts (*Acad.* 1.41; *Fin.* 3.1.3; *N.D.* 1.44).

118. Cf. Ex 34.33–35.

119. Cf. Ex 40.3.

120. See G. Striker, "Cicero and Greek Philosophy," *HSCP* 97 (1995): 53–61; J. Powell, "Cicero's translations from Greek," in *Cicero the Philosopher: Twelve Papers*, ed. J. Powell (Oxford: Oxford University Press, 1995), 273–300.

121. Gal 1.1.

on the road to Damascus, where he was found worthy to hear Christ's voice and gazed with his blinded eyes at the true light of the world.[122]

1.13–14. *You have heard of my former conduct in Judaism, that I persecuted the church of God beyond measure and tried to exterminate it. I advanced in Judaism beyond many who were my age, being far more zealous than they were for the traditions of my forefathers.*

This narrative is of enormous benefit to the Galatians because it relates how Paul, once a scourge of the church and a passionate defender of Judaism, suddenly came to believe in Christ at a time when the crucified one was first being preached and the new teaching was being opposed by Jews and Gentiles alike in many sectors throughout the world. Paul had been indoctrinated by the Pharisees from a young age and had surpassed all of his contemporaries in the Judaic tradition,[123] but he now defends the very church he used to persecute rabidly, and he would rather have the grace and newness offered by Christ (even if that means being hated by all) than the old Law and popular praise. When confronted with someone like this, the Galatians could ask: What should we Gentile converts to Christianity do? Paul strategically inserts the phrase "I persecuted the church of God beyond measure" in order to inspire admiration for his conversion experience by emphasizing that he had not been some casual persecutor of the church but had outdone all others in his efforts. And, in the midst of recounting other things, he cleverly intimates that he had observed not so much the Law of God as the traditions of his forefathers, the Pharisees, who teach the doctrines and mandates of men and reject the Law of God in favor of establishing their own traditions.

Note how carefully Paul weighs his words. "You have heard

122. Cf. Acts 9.1–9.
123. According to N. T. Wright, *What Saint Paul Really Said* (Grand Rapids: W. B. Eerdmans, 1997), 26–29, Paul was a Shammaite Pharisee and therefore the strictest kind of Pharisee. See further A. F. Segal, *Paul the Convert: The Apostolate and the Apostasy of Saul the Pharisee* (New Haven: Yale University Press, 1990); T. Seland, "Saul of Tarsus and Early Zealotism: Reading Gal 1,13–14 in Light of Philo's Writings," *Bib* 83 (2002): 449–71.

of my former conduct in Judaism." He says "conduct," not "esteemed behavior," "former" instead of "current," and "in Judaism" rather than "in the Law of God."[124] Also noteworthy is the statement, "I persecuted the church of God beyond measure and tried to exterminate it." Paul did not persecute like everyone else but did so "beyond measure." Nor was persecution enough, however violent it was: Paul ravaged the church like a riotous troublemaker and robber. He does not say "the church of Christ," as he regarded it at the time and which he held in contempt and persecuted. Now, however, he believes it is "the church of God" and thus implies either that Christ himself is God or that this is the church of the same God who had been the giver of the Law.[125] He says further, "I advanced in Judaism beyond many who were my age, being far more zealous than they were for the traditions of my forefathers." Again he calls it advancement not in the Law of God but in Judaism. He does not say "beyond all" but "beyond many who were my age," rather than "beyond my elders," so as to recount his zeal for the Law without coming off as being boastful. By specifying "the traditions of my forefathers" rather than "the commandments of the Lord,"[126] he indicates that he was a Pharisee of Pharisees and that his zeal for God was not according to understanding.[127] Down to the present day, those who interpret Scripture according to a Jewish mentality persecute the church of Christ and devastate it not out of zeal for the Law of God but because they have been corrupted by the traditions of men.

---

124. *Audistis, inquit, conversationem meam aliquando in Iudaismo; conversationem non gratiam, aliquando non modo, in Iudaismo non in lege Dei.* Cf. Eusebius of Emesa, *Comm. Gal.* 1.13–14 (Staab, p. 48): Ἠκούσατε γὰρ τὴν ἐμὴν ἀναστροφήν ποτε ἐν τῷ Ἰουδαϊσμῷ. Καὶ οὐκ εἶπεν ἐν τῷ νόμῳ.

125. In one and the same sentence Jerome emphasizes both Christ's divinity and the continuity between the OT and NT, and thus he may have Marcion in mind.

126. *Nec supra omnes sed supra plurimos, nec supra senes sed supra coaetaneos, ut et studium suum referret in lege et iactantiam declinaret. Paternas autem traditiones, non Domini mandata commemorans . . .* Cf. Eusebius of Emesa, *Comm. Gal.* 1.13–14 (Staab, p. 48): πολλοὺς καὶ οὐ πάντας διὰ τὸ σύμμετρον, συνηλικιώτας δὲ διὰ τὸ μὴ κατὰ τῶν πρεσβυτέρων δοκεῖν ἐπαίρεσθαι . . . πατρικῶν δὲ παραδόσεων εἶπεν καὶ οὐ νομίμων.

127. Cf. Rom 10.2.

1.15–16a. *But when it pleased God, who separated me from my mother's womb and called me through his grace, to reveal his Son in me so that I might preach him among the nations . . .*

Here and in his epistle to the Romans Paul writes that he has been set apart for the Gospel of God.[128] God knew Jeremiah and sanctified him before he was formed and conceived in his mother's womb.[129] The righteous man, or (as some think) the Savior, says, "I was cast upon you from birth; from my mother's womb you have been my God."[130] It is different with sinners, as David declares, "Behold, I was brought forth in iniquity, and in sin my mother conceived me."[131] He says elsewhere, "Sinners are estranged from the time they are in the womb."[132] Finally, as a joint illustration of people being either sinful or righteous from the womb, God loved Jacob but hated Esau before they were born.[133]

Here a foothold is gained by the heretics who fancy two different but interdependent natures, one spiritual and redeemable, the other material, animal-like, and destined to perish.[134] It could never be the case, they argue, that a righteous man is chosen by God before doing good or that a sinner is despised before sinning, unless the damned and the saved had different natures. There is an easy solution to this conundrum. God's foreknowledge allows him to love whom he knows will be righteous even before they emerge from the womb, and to hate whom he knows will be sinners even before they ever commit a sin. God is not unjust in terms of whom he loves or hates. He

128. Cf. Rom 1.1. For Paul's personal conviction about the divine mandate of his apostolic mission, see A. Hultgren, "The Scriptural Foundations for Paul's Mission to the Gentiles," in *Paul and His Theology*, ed. S. Porter (Leiden: E. J. Brill, 2006), 21–44.

129. Cf. Jer 1.5.   130. Ps 22.10.
131. Ps 51.5.   132. Ps 58.3.
133. Cf. Mal 1.2–3.

134. In this paragraph Jerome refutes the Gnostic doctrine of natures (cf. below, 3.6.1). According to its proponents (e.g., Basilides and Valentinus), all human beings are born with either a good or an evil nature, and their salvation or damnation depends on this pre-ordained nature and not on their individual merits in this life. Jerome's argument undoubtedly comes directly from the pages of Origen (see, e.g., *Peri Archōn* 2.9.5; 3.1.6; *Comm. Rom.* 1.3.3; 2.4.7; 2.10.2; 4.12.1; 8.8.7; 8.11.2).

simply cannot be otherwise disposed towards those whom he knows will be either righteous or sinful. We humans can pass judgment only about matters in the here and now, but God, before whom the future has already unfolded, determines his verdict on the basis of how things end up, not on how they began. This explanation, which offers a concise and comprehensible solution to the problem at hand, should be enough to ease whatever concerns the reader may have.

Some who try to prove that God is unjust cite the above-quoted passage, "Sinners are estranged from the time they are in the womb," in conjunction with another, "They have gone astray from the womb, they have spoken lies."[135] How can this be true, they ask, seeing that sinners cannot speak or think while in the womb? How can the foreknowledge of God be fair when it loves and cares for one before he is born but despises another? These skeptics tie this objection with the notion of the pre-existence [of souls] and claim that each person, from the very moment [his soul] is conceived, is assigned to the guardianship of either good or bad angels according to his merit. They also allege that the entire passage about Jacob and Esau, of which I just made mention, was directed at the Roman Christians so that they would find the answer to their question only after expending much effort and drinking Chrysippus's hellebore.[136]

"To reveal his Son *in me*" does not mean the same thing as "to reveal his Son *to me*." In the first case, the thing revealed was in him already but then later revealed.[137] In the second, what was not in him beforehand is able to be revealed. We find a parallel in the Gospel, "One stands among you whom you do not know,"[138] and elsewhere, "He was the true light that gives light

---

135. Ps 58.3.

136. According to Lucian (*Ver. Hist.* 2.18), the third-century BC Stoic philosopher Chrysippus of Soli drank hellebore as a cure for madness.

137. Cf. G. Fee, *Pauline Christology: An Exegetical-Theological Study* (Peabody: Hendrickson Publishers, 2007), 221–22. Fee, like Jerome, emphasizes the locative force of Paul's ἐν ἐμοί: the revelation of which Paul speaks in v. 12 took place in him in such a vivid way that his apostleship has become indistinguishable from the Gospel of Christ.

138. Jn 1.26.

to every man coming into the world."[139] It is clear from this that the knowledge of God is innate in all humans and that no one is born without Christ and that none lacks within himself the seeds of wisdom, righteousness, and the rest of the virtues. This is why many unbelievers act prudently and uprightly in some respects, such as when they obey their parents, extend a helping hand to someone in need, and do not bully their neighbors or steal others' property. Furthermore, they become more vulnerable to the judgment of God, for although they possess the fundamentals of the virtues and the seeds of God, they do not believe in him without whom these things could not exist.

Finally, in Paul's epistles the phrase "the Son of God [who has been] revealed" refers to the fact that Christ, thanks to the preaching of Paul, is recognized by the nations who did not know him beforehand.

1.16b. *I gave no rest* (non acquievi) *right away to flesh and blood.*

A more accurate translation from the Greek is, "I did not confer (*non contuli*) right away with flesh and blood."[140] I know that many think this refers to the apostles. Even Porphyry claimed that Paul, after Christ had revealed himself to him, did not think it appropriate to confer with other human beings, lest after receiving teaching directly from God he take instruction from flesh and blood. But far be it from me to reckon Peter, John, and James as flesh and blood, which cannot possess the kingdom of God.[141] If spiritually-minded apostles count as flesh and blood, then what about earthly-minded people? It is obvious that Paul

139. Jn 1.9. In Jerome's quotation the participle "coming" modifies "man," not "light."

140. Marius Victorinus, following the Old Latin reading *non acquievi*, gave this interpretation: "When Paul is busy bringing the news of divine things, things containing God's grace, it's no labour for his mind. The labour falls rather on flesh and blood: hustling to and fro, bearing the labour of the road, travelling through provinces and countries. I gave no rest, he says, to flesh and blood. Flesh and blood mean the whole external person": S. A. Cooper, *Marius Victorinus' Commentary on Galatians: Introduction, Translation, and Notes* (Oxford: Oxford University Press, 2005), 264. Jerome rightly saw *non acquievi* as a mistranslation of the Greek οὐ προσανεθέμην and emended it to *non contuli*.

141. Cf. 1 Cor 15.50.

did not confer with flesh and blood after receiving revelation from Christ because he would not throw pearls to swine or give what is holy to dogs.[142] Take note of what Scripture has to say about sinners, "My spirit shall not remain in these people because they are flesh."[143] The Apostle did not confer about the Gospel revealed to him with people who were flesh and blood (these people did not reveal the Son of God to Peter, either).[144] Rather, he converted them gradually from flesh and blood to the Spirit and then vouchsafed to them the hidden mysteries of the Gospel.

Someone may say: Even if he did not confer about the Gospel right away with flesh and blood, he nevertheless implies that he did so a short time later, and this means that the apostles must be flesh and blood after all, though nevertheless he who did not initially confer with flesh and blood did so later, as I have said. This line of reasoning constrains us to avoid coupling "immediately" or "right away" with "flesh and blood," and instead to construe it as part of the preceding verset, "But when it pleased God, who separated me from my mother's womb, to reveal his Son in me, so that I might preach him among the nations right away." So, "I did not confer with flesh and blood" is its own self-contained sentence. This reading better preserves the sense of the passage, for after Christ was revealed to him, Paul was dispatched immediately to announce the good news to the nations. He did not linger or waste any time going to the apostles or conferring with others about the revelation the Lord had given him. Rather, he went to Arabia and, returning to Damascus after three years, preached the Gospel and at last went to Jerusalem to meet with Peter, John, and James.

1.17a. *Nor did I go to Jerusalem to those who were apostles before me.*

If he had been referring to the apostles when he said, "I did not confer with flesh and blood," why did he find it necessary to repeat himself by saying, "Nor did I go to Jerusalem to those who were apostles before me"? The meaning I gave above, then, must stand.

142. Cf. Mt 7.6. 143. Gn 6.3.
144. Cf. Mt 16.17.

1.17b. *But I went to Arabia and returned again to Damascus.*

The sequence of events presented here seems to be at odds with Luke's account in the Acts of the Apostles, which runs as follows. After coming to faith in Christ, Paul courageously pro-claimed the Gospel at Damascus for many days. But when plots were hatched to kill him, he was lowered in a basket through the city wall and went to Jerusalem and tried to join the disciples. When they shied away from him and refused to come near him, Barnabas brought him to the apostles, and Paul related how he had seen the Lord on his journey and how at Damascus he had spoken boldly in the name of Jesus.[145] "He was with them at Jerusalem, coming in and going out and speaking boldly in the name of the Lord. He also conversed and debated with some Greeks, but they were looking for a way to kill him. When the brothers realized this, they escorted him to Caesarea and sent him off to Tarsus."[146] Paul says, however, that he went first to Arabia, then back to Damascus, and after three years traveled to Jerusalem, where he met with Peter and stayed with him for fifteen days but did not meet with anyone else besides James, the brother of the Lord. Since the facts might seem dubious to those who were not there, Paul emphasizes the veracity of his account by swearing under oath, "Concerning the things I write to you, I do not lie before God."[147]

We can surmise therefore that, as Luke relates, Paul went to Je-rusalem not to see those who were apostles before him so that he might learn from them, but to evade persecution that had been stirred up against him at Damascus on account of the Gospel of Christ. He went to Jerusalem as if it were any other city, depart-ed right away because of the plot against him, arrived in Arabia or Damascus, and then after three years returned to Jerusalem to spend time with Peter. The following is a plausible recon-struction of the chain of events. As soon as he was baptized and refreshed with a meal, he remained for several days with the dis-ciples who were in Damascus and stupefied all those around him by preaching incessantly in the synagogues of the Jews that Je-sus is the Son of God. Then he went to Arabia and from there

145. Cf. Acts 9.19–27.   146. Acts 9.28–30.
147. Gal 1.20.

turned back to Damascus, where he spent three years. Scripure attests to this, "When many days had passed, the Jews concocted a plot to kill Saul [Paul]. But their plot became known to Saul. They watched the city gates day and night to kill him. Then the disciples took him at night and let him down the city wall in a basket. When Saul had come to Jerusalem, he tried to join the disciples."[148] Luke neglected to mention Arabia because Paul perhaps did nothing notable there as far as his apostolic preaching was concerned, and he instead gave a compendious account of what Paul had accomplished that seemed worthy of Christ's Gospel.

We should not think that the Apostle's trip to Arabia was wasted or in vain; it was according to God's plan and will that he did not preach there. For we later read that Paul, after leaving Silas's side, was prohibited by the Holy Spirit from saying a word in Asia [Minor].[149] Otherwise, of what benefit to me is the detail, "But I went to Arabia and returned again to Damascus," if I read that Paul, immediately after receiving a revelation from Christ, went to Arabia and then doubled back to Damascus, even though I do not know what he did there or what purpose his travels served? In the same epistle the Apostle provides me with an opportunity for deeper understanding when he discusses Abraham, Hagar, and Sarah. "These things are to be taken figuratively. For the women represent two covenants. One covenant is from Mount Sinai and bears children who are to be slaves: this is Hagar. Now Hagar stands for Mount Sinai in Arabia and corresponds to the present city of Jerusalem."[150] He teaches that the Old Testament, that is, the son of the maidservant Hagar, was established in Arabia, which means "lowly" and "falling." And so, as soon as Paul believed, he turned to the Law, the prophets, and the mysteries of the Old Testament, which itself had already come to an end.

148. Acts 9.23–26. Cf. 2 Cor 11.32–33.

149. Cf. Acts 16.6. It has been suggested that Paul's mission here may have been hampered by pockets of Jewish resistance in strategic stopping-points. See C. Breytenbach, "Probable Reasons for Paul's Unfruitful Missionary Attempts in Asia Minor (A Note on Acts 16:6–7)," in *Die Apostelgeschichte und die hellenistische Geschichtsschreibung: Festschrift für Eckhard Plümacher zu seinem 65. Geburtstag*, ed. C. Breytenbach and J. Schröter (Leiden: E. J. Brill, 2004), 157–69.

150. Gal 4.24–25.

In these mysteries he sought Christ, whom he had been commanded to preach among the nations. Once he found Christ, he
did not tarry any longer there but returned to Damascus, that is,
to the blood and suffering of Christ. Emboldened by his reading
of the prophets, he departed thence for Jerusalem, the place of
vision and peace, but his intention was not as much to learn anything from the disciples as it was to confer with them about the
Gospel which he had already been teaching.

1.18a. *Then after three years I went to Jerusalem to see Peter.*
He did not go to see Peter's eyes, cheeks, or face; whether he
was lean or plump; whether his nose was curved or straight; or
whether he had hair covering his forehead or (as Clement re-
ports in the *Travels of Peter*)[151] was bald.[152] In my estimation, it is
not characteristic of the Apostle's gravity to go through such intense preparation for three years, only to care about gazing at
the human element in Peter. He saw Peter with the same eyes
with which he himself is now seen in his own epistles; Paul saw
Cephas with the very same eyes with which every discerning
reader views him. Now, if this is not clear in the present passage,
let the reader recall the meaning of the previous passage: The
apostles did not confer anything on Paul, but he was seen going
to Jerusalem to meet with the Apostle Peter because he wanted

151. *Vt Clemens in Periodis eius refert.* This work may have been a source, known
by this title (Εν ταῖς περιόδοις), underlying the Ps.-Clementine *Recognitions*. This
possibility suggests that Origen perhaps supplied Jerome with this reference: see
P. Courcelle, *Les lettres grecques en Occident de Macrobe à Cassiodore* (Paris: E. de Boccard, 1948), 82; M. Schatkin, "The Influence of Origen upon St. Jerome's Commentary on Galatians," *VChr* 24 (1970): 49–58 (57).

152. For another instance of the early Christian fascination with the apostles' physical appearance, see the description given of Paul in the late-second-
century apocryphal *Acts of Paul and Thecla:* "A man small of stature, with a bald
head and crooked legs, in a good state of body, with eyebrows meeting and nose
somewhat hooked, full of friendliness": trans. R. M. Wilson in Schneemelcher,
NTA, 2.239. For an excellent discussion of how Paul was depicted in Christian
iconography down to the fourth century, see Cooper, *Marius Victorinus' Commentary on Galatians,* 49–87; see further D. MacDonald, "Apocryphal and Canonical
Narratives about Paul," in *Paul and the Legacies of Paul,* ed. W. S. Babcock (Dallas:
Southern Methodist University Press, 1990), 55–70.

to pay his respects to the chief apostle and not because he wanted to be a student, for both his and Peter's preaching ministries had the same [divine] author.

1.18b. *And I stayed with him for fifteen days.*

Because he had prepared himself for such a long time to see Peter, he did not need a great deal of instruction. Although it seems pointless to some to look for symbolism behind the numbers in Scripture,[153] I have good reason to believe that the fifteen days that Paul spent with Peter signify complete knowledge and perfect doctrine, seeing that there are fifteen songs in the Psalter and fifteen steps that the righteous man climbs in order to sing to God and stand in the Temple court.[154] Hezekiah, who had fifteen years added to his life, was found worthy to receive a sign from God on the degree-markings on the sundial.[155] Finally, the feasts in honor of God began on the fifteenth day.[156]

Since we seek to understand Scripture on two levels, it is useful to note that Paul writes "fifteen days" to show that he would not have had much time to learn from Peter anyway. Consequently, all of this is meant to support his initial argument that he was taught by God and not by men.

1.19. *I saw none of the apostles except James, the brother of the Lord.*

I recall that while I was in Rome, I wrote, at the instigation of the brothers, the book *On the Perpetual Virginity of Holy Mary* [*Against Helvidius*]. In it I was compelled to explain what Scripture means when it speaks of the brothers of the Lord.[157] I must

153. Origen was especially fond of speculating about the mystical significance of numbers in the Bible. See J. Pettis, "Number symbolism," in *The Westminster Handbook to Origen*, ed. J. A. McGuckin (Louisville: John Knox Press, 2004), 158–59.

154. During the Feast of Tabernacles, the Levites would sing the fifteen so-called Psalms of Ascent (Pss 120–34) in the Temple at Jerusalem as they climbed the fifteen steps that led up to the Court of Israel. See H. Ulfgard, *The Story of Sukkot: The Setting, Shaping and Sequel of the Biblical Feast of Tabernacles* (Tübingen: Mohr Siebeck, 1998), 152 n. 271.

155. Is 38.5–8.

156. Ex 12.2–6.

157. Helvidius was a Roman priest or layman who wrote a now-lost treatise

remain content with whatever I wrote there. For now let it be enough to say that James, on account of his outstanding character, incomparable faith, and superior wisdom, is called the "brother of the Lord" and was the first person to preside over the first Jewish church to believe in Christ and congregate as a community. The rest of the apostles are also called the brothers of the Lord, just as they are in the Gospel, "Go, tell my brothers that I am going to my Father and to your Father, to my God and to your God."[158] And in the Psalm, "I shall declare your name to my brothers; in the midst of the assembly I shall praise you."[159] The man to whom the Lord had entrusted the sons of his mother as he was on his way to meet the Father especially deserves to be called "brother."[160] Job and the rest of the patriarchs are called servants of God, and Moses had such an exemplary quality about him that it was written about him, "Not so with my servant Moses."[161] Likewise, the blessed James is, as I said earlier, given the special appellation "brother of the Lord."

As for why some besides the Twelve are called apostles, it is be-

---

in the early 380s arguing that Mary had been a virgin prior to Jesus' birth but afterward consummated her marriage to Joseph and gave birth to many more children. Jerome, driven by the conviction that virginity is intrinsically superior to marriage, was appalled by the suggestion that Mary ceased to be a virgin at any point in her life. In 383, he leapt into the fray with a treatise of his own (*Adversus Helvidium*) in which he argued that whenever Scripture refers to James and others as the "brothers" of Jesus, it actually means cousins and not brothers in the strict sense of the word. For a summary of Jerome's argument, see J. McHugh, *The Mother of Jesus in the New Testament* (London: Darton, Longman & Todd, 1975), 223–33. Giancarlo Rocca, in *L'Adversus Helvidium di san Girolamo nel contesto della letteratura ascetico-mariana del secolo IV* (Bern: Peter Lang, 1998), analyzes the controversy with Helvidius in the broader context of spirituality in the late fourth century. In the brief aside he gives above, Jerome does not restate his case at length but says only that James was called the "brother of the Lord" on account of his great faith. Incidentally, Marius Victorinus was the only patristic Latin commentator on Galatians to hold that James was Jesus' blood brother. Today, Protestant Biblical scholars overwhelmingly accept Helvidius's argument, while Jerome's view has prevailed among Roman Catholic scholars. Eastern Orthodox scholars, too, reject the idea that Mary bore any children other than Jesus.

158. Jn 20.17.   159. Ps 22.22.
160. I.e., John the Apostle (see Jn 19.26–27).
161. Nm 12.7.

cause all who had seen the Lord and afterward preached about
him were referred to as apostles, as it is written to the Corinthians, "After that he appeared to the Eleven, then to more than five
hundred brothers at the same time, many of whom are still alive,
though some have fallen asleep. Then he appeared to James and
then to all of the apostles."[162] A little while after that, others were
ordained apostles by the ones the Lord had chosen, just as that
passage in the epistle to the Philippians declares, "But I think it
is necessary to send back to you Epaphroditus, my brother, fellow
worker and fellow soldier, who is also your messenger (*apostolus*),
whom you sent to take care of my needs."[163] And to the Corinthians it is written about such men, "The apostles of the churches
are the glory of God."[164] Silas and Judas are also called "apostles"
by the apostles.[165]

That writer[166] was seriously deluded who confused James the
Apostle with being the brother of John from the Gospel, the one
who the Acts of the Apostles says shed his blood for Christ after
Stephen did.[167] The apostle, who was nicknamed "the Just," was
the first bishop of Jerusalem and a man of such great holiness
and repute among the people that they would go out of their
way just to touch the edge of his cloak. He was later heaved off
the top of the Temple by the Jews. His successor was Symeon,
who according to tradition was crucified for the Lord.[168]

---

162. 1 Cor 15.5–7.   163. Phil 2.25.
164. 2 Cor 8.23.   165. Cf. Acts 15.22.
166. The identity of this writer is unknown.
167. Cf. Acts 12.2.
168. The source(s) informing this paragraph may have included the *Memoirs* of Hegesippus (d. c. 180), Clement of Alexandria, and Eusebius of Caesarea, who relied heavily on Hegesippus and to a lesser extent on Clement for his
narrative about James in the second and third books of the *Ecclesiastical History*.
For an overview of their contributions to early traditions about James, see P. J.
Hartin, *James of Jerusalem: Heir to Jesus of Nazareth* (Collegeville: Liturgical Press,
2004), 119–27; see further J. Painter, *Just James: The Brother of Jesus in History
and Tradition* (Columbia: University of South Carolina Press, 2004). In his notice on James in *Vir. ill.* 2, Jerome preserves a number of other interesting details taken over from Hegesippus: "This one was holy from his mother's womb.
He drank neither wine nor strong drink, ate no meat, never shaved or anoint-
ed himself with ointment or bathed. He alone had the privilege of entering the
Holy of Holies, since indeed he did not use woolen vestments, but linen, and
went alone into the Temple and prayed on bended knees on behalf of the peo-

Paul denies that he met with any of the apostles except Peter and James in order to remove a possible latent contradiction from his narrative: Even if you were not taught by Peter, you had other apostles to teach you. Moreover, he failed to see the other apostles, not because he was purposefully snubbing them, but because they had been scattered throughout the entire world to preach the Gospel.

1.20. *Concerning the things I write to you, I do not lie before God.*

This may be simply taken as follows: What I write to you is true and I affirm, with God as my witness, that it has not been embellished with any lie or verbal artifice. Or perhaps it could be taken in a deeper sense: What I write to you is before God, that is, it is worthy of being seen by God. But why worthy of God's countenance? Because I do not lie. And just as the Lord fixes his eyes on the righteous but turns his face away from the unholy, so also now what I write is before the Lord. I who write do not lie; if I *were* to lie, my writing would not be before God. This holds true not only for what he writes now to the Galatians but also generally for all of his epistles inasmuch as he does not write what is untrue and his heart and words are never at odds with each other.

1.21. *Then I went to parts of Syria and Cilicia.*

After seeing [James] in Jerusalem Paul went to Syria, which means "high and lofty," and then on to Cilicia, which he was determined to win over for Christ, preaching there a call to repentance. "Cilicia," not coincidentally, means the "acceptance of mourning" or "a call to be mournful."

1.22–24. *I was personally unknown to the churches of Judea that are in Christ Jesus. They only heard that the man who once persecuted us now is preaching the faith he formerly attacked. And they praised God because of me.*

The churches of Judea had known Paul only by reputation, and many of them had perceived him to be a persecutor rath-

---

ple, so much so that his knees were supposed to have acquired the hardness of camels' knees (trans. Halton, FOTC 100:7).

er than an apostle. But [the churches in] Syria, parts of Cilicia, Arabia, and Damascus perhaps knew him in person also [and not only by reputation] because he was the teacher of the Gentiles and accordingly preached the Gospel to them and not to the Jews. The point he is trying to make is that he would never have been able to go from being a persecutor to a praiseworthy figure in the eyes of his former victims unless his preaching had met with the approbation also of those who hardly knew him beforehand. He discreetly returns to the main issue and establishes that he had spent such a short time in Judea that he was unknown by face even to the believers. Thus, he demonstrates that he had no teachers—not Peter, not James, not John, but only Christ, who had revealed the Gospel to him.

It should also be noted that earlier[169] he is said to have attacked the church but here to have attacked the faith (in the former case, he attacked people; in the latter, an entity). Hence, it may now be fittingly said, "He preaches the faith he formerly attacked." For he was not able to say the same thing about the church.

2.1–2. *Then after fourteen years I went up again to Jerusalem with Barnabas and Titus. I went in response to a revelation and conferred with them about the Gospel that I preach among the Gentiles. But I did this privately to those who seemed to be leaders, for fear that I was running or had run my race in vain.*

What the Latin translator rendered as *acquievi* ["I gave rest"] in a previous passage[170] where it is written, "I gave no rest right away to flesh and blood," he here renders as *contuli* ["I conferred"]. To speak more truly, the Greek word ἀνεθέμην has a somewhat different connotation for us Latins. It refers to when we confide in a friend and place whatever we know into his trust and awareness, such that the decisions we make must be approved or rejected by mutual consent.

After fourteen years Paul went up to Jerusalem. The same man who had gone there earlier only to see Peter and who stayed with him for fifteen days now says that the purpose of his trip was

169. Gal 1.13.   170. Gal 1.16.

to confer with the apostles about the Gospel. He took with him Barnabas, a circumcised Jew, and Titus, an uncircumcised Gentile, so that everything he said would be verified by the presence of two or three witnesses.[171] It is one thing to confer, quite another to learn. Those who confer are on an equal footing with one another, but the student is always inferior to the teacher. When Paul first came to the faith, he saw the apostles in passing. But, as he himself says, after seventeen years had gone by he spoke openly with them and humbled himself before them. He sought, for two reasons, to make sure that he neither was running nor had run his race in vain. One was to show his humility, that he had run to his predecessors, the apostles, even though he was already a reputed teacher of the Gentiles throughout the world. The other was to inform the Galatians that the leaders of the Judean churches had not corrupted his Gospel. He simultaneously shows that he acted from his faith in Christ and a sense of evangelical freedom and had the courage to bring Titus, an uncircumcised man, before the very people who knew much about him, namely, that he had broken with the Law, toppled Moses, and had done away completely with circumcision. He shows also that neither he nor Titus was compelled out of fear to cave in to pressure when confronted by a good many Jews and his own personal enemies whose zeal for the Law made them want to assassinate him. Had they succumbed, they could be forgiven on the basis of the circumstances for not wanting to endure too much ill will all at once—where they were, the elders' authority, the sheer number of Jewish Christian churches, or the timing of the confrontation.

Some say that Paul's visit to Jerusalem after fourteen years occurred when, as related in the Acts of the Apostles, a dispute arose among the believers at Antioch about whether the Law should be observed or abrogated,[172] and when Paul and Barnabas were dispatched and were obliged to go to Jerusalem and seek out the verdict of the elders. They say further that the reading found in the Latin manuscripts, "We gave in to them for

171. Cf. Dt 19.15.

172. The scope of the Law in first-century AD Judaism is discussed by W. D. Davies, *Jewish and Pauline Studies* (Philadelphia: Fortress Press, 1984), 3–26.

a moment, so that the truth of the Gospel might remain with you,"[173] indicates that Paul and Barnabas allowed themselves to be sent there over a matter that they knew to be clear-cut but nevertheless pretended was ambiguous, so that evangelical grace might be approved by the elders [as being wholesome] for believers and so that there would be no doubt from that point on that circumcision had been done away with, inasmuch as a written edict from the apostles had removed the burden of the Law from Gentile Christians.

As for Paul's statement about meeting privately,[174] this can be taken to mean that the grace of evangelical freedom and the obsolescence of the abolished Law were discussed in confidence due to the many Jewish believers who had not yet had the chance to hear that Christ was the fulfillment and end of the Law. In Paul's absence these men had boasted in Jerusalem that he was running or had run his race in vain because he thought that the old Law ought not to be followed. Paul did not fear that he had preached a false gospel among the Gentiles for seventeen years, but he wanted to prove to his predecessors that he was not running nor had run his race in vain, as the ignorant believed about him.

2.3–5. *But not even Titus, who was with me, was compelled to be circumcised (even though he was a Gentile) on account of false brothers introduced in secret who infiltrated our ranks to spy on the freedom we have in Christ Jesus and to make us slaves. We did not give in to them for a moment, so that the truth of the Gospel might remain with you.*

Jerusalem was the capital city of the Jews and the place where Paul was suffering from such treacherous allegations of blasphemy against the Law of Moses that the Jews almost succeeded in murdering him, when he was set free by the tribune and [for his own protection] was apprehended and sent to Rome to see Caesar.[175] If Titus, although a Gentile, could not be frightened into being circumcised in Jerusalem, then why do some think that

173. Gal 2.5.

174. Here Jerome quotes the epistle passage again: "I conferred with them . . . . my race in vain."

175. Cf. Acts 21.31–32; 23.10.

the phrase "we gave in to them for a moment, so that the truth of the Gospel might remain with you" should be understood to imply that Titus yielded and was circumcised, even though earlier he had not been forced to be circumcised? What does the "truth of the Gospel" entail? Giving in to the hypocrisy of the Jews and upholding the things that you used to condemn as refuse and ruin? Pronouncing them valuable even when they are worthless? This contradicts the spirit of his epistle. By inviting the Galatians to turn away from circumcision in this sequence of his discussion, he tries to prove that while he had been a Hebrew among Hebrews and a conscientious observer of all aspects of the Law and had been circumcised on the eighth day and also had been a Pharisee according to the Law,[176] he nevertheless considered all of this to be of little importance in light of Christ's grace. For when he had gone to Jerusalem and the false brothers from the circumcision party intended to force him to circumcise Titus, neither he nor Titus yielded to the threat of violence, and by standing their ground each guarded evangelical truth. Moreover, if Paul were to say that he was compelled to circumcise Titus, how would he be able to summon the Galatians away from circumcision, the very thing from which he was not able to exempt Titus, his Gentile companion, at Jerusalem?

Therefore, either we follow the Greek manuscripts and take "so that the truth of the Gospel might remain in you" as the consequence of "we did not give in to them for a moment," or, if anyone is inclined to put faith in the Latin exemplar, we must take the "giving in for a moment" as referring to the journey to Jerusalem, not to the circumcision of Titus. That is to say, Paul and Barnabas "gave in" and went to Jerusalem after the controversy about the Law had been stirred up at Antioch so that Paul's own opinion on the matter might be vouched for by a letter from the apostles and so that evangelical truth might remain among the Galatians—not in the letter but in the Spirit, not in fleshly understanding but in spiritual apprehension, not in patent Judaism but hidden from plain view.[177]

The conjunction "but" (*autem*) in the present passage, "but

176. Cf. Phil 3.5–6.
177. Cf. Rom 2.29.

on account of false brothers introduced in secret" (*propter sub-introductos autem falsos fratres*), is superfluous. If it were to be retained in the reading, it would have nothing to follow from it and finish its thought. Here is how we should construe the order of the narrative and its meaning. Immediately after saying, "But not even Titus, who was with me, was compelled to be circumcised (even though he was a Gentile)," Paul gives the reason why he might have been coerced into circumcision against his will: "On account of false brothers introduced in secret who infiltrated our ranks to spy on the freedom we have in Christ Jesus and to make us slaves." Although they used threats, intimidation, and their strength in numbers to deter us from the freedom we enjoyed in Christ and to make us slaves of the Law, we did not give in to them even for a moment and circumcise Titus, especially when a desire for peace among the churches could have excused us from blame for doing so. We did all of this so that you would have no motive to abandon evangelical grace. While at Jerusalem we faced very formidable Jewish foes in the form of false brothers making sneaky advances here and there and of church elders who did not exactly favor our cause. If we could not be compelled by either physical force or persuasion to observe circumcision, which we knew to be obsolete, [how shameful is it that] you Gentiles in Galatia—you!—abandon grace and revert to the abolished Law when nobody is forcing you to do so?

2.6a. *As for those who seemed to be important, whatever they were does not matter to me: God does not make distinctions between persons.*

In other words: Even though the apostles Peter and John personally witnessed the Lord being transfigured on the mountain,[178] and even though the church is built upon them,[179] it matters nothing to me, for I do not speak against those who followed the Lord at that time but against those who now give the Law priority over grace. I neither take anything away from my predecessors nor by any means do I bring an accusation against the elders. I say only that God does not make distinctions between persons.

God did not show favoritism to Moses, David, or any others.

178. Cf. Mt 17.1–2. 179. Cf. Eph 2.20.

Nor will he do so to those who appear to cave in momentarily to others, even if they are in agreement with Paul. Thus Peter says, "I realize how true it is that God does not make distinctions between persons but shows favor to people from every nation who fear him and do what is right."[180] The holy apostle Peter himself used this argument against those scandalized by Cornelius, a Gentile believer who had been baptized but not circumcised,[181] and he appeased them by asserting that he could not deny baptism to recipients of the Holy Spirit.[182] In the same manner, the holy Apostle Paul now opposes Peter and maintains that God does not make distinctions between persons but judges each person for how he really is. Therefore, he cautiously takes the middle ground between praising and rebuking Peter so as to defer to his apostolic predecessor while at the same time opposing him boldly to his face in obedience to his strong personal conviction about the truth.[183]

2.6b. *For those who seemed to be important conferred nothing on me.*

As we saw above, Paul met with them and told them about the many things he had accomplished among the Gentiles. They conferred nothing on him but only approved his report, joined their right hands in agreement,[184] and established that their gospel was the same as Paul's. I pointed out earlier, and do so now again, that the Greek text contains the equivalent of the word *contulerunt* ["they conferred"].

2.7–9. *On the contrary, when they saw that the Gospel for the uncircumcised had been entrusted to me, as the Gospel for the circumcised was to Peter, for God, who was at work in the ministry of Peter as an apostle to the Jews, was also at work in my ministry as an apostle to the Gentiles, and when James, Peter, and John, who seemed to be pillars, recognized the grace given to me, they extended their right hands to me and Barnabas in fellowship so that we should go to the Gentiles and they to the Jews.*

This intricate passage, full of intervening matter, may be simplified as, "Those who seemed to be important conferred noth-

180. Acts 10.34–35.   181. Cf. Acts 11.2–3.
182. Cf. Acts 10.47; 11.17.   183. Cf. Gal 2.11.
184. In antiquity the handshake was a commonly used gesture by which par-

ing on me but, on the contrary, extended their right hands
to Barnabas and me in fellowship." Paul hides this alternative
sense beneath the surface so as to avoid boasting about himself:
Those who seemed to be important conferred nothing on me;
to the contrary, I conferred something on them inasmuch as
they became more steadfast in evangelical grace.[185]

Paul's argument may be summarized as follows. One and the
same God entrusted me with preaching to the uncircumcised,
and Peter with preaching to the circumcised, and he sent me to
the Gentiles and stationed Peter in Judea. Gentile adults found
it intolerable to undergo the unnecessary pain of circumcision[186]
and to abstain from their usual foods, which God had created
for consumption.[187] Likewise, circumcised Jewish believers who
thought they were superior to other nations because of a custom that was like second nature to them did not find it easy to
renounce what had been the cause of their boasting. In order
to make sure that circumcision did not under any circumstance
ever become an impediment to anyone's belief, God in his provi-
dence appointed one apostle for the circumcised, who appeared
to take comfort in the shadows of the Law, and another for the
uncircumcised, who realized that the grace of the Gospel con-
sists not in slavery but in a faith that liberates.

In the Acts of the Apostles, Peter declares that no man is unclean[188] and learns from his vision of the sheet let down from

---

ties ratified mutual agreements. See G. Herman, *Ritualised Friendship and the Greek City* (Cambridge: Cambridge University Press, 1987), 49–53.

185. Jerome shares Origen's high view of Paul as an independently authoritative teacher of the Gentiles as opposed to an underling of the original apostles. Cf. Origen, *C. Cels.* 7.21 (Chadwick, 412): "And since the divine truths were
made known to him by revelation and he was illuminated in his soul by the divinity of the Logos, for this reason he did not borrow, nor did he need anyone
to minister the word to him. . . . By the power conferred by the Logos he subjected the Gentiles to the teaching of Christ Jesus and ruled them, and was never made subject even for an hour to any men as his superiors."

186. Circumcision was the last and often the most difficult hurdle for Gentiles who wished to become full converts to Judaism. See P. Fredriksen, "Judaism, the Circumcision of Gentiles, and Apocalyptic Hope: Another Look at Galatians 1 and 2," *JThS,* n.s., 42 (1991): 532–58.

187. Cf. 1 Tm 4.3–5.

188. Cf. Acts 10.34–35.

heaven by its four corners that there is no difference between Jew and Gentile.[189] I am not saying that this Peter forgot the fundamentals, so to speak, and believed that grace should be discarded in favor of keeping the Law. Rather, I am saying that he pretended to keep the Law in order to rescue the Jews, one step at a time, from their previous way of life. For they were not capable of instantaneously casting to the wayside their enormous effort in observing the Law and their time-honored, extremely fastidious manner of living. Hence, Peter, James, and John extended their right hands to Paul and Barnabas in fellowship so that Christ's Gospel would not seem to be divided due to a multiplicity of customs and so that the circumcised and uncircumcised might comprise a single community.

Paul advisedly says, "For God, who was at work in the ministry of Peter as an apostle to the Jews." He does not want anyone to think that he is insulting Peter. To the contrary, he gives the impression from this explicit compliment that Peter was somewhat favorable to circumcision, but only for the purpose of winning over Jewish believers entrusted to his apostolic care and establishing them in the faith and Gospel of Christ.[190] Paul condones Peter for following Jewish custom and for temporarily observing what was not permissible because his intention was to lose none of those who had been entrusted to him. But Paul had an obligation to the Gospel truth to do the same thing he was charged with doing among the uncircumcised, namely, to ensure that the Gentiles would not be deterred by the burdensomeness and rigor of the Law and depart from their faith and belief in Christ.

A subtle dilemma suggests itself: If Peter had found [potential converts] among the Gentiles, would he have refrained from bringing them to the faith? And conversely: If Paul had found some [potential converts] among the Jews, would he have refused to invite them to be baptized in Christ? This twofold question may be answered in the following way. The principal commission over Jews and Gentiles was given to specific people so that Jewish defenders of the Law might have someone to fol-

189. Cf. Acts 10.11; 11.5.
190. Cf. 1 Cor 9.21.

low and so that champions of grace rather than law might have their own teacher and guide. Yet they shared the common goal of populating the church for Christ with people from every race. Thus we read that Peter baptized the Gentile Cornelius[191] and that Paul regularly preached Christ in the synagogues of the Jews.[192]

"Peter, John, and James, who seemed to be pillars." On three occasions above it is said of the apostles, "Privately to those who seemed to be [leaders]";[193] "as for those who seemed to be important";[194] "for those who seemed to be important conferred nothing on me."[195] I had been wondering what the phrase "who seemed" referred to, but now Paul has banished all question from my mind, when he describes them as those "who seemed to be pillars." This means that the pillars of the church are the apostles, and especially Peter, James, and John, two of whom were deemed worthy to climb the mountain with the Lord.[196] One of them introduces the Savior in Revelation,[197] saying, "Whosoever

191. Cf. Acts 10.47–48.   192. Cf. Acts 9.20.
193. Gal 2.2.   194. Gal 2.6.
195. Ibid.

196. Cf. Mt 17.1–8. When Ambrosiaster and Augustine commented on Paul's reference to Peter, James, and John as "pillars," they both noted how all three had been present at the Transfiguration. They were, however, confusing James the son of Zebedee, who witnessed the Transfiguration, with James the brother of Jesus, who is one of the "pillars." Jerome does not make the same mistake. In addition, he is right to identify John the Apostle (son of Zebedee), who had been at the Transfiguration along with his brother James and Peter, as the "John" mentioned by Paul. This is the only place Paul mentions John in his epistles; cf. Acts 3.1–4.22 and 8.14–25, where he appears as Peter's (silent) associate.

197. The author of Revelation identified himself simply as "John" (Rv 1.1, 4, 9; 22.8). Jerome took him to be John the Apostle and son of Zebedee here and also in *Vir. ill.* 9.6. Several early patristic writers (e.g., Justin Martyr, *Dial.* 81.4, and Irenaeus, *Adv. haer.* 4.20.11) affirmed the apostolic authorship of Revelation. In the middle of the third century, Dionysius of Alexandria conjectured that the author was John Mark, a young man who accompanied Paul and Barnabas on their first missionary trip to Asia (Acts 13.5); Eusebius quotes Dionysius at length in *H.E.* 7.25. Eusebius (*H.E.* 3.39) speculated that the author was John the Elder, whom Papias distinguished from John the Apostle. Modern scholars are divided about who exactly this John was, though most agree that John was his real name rather than a pseudonym. For a brief review of the scholarly debate, see G. K. Beale, *The Book of Revelation* (Grand Rapids: W. B. Eerdmans, 1999), 34–36.

will be victorious, I shall make him a pillar in the temple of my God."[198] This verse teaches us that all believers who have conquered Satan can become pillars of the church. But to Timothy, Paul writes, "So that you may know how to conduct yourself in the house of God, which is the church of the living God, the pillar and foundation of truth."[199] These and other passages inform us that the apostles and all believers, not to mention the church itself, are called pillars in Scripture and that there is no distinction between body and its limbs because the body is divided into members which comprise it.[200]

Peter, James, and John, who seemed to be pillars, extended their right hands to Paul and Barnabas in fellowship, but they did not do so to their companion Titus. For he had not yet reached the point where he could be trusted, along with the elders, with the wares of Christ and become, along with Barnabas and Paul, a wholesaler of these wares, just as "we [were sent] to the Gentiles and they to the circumcised."

2.10. *They asked only that we should remember the poor, the very thing I was eager to do.*

The holy poor, the care of whom was specially committed by the apostles to Paul and Barnabas, are Jewish believers. Either they lay at the feet of the apostles their most valuable possessions[201] to be distributed to the needy, or they were reviled and persecuted by their kin, family, and parents for deserting the Law and believing in a crucified man.[202] The letters of the holy apostle Paul testify to how much effort he poured into ministering to them, as he wrote to the Corinthians, Thessalonians, and all of the churches of the Gentiles to ask them to prepare this offering to be taken to Jerusalem through himself or other ministers acceptable to them.[203] For this reason he now says confidently, "The very thing I was eager to do."

The "poor," understood another way, may refer also to those

---

198. Rv 3.12. 199. 1 Tm 3.15.
200. Cf. 1 Cor 12.12–17. 201. Cf. Acts 4.34–35.
202. Cf. Lk 21.16–17.

203. Paul set up a relief fund in the Gentile churches for the believers in the Jerusalem church. See Rom 15.25–28; 1 Cor 16.1–4; 2 Cor 8.1–9.15.

about whom the Gospel speaks: "Blessed are the poor in spirit, for theirs is the kingdom of heaven."[204] Such people undoubtedly deserve to be remembered by the apostles. Solomon writes about them as well: "The ransom of a man's life is his riches, but the poor man does not hear rebuke."[205] For the man who is poor in grace or faith is unable to hear the warning about the punishment that is to come because he does not have spiritual riches or a knowledge of Scripture, which is compared to gold, silver, and a precious gem.[206] Therefore, because it is the sick and not the healthy that need a doctor, the apostles agreed by the clasping of right hands not to look down on the poor or be contemptuous of sinners but always to remember them, just as Paul remembered the man whom in his first letter to the Corinthian church he had chastised momentarily in the hope that he would put his body through rigorous repentance and thereby save his spirit.[207] He wrote to this man in his second letter [to the same church] to summon him back to the fold so that he would not be swallowed up by more sorrow, and he asked all the members of the congregation to forgive their brother and reaffirm their love for him, just as Paul himself forgave each of them before Christ, thus fulfilling the promise he had made at Jerusalem always to remember the poor.[208]

2.11–13. *When Peter came to Antioch, I opposed him to his face, because he was in the wrong. Before certain men came from James, he used to eat with the Gentiles. But when they arrived, he began to draw back and separate himself [from the Gentiles] because he was afraid of those who belonged to the circumcision group. The other Jews joined him in his hypocrisy, so that even Barnabas was led astray.*

The fact that Peter would eat with Gentiles before certain men came from Jerusalem to Antioch shows that he had not forgotten the injunction not to call anyone common or unclean.[209] But because of the Judaizers he withdrew from the Gentile gathering. As a result, the rest of the Jews followed suit—and even Barnabas, who together with Paul had preached

204. Mt 5.3.   205. Prv 13.8.
206. Cf. Ps 119.72.   207. Cf. 1 Cor 5.5.
208. Cf. 2 Cor 2.6–10.   209. Cf. Acts 10.28.

the Gospel among the Gentiles, was compelled to do so. Uncircumcised Gentile believers in Antioch were being forced to comply with the burdensome requirements of the Law and did not apprehend the dispensation by which Peter hoped for all Jews to be saved although they thought that they were the ones who properly understood the Gospel. When the Apostle Paul saw the grace of Christ in peril, the fighter in him employed a new battle tactic to counter Peter's plan of saving the Jews with a plan of his own and to oppose him to his face, without making known his plan but acting in public as if he were contradicting Peter so that the Gentiles might be protected by his actions.[210]

Now, if anyone thinks that Paul really opposed Peter and fear-

210. In general, the Latin tradition—represented by Tertullian, Cyprian, Hilary, Ambrose, Marius Victorinus, Ambrosiaster, and Augustine—assumed that Peter was in the wrong and defended Paul's right to chastise him: see G. Raspanti, "San Girolamo e l'interpretazione occidentale di *Gal* 2,11–14," *REAug* 49 (2003): 297–321. Jerome, wanting both to uphold Paul's apostolic authority and to clear the chief of the apostles of the charge of temporary apostasy, took a different approach. He argued that Peter and Paul had agreed beforehand to stage a public confrontation for the benefit of the Gentile and Jewish believers. He later claimed that he obtained this interpretation from Origen (*Ep.* 112.6; in the same section he cites John Chrysostom as another authority who believed the dispute was scripted). It has been pointed out, however, that in his surviving works Origen nowhere advocates the reading attributed to him by Jerome and in fact he seems to assume that the confrontation was not a pretense: see F. Cocchini, "Da Origene a Teodoreto," in *Origeniana Septima: Origenes in den Auseinandersetzungen des 4. Jahrhunderts,* ed. W. A. Bienert and U. Kühneweg (Leuven: Leuven University Press, 1999), 292–309. Cocchini suggests that Jerome took this interpretation not from Origen but from Chrysostom's homily *In faciem ei restiti* (PG 51:383). This hypothesis, however, is untenable. Chrysostom preached this particular homily at Antioch no earlier than February 386, and possibly much later (its exact date is uncertain: see W. Mayer, *The Homilies of St John Chrysostom—Provenance. Reshaping the Foundations* [Rome: Pontificium Institutum, 2005], 319 n. 21, 470), and so it is very unlikely that Jerome could have had access to it by the summer of 386. In any event, Augustine objected to Jerome's interpretation of the Antioch incident because it meant that the apostles were knowingly deceitful, and this presents a problem because Scripture forbids lying. The debate between Augustine and Jerome about this issue is analyzed in great detail by Alfons Fürst in his monograph *Augustins Briefwechsel mit Hieronymus* (Münster: Aschendorff, 1999). For a concise overview of the various patristic opinions about the Paul-Peter confrontation, see R. Kieffer, *Foi et justification à Antioche: interprétation d'un conflit (Ga 2, 14–21)* (Paris: Éditions du Cerf, 1982), 81–99.

lessly insulted his predecessor in defense of evangelical truth, he will not be moved by the fact that Paul acted as a Jew among fellow Jews in order to win them for Christ.[211] What is more, Paul would have been guilty of the same kind of dissimulation on other occasions, such as when he shaved his head in Cenchrea,[212] when he made an offering in Jerusalem after doing this,[213] when he circumcised Timothy[214] and went barefoot—all of which are clearly aspects of Jewish religious ritual. The preacher to the Gentiles did some things that were contrary to evangelical freedom in order to avoid scandalizing the Jews, and he thought it necessary to say, "Do not cause Jews or the church of God to stumble, just as I please everybody in every way, seeking not my own good but the good of many, so that they may be saved."[215] On what authority, or with what affront, then, did Paul dare to rebuke Peter, the apostle of the circumcised, for the very thing that he, as the apostle of the uncircumcised, had done? As I already noted, he opposed Peter and the rest so that, as far as public appearances were concerned, their hypocrisy in observing the Law, which was harmful to Gentile believers, might be corrected by his own hypocrisy in reproaching them. This was done so that both Jews and Gentiles might be saved, for the advocates of circumcision would follow Peter, and their opponents would preach the liberty espoused by Paul. When he says that Peter was in the wrong, he tempers his words to give us the impression that Peter's conduct did not so much offend him as it did the brothers with whom he had been eating but from whom he later withdrew.

For another example of how temporary deception can be expedient, let us consider Jehu, the king of Israel. He would not have been able to kill the priests of Baal unless he had feigned a desire to worship this false god, and he said, "Assemble all the priests of Baal for me, for Ahab served Baal in a few respects, I shall serve him in many."[216] Another example is when David altered his appearance, pretending to be somebody else in Abimelech's presence, and Abimelech dismissed him.[217] That even

211. Cf. 1 Cor 9.20.
212. Cf. Acts 18.18.
213. Cf. Acts 21.23–26.
214. Cf. Acts 16.3.
215. 1 Cor 10.32–33.
216. 2 Kgs 10.18–19.
217. Cf. 1 Sm 21.13.

very righteous men resort to temporary dissimulation for the sake of their own or others' salvation is not surprising when we recall that our Lord himself, who was free of iniquity and whose flesh was not sinful, pretended to take on sinful flesh so that by condemning sin in his flesh he might make us the righteousness of God. Paul certainly had read in the Gospel where the Lord teaches, "If your brother sins against you, go and rebuke him privately; if he listens to you, you have won your brother over."[218] So how, after Christ ordered that this be done with regard to the least of the brothers, could Paul venture to rebuke publicly the greatest of the apostles so resolutely and firmly, unless Peter had consented [beforehand] to this? Paul accordingly would not have insulted the man whose praises he had sung in many instances, including the following. "I went to Jerusalem to see Peter and I stayed with him for fifteen days and I did not see any other of the apostles [except James the brother of the Lord]."[219] "For God, who was at work in Peter's ministry to the Jews."[220] "Peter, James, and John, who seemed to be pillars."[221]

As a young man, I would deliver rhetorical declamations in Rome and would engage in real contests in which I argued mock court cases.[222] Many times I rushed to the courtroom and watched extraordinary orators argue so bitterly that at times they would momentarily forget the case at hand and become sidetracked with their own personal quarrels, trading sarcastic barbs with each other. If they do this to keep from arousing suspicion from the guilty parties on trial that they are in collusion

---

218. Mt 18.15.   219. Gal 1.18–19.

220. Gal 2.8.   221. Gal 2.9.

222. Jerome is remembering his student days in Rome in the 360s. Declamations were speeches that addressed sets of circumstances such as the kind that one might encounter in an actual deliberative or judicial setting. Specialized training in composing and delivering these represented the culmination of the classical and late Roman rhetorical curriculum: see S. F. Bonner, *Education in Ancient Rome. From the Elder Cato to the Younger Pliny* (Berkeley: University of California Press, 1977), 250–327. One of Jerome's most famous letters (*Ep.* 117), in which he rebukes a virgin and her widowed mother for cohabiting with men of the cloth under the pretext of religion, is cast ostensibly as a rhetorical declamation: see A. Cain, "Jerome's *Epistula* 117 on the *subintroductae:* Satire, Apology, and Ascetic Propaganda in Gaul," *Augustinianum* 49 (2009): 119–43.

and they end up deceiving the audience, what do we think such great pillars of the church and vessels of wisdom as Peter and Paul should have done to reconcile the bickering Jews and Gentiles, except to feign a quarrel to bring about peace among the believers and harmonize the faith of the church by means of a holy dispute between themselves?

Some suppose that the Cephas whom Paul claims to have confronted is not Peter but one of the seventy disciples who went by the same name.[223] They claim that there is no way Peter could have been capable of withdrawing from fellowship with the Gentiles. After all, he had baptized Cornelius.[224] And when he had gone up to Jerusalem, the circumcised believers criticized him and asked, "Why did you enter the houses of uncircumcised men and eat with them?"[225] After recounting his vision he answered their question directly: "'If God gave the same grace to them as he did to us who believed in the Lord Jesus Christ, who am I to stand in God's way?' Upon hearing his words they fell silent and praised God, saying, 'God has given to the Gentiles the repentance that leads to life.'"[226] Most compelling of all is that the historian Luke was silent about this quarrel [in the Acts of the Apostles], and he also does not say that Peter was ever in Antioch with Paul. That blasphemer Porphyry scores a victory if it is believed that either Peter erred or Paul rashly rebuked the chief of the apostles.

Those who believe that Cephas and Peter are two different people can be refuted, first of all, by the fact that we do not

223. Cf. Lk 10.1. One of those meant here must be Clement of Alexandria, who made the same argument in the fifth book of his now-lost *Hypotyposeis*. Jerome could have gotten this via Eusebius (*H.E.* 1.12.2), who summarizes Clement's position, or else directly from the *Hypotyposeis*, which he did know firsthand: on his reading of this work, see R. T. France, *The Gospel of Mark* (Grand Rapids: W. B. Eerdmans, 2002), 38. The question about whether Peter and Cephas were the same or different people continues to be debated in modern scholarship. Earlier in the twentieth century a handful of scholars (e.g., M. Goguel, K. Lake, D. W. Riddle) argued that Peter and Cephas were two separate individuals. More recently, this minority position has been championed by B. D. Ehrman, "Cephas and Peter," *JBL* 109 (1990): 463–74. For a decisive rejoinder to Ehrman, see D. C. Allison, "Peter and Cephas: One and the Same," *JBL* 111 (1992): 489–95.

224. Cf. Acts 10.48.   225. Acts 11.2–3.

226. Acts 11.17–18.

know of any other person named Cephas besides the one who shows up in the Gospels and other Pauline letters, in some of which he is called Cephas, in others, Peter. It is not that "Peter" and "Cephas" signify different things, but what we call *petra* ["stone"] in Latin and Greek, the Hebrews and Syrians[227] call *cephas* because of the similarity of their languages. Secondly, the entire argument of the epistle, namely, its subtext about Peter, James, and John, militates against this interpretation. It is not surprising that Luke failed to mention this detail, seeing that there are many other things that Paul claims to have suffered which [Luke, invoking his] license as an historian, omits. There is no contradiction involved if one of them deemed an event worthy of being recounted while the other consigned it to oblivion. Furthermore, we accept that Peter was the first bishop of the church at Antioch and later moved to Rome—information that Luke altogether disregarded. Finally, if in our attempt to refute Porphyry's blasphemy we invent another Cephas just so that we can acquit Peter of error, then we must purge from divine Scripture an untold number of passages that Porphyry calumniated because he did not understand them. But if Christ will command it, I shall take aim at Porphyry in another work.[228] But for now, let us continue the present discussion.

2.14a. *But when I saw that they were not walking uprightly in the truth of the Gospel, I said to Peter in front of them all . . .*

Just as people who walk normally but pretend to limp do not have a problem with their feet, though there is a reason why they [pretend to] limp, so also Peter, aware that neither circum-

227. Jerome's appeal to Syriac philology here and elsewhere in his writings may seem impressive to the casual observer. As Daniel King points out, however, "Jerome's knowledge of Aramaic/Syriac was somewhat shaky and was used with an eye to making an impression upon the reader rather than to elucidating philological problems *per se*": "*Vir Quadrilinguis?* Syriac in Jerome and Jerome in Syriac," in *Jerome of Stridon*, ed. A. Cain and J. Lössl, 223.

228. Jerome never followed through with this wish. He was an extremely ambitious writer and often planned projects with which he never ended up carrying through. For example, in the prologue to his *Life of Malchus*, he announces his plans to write a comprehensive church history covering the apostolic period down to his own age, but this work never materialized.

cision nor uncircumcision matters but only keeping the commandments of God,[229] ate beforehand with Gentiles but for a time withdrew from them to avoid alienating the Jews from their faith in Christ. Paul likewise employed the same pretense as Peter and confronted him and spoke in front of everyone, not so much to rebuke Peter as to correct those for whose sake Peter had engaged in simulation. Now, if anyone is not convinced by this interpretation, that Peter was not in error and Paul did not rashly rebuke his elder, he must account for why Paul criticized another for doing the same thing he had done.

2.14b. *Although you are a Jew, if you live like a Gentile and not like a Jew, how is it that you force Gentiles to follow Jewish customs?*

He corners Peter with an irrefutable argument, or rather through the person of Peter he corners those who compelled Peter to act at odds with his convictions. What Paul says is this: If you, Peter, a Jew by birth, were circumcised at a young age and obeyed all of the Law's precepts and now by the grace of Christ realize that these are worthless in themselves and are types and symbols of things to come, and you break bread with Gentiles and do not (as before) live superstitiously but in freedom and without prejudice—how can you force Gentile believers, from whom you now withdraw and separate yourself as if they were unclean, to follow Jewish customs? For if they are unclean (you shun them because they are uncircumcised), you force them to be circumcised and become Jews, even though you live like a Gentile, despite being a Jew by birth. Paul subtly indicates that the reason for his dispute with Peter was that Peter, through his simulation, was forcing Gentiles who aspired to pattern themselves after him to live like Jews.

2.15. *We who are Jews by nature and not Gentile sinners.*

The heretics sneak up here with their ridiculous and dimwitted fabrications and allege that the spiritual nature cannot sin and that the earthly one cannot do anything righteous. Let us ask them: Why are branches broken off from a cultivated ol-

229. Cf. 1 Cor 7.19.

ive tree and then branches from a wild olive tree grafted into its
root, if nothing can either fall from good or grow out of evil?
Put another way: How could Paul initially have persecuted the
church if his nature was spiritual, or later have been made an
apostle if he came from earthly dregs? Now, if the heretics con-
tend that his nature was not earthly, let us recall his words: "Like
the rest, we were by nature sons of divine wrath."[230] A Jew by nature is someone of Abraham's stock circumcised by his parents
on the eighth day. Someone who is a Jew but not by nature is a
Gentile who later became a Jew.

To summarize briefly the entire argument, the sense of the
text is as follows. We—you and I, Peter (Paul used the inclusive
"we" so as not to appear to insult Peter)—are Jews by nature, doing the things that were prescribed by the Law. We are not Gentile sinners who are sinners in a generic sense; that is, we do not
worship idols and are not like those sinners whom we now regard as unclean. We know that we cannot be saved by the works
of the Law but by faith in Christ. We have believed in Christ so
that our faith in him might give us what the Law could not. We
abandoned the Law in which we could not be saved, and we
have gone over to faith, in which the devotion of a pure heart is
demanded, not the circumcision of the flesh. By now withdrawing from the Gentiles we declare that whoever is uncircumcised
is unclean. Therefore, is faith in Christ, by which we previously thought we were saved, the agent of sin rather than of righteousness, which abolishes [the need for] circumcision, the very
thing without which one is deemed unclean? God forbid that
I should uphold what I once attacked and knew would never
again be beneficial to me. When I decisively departed from the
Law, I died to it that I might live in Christ and be nailed to his
cross and that I might be reborn as a new man and live by faith,
not by the flesh, and leave the world in Christ. I remain steadfast
in my original resolve. Christ did not die for me for nothing. If I
was able to be saved by keeping the old Law instead of by having
faith in him, then I have believed in Christ in vain.

230. Eph 2.3.

2.16a. *We know that a man is not justified by observing the Law, but by faith in Jesus Christ. We too have put our faith in Christ Jesus so that we may be justified by faith in him and not by observing the Law.*

Some[231] say that if Paul is right to assert that no one is justified by the works of the Law but by faith in Jesus Christ, then the patriarchs, prophets, and saints who lived prior to Christ's advent were lacking in something. We must remind these objectors that Paul is talking here about those who have not pursued righteousness and who believe that they can be justified only by works. The saints who lived long ago, however, were justified by faith in Christ. Abraham foresaw the day of Christ and rejoiced.[232] "Moses regarded disgrace for the sake of Christ as of greater value than the treasures of Egypt, because he was looking ahead to his reward."[233] Isaiah beheld the glory of Christ, as John the Evangelist notes.[234] Jude speaks generally about all [the saints of old]: "Although you already know all this, I want to remind you that Jesus delivered his people out of Egypt but later destroyed those who did not believe."[235]

Thus it is not so much the works of the Law that are condemned as those who are confident that they can be justified by them.[236] The Savior says to his disciples, "Unless your righteousness surpasses that of the Pharisees and the teachers of the Law, you will not enter the kingdom of heaven."[237] It is fitting to point out how many precepts the Law contains that no one is able to fulfill. It must also be said that some works of the Law are done even by those who are ignorant of it. But doers of the Law are not justified because their deeds are done without faith

231. Marcion may be meant. According to Irenaeus (*Adv. haer.* 1.27.3; 4.8.1), Marcion held that when Christ descended into Hades to rescue the souls of the holy men and patriarchs of the OT (e.g., Abel, Enoch, Noah, Abraham), they rejected him, thinking that this was yet another cruel joke that Yahweh the Demiurge was playing on them, and thus they were excluded from salvation.

232. Cf. Jn 8.52.   233. Heb 11.26.

234. Cf. Jn 12.41.   235. Jude 5.

236. Cf. Origen, *Comm. Rom.* 8.7.6 (trans. Scheck, FOTC 104:159): "One should know that the works that Paul repudiates and frequently criticizes are not the works of righteousness that are commanded in the Law, but those in which those who keep the Law according to the flesh boast; i.e., the circumcision of the flesh, the sacrificial rituals, the observance of Sabbaths or new moon festivals."

237. Mt 5.20.

in Christ. Take, for example, these commandments: Do not lie with a man as you would with a woman; do not commit adultery; do not steal; honor your father and mother; and so on. If critics adduce examples of saintly men who lived by the Law and fulfilled its commandments, we will answer [with Paul's words], "The Law was established not for the righteous but for lawbreakers and rebels, the ungodly and sinful, the unholy and irreligious."[238] Moreover, the person taught by God does not need to be taught—at least, about love—by Paul, who says, "Now about brotherly love I do not need to write to you, for you yourselves have been taught by God to love each other."[239]

2.16b. *Because no flesh will be justified by observing the Law.*[240]

The flesh about which it is said, "All flesh is like grass, and all of its glory is like the flowers of the field,"[241] is not justified by the works of the Law. But the flesh spoken of in the mystery of the resurrection, "All flesh will see God's salvation,"[242] is justified through faith in Jesus Christ. According to the more common understanding, it used to be that the only flesh redeemable by the Law were those who lived in Palestine. Now, however, all flesh is justified by faith in Jesus Christ, as his churches are being established all over the world.

2.19a. *For through the Law I died to the Law so that I might live for God.*

It is one thing to die *through* the Law, quite another to die *to* it. If someone dies to the Law, it means that he used to live for it and observed the Sabbath, new moons, festivals, bizarre periodic animal sacrifices, and Jewish fables and genealogies. But with the advent of Christ and the Law about which it is said, "We know that the Law is spiritual,"[243] he died to the original Law through the Law of the Gospel. And the soul, which according

---

238. 1 Tm 1.9.   239. 1 Thes 4.9.

240. All but one modern editor of Jerome's *Commentary on Galatians* has added verses 17–18 to this quotation. Raspanti (CCSL 77A:249–50) rejected this interpolation for two reasons: it is not supported by any manuscript witness, and Jerome's comments are restricted only to v. 16b. It is not clear why Jerome omitted vv. 17–18.

241. Is 40.6 (LXX).   242. Lk 3.6.
243. Rom 7.14.

to the epistle to the Romans would be called an adulteress if she remarried while her first husband was still alive, wed the spiritual Law so that she might bear fruit for God, when her husband, the old Law, died.[244] Thus, in Hosea the Lord says to this soul, "Your fruitfulness comes from me,"[245] and [the next] verse mystically says to it, "Who is wise and will understand these things, or who is discerning and will recognize them?"[246] Therefore, he lives for God who through the spiritual Law dies to the literal Law. He is not however without the Law of God because he is in the Law of Christ. Whoever dies to the Law is dead with regard to sin, but this does not necessarily mean that he lives for God.

In another place the Apostle teaches that there is another Law, a spiritual one, apart from the literal Law:[247] "So, then, the Law is holy and the commandment is holy, righteous, and good."[248] Ezekiel speaks in the *persona* of God: "I led them— that is, the Jewish people—out of Egypt and brought them into the desert. I gave them my decrees and made known to them my laws, for the man who obeys them will live by them."[249] Further on, he references the Law to which the Apostle died—the one that brings [divine] wrath:[250] "I also gave them precepts that were not good and laws they could not live by."[251] The same idea is expressed in the Psalter, "I shall proclaim the Lord's mightiness because I do not comprehend its limits."[252]

2.19b. *I have been crucified with Christ.*

Paul clarifies how he died to the Law through the spiritual Law. He took up his cross and followed Christ[253] and beseeched him during his very Passion: "Remember me when you enter into your kingdom."[254] He immediately heard [Christ respond], "Today you will be with me in paradise."[255] If anyone has put

---

244. Cf. Rom 7.2–4.

245. Hos 14.8.

246. Hos 14.9.

247. Cf. Origen, *C. Cels.* 7.20, on how Ezekiel was referring to the literal interpretation of the Law when he said that God gave Israel laws that were not good.

248. Rom 7.12.   249. Ezek 20.10–11.

250. Rom 4.15.   251. Ezek 20.25.

252. Ps 71.15.   253. Mt 16.24.

254. Lk 23.42.   255. Lk 23.43.

to death what belongs to his earthly nature,[256] has died to the world, and has been conformed to the death of Jesus Christ,[257] he is crucified with Jesus and has nailed to the cross of the Lord's suffering the trophy of his own self-mortification.[258]

2.20a. *I no longer live, but Christ lives in me.*

The man who once lived according to the Law and persecuted the church no longer lives, but Christ lives in him, as do wisdom, fortitude, eloquence, peace, joy, and the rest of the virtues.[259] He who is without these virtues cannot say, "Christ lives in me." Paul, speaking in his own person, directs all of this at Peter, against whom he is arguing.

2.20b. *The life I now live in the body.*

It is one thing to *be* in the flesh, another to *live* in the flesh. For those who are in the flesh are unable to please God,[260] but to those living uprightly it is said, "You are not in the flesh."[261]

2.20c. *I live by faith in the Son of God, who loved me and handed himself over for me.*

Paul tells the Romans that God did not spare his own Son but handed him over for us,[262] but now he says that Christ handed himself over: "who loved me and handed himself over for me." In the Gospel, Judas Iscariot, the one who handed him over,[263]

---

256. Cf. Col 3.5.   257. Cf. Phil 3.10.
258. Cf. Col 2.14.

259. Jerome most likely borrowed this idea about the cohabitation of Christ and the virtues in the Christian from Origen: cf. Origen, *Comm. Rom.* 7.13.2 (trans. Scheck, FOTC 104:105): "The truth of Christ is there where the rest of the virtues, which Christ is said to be, exist. That is, where there is righteousness, where there is peace, where there is the Word of God, there also is the truth of Christ." Wiles, *The Divine Apostle*, 115, succinctly summarizes this point in Origen's teaching: "Our relationship to Christ is automatically our relationship to wisdom, righteousness, truth and all the other virtues. To be 'in Christ' is to be 'in' all the virtues; to have Christ in us is to have them in us. To be 'in Christ' is the same as to serve him, and to be his servant is to be the servant of all the virtues. To put on Christ is to put on all the virtues, and conversely to put on the armour of God is to put on Christ."

260. Cf. Rom 8.8.   261. Rom 8.9.
262. Cf. Rom 8.32.   263. Cf. Mt 10.4.

is named where the [names of the] twelve apostles are listed: "and Judas Iscariot, who handed him over"; he is mentioned again in the same Gospel: "Behold, he who will hand me over has come."[264] Scripture relates how the chief priests and the elders of the people sentenced Jesus to death, tied him up, led him away, and handed him over to the governor Pilate,[265] who "released Barabbas to them. But he had Jesus flogged and handed him over to them to be crucified."[266] Thus, the Father handed over his Son, the Son gave himself over, Judas and the priests and elders of the people handed him over, and Pilate, to whom he was finally handed over, handed him over [to the people]. But the Father handed him over in order to save the doomed world, and Jesus gave himself in accordance with the Father's will and his own. Judas, the priests, the elders of the people, and Pilate, however, all unwittingly handed Life [that is, Christ] over to death. Since Life surrendered himself for our salvation, that person is blessed and happy indeed who has Christ living within him and who is able to declare in his thoughts and through his deeds, "I live by faith in the Son of God, who loved me and handed himself over for me."

2.21. *I do not cast aside the grace of God, for if righteousness could be attained through the Law, then Christ died for nothing.*

If one receives the Gospel yet continues to live according to the Law, he casts aside the grace of God; so, too, does one who is baptized and is then defiled again by sin. But he who can affirm with the Apostle that, "His grace was not without effect in me,"[267] can also say with confidence, "I do not cast aside the grace of God."

What comes next is crucial for Paul's case against [Judaizing] Christians who think that the Law must still be observed. They must be told, "If righteousness could be attained through the Law, then Christ died for nothing." Or else, if works do indeed bring about righteousness, then the burden of proof is on them to show how Christ did *not* die in vain. However dim-witted they are, they will not dare to say that Christ died for no reason. As

264. Mt 26.46.
266. Mt 27.26.
265. Cf. Mt 27.1–2.
267. 1 Cor 15.10.

for the syllogism, "If righteousness could be attained through the Law, then Christ died for nothing," we must assume the logical and undeniable consequence that Christ did *not* die in vain, and we conclude that righteousness does not come through the Law.

Up until this point Paul has been dealing with Peter, but now he returns to the Galatians.

3.1a. *You foolish Galatians, who has cast a spell on you?*

This passage can be taken in either of two ways. The Galatians are called foolish either because they started out in the Spirit but finished in the flesh and thus reverted from greater to lesser things, or because each locale has its own peculiar behaviors.[268] The Apostle approvingly cites the poet Epimenides, who called the Cretans "perpetual liars, evil brutes, and lazy gluttons."[269] The Latin historian[270] ridicules the Moors for their levity and the Dalmatians for their cruelty.[271] All the poets belittle the Phrygians for being cowards.[272] The philosophers boast that the best minds are born in Athens. In a speech delivered in Cae-

---

268. Jerome's catalogue is modeled closely on the one devised by Tertullian in *De an.* 20.2–3 to illustrate that the influence of local customs accounts for why souls develop different attributes despite sharing the same universal nature: "It has been said that dull and brutish persons are born at Thebes; and the most accomplished in wisdom and speech at Athens. . . . The subject of national peculiarities has grown by this time into proverbial notoriety. Comic poets deride the Phrygians for their cowardice; Sallust reproaches the Moors for their levity, and the Dalmatians for their cruelty; even the Apostle brands the Cretans 'liars'" (ANF 3:201). See A. Cain, *REAug* 55 (2009): 38–41.

269. Ti 1.12.

270. I.e., Sallust, who was, for Jerome, "the Roman historian *par préférence*": H. Hagendahl, *The Latin Fathers and the Classics: A Study on the Apologists, Jerome, and Other Christian Writers* (Göteborg: Elanders Boktryckeri Aktiebolag, 1958), 292.

271. This detail about the Moors and Dalmatians comes ultimately from Sallust's now-fragmentary *Histories*. On other occasions Jerome worked firsthand from this work: see, e.g., N. Adkin, "Hieronymus Sallustianus," *GB* 24 (2005): 93–110. On the present occasion, however, Jerome retrieved his information indirectly through the intermediary of Tertullian.

272. Phrygian effeminacy had been a theme in Greek drama as far back as the fifth century BC as well as in Roman poetry (e.g., Virgil and Ovid). See E. Hall, *Inventing the Barbarian: Greek Self-Definition through Tragedy* (Oxford: Oxford University Press, 1989), 73–74, 103, 113–14.

sar's presence, Cicero pummeled the Greeks for being fickle: "[The habits] of either the fickle Greeks or the savage barbarians,"[273] and in his speech on behalf of Flaccus he says, "Fickleness is innate and vanity learned."[274] All of Scripture reproaches Israel for having a hardened heart and a stiff neck.[275] I reckon that it is along these same lines that the Apostle ridicules the Galatians because of the behavioral peculiarities endemic to their region.

Some, under the guise of refuting the heresy which holds that there are different natures,[276] delve into arcane questions and claim that the Tyrians, Sidonians, Moabites, Ammonites, Edomites, Babylonians, Egyptians, and all the nations mentioned in Scripture have certain idiosyncrasies that arise from antecedent causes and from their conduct in the past. They allege that the integrity of God's righteousness is preserved by the fact that each nation supposedly has good or bad qualities that another nation does not have. We shall shy away from these complexities and pursue a sounder line of reasoning. Either the Galatians are denounced for foolishness, which prevented them from distinguishing between the spirit and letter of the Law, or they are chided on account of a national vice, because they are unteachable, senseless, and slow-minded in their quest for wisdom.

The phrase "Who has cast a spell on you?" must be expounded in a manner worthy of Paul, who, although inelegant in speech, is nevertheless not so in knowledge. He does not suspect the involvement of witchcraft, which common folk believe causes harm. Rather, he has employed a colloquial expression, and here, as on other occasions, he has adopted a word from everyday conversation. We read among the Proverbs, "A gift

273. *Lig.* 11. The stereotype of Greek unreliability, which Cicero invoked occasionally in his speeches, continued to have currency into the imperial period. See M. Garrett, "Rome," in *Encyclopedia of Ancient Greece,* ed. N. G. Wilson (London: Routledge, 2005), 632.

274. *Flac.,* frag. 9. Jerome had already quoted this Ciceronian line a decade earlier in a letter (*Ep.* 10.3) to the centenarian Paul of Concordia.

275. E.g., Ex 32.9.

276. I.e., the Gnostic doctrine of natures taught by Valentinus, Basilides, and others.

from an envious person troubles the eyes."[277] The Latin word
invidus ["envious one"] translates into Greek more poignantly
as "spellcaster." In the Book of Wisdom, which is attributed to
Solomon, we read, "The bewitching of malice obscures good
things."[278] These passages teach us that the envious man is tortured by another's good fortune or, alternatively, that the person in whom there is good is harmed by another who casts a
spell on him, that is, who envies him. The spellcaster is said to
bring trouble especially for infants and young children as well
as for those who do not yet walk with a firm gait. This is why a
certain heathen poet writes, "Some evil eye casts a spell on my
tender lambs."[279] God sees whether this holds true or not. It is
possible that demons serve this wicked purpose and avert from
doing good deeds everyone whom they recognize to be either
a beginner or a veteran in the work of God. I reckon that Paul
borrowed the example in question from popular usage in order
to express that, just as tender youths are said to be harmed by
witchcraft, so also the Galatians, recently born in faith in Christ
and nourished with milk, not solid food,[280] have been harmed
as though someone has cast a spell on them, and they have vom-
ited up the food of the Holy Spirit because the stomach of their
faith is upset. If anyone disagrees, let him explain how it is that
certain [Biblical] expressions are adopted from common usage:
the valley of the giants in the Books of Kingdoms;[281] the sirens
and onocentaurs in Isaiah;[282] Arcturus, Orion, and the Pleiades
in Job;[283] and other comparable examples, which trace their origins and names back to heathen fables.

Let us here inquire of Marcion, the repudiator of the prophets, how he would interpret what follows below:

3.1b. *Before your very eyes Jesus Christ was clearly portrayed as crucified.*
Christ is rightly said to be portrayed clearly before us because
the whole chorus of the [Old Testament] prophets foretold his

---

277. Sir 18.18.   278. Wis 4.12.
279. Virgil, *Ecl.* 3.103.   280. Cf. 1 Cor 3.2.
281. Cf. 2 Sm 23.13.
282. Cf. Is 13.21–22; 34.13–14 (LXX).
283. Cf. Jb 9.9 (LXX).

torture, suffering, and the blows and whippings he would receive. As a result, we know about the cross not only from the
Gospel, which relates the story of his crucifixion, but also [from
writings penned] long before he deigned to come down to
earth and assume the form of a crucified man. It is much to
the Galatians' credit that they believed in Christ crucified as he
had previously been portrayed for them. They of course had
been led in due course to this belief by continually reading the
prophets and by knowing all of the ordinances of the old Law.

Some manuscripts contain the reading, "Who has cast a spell
on you so that you would not believe the truth?" I have not included it here because it is not found in the copies[284] of Adamantius.[285]

3.2. *I want to learn just this one thing from you. Did you receive the
Spirit by performing works of the Law or by believing what you heard?*

Many lines of inquiry, he says, can induce you to choose the
Gospel over the Law, but seeing that you are foolish and unable
to grasp them, I shall address you in simple terms and question
you about the matter at hand: Did you receive the Holy Spirit by performing works of the Law—the Sabbath, circumcision,
and superstitious new moon festivals—or by believing what you
heard? If there is no question that the Holy Spirit as well as the
virtues that accrue to the new believer after he receives the Spirit are granted on the basis of having faith in Christ and not of
keeping the Law, it is clear that you [Galatians] made a good
beginning but have now fallen into a deplorable state.

Let us take special note of the fact that Paul did not say sim-

284. A. Souter, *The Earliest Latin Commentaries on the Epistles of St. Paul* (Oxford: Oxford University Press, 1927), 115, suggested that these *exemplaria* were
Origen's personal copies of Galatians (in Greek) that were kept at the ecclesiastical library at Caesarea.

285. "Adamantius" means "man of bronze" and was the nickname applied to
Origen by Eusebius (*H.E.* 6.14.10) and others thereafter because of his scholarly
prodigiousness. Thus Jerome says in *Ep.* 33.4: "You will ask why I have mentioned
Varro and the man of bronze of the Greeks. To come to our own Adamantius
and man of bronze, of course. He put so much work into his commentaries on
Holy Scripture that he has quite rightly been referred to as being made of steel:
would you like to know how many written works he has left behind?"

ply, "I want to learn if you received the Spirit on the basis of your works." He instead added "by performing works of the Law." For he knew that the centurion Cornelius had received the Spirit because of his works (but not because of the works of the Law, of which he was ignorant).[286] If anyone uses this as evidence that the Spirit can be received without hearing and then having faith, we will respond that Cornelius received the Spirit by believing what he had heard and by obeying the natural law, which speaks in our hearts and directs us to do good and to shun evil. It was by this law that Abraham, Moses, and the rest of the saints of old were justified. This natural law can then be augmented by observance of the Law and the righteousness that comes from the Law—not the fleshly law, which has passed away, but the spiritual Law, for the Law is spiritual.[287] By privileging faith we do not do away with the works of the Law, nor do we say, as some allege we do, "Let us do evil that good may result."[288] Their condemnation is well deserved. We put grace ahead of slavery [to the Law], and we maintain that we do out of love what the Jews do out of fear. They are servants, we are sons. They do good under compulsion, we do it of our own accord. Therefore, freedom to sin is not the fruit of faith in Christ. Rather, a willingness to do good works is enhanced by love for one's faith. We do good deeds not because we fear the Judge but because we know that they are pleasing to him in whom we believe.

Someone may ask: If faith comes only from hearing, how can people born deaf become Christians? To be sure, anyone can come to an understanding of God the Father through the beauty and grandeur of [his] creatures; the Creator is recognized by what he has made.[289] But Christ's nativity, cross, death, and resurrection can only be apprehended by hearing. So, either the deaf are not Christians, or, if they are, then the Apostle has lied when he claimed elsewhere in his writings that "faith comes from hearing, and hearing from the word of God."[290] One who is content with a simplified solution to this quandary holds that

286. Cf. Acts 10.44–48.   287. Cf. Rom 7.14.
288. Rom 3.8.   289. Cf. Rom 1.19–20.
290. Rom 10.17.

Paul was not making a sweeping statement. Everyone's faith comes from hearing, but the phrase "faith from hearing," which can be construed in both partial and absolute terms, refers to the faith of those who hear and believe. Moreover, one who tries to solve this conundrum will first attempt to assert that the deaf are able to learn the Gospel by means of nods, everyday routines, and the so-called talking gesticulation of the entire body. Then he will point out that the words of God, to which nothing is deaf, speak instead to the ears about which God himself says in the Gospel, "He who has ears, let him hear,"[291] and in Revelation, "He who has an ear, let him hear what the Spirit says to the churches."[292] Finally, Isaiah declares, "The Lord has given me the ability to hear."[293] Isaiah was another person to whom God spoke in private and who cried out "Abba, Father"[294] in his believing heart.

Furthermore, as I have explained on many occasions, the soul, like the body, has its own limbs and sensory faculties, among which are these [figurative] ears. Whoever has these will not need physical ears to apprehend the Gospel of Christ. Also realize that we do not need any additional aid in order to come to a knowledge of the Holy Spirit. We obtain him by virtue of a gift, and not a gift of human origin. It is written about him elsewhere, "The imperishable Spirit is in all things,"[295] and, "The Spirit himself testifies with our spirit."[296] And in another place, "No one knows the [thoughts] of a man except the man's spirit within him."[297] And in Daniel, "Bless the Lord, you spirits and souls of the righteous."[298]

3.3. *Are you so foolish? Although you began in the Spirit, are you now trying to reach perfection by the flesh?*

How were the Galatians foolish if they had received the Holy Spirit? The answer to this question comes right away: They had begun in the Spirit but tried to achieve perfection by the flesh, and so the Spirit was taken away from them. Therefore, they suf-

---

291. Mt 11.15.
293. Is 50.5.
295. Wis 12.1.
297. 1 Cor 2.11.

292. Rv 2.11.
294. Cf. Rom 8.15; Gal 4.6.
296. Rom 8.16.
298. Dn 3.86.

fered so much for nothing.[299] David begged God not to allow [the same fate] to befall him after he had sinned: "Do not take your Holy Spirit away from me."[300]

Be mindful that the person who follows Scripture to the letter is said to reach for perfection by the flesh. For this reason what Paul wrote to the Corinthians, "Although we live in the flesh, we do not wage war as the flesh does,"[301] may be better understood as follows. Those who expound the Old Testament in an earthly fashion are said to wage war in the flesh. But those who pursue spiritual knowledge are simply "in the flesh" because, while they adhere to the same letter of the Law as the Jews, they nevertheless have crossed over from the flesh to the Spirit and do not wage war as the flesh does. Suppose a Gentile believer has initially followed the lead of some wise teacher. He has put his hand to the plow of Christ[302] and has advanced from the Law to the Gospel, such that he regards the prescriptions about the Sabbath, unleavened bread, circumcision, and sacrifices in a way that is pleasing to God. Then, after an encounter with the Gospel, some Jew or ally of the Jews convinces him to leave behind these allegorical mists and shadows and to interpret Scripture strictly according to the letter. You may then say to him, "Are you so foolish? Although you began in the Spirit, are you now trying to reach perfection by the flesh?"

3.4. *Have you suffered so much for nothing—if it nevertheless was for nothing!*

Let us ponder the enormity of the superstition and burden of observing the Law under which the unhappy Jews live among the other nations, with their prohibitions, "Do not touch," "Do not taste," "Do not handle." When we do this, we will understand that what Paul says is true: "Have you suffered so much for nothing?" He does not pass judgment on them right away but remains irresolute and adds, "If it nevertheless was for nothing," because he is referring to people who might come back to the Gospel after [their stint under] the Law.

299. Cf. Gal 3.4.   300. Ps 51.11.
301. 2 Cor 10.3.   302. Cf. Lk 9.62.

The import of this passage may be better grasped in the following terms. The Galatians initially believed in the Crucified One and suffered many indignities at the hands of Jews and Gentiles alike. They underwent severe persecutions, but they are rebuked for having suffered in vain if they fall away from the grace of Christ, for which they suffered so much. At the same time, there is the hope that whoever exerts himself for his faith in Christ but afterward lapses into sin will not again lose the initial progress he has made, provided that he returns to his original faith and former zeal, just as he is said to have suffered for nothing while living in sin. Put another way: If you think you should observe circumcision after receiving the grace of Christ, all that you have suffered is rendered meaningless because you have lived up until now without circumcision. It accordingly seems to me that you have not suffered in vain, for I know that the Law avails nothing once you receive the Gospel. To put it still another way: If by embracing circumcision you lost the substantial progress you initially made in faith, the damage done was not slight. But now this loss is compounded by punishment for straying from the truth. Not only have you suffered in vain in the past, but you also will be tormented in the future.

Some interpret the passage more rigidly: Compare the freedom of grace you originally enjoyed and the burden of observing the Law you are experiencing now, and you will see how many things you have done out of futile zeal. Nevertheless, do not completely despair over the outcome of that mistake, as long as you have been led to this [revelation] by zeal for God. For you can be granted leniency for acting out of ignorance, provided that you take a better course and prove that it was your knowledge rather than your zeal that fluctuated.

3.5. *Does God give you his Spirit and work miracles among you because you observe the Law or because you believe what you heard?*

Paul uses the present tense ("does give") to show that the Holy Spirit ministers perpetually—every hour and every minute—to those who are worthy, and that the more one advances in the work of God and in love for him, the more he manifests in himself the Holy Spirit's virtues, which are made complete by believing what he has heard rather than by doing the works of the Law. This does not mean that the works of the Law ought to be discarded and that a one-dimensional faith devoid of works is the goal. It means rather that faith in Christ enriches these works. Indeed, that saying of the wise man is well known, "The faithful man does not live by righteousness, but the righteous man lives by faith."[303] Paul simultaneously shows that after the Galatian Christians had come to faith and received the Holy Spirit, they were invested with the gifts and powers of prophecy, speaking in tongues, healing sicknesses, and other things listed among the spiritual gifts in his letter to the Corinthians.[304] And yet even after they had come into possession of such great gifts, they were ensnared by false teachers, perhaps because they lacked the grace to discern between [good and evil] spirits.

Note also that miraculous powers are said to be at work in those who do not possess the truth of the Gospel,[305] just as they had been at work in those who in the Lord's time did not follow him yet would perform signs and wonders in his name. John complained bitterly about them, "Teacher, we saw a man driving out demons in your name, and we tried to stop him, because he is not one of us."[306] This is a rebuke of heretics who consider their faith to be authentic because they have performed a miracle. Although they have eaten and drunk in the Lord's name (they have a blasphemous altar of their own)[307] and boast that they have performed many signs and wonders with the Savior's help, they will fittingly hear on Judgment Day, "I do not know you. Depart from me, you evildoers."[308]

3.6. *Abraham believed God, and it was credited to him as righteousness.*
Marcion omitted from his version of the Apostle's epistle this and the next two verses, and he resumed with the verse [9], "Those who have faith will be blessed along with Abraham, the

303. Hab 2.4; Rom 1.17; Gal 3.11; Heb 10.38.
304. Cf. 1 Cor 12.4–11.   305. Cf. Mt 14.2.
306. Lk 9.49.
307. The mention of a "blasphemous altar" makes it clear that the eating and drinking in the Lord's name refers to the Eucharist.
308. Mt 7.23.

man of faith." But what was the point of doing this, seeing that the parts he left intact refute his madness?

Abraham believed God and left his homeland for a land he did not know. He trusted that his ninety-year-old sterile wife Sarah would give birth to a child. He heard God's promise that his seed would be called in Isaac, the very one he offered as a sacrifice, and all the while he never doubted the Lord's promise.[309] Faith is rightly credited as righteousness to such a man as this who went above and beyond the works of the Law and found favor with God by loving him, not fearing him.

3.7. *You recognize that those with faith are children of Abraham.*

In his epistle to the Romans Paul elaborates on how faith was credited to Abraham as righteousness while he was still uncircumcised.[310] Keeping this at the forefront of his mind, he teaches that the children of Abraham are whoever have believed in the manner of an uncircumcised Abraham, who rejoiced at the thought of seeing the day of the Lord's arrival, saw it, and was glad.[311] For this reason Christ says to the unbelieving Jews, "If you were the children of Abraham, you would do what Abraham had done."[312] Moreover, what deeds did the Lord expect from his contemporaries other than belief in the Son of God whom the Father had sent and who said, "He who believes in me does not believe in me only, but in him who sent me"?[313] In another place he replied to Jews who applauded themselves for the antiquity and nobility of their ethnicity, "Do not say, 'We have Abraham as our father,' for God is capable of raising up children for Abraham out of these stones."[314] There is no question that the stones here symbolize the Gentiles' hardened hearts, which were later softened and received the seal of faith. My attentive reader, count up the virtues by which Abraham pleased God even before being circumcised. Whatever people you may find who have conducted themselves as he did, pronounce them to be the children of Abraham, who was justified while still uncircumcised and received circumcision

309. Cf. Heb 11.8–18.   310. Cf. Rom 4.9–10.
311. Cf. Jn 8.56.   312. Jn 8.39.
313. Jn 12.44.   314. Mt 3.9.

as an outward sign of the faith he already had and not because he earned it by works.

Since Christ was supposed to come from Abraham's seed, in which all nations had been promised a blessing, and since many centuries would intervene between Abraham and Christ, God had the foresight not to allow the stock of his beloved Abraham to intermingle with other nations, lest his bloodline gradually become muddled. He branded the [male] population of Israel with circumcision in order to make them distinct from the Egyptians, Assyrians, Babylonians, and Chaldeans among whom they lived. Furthermore, nobody was circumcised [when the Israelites wandered] in the desert for forty years, for they lived in solitude and did not have contact with any other nation.[315] As soon as the Jews crossed *en masse* over the shore of the Jordan River and poured into the land of Palestine, circumcision became a necessary precaution against future straying that might occur due to the intermingling of nations. The fact that (according to Scripture) Joshua, the second leader of Israel, had the people circumcised[316] indicates both that the practice of circumcision, which had for good reason been observed while the Israelites were in Egypt, was suspended in the desert, and that Christians must be purified by our Lord Jesus Christ by means of spiritual circumcision.[317]

3.8–9. *Scripture foresaw that God would justify the Gentiles by faith and announced to Abraham in advance: "All nations will be blessed through you."*[318] *Therefore, those who have faith will be blessed with Abraham, the man of faith.*

This does not mean that [the physical form of] Scripture itself—the ink and the parchment (which are insensate)—can foreknow the future, but that the Holy Spirit and the sense that lies hidden among the letters have foretold what would come to pass many centuries later.

The embedded passage from Genesis is worded as follows in its own book: "All the nations of the earth will be blessed

---

315. Cf. Jos 5.5–6.   316. Cf. Jos 5.2–3.
317. Cf. Rom 2.29; Col 2.11.   318. Gn 12.3.

through your seed."[319] The Apostle interprets it with Christ in mind: "Scripture does not say 'and to seeds,' meaning many people, but 'and to your seed,' meaning one person, namely, Christ."[320] When dealing with almost all Old Testament quotations in the New Testament, we must bear in mind that the writers of the Gospels and the apostles had committed the Old Testament to memory and they often altered the word order of a given passage when explaining its meaning, and sometimes they either added or omitted words. No one doubts that not all nations have been blessed through Isaac, Jacob, the twelve patriarchs, and the rest of Abraham's descendants. They have, however, been blessed through Christ Jesus, because of whom all nations praise God and a new name is blessed on earth. The Apostle could have cited an example pertaining to [Abraham's] offspring from elsewhere in Genesis: "God took him (Abraham, undoubtedly)[321] outside and said to him, 'Look up at the heavens and count the stars, if you can count them.' Then he said to him, 'So shall your offspring be.' Abraham believed God and it was credited to him as righteousness."[322]

Moreover, believers will be blessed along with Abraham the man of faith, who by virtue of his exemplary faith in God is said to have been the first person to put his trust in God. Similarly, when Scripture says that Enosh, on account of his hope in God that was unrivaled among other mortals, hoped to call upon the Lord God,[323] it does not mean that Abel, about whom the Lord said, "Your brother's blood cries out to me,"[324] and others after him did not hope to call upon God, but that each one is honored according to his individual capacity [for hope].

---

319. Gn 22.18.   320. Gal 3.16.
321. The parenthetical addition is Jerome's.
322. Gn 15.5–6.   323. Cf. Gn 4.26 (LXX).
324. Gn 4.10.

BOOK TWO (GALATIANS 3.10–5.6)

N THE FIRST book of this commentary on Galatians, I discussed peculiarities endemic to each nation.[1] It behooves me now to address, in the second book, what I did not cover there. Who were the Galatians? Where did they come from? With regard to the land they now inhabit, are they natives or foreign settlers? Did they lose their original language as a result of intermarriage, or did they learn a new language and fail to retain their own?

That incredibly scrupulous investigator of antiquities Marcus Varro,[2] as well as his imitators, have preserved for us many noteworthy details about the Galatians. Because, however, I have no intention of introducing uncircumcised men into the temple of God[3] and because—if I may frankly confess—it has been many years since I stopped reading secular literature,[4] I shall quote the conjecturings that our own Lactantius recorded about this people in the third volume of his work addressed to Probus: "From ancient times the Gauls were called Galatians due to their shiny complexion, and the Sibyl refers to them as such. This is what the poet meant when he said, 'Their milky-white

---

1. See Jerome's remarks on Gal 3.1a.

2. Marcus Terentius Varro (116–27 BC) was an extremely prolific Roman polymath who wrote books on history, philosophy, culture, and the arts. Very little of his vast literary output survives today. Jerome's allusion is to one of Varro's lost works, the forty-one-volume *Antiquities of Human and Divine Matters* (*Antiquitates rerum humanarum et divinarum*).

3. Ironically, Jerome rejects Varro here but then cites him as a source anyway further down in the same paragraph.

4. This is an allusion to the vow he made in his famous Ciceronian dream never again to read the Latin classics. See *Ep.* 22.30. He refers to this dream again in the preface to Book 3.

necks are decked in gold,'[5] though he could have used the word 'shiny.' It is clear from this that the province where the Gauls arrived and intermingled with the Greeks was called Galatia. For this reason the region was named Gallo-Graecia and afterward Galatia."[6]

Given the well-known fact that hordes of settlers from Greece and the eastern world immigrated to the remotest regions of the west, it comes as no surprise that Lactantius would relate, in regard to the Galatians, that a western people settled in a region of the east after having traversed such a vast distance in between. The Phocaeans founded a colony at Massilia.[7] According to Varro, they spoke three languages: Greek, Latin, and a Gallic dialect. The Rhodians made Rhoda their home; this is how the Rhone River got its name. I say nothing of the Tyrians who founded Carthage, Agenor's city.[8] I pass over Thebes, which Liber established in Africa; it is now called Tebessa.[9] I also say nothing of the part of Libya that is densely populated with Greeks. I turn now to Spain. Did not Greeks setting out from the island of Zacynthus found Saguntum? And is it not believed that Greek men from Ionia colonized the town of Tartessus, which is now called Carteia? As for the mountains of Spain—the Calpe, Hydria, and Pyrene—and in like manner the islands of Aphrodisias and Gymnasia, which are called the Balearic islands, do not their names bear the mark of Hellenistic influence? Italy itself used to be called Greater Greece because it had been occupied by Greeks. Certainly it cannot be denied that the Romans were born from the stock of Aeneas, a man from Asia. As a result, in the west specimens of Greek acumen are often found, while in the east they have the scent of barbarian obtuseness. We do not say that diverse specimens are not born from each region, but that to a great extent even the oth-

5. Virgil, *Aen.* 4.138.

6. In *Vir. ill.* 80 Jerome informs us that this work consisted of four books of letters to Probus. The quotation presented above is one of only four fragments that survive from it.

7. Modern-day Marseilles. The Phocaeans lived on the western coast of Anatolia. Around 600 BC, they abandoned their home to escape Persian rule under Cyrus, and most of them settled in Massilia.

8. Cf. Virgil, *Aen.* 1.338.

9. Tebessa is a city in modern-day southeastern Algeria.

ers that are not like them are lumped into the same category. It is
no wonder that Paul called the Galatians foolish and slow to understanding when Hilary, the Rhone River of Latin eloquence,[10]
and himself a Gaul born at Poitiers, called the Gauls unteachable
in the hymns he composed.[11] The fact that Gaul is so rich in orators has to do not as much with the hard work of the region as it
does with the sheer loudness of its rhetoric, especially seeing that
Aquitania vaunts its Greek roots and the Galatians originated not
from the Greek world but from the more savage Gauls.[12]

Do you wish to know, Paula and Eustochium, how the Apostle delineates each geographical area according to its unique
characteristics? To this day, the same traces of virtues or vices remain. For example, the Roman people are lauded for their faith.
Where else [but in Rome] do [Christians] so enthusiastically
rush in droves to the churches and martyrs' tombs?[13] Where else
does "Amen" reverberate like thunderclaps in the sky, and where

10. For the significance of this epithet, see P. Antin, "*Hilarius latinae eloquentiae Rhodanus* (Jérôme, *In Gal.* prol. 2)," *Orpheus* 13 (1966): 3–25.

11. The particular hymn to which Jerome refers no longer survives.

12. For some modern scholarly perspectives on the ethnogenesis of the Galatians, see W. Leschhorn, "Die Anfänge der Provinz Galatia," *Chiron* 22 (1992):
315–36; G. Darbyshire, S. Mitchell, and L. Vardar, "The Galatian settlement in
Asia Minor," *AS* 50 (2000): 75–97; K. Strobel, "State formation by the Galatians
of Asia Minor: politico-historical and cultural processes in Hellenistic central
Anatolia," *Anatolica* 28 (2002): 1–46; idem, "Galatien, die Galater und die *Poleis*
der Galater: historische Identität und ethnische Tradition," *Eirene* 42 (2006):
89–123.

13. When he was a student in Rome in the 360s, Jerome made regular visits
to martyrs' tombs with his Christian friends. In his *Commentary on Ezekiel* 40.5–13
(CCSL 75:468), written when he was in his early seventies, Jerome reminisced
about his experiences: "When I was a youth at Rome studying liberal arts, it was
my custom on Sundays, along with companions of the same age and the same
conviction, to make tours of the tombs of the apostles and the martyrs. Often
we would enter those crypts which have been hollowed out of the depths of
the earth and which, along the walls on either side of the passages, contain the
bodies of buried people. Everything was so dark that the prophet's saying, 'Let
them go down to living hell,' seemed almost to have been fulfilled. Here and
there a ray of light admitted from above relieved the horror of blackness, yet in
such a way that you imagined it was not so much a window as a funnel pierced
by the light itself as it descended. Then we would walk back with gingerly steps,
wrapped in unseeing night, with Vergil's line recurring to us, 'Everywhere dread
fills the heart; the very silence dismays.'"

else are the empty shrines of false gods shaken to the core? The Romans' faith is no different from the faith that all of Christ's churches have, though their sense of pious devotion and the innocence of their belief are superior to all. And yet Paul rebuked them for being prideful and too easily swayed by bad influences. He reproves them for their gullibility in this passage: "I urge you, brothers, to watch out for those who cause divisions and put obstacles in your way that are contrary to the teaching you have learned. Stay away from them. For such people serve not our Lord Christ but their own appetites. By smooth talk and flattery they deceive the minds of naïve people. Your obedience is known everywhere. I therefore rejoice over you and want you to be wise about what is good, and innocent about what is evil."[14] Paul rebukes them for their pride here: "Do not be haughty, but be afraid."[15] And also: "I do not want you to be ignorant of this mystery, brothers, so that you may not be conceited."[16] And further on: "By the grace given to me I say to every one of you: Do not think of yourself more highly than you ought, but rather think of yourself with sober judgment."[17] Elsewhere he was more emphatic: "Rejoice with those who rejoice, and mourn with those who mourn. Live in harmony with one another. Do not be proud, but associate with people of low position. Do not be conceited."[18] Regarding the Corinthians, Paul noted that their women do not cover their heads,[19] the men grow long hair,[20] they feast in temples without discretion,[21] and they are puffed up with pride in their worldly wisdom and deny the bodily resurrection.[22]

Anyone who visits Achaia will not doubt that these criticisms to some extent still hold true today. [The Christians] in Macedonia are praised for their charity as well as for their hospitality and eagerness to host fellow believers. Thus Paul wrote to them, "We do not need to write to you about brotherly love, for you yourselves have learned from God how to love one another. And in fact you do love all the brothers throughout Macedo-

---

14. Rom 16.17–19.
15. Rom 11.20.
16. Rom 11.25.
17. Rom 12.3.
18. Rom 12.15–16.
19. Cf. 1 Cor 11.13.
20. Cf. 1 Cor 11.14.
21. Cf. 1 Cor 11.20–21.
22. Cf. 1 Cor 4.6, 18.

nia."[23] Nevertheless, Paul upbraided them for idly visiting others' houses, expecting others to give them food, making it their goal to please certain individuals, and running to and fro gossiping about one person or another. "We urge you, brothers, to do so more and more and to make an effort to lead a quiet life, to mind your own business, and to work with your hands, just as we instructed you, so that you may walk uprightly in the eyes of outsiders and not be dependent on anybody."[24] Lest anyone think that this admonition was prompted more by Paul's duty to teach than by the vice of his audience, in his second letter to the same [Christians] he inculcates this exact thing. "For even when we were with you, we laid down the rule that if a man will not work, he shall not eat. We hear that some among you are restless. They are not busy; they are busybodies. We command such people and urge them in the Lord Jesus Christ to settle down and earn the bread they eat."[25]

It would be tedious to produce from Paul's epistles and the rest of Scripture a roll-call of the virtues and vices of individual nations, for we have returned to the original point that the Galatians were pronounced foolish and senseless. Anyone who has visited Ancyra, the capital city of Galatia, knows, as I do,[26] by how many schisms it has been ripped apart and with how many doctrinal differences it has been blotted. I say nothing of the Cataphrygians,[27] Ophites,[28] Borborites,[29] and Manichaeans, as

23. 1 Thes 4.9–10.   24. 1 Thes 4.10–12.

25. 2 Thes 3.10–12.

26. Jerome passed through Ancyra during the early 370s *en route* to Antioch. See J. N.D. Kelly, *Jerome: His Life, Writings, and Controversies* (New York: Harper & Row, 1975), 37.

27. This was the most common name for the earliest Montanists, who flourished in Phrygia around the middle of the second century. See C. Trevett, *Montanism: Gender, Authority and the New Prophecy* (Cambridge: Cambridge University Press, 1996).

28. "Ophites," from ὄφις *("serpent")*, was a generic designation for any number of Gnostic sects in Syria and Egypt starting in the second century that honored the serpent in Genesis 3 as a revealer of redemptive gnosis. See T. Rasimus, "Ophite gnosticism, Sethianism and the Nag Hammadi Library," *VChr* 59 (2005): 235–63.

29. The Borborites, from βόρβορος ("filth"), were an offshoot of the Ophites. According to Epiphanius, *Pan.* 25.2–5, they were libertines and engaged in unspeakable sexual acts.

these are already familiar names of human woe. Who has ever heard of the Passalorynchites,[30] Tascodrougitae,[31] and Artotyrites,[32] and other groups which are monstrosities rather than mere names in another part of the Roman world? The vestiges of ancient foolishness persist down to the present day.

I must make one final remark in order to fulfill the promise I made at the beginning. In addition to Greek, which the entire east speaks, the Galatians have their own language [that is, Celtic][33] and it is almost identical to the one spoken by the people of Trier.[34] It does not matter if the Galatians have corrupted some aspects of the Greek tongue. After all, the Africans have altered the Phoenician language somewhat, and Latin itself undergoes constant changes depending on when and where it is spoken. But let us now return to the task at hand.

30. From πάσσαλος ("peg") and ῥύγχος ("snout"), "Passalorynchites" was a derogatory epithet for the Tascodrougitae, on whom see the note immediately below.

31. Various heresiological writers refer to them alternatively as *Tascodrogitae, Ascodrugitae, Ascodrobi, Ascodrogi*, and Ἀσκοδρούτοι. Epiphanius (*Pan.* 48.14) ridicules them as "Peg-noses" (Τασκοδρουγῖται) due to their habit of placing their forefinger (the τασκός, or peg) on their nose (δροῦγγος) when they pray, apparently as an expression of piety: on this custom, see C. Trevett, "Fingers up Noses and Pricking with Needles: Possible Reminiscences of Revelation in Later Montanism," *VChr* 49 (1995): 258–69. Τασκός and δροῦγγος are the only two known non-onomastic words that can definitely be assigned to the lexicon of the Galatians; hence, the compound Τασκοδρουγῖται is of Celtic origin. J. Katz, "How the Mole and Mongoose Got Their Names: Sanskrit Ākhú- and nakulá-," *JAOS* 122 (2002): 296–310 (299), demonstrates on linguistic grounds that this name did not originally mean "Peg-noses" at all (*pace* Epiphanius's etymology), but rather "Badger-noses" or "Mole-noses," though he confesses ignorance as to how they might have acquired these nicknames to begin with.

32. A sect of the Montanists referred to as the "Bread-and-cheesers" (ἀρτός + τυρός) because they celebrated the Eucharist with bread and cheese (or possibly yogurt). See Epiphanius, *Pan.* 49.2.6; Augustine, *De haer.* 86; Praedestinatus, *Haer.* 1.28.

33. For a recent study of the Galatian language, see P. Freeman, *The Galatian Language: A Comprehensive Survey of the Language of the Ancient Celts in Greco-Roman Asia Minor* (Lewiston: Edwin Mellen Press, 2001).

34. Jerome may be speaking from personal experience, as he lived in Trier for several years, from the late 360s until the early 370s: see J. Steinhausen, "Hieronymus und Laktanz in Trier," *TZ* 20 (1951): 126–54.

BOOK TWO

3.10. *All who rely on keeping the Law are under a curse, for it is written: "Cursed is everyone who does not continue in all of the things written in the book of the Law and do them."*[35]

Whenever the apostles quote from the Old Testament, it is my custom to revert to the sources of these quotations and to scrutinize the quotations in their original context. I have found that this verse from Deuteronomy is rendered by the translators of the Septuagint as, "Cursed is everyone who does not continue in all of the words of this law and do them; and all the people will say, 'Let it be done!'" In Aquila's[36] translation it reads, "Cursed is he who does not uphold the words of this law and do them; and all the people will say, 'Truly!'" In Symmachus's[37] version we read, "Cursed is he who does not make strong the words of this law and do them; and all the people will say, 'Amen!'" Furthermore, Theodotion[38] translated as follows: "Cursed is he who does not lift up the words of this law and do them; and all the people will say, 'Amen!'"

From the above we infer that the Apostle, here as on other occasions, has captured the sense of a passage rather than its mere words. We do not know for certain whether the Seventy added "everyone" and "in all" or whether these words had been present in the original Hebrew text but later excised by the Jews. I am inclined to believe that the Apostle, a man of Hebrew learning and exceptionally well-versed in the Law, would never

35. Dt 27.26.

36. Aquila, a native of Sinope in Pontus, was a convert to Judaism in the second century AD. Around 130 he produced an extremely literal Greek translation of the Hebrew OT.

37. Symmachus, a prominent member of the Ebionite sect, translated the Hebrew Bible into Greek in the late second century AD.

38. The Hellenistic Jewish scholar Theodotion authored his Greek translation of the Hebrew OT around 180 AD. His edition is quoted in two second-century Christian works, the *Shepherd of Hermas* and Justin Martyr's *Dialogue with Trypho.* It is now generally accepted that Aquila, Symmachus, and Theodotion produced their translations to fill the void left by the Septuagint, which Hellenistic Jews rejected once the Christians adopted it as their authoritative version of the OT.

have added these words, as if they were necessary to prove that all who rely on keeping the Law are under a curse, unless they were in the Hebrew manuscripts. This led me to read through the Hebrew manuscripts of the Samaritans. I found the word *chol*, which means "everyone" or "in all" and agrees with the Septuagint translators. The Jews expunged these words to avoid looking as if they were under a curse for failing to comply with everything that is written. Their efforts, however, were in vain, for the ancient literature of another nation testifies that these words had originally been present.

Paul confirms elsewhere that no one is able to fulfill the Law and comply with everything that is commanded. "For what the Law was powerless to do in that it was weakened by the flesh, God did by sending his own Son in the likeness of sinful flesh and condemned sin in the flesh."[39] If this is true, an objection can be raised: Are Moses, Isaiah, and the rest of the prophets under a curse because they relied on keeping the Law? One will not be afraid of agreeing with this sentiment if he reads the words of the Apostle: "Christ redeemed us from the curse of the Law by becoming a curse for us,"[40] and maintains that each and every one of the saints in the Old Testament became a curse for the people in his lifetime. By according righteous men this [honor], he will not appear to take anything away from the Savior (as if the one who became a curse for us were not an exceptional case), inasmuch as they became a curse for others. For no matter how great a curse each one became, not one of them freed anyone from a curse; only the Lord Jesus Christ did. With his precious blood[41] he redeemed all of us and them (that is, Moses, Aaron, and all of the prophets and patriarchs) from the curse of the Law. Do not imagine that I have concocted this idea on my own. Scripture testifies that Christ is the grace of God,[42] or, as it is worded in some manuscripts, "he died for all"[43] except God. Moreover, he died for all—for Moses and every one of the prophets, none of whom was able either to erase the old code of the Law which had been written against us or to

---

39. Rom 8.3.
41. Cf. 1 Pt 1.18–19.
43. 2 Cor 5.15.

40. Gal 3.13.
42. Cf. Rom 5.15.

nail it to a cross.[44] "All have sinned and fall short of the glory of God."[45] Ecclesiastes supports this notion, "There is not a righteous man on earth who does good and does not sin."[46] Finally, what the Apostle says below shows unambiguously that neither Moses nor any man from ancient times could be justified before God through the Law. Paul continues:

3.11–12. *It is clear that no one is justified before God by the Law because, "The righteous man lives by faith."*[47] *The Law is not based on faith; to the contrary, "The man who does these things will live by them."*[48]

Paul has taken from the prophet Habakkuk an example to prove that the righteous man lives by faith and not by works. The Septuagint translators rendered the phrase as, "The righteous man lives by faith in me." Aquila and Theodotion translated it as, "The righteous man lives by faith in him," that is, in God. We should note that he did not say that just any man lives by faith, lest he provide an excuse for the devaluation of virtuous deeds. Rather, he said that the righteous man lives by faith. This means that before having faith and the intention to live by it, one must already be righteous and must by the purity of his life have climbed certain steps that lead to faith. It is therefore possible for someone to be righteous without yet living by faith in Christ. If this is troublesome to the reader, let him consider what Paul said about himself: "As for righteousness according to the Law, I was faultless."[49] At the time, Paul was righteous in terms of keeping the Law, but he was not yet able to live [by faith] because he did not have Christ in him saying, "I am the Life,"[50] for he subsequently believed in Christ and began to live [by faith]. Let us formulate similar variations on the phrase "The righteous man lives by faith." The chaste man lives by faith; the wise man lives by faith; the courageous man lives by faith. Let us apply a similar principle with respect to the rest of the virtues to show unbelievers who reckon themselves to be courageous, wise, temperate, or righteous, that no one lives

44. Cf. Col 2.14.
46. Eccl 7.21.
48. Lv 18.5.
50. Jn 11.25.

45. Rom 3.23.
47. Hab 2.4.
49. Phil 3.6.

without Christ and that without him every virtue is like vice.[51]

The verse in question can also be taken in such a way that "[he] lives" is inferred from the phrase "because the righteous man by faith." But by saying, "The Law is not based on faith; to the contrary, 'The man who does these things will live by them,'" he is very clearly not referring to life in general but to the life which has a specific goal: The righteous man lives by faith ("by these or those things" is not added). He who does these things while living by the Law will live by them, that is, by the things he has done which he has regarded as good. For his hard work, he has as recompense only what he has accomplished, be it a long life (as the Jews think) or an evasion of the punishment by which the transgressor of the Law is put to death.

But let us not mistake the words "live by them" for being the Apostle's. They are the prophet Ezekiel's, who said, "I brought them into the wilderness and gave them my commandments and made known to them my ordinances, which if a man shall do, he shall also live by them."[52] After saying that they would live if they walked in the commandments and ordinances, he added, "I gave them commandments that were not good and ordinances in which they shall not live."[53] How carefully these words are weighed! When he said, "I gave them commandments and ordinances" in which they should live, he did not add the word "good." When he wrote, "In which they shall not live," he also said, "I gave them commandments that were not good and ordi-

51. Jerome seems to take a harder line than Origen does in *Comm. Rom.* 2.7.6 (trans. Scheck, FOTC 103:125–26): "But also a Greek, i.e., a Gentile, who, though he does not have the Law, is a law to himself, showing the work of the Law in his heart and moved by natural reason, as we see is the case in not a few Gentiles, might hold fast to justice or observe chastity or maintain wisdom, moderation, and modesty. I grant that such a man might seem a stranger to eternal life, since he has not believed in Christ, and cannot enter into the kingdom of heaven, for he has not been born again of water and the Spirit. Nevertheless it seems that from what the Apostle has said here, he cannot completely lose the glory of the good works he has accomplished. . . . I do not think it can be doubted that the one who had merited condemnation on account of his evil works will be considered worthy of remuneration for his good works, if he indeed had performed good works."

52. Ezek 20.10–11 (LXX).

53. Ezek 20.25 (LXX).

nances in which they shall not live." Be that as it may, these matters pertain more to Ezekiel. For now let us return to the ordering of the epistle [to the Galatians].

3.13a. *Christ redeemed us from the curse of the Law by becoming a curse for us.*

Marcion creeps up here with his talk about the sovereignty of the Creator, whom he maligns as a cruel, bloodthirsty judge, and with his claim that we have been redeemed by Christ, the son of the other, good God. Had he understood the difference in meaning between "procure" (*emere*) and "redeem" (*redimere*)—that is, the procurer gets something that does not belong to him and the redeemer gets back what once was his—he would never have twisted the plain words of Scripture in such a way as to condemn his own teaching.

Christ redeemed us from the curse of the Law. This was a curse put in place for sinners, whom [Christ] censures through the prophet: "Because of your sins you were sold, and because of your transgressions I sent away your mother."[54] The Apostle echoes this sentiment: "I am unspiritual, sold as a slave to sin."[55] The curses of the Law set down in Leviticus and Deuteronomy are not brought to pass by God, as if he were the author of them. Rather, future outcomes are announced prophetically to those who will commit sin. Now if [Marcion] wanted to bind us by the testimony of the Apostle who says, "All who rely on keeping the Law are under a curse, for it is written, 'Cursed is everyone who does not continue in all of the things written in the book of the Law and do them,'"[56] and if he wanted to assert that everyone under the Law had been cursed, let us ask him whether or not those who are under the Gospel of Christ but do not keep his commandments are cursed. If he answers that they are cursed, he will encounter the same curse in the Gospel that we face in the Law. If he denies that they are cursed, then the precepts of the Gospel have been given in vain and those who have kept them will be without a reward. Both issues are resolved in

54. Is 50.1.   55. Rom 7.14.
56. Gal 3.10.

this way: Christ Jesus, by becoming a curse for us, has freed us not only from the curse of the Law but also from the curse of the Gospel which has been put in place for those who do not keep his commandments. For he knows not to take away the smallest portion of a talent and to exact the very last quarter as payment.

3.13b–14. *For it is written, "Cursed is everyone who is hung on a tree."*[57] *He redeemed us in order that the blessing given to Abraham might come to the Gentiles through Christ Jesus, so that by faith we might receive the promise of the Spirit.*

Before we delve into the meaning of the Apostle's words, it seems appropriate to go over the passage in Deuteronomy from which he extracted this versicle and to examine its wording in the various translations [of the Old Testament]. The Septuagint translators rendered it: "If there is sin in anyone and the judgment of death is upon him, and he is put to death and you hang him on a tree, do not let his body rest on the tree all night, but bury him on that very day. For everyone who is hung on a tree is cursed by God. And do not defile your land which the Lord your God will give you as an inheritance."[58] This is what Aquila has: "When there is sin in a man and the judgment of death is upon him, and he is killed and you hang him on a tree, do not let his dead body remain on the tree, but bury him on that very day. For he who has been hung on a tree is a curse in the eyes of God. And do not defile your land which the Lord your God will give to you as an inheritance." Symmachus translates as follows: "If a man has sin that leads to a judgment of death, and he is killed and you hang him on a tree, do not let his corpse stay on the tree for the night, but bury him on that very day. For he has been hung for committing blasphemy against God. And do not defile your land which the Lord your God will give to you as an inheritance." [Finally,] Theodotion renders the passage: "Because sin is in a man, and the judgment of death is upon him, he will die, and then hang him on a tree; do not let his dead body rest on the tree, because you must bury him on that

57. Dt 21.23.
58. Dt 21.22–23 (LXX).

very day, for he who has been hung is a curse in the eyes of God. And do not defile your ground (*adama*) which the Lord your God will give to you as an inheritance."

In Hebrew, *adama* means either land or earth. Where Aquila and Theodotion produce a similar translation: "For he who has been hung is a curse in the eyes of God," the Hebrew has *chi klalat eloim talui* ["For he who is hanged is cursed by God"]. The half-Christian, half-Jewish heresiarch Ebion took it as, ὅτι ὕβρις θεοῦ κρεμάμενος, that is, "He was hung for being an outrage to God." I recall reading in the Greek *Debate between Jason and Papiscus*[59] the words λοιδορία θεοῦ ὁ κρεμάμενος, which mean, "The one who is hanged is a curse in the eyes of God." A Jew who gave me some instruction in Scripture[60] told me that the phrase could even be construed as, "Because God was hanged in a disgraceful manner."

I have compiled all of these data because a notorious issue is at stake. The Jews, intent upon bringing dishonor on our religion, [are fond of alleging] that our Lord and Savior was under the curse of God.[61] First of all, we must realize that not everyone who hangs on a tree is cursed before God. The one who

59. This second-century work, which survives only in a few fragments, purported to be a transcript of a debate at Alexandria between a Jewish Christian (Jason) and a Jew (Papiscus) about whether Jesus is the Messiah prophesied in the OT; it ends with Papiscus becoming a Christian. The authorship of the *Debate* is traditionally ascribed to Aristo of Pella (fl. c. 150): see most recently S. Borzì, "Sull'attribuzione della Disputa fra Giasone e Papisco ad Aristone di Pella," *VetChr* 41 (2004): 347–54. As he indicates above, Jerome knew this writing firsthand: see P. Courcelle, *Les lettres grecques en Occident de Macrobe à Cassiodore* (Paris: E. de Boccard, 1948), 87–88.

60. The private instruction in Hebrew philology and exegesis Jerome received from contemporary Jews is discussed by Gustave Bardy in "Saint Jérôme et ses maîtres hébreux," *RBén* 46 (1934): 145–64, and also by Ilona Opelt in "S. Girolamo ed i suoi maestri ebrei," *Augustinianum* 28 (1988): 327–38.

61. Prior to his conversion, Paul believed that Christ had been justly executed as a criminal, though he does not specify in his epistles the crimes of which he believed Christ to have been guilty. After his conversion, he came to believe that Christ had been innocent but put to death for humanity's misdeeds. See P. Borgen, "Crucified for his own Sins—Crucified for our Sins: Observations on a Pauline Perspective," in *The New Testament and Early Christian Literature in Greco-Roman Context: Studies in Honor of David E. Aune*, ed. J. Fotopoulos (Leiden: E. J. Brill, 2006), 17–35.

sins and is condemned to death and is raised up on a cross because of a crime *is* cursed before God. One is not cursed, then, because he was crucified but rather because he was convicted of an offense grave enough to warrant crucifixion. Secondly, we should point out that at the end of the above-quoted passage from Deuteronomy the reason for the suffering is explained. Scripture reveals that the man was crucified for cursing and blaspheming God. Symmachus translated this more clearly, "He was hung [on a tree] for blaspheming God."

Finally, let us issue a challenge to [our Jewish] critics. If Ananias, Azarias, and Misael had been hung on a tree for refusing to worship the statue in Nebuchadnezzar's likeness,[62] and if the nonagenarian Eleazar and the seven Maccabean brothers along with their glorious mother [had met with the same fate] during the reign of Antiochus the king of Syria, would they deem them cursed or very worthy of being blessed?[63] To be sure, if Haman had not climbed the gallows (and deservedly so) which he had prepared for Mordecai, I reckon that Mordecai would have climbed them as a holy rather than cursed man.[64] These and similar examples confirm that the perpetrator of a crime deserving of crucifixion is cursed, but not a man who is crucified because of the inequity of judges, the influence of his enemies, the outcry of the masses, envy for his virtues, or the anger of a king. Long ago the entire city of Jezreel, in obedience to the orders Jezebel sent them by letter, murdered Naboth.[65] But many centuries later, Naboth's blood was avenged, being as it was a symbol for Christ. The Lord says to Hosea in condemnation of the Jews, "Call him Jezreel, because I will soon punish the house of Jehu for the massacre at Jezreel."[66]

But to bring the discussion back to us [Christians], I cannot ascertain why the Apostle either added to or took away from the statement, "Everyone who hangs on a tree is cursed by God." For if he was exclusively following the authority of the Septuagint translators, he was obligated to insert the phrase "by God," just as they had done. But if, as a Jew among Jews, he thought that what

62. Cf. Dn 3.16–18.
63. Cf. 2 Mc 6.18–31.
64. Cf. Est 7.9–10.
65. Cf. 1 Kgs 21.8–22.
66. Hos 1.4.

he had read in his own language was the closest to the truth, he had to omit both "everyone" and "on a tree," which are not found in the Hebrew original. This leads me to believe either that the ancient manuscripts of the Jews contained a different reading than they do now, or that the Apostle (as I said above) captured the sense rather than literal meaning of Scripture. It is more plausible that after Christ had suffered on the cross, someone added "by God" to both the Hebrew manuscripts and our own so as to shame us for believing in Christ, who [according to this reading] was cursed by God. I enter fearlessly into this fray so that I may call people's attention to the text and to the fact that it is nowhere written that anyone was cursed by God.

Wherever the word "curse" occurs, the word "God" is never found in juxtaposition. The Lord said to the serpent, "You are cursed above all animals."[67] He said to Adam, "The ground is cursed because of your deeds."[68] He said to Cain, "You are cursed from the earth."[69] And, "Cursed be Canaan; he will be a slave to his brothers."[70] In another place, "Cursed be their anger because it is fierce, and cursed be their wrath because it is cruel."[71] It would be tedious to list all of the curses found in Leviticus, Deuteronomy, and Joshua. And yet no mention of God is made in connection with any of them. Even when Satan promised that Job would blaspheme God under duress, he did not use explicitly imprecatory language: "And see if he does not bless you to your face."[72] Additionally, in the Books of Kingdoms Naboth is said to have been stoned because he blessed God and the king.[73]

Moreover, nobody should be disturbed by the idea that Christ became a curse for us, seeing that God himself, who Scripture says made him a curse, made Christ to be sin for us even though he had no sin.[74] The Savior emptied himself of the Father's fullness and assumed the form of a servant.[75] Life succumbed to death, and the wisdom of God was called madness so that the foolishness of God might become wiser than men.[76] In the

67. Gn 3.14.
68. Gn 3.17.
69. Gn 4.11.
70. Gn 9.25 (LXX).
71. Gn 49.7.
72. Jb 1.11.
73. Cf. 1 Kgs 21.13.
74. Cf. 2 Cor 5.21.
75. Cf. Phil 2.7.
76. Cf. 1 Cor 1.25.

sixty-eighth Psalm he speaks of himself: "You know my folly, God, and my transgressions are not hidden from you."[77] An insult to the Lord is therefore a reason for us to boast. He died so that we might live. He descended into Hades so that we might rise to heaven. He became foolish so that we might become wise. He emptied himself of the fullness and form of God and assumed the form of a servant so that the fullness of divinity might dwell in us[78] and so that we might go from being servants to masters.[79] He hung on a tree so that by means of a tree he might erase the sin we had committed through the tree of the knowledge of good and evil.[80] His cross made bitter waters sweet,[81] and, when cast into the waves of the Jordan River, it caused the axhead that had been lost and submerged under water to float.[82]

One final comment is in order about Christ being made a curse. I maintain that he became a curse but was not born one. This means that the blessings promised to Abraham were redirected to the Gentiles on his authority and initiative and that the promise of the Holy Spirit through faith in him would be fulfilled in us. We must understand this as a twofold reference to either the spiritual gifts of virtues[83] or the spiritual understanding of Scripture.[84]

3.15–18. *Brothers, I speak in the manner of men. No one can set aside or add to a human covenant that has been duly established. The promises were spoken to Abraham and to his seed. [Scripture] does not say "and to seeds," meaning many people, but "and to your seed," meaning one person, namely, Christ. What I mean is that the Law, introduced four hundred thirty years later, does not do away with the covenant previously established by God and thus do away with the promise. For if the inheritance depends on the Law, then it no longer depends on a promise. God, however, gave it to Abraham through a promise.*

The Apostle became all things to all people in order to win them for Christ.[85] He had a responsibility to Greeks and barbar-

77. Ps 69.5.
78. Cf. Col 2.9–10.
79. Cf. Jn 15.14–15.
80. Cf. Gn 2.9,17; 3.11.
81. Cf. Ex 15.22–25.
82. Cf. 2 Kgs 6.1–6.
83. Cf. 1 Cor 12.7–11.
84. Cf. Col 1.9.
85. Cf. 1 Cor 9.22.

ians and to the wise and fool alike[86] and became a fool also for
the sake of the Galatians, whom a little earlier he had called
fools.[87] For he did not use the same arguments with them as
he did with the Romans, but simpler ones that both fools and
common folk on the street could understand. To show that he
did so deliberately and not haphazardly, he first assuages the
enlightened reader and tempers what he is about to say with
a prefatory remark: "Brothers, I speak in the manner of men."
What I am about to say, I say not in the manner of God, nor
of recondite wisdom, nor of those who can eat solid food, but
I speak in the manner of those who feed on milk because of
their delicate stomachs[88] and who are wholly incapable of com-
prehending deeper matters. Hence to the Corinthians—among
whom there was a rumored incidence of fornication unheard
of even among the heathens—Paul writes, "It is I who speak,
not the Lord."[89] In his second letter to the same [Christians]
he says, "What I say, I say not as the Lord would but as a fool."[90]

Some think that Paul said, "Brothers, I speak in the manner
of men," because he is about to discuss a human covenant, the
death of a testator, and other examples taken from the human
sphere. This is certainly the case, but he said this also because
of what follows: "[Scripture] does not say 'and to seeds,' meaning many people, but 'and to your seed,' meaning one person,
namely, Christ." Traversing the entire Bible in my thought and
my memory, I have never come upon the word "seed" in the
plural, but only in the singular, used in either a good sense or
a bad. As for his statement, "What I mean is the covenant established by God," if anyone carefully compares the Hebrew
manuscripts and other editions with the rendering done by the
Septuagint translators, he will find that wherever *testamentum* is
written, what is meant is not "testament" but "agreement" [or
"covenant": Lat., *pactum*], which is equivalent to the Hebrew
berith. It is thus clear that the Apostle has done as he promised,
that is, he has not used deeper meanings in addressing the Galatians, but everyday ones and even trivial ones which might

86. Cf. Rom 1.14.   87. Gal 3.3.
88. Cf. 1 Cor 3.1–2.   89. 1 Cor 7.12.
90. 2 Cor 11.17.

have displeased the erudite if he had not said first, "I speak in the manner of men."

At this point we should count up the number of years that elapsed between the Lord saying to Abraham, "All the nations of the earth will be blessed through your seed,"[91] and Moses' giving of the Law. Then let us determine whether that number comes to four hundred thirty, and also how in Genesis the Lord promises Abraham that after four hundred years his descendants will leave the land of captivity.[92] This is an important issue over which many have puzzled, and I am not aware of anyone having settled it. What we read about Tamar and her two newborn sons in Genesis—that the first, Zerah, stuck out his hand and the midwife tied a scarlet thread on it, and then, when he pulled it back, the second one, Perez, extended his hand[93]—is applicable here. For it illustrates how Israel, by keeping the Law, pulled back its hand sullied with the blood of the prophets and of the Savior himself, and how the Gentiles then emerged, on account of whom the barrier and the wall that had separated the Jews and them were torn down and destroyed,[94] so that there could be one flock and one shepherd,[95] and glory, honor, and peace to everyone who does good, first to the Jew and then to the Greek.[96]

The literal sense put together in this passage is this: The Apostle shows that the promises previously made to Abraham cannot be nullified by the Law, which was given afterward, and that what comes later is prejudged by what came before it, inasmuch as the promises to Abraham that all nations would be blessed through him had been given four hundred thirty years earlier, whereas four hundred thirty years later the Law, by which he will live who observes it, was given to Moses on Mount Sinai. An objection could be registered here: Why was it necessary for the Law to be given so long after the promise, seeing that its introduction might cause suspicion that the promise became obsolete and that as long as the promise was in effect, the Law would offer no benefit? The Apostle anticipates this question, poses it to himself, and then answers it in the verses that follow:

---

91. Gn 22.18.
93. Cf. Gn 38.27–30.
95. Cf. Jn 10.16.

92. Cf. Gn 15.13.
94. Cf. Eph 2.14.
96. Cf. Rom 2.10.

3.19–20. What, then? The Law was put in place because of transgressions until the seed to whom the promise referred had come. It was set up through angels by the hand of a mediator. A mediator, however, does not represent just one party; but God is one.

Since it seemed that the Law given later through Moses had been imposed in vain as long as the promise made to Abraham was still in effect, Paul explains that it had been given "because of transgressions." For it was after the offense of the people in the wilderness[97] and after their adoration of the calf[98] and grumbling against the Lord that the Law came to forbid transgressions. "The Law was put in place not for the righteous but for lawbreakers and rebels, the ungodly and sinful."[99] Furthermore, after their idolatry, to which they had been so enslaved in Egypt that they forgot the God of their fathers and would say, "These are your Gods, Israel, who brought you out of the land of Egypt,"[100] rituals prescribing how properly to worship God and to punish wrongdoers were instituted through the hand of the mediator, Christ Jesus.[101] For "all things were made through him, and without him nothing was made"[102]—this goes not only for heaven, earth, the sea, and everything we see, but also for the provisions of the Law that were imposed as a yoke by Moses on a stiff-necked people. Also, Paul wrote to Timothy, "For there is one God, and one mediator between God and men, the man Christ Jesus."[103] After he deigned to be born from the womb of the Virgin for the sake of our salvation, the man Christ Jesus was called the broker between God and men. But before he took on a human body, when he was with the Father in the beginning as God[104] and was the Word to all the holy people (such as Enoch, Noah, Abraham, Isaac, Jacob, Moses, and all the prophets whom Scripture mentions), he served as God's

97. Cf. Ex 17.1–7.   98. Cf. Ex 32.5–6.
99. 1 Tm 1.9.   100. Ex 32.4.
101. Jerome and other ancient commentators (e.g., Origen and Augustine) who applied a systematic Christological reading to the OT thought that Paul's mediator was Christ. The majority of modern commentators, however, identify this mediator as Moses.
102. Jn 1.3.   103. 1 Tm 2.5.
104. Cf. Jn 1.1–2.

mouthpiece to them and was only called a mediator although he had not yet assumed human nature.[105]

This is what he means by the Law being set up through angels: Wherever in the Old Testament it is initially reported that an angel has appeared and later it is inferred that God is the one speaking, the angel who appears is one of a multitude of ministers, but the mediator [that is, Christ] speaks in him and says, "I am the God of Abraham, the God of Isaac, and the God of Jacob."[106] It is no wonder that God speaks in angels, seeing that he speaks through the angels who are in men, that is, in the prophets. Haggai[107] says, "The angel who spoke in me said,"[108] and later he adds, "Thus says the Lord Almighty."[109] The angel said to be in the prophet did not dare to say on his own behalf, "Thus says the Lord Almighty." We must understand the "hand of the mediator" as the strength and power of him who by virtue of his deity is one with the Father but by virtue of his mediatorial duties is someone other than he.

Since the word order is jumbled and its flow is disrupted by hyperbaton,[110] we should restructure the passage as follows: "The Law was set up through angels by a mediator and put in place through angels because of transgressions until the seed to whom the promise referred had come." The "seed" undoubtedly signi-

---

105. Cf. Origen, *Comm. Gal.* 3.19, preserved by Pamphilus in *Apol. pro Orig.* 120: "The Law was given to Moses by angels through the hand and power of Christ the mediator, who, although 'he was the Word of God in the beginning and was with God and was God' [Jn 1.1], did the Father's bidding in all things. For 'all things were made through him' [Jn 1.3]; that is to say, not only creatures but also the Law and the prophets, and the Word himself is the 'mediator between God and men' [1 Tm 2.5]. At the conclusion of the ages this Word became man, Jesus Christ. But before this coming in the flesh had been made manifest, he was indeed the mediator of everything, though he was not yet a man" (translated from Rufinus's Latin [SC 464:194–96]).

106. Ex 3.6.

107. Jerome ascribes the first of these verses to Haggai when it in fact belongs to Zechariah. Such misattributions are few and far between in the *Commentary on Galatians*, evidence of Jerome's extraordinary memory and command of the Bible.

108. Zec 1.14.

109. Hg 2.12.

110. See p. 72 n. 77 in Book 1, above.

fies Christ, whom the prologue to Matthew's Gospel verifies to be the son of Abraham: "A record of the genealogy of Jesus Christ the son of David, the son of Abraham."[111]

3.21–23. Is the Law therefore opposed to the promises of God? Absolutely not! For if the Law had been given that could impart life, then righteousness would certainly have come by the Law. But Scripture declares that the whole world is a prisoner of sin, so that what was promised, being given through faith in Jesus Christ, might be given to those who believe. But before this faith came, we were held prisoners by the Law, locked up until the faith should be revealed.

Just as the mediator between God and men interceded between the giver and receiver of the Law, so also did the Law itself, which was given after the promise had been made, insert itself as the intermediary between the promise and its fulfillment. We should not imagine that the Law nullifies the promise because it appeared after the promise and seemed to abolish what came before. Rather, because the Law could not impart life or accomplish what the initial promise offered, it clearly was given in order to preserve the promise, not to subvert it. For if the Law had been given to bring life and deliver what the promise had vowed, the promise would be reckoned void on account of the Law. But now the Law rebukes sinners even more, for, as I said above, it was put in place because of transgressions. It was given to them after the promise as a protector and as a prison, so to speak, so that the blameless, because they had been unwilling to await the promise through the use of their free-will, might be bound by the chains of the Law and be forced to obey its commandments and thus be safeguarded until faith in Christ arrived to bring closure to the promise.

We should not surmise that Scripture is the author of sin because it states that the whole world is a prisoner of sin. It conveys the commandments prescribed by the Law and condemns sin but it is not the cause of sin any more than a judge is the author of a crime for subduing malefactors. The judge imprisons them and by his legal authority pronounces them to be danger-

111. Mt 1.1.

ous, but he leaves open the option of showing mercy and absolving the guilty from their initial punishment, if he so desires.

3.24–26. Therefore, the Law was our pedagogue [to bring us] to Christ Jesus, so that we might be justified by faith. But after faith has come, we are no longer under a pedagogue. For all of you are children of God through faith in Christ Jesus.

A pedagogue is assigned to the very young to restrain their lascivious nature and to hold in check, by fear of punishment, their vice-prone hearts while they are guided in their studies during their tender years and readied for learning the more advanced disciplines of philosophy and civic leadership. Nevertheless, a pedagogue is not a teacher or father, and the child does not expect to receive either an inheritance or knowledge from him. He takes care of another person's son and will leave his side once the child reaches the age at which he can legally collect his inheritance.[112] Furthermore, the meaning of the word "pedagogue" is self-evident: one who leads or guides children. Moses, acting as a kind of harsh pedagogue, gave the Law to a lascivious people to keep watch over them and prepare them for the faith that was to come. Now that this faith has come and we have believed in Christ, we are no longer under a pedagogue. Our tutor and overseer has left us, and now that we have reached the legal age of adulthood, we are truly called sons of God. It is not the abolished Law that gives birth to us but our mother, the faith which is in Christ Jesus.

If anyone has reached the age of maturity at which he is called an heir, a free man, and a son, but still wishes to be under the care of a pedagogue, he should realize that he cannot live by the same rules as the very young do. Since Jerusalem has been overthrown and the Temple reduced to rubble, where can one comply with the injunction, "Three times a year every male among you is to appear before the Lord your God"?[113] Where can one

112. The pedagogue was usually a slave in charge of escorting the master's children to school and watching over them when they were at home. He was expected to be a strict disciplinarian and had the authority to punish them if they misbehaved.

113. Ex 23.17.

make atonement sacrifices for sin? Now that the altar has been completely destroyed, where is the eternal fire of whole burnt offerings that resembles the stars in the heavens?[114] While the Jews remain subservient and the Romans in power, what punishment can be meted out to the wayward, as Scripture says, "Purge the evil from your midst"?[115] And so, as long as the Law is impossible to fulfill once faith has superseded it, and as long as a person looks to the Law as his pedagogue but has no faith, he will live under the care of neither a father nor a pedagogue.

3.27–28. *For all of you who were baptized into Christ have clothed yourselves with Christ. There is neither Jew nor Greek, slave nor free, male nor female, for you are all one in Christ Jesus.*

When he says, "For all of you who were baptized into Christ have clothed yourselves with Christ," Paul shows how we are born "children of God through faith in Christ Jesus."[116] The idea that Christ is [metaphorical] clothing[117] is confirmed not only by the present passage but also by another, in which the same Paul exhorts, "Clothe yourselves with the Lord Jesus Christ."[118] If those who were baptized into Christ clothed themselves with him, it is clear that those who did not clothe themselves with Christ had not been baptized into him. To those who are reckoned to be faithful and to have embraced the baptism of Christ it was said, "Clothe yourselves with the Lord Jesus Christ." If anyone has received only the bodily baptism of water that is visible to fleshly eyes, he has not clothed himself with the Lord Jesus Christ. For Simon [the magician] in the Acts of the Apostles had received the baptism of water, yet he had not clothed himself with Christ because he did not have the Holy Spirit.[119] Fur-

114. Cf. Origen, *Hom. Jos.* 17.1 (trans. Bruce, FOTC 105:157–58).

115. Dt 13.5.

116. Gal 3.26.

117. For the Greco-Roman and Jewish roots of this metaphor of putting on and taking off identities, see N. Alstrup Dahl and D. Hellholm, "Garment-Metaphors: the Old and New Human Being," in *Antiquity and Humanity: Essays on Ancient Religion and Philosophy*, ed. A. Yarbro Collins and M. M. Mitchell (Tübingen: Mohr Siebeck, 2001), 139–58.

118. Rom 13.14.

119. Cf. Acts 8.9–24.

thermore, the heretics, hypocrites, and those who lead morally reprehensible lives appear on the surface to receive baptism, but I do not know if they have the clothing of Christ. Therefore, let us take heed lest by chance someone among us be taken by surprise and rebuked for not having been baptized into Christ because he does not have the clothing of Christ.

When someone definitely clothes himself with Christ and is cast into the flame and glimmers with the intense brightness of the Holy Spirit, it is impossible to tell whether he is gold or silver. As long as the lump of material is surrounded by heat, it has a uniform fiery color, and all diversity of its nature, condition, and physical properties is taken away by this cloak [of fire]. "For there is neither Jew nor Greek." In place of "Greek" we must understand "Gentile," for the word Ἕλλην signifies both "Greek" and "heathen." The Jew is not superior because he is circumcised, nor is the Gentile inferior because he is uncircumcised. Rather, the Jew or Gentile is superior or inferior depending on the quality of his faith. Also, slaves and free men are distinguished by faith and not by social standing, for the slave is able to be superior to the free man, and the latter is able to surpass the former in the quality of his faith. Likewise, men and women are distinguished by their bodily strength and weakness, but faith is measured by devotion of the mind, and it often happens that a woman becomes the reason a man is saved and that a man precedes a woman in matters of religion.

Since this is how things go and since being baptized in Christ and putting him on as a garment take away all diversity of [our] nature, condition, and physical properties, we are all one in Christ Jesus, so that just as the Father and the Son are one with each other, so are we one in them.

3.29. *If you belong to Christ, then you are Abraham's seed and heirs according to the promise.*

The promises were made to Abraham and his seed (that is, Christ Jesus), and so it follows that the children of Christ, who are his seed, are also said to be the seed of Abraham; they are the seed from his seed. Whenever our Lord Jesus is called the seed of Abraham, it is to be understood in a physical sense, that

he is born from his stock. And whenever we receive the word of
the Savior, believe in him, and countenance the nobility of the
race of Abraham, to whom the promise was made, we must accept spiritually the seed of faith and the seed of the [Gospel]
message.

Next we should note how Paul uses the plural "promises"
when he says of the Lord, "The promises were spoken to Abraham and to his seed,"[120] that is, to Christ Jesus. But when he
speaks of those who are the seed of Abraham through Christ,
he uses the singular "promise," as he does in the present verse:
"Then you are Abraham's seed and heirs according to the
promise." It was appropriate that what was expressed in the plural with reference to the one Christ might be expressed in the
singular with reference to many people. Paul continues:

4.1–2. *What I am saying is that as long as the heir is a child, he is no
different from a slave, although he is the master in charge of everything.
He is subject to guardians and trustees until the time set by his father.*

The child-heir described above symbolizes the entire human race, and the pre-appointed time stands for the coming of
Christ or, to speak more broadly, the end of the world. For just
as all not yet born die in the first man Adam, so are all made
alive in the second Adam, even if they had been born prior to
Christ's coming.[121] And so it is that we obeyed the Law in the fathers and are saved by grace in the sons. This way of thinking is
agreeable to the universal church, which maintains that one divine plan unites the Old and New Testaments and does not distinguish in time those whom it binds together by condition. We
have all been built upon the foundation of the prophets and
apostles and are stabilized by the cornerstone, our Lord Jesus
Christ.[122] He has made the two one, he has destroyed in his own
flesh the dividing wall of hostility between Jews and Gentiles,[123]
and he has replaced the difficulty in keeping the old Law with
the purity of the Gospel teachings. In Christ we truly are all
one bread,[124] and as two we have agreed on something on earth

120. Gal 3.16.   121. 1 Cor 15.22.
122. Cf. Eph 2.20.   123. Cf. Eph 2.14.
124. Cf. 1 Cor 10.17.

[and so it will be granted us by our Father in heaven].¹²⁵ Just as we are built upon the foundation of the prophets, so also the patriarchs stood on the foundation of the apostles.

The "guardians" and "trustees" can be taken as the prophets, by whose words we used to be alerted daily to the coming of the Savior, just as the Law of Moses is described above as a pedagogue and as the guardian angels of children who daily see the Father's face¹²⁶ and intercede on their behalf. Scripture speaks of them: "The angel of the Lord will encamp around those who fear him and will deliver them."¹²⁷ Those who have the spirit of fear and are not yet worthy to receive the spirit of freedom and adoption¹²⁸ are rightly said to be subject to guardians and trustees. For the age of infancy is afraid of making mistakes; it fears the pedagogue and does not trust in its own freedom, even if it is a master by nature. And according to the twofold understanding that equates guardians and trustees with prophets or angels, the child is subject to trustees and guardians until he reaches the legally appointed time when he becomes a mature adult.¹²⁹

The legal age of adulthood, according to Roman law, comes by the age of twenty-five.¹³⁰ Similarly, the advent of Christ has reference to the maturation of the human race. As soon as Christ comes and all of us grow up to be mature adults, the pedagogue and guardian leave our side. Then we enjoy the authority of being a master and possessing an inheritance, whereas prior to this we were considered to be children of someone else.

4.3. *So also, when we were children, we were in slavery under the basic elements of the world.*

By "the basic elements of the world" Paul means the guardians and trustees about which he has just spoken. We were initially placed under the care of these overseers and were instruct-

125. Cf. Mt 18.19.　　126. Cf. Mt 18.10.
127. Ps 34.7.　　128. Cf. Rom 8.15.
129. Cf. Eph 4.13.

130. Beginning around 200 BC (with the *Lex* [*P*]*laetoria*) and continuing down to the late fourth century AD, the most fundamental age distinction in Roman law was that between *minores* and *maiores*. A minor (*minor*) was anyone under twenty-five, and an adult (*maior*) with full legal competence was anyone twenty-five or older.

ed through the world because we could not yet fathom that the
Son of God had come to us. Some are of the opinion that these
are angels who preside over the four elements of the world
(earth, water, fire, and wind) and that one must be governed
by these rulers before believing in Christ. A great many people
think that heaven, earth and the things in them are called the
elements of the world because the sages of Greece, the barbarian peoples, the Romans—the cesspool of all superstition—worship the sun, moon, seas, and the gods of the forests and mountains. When Christ came, we were freed from such superstitions
and understood that these are creatures, not divine beings.
Others interpret the basic elements of this world as the Law of
Moses and the utterances of the prophets.[131] For it is through
the Law and the prophets, which are analogous to the first les-
sons in writing, that we come to acquire a fear of God, which
is the beginning of wisdom.[132] In his letter to the Hebrews, the
Apostle addresses those who were already supposed to be [spiri-
tually] mature but who cast aside the truth and still clung to the
rudimentary principles of learning. "In fact, though by this time
you ought to be teachers, you need someone to teach you the
elementary truths of God's word all over again."[133]

Some may object that the Apostle Paul had something else
in mind when he wrote to the Colossians about the basic ele-

131. Like the ancients, modern commentators on Galatians disagree about
what these "basic elements" are. There are four main possibilities. First, they
are precursors to more advanced stages (Jerome favors the view that they are
the Law and the prophets, which paved the way for the Gospel): e.g., R. N. Longenecker, *Galatians* (Dallas: Word Books, 1990), 165–66. Second, they are the
elemental substances of which the natural world is composed, i.e., earth, wind,
fire, and water: e.g., J. Blinzler, "Lexikalisches zu dem Terminus *ta stoicheia tou
kosmou* bei Paulus," in *Studiorum Paulinorum Congressus internationalis catholicus
1961*, 2 vols. (Rome: Pontificium Institutum Biblicum, 1963), 2.429–43. Third,
they are elementary spirits associated with the physical elements: e.g., H. D.
Betz, *Galatians* (Philadelphia: Fortress Press, 1979), 205. Fourth, and somewhat
related to the third possibility, they are demonic principalities: e.g., C. E. Arnold, "Returning to the Domain of the Powers: *Stoicheia* as Evil Spirits in Galatians 4:3, 9," *NovTest* 38 (1996): 55–76; cf. Athenagoras, *Apol.* 10; Origen, *Hom.
Nm.* 14.2; *Hom. Jer.* 10.6.

132. Cf. Prv 1.7.

133. Heb 5.12.

ments of this world. He said, "Make sure that no one takes you captive through philosophy and empty deceit, which depend on human tradition and the basic elements of this world rather than on Christ."[134] By adding "which depend on human tradition" and "empty deceit," he shows that he is not talking about the same basic elements in his epistles to the Colossians and Galatians. The basic elements in the latter epistle are those from which we are freed after the fullness of time, when we progress toward greater things and are adopted as sons.[135] Nothing of this kind is said to result from the basic elements mentioned in the other epistle, where they refer to secular learning. Thus, as I have said, the Law of Moses and the prophets are comparable to the basic elements of writing, because through them syllables and names are put together. They are learned not so much for their own sake as for their utility, so that we can read a finely composed oration in which we pay more attention to the sense and the word order than the rudiments of the letters.

As for our interpretation of the Law and prophets as the basic elements of this world, "world" usually stands for the people who are in the world, as the same Paul says, "God was reconciling the world to himself in Christ,"[136] and as we read in the Gospel, "The world was made through him, but the world did not accept him."[137] Some even venture more freely into speculation, and wonder whether, given that the Law is a shadow of good things to come,[138] we were initially young children in another world about which the Savior speaks, "I am not of this world,"[139] and also made subject to the basic elements of first things, but then we progress little by little toward perfection and receive the adoption which we formerly lost.

4.4–5. *But when the fullness of time came, God sent his Son, made of a woman and put under the Law to redeem those under the Law, so that we might receive the full rights of [adopted] sons.*

Take note that he did not say "made through a woman"— phrasing opted for by Marcion and other heresies which pre-

---

134. Col 2.8.　　　　　　　　135. Cf. Gal 4.4–5.
136. 2 Cor 5.19.　　　　　　 137. Jn 1.10.
138. Cf. Heb 10.1.　　　　　 139. Jn 8.23.

tend that the flesh of Christ was imaginary—but "made of a woman,"[140] in order to support the belief that Christ was born of a woman and not through her.[141] As for his calling the holy and blessed mother of the Lord a woman instead of a virgin, this same thing is written both in the Gospel according to Matthew, where she is referred to as the wife of Joseph,[142] and [in the Gospel according to John, where] the Lord himself scolds her as a woman.[143] It was not necessary always to use the term "virgin," as if being circumspect and cautious, for the word "woman" denotes gender more than it does union with a man, and the Greek γυνή can be translated as either "wife" or "woman." But let us leave all of this aside. Just as Christ was put under the Law to redeem those under the Law, so also did he want to be born of a woman for the sake of those who had also been born of a woman. For although he was free from sin, he received the baptism of repentance in the Jordan River ostensibly to inculcate in others, who are worldly, the need to be cleansed through baptism and be born as sons by a new spiritual adoption. John the Baptist did not by any means comprehend this and he accordingly prohibited Jesus from approaching the baptismal bath, saying, "I should be baptized by you."[144] Immediately thereafter the sacrament is revealed. "Let it be so now, for it is proper for us to fulfill all righteousness,"[145] lest he who had come to save mankind should neglect human customs.

Someone might raise the following issue. If Christ was put under the Law to redeem those under the Law because he could

140. Irenaeus (*Adv. haer.* 3.22.1) quoted the verset "God sent his Son, made of a woman" when defending the full humanity of Christ against the Docetics, who believed that Christ was only God and that he passed through Mary as if through a funnel without partaking in her humanity or receiving from her a fleshly body.

141. Cf. Origen, *Comm. Gal.* 4.4, preserved by Pamphilus in *Apol. pro Orig.* 113: "We need not give a hearing to those who say that Christ was born through Mary and not of Mary, because the Apostle, in his foresight, said in anticipation of this, 'But when the fullness of time came, God sent his Son, made of a woman and put under the Law to redeem those under the Law.' You see why he did not say 'made through a woman' but rather 'made of a woman'" (translated from Rufinus's Latin [SC 464:190]).

142. Cf. Mt 1.18. 143. Cf. Jn 2.4.
144. Mt 3.14. 145. Mt 3.15.

not otherwise have redeemed them, either he was not put under it to redeem those not under the Law, or, if he was put under the Law, he did not redeem those who had not been under it, because if those without the Law could be redeemed, such that he himself would not be without the Law, it was pointless for him to be put under the Law to redeem those subject to it. This quandary can be cleared up in short order by citing the verse, "And he was numbered among those who were without the Law."[146] In the Latin manuscripts the reading "he was numbered among the transgressors" has been corrupted due to the ineptness of translators, but nevertheless we should realize that ἄνομος, which is found in the Greek manuscripts, means something different than ἄδικος, the equivalent of which is contained in the Latin manuscripts. For the person who is ἄνομος is not under the Mosaic Law and in fact is not bound by any law, while the person who is ἄδικος is a transgressor or unrighteous. Hence, the Apostle himself says elsewhere, "Although I am not free from God's Law but am under Christ's Law."[147] Indeed, ἄνομος is used in the Greek in this passage as well, and he who translated it correctly here was able to translate the same word correctly in another passage, unless the ambiguity had confused him.

Another will probe the word "redeem" and conclude that by the redeemed are meant those who initially belonged to God but ceased to be so, while those who were not under the Law were not so much redeemed as purchased. Thus, Paul wrote to the Corinthians, among whom there was reported to be sexual immorality of a kind that is unheard-of even among unbelievers,[148] "You were bought at a price"[149]—not "redeemed," for they had not been subject to the Law. We therefore receive the full rights of [adopted] sons of God. After having been redeemed by Christ, we ceased to be under slavery to the basic elements of this world and under the power of trustees. Moreover, just as we have highlighted the difference between "redeem" and "purchase," let us also consider the difference between accepting and receiving full rights as [adopted] sons.

---

146. Is 53.12; Lk 22.37.
148. Cf. 1 Cor 5.1.

147. 1 Cor 9.21.
149. 1 Cor 6.20.

4.6. *Because you are sons of God, God sent the Spirit of his Son into our hearts, the Spirit who calls out, "Abba, Father."*

Paul plainly mentions three distinct spirits: the Spirit of the Son of God, as in the present verse: "He sent the Spirit of his Son into our hearts"; the Spirit of God, as mentioned elsewhere: "As many as are led by the Spirit of God are sons of God";[150] and the Holy Spirit, as here: "Your bodies are a temple of the Holy Spirit, who is in you."[151] A passage in the Gospel manifestly proves that the Holy Spirit is different from the Son of God, "Anyone who speaks a word against the Son of Man will be forgiven, but anyone who speaks against the Holy Spirit will not be forgiven, either in this age or in the age to come."[152] Paul says this because many in their ignorance of Scripture assert that the Holy Spirit is interchangeably called the Father and the Son (Lactantius is guilty of doing this in the eighth book of his letters to Demetrianus).[153] Although we unquestionably believe in the Trinity, these people take away the Third Person and want the name to remain but not the reality behind the name. Not to belabor the point—this is, after all, a commentary and not a dialogue—but let me show briefly that three spirits are named in the fiftieth Psalm. The prophet says, "Create in me a pure heart, O God, and renew a steadfast spirit within me. Do not cast me from your presence or take your Holy Spirit from me. Restore to me the joy of your salvation and uphold me by your leading spirit."[154] He calls the Father the leading Spirit because the Son is of the Father but the Father is not of the Son. By "steadfast spirit" of truth and righteousness[155] he means Christ the Lord, for the Father has handed over all authority to judge to the Son.[156] "Bestow your authority to judge upon the king, O God, and your righteousness upon the son of the king."[157] Last-

---

150. Rom 8.14.   151. 1 Cor 6.19.
152. Mt 12.32.

153. Cf. Jerome, *Ep.* 84.7: "In his books and especially in his letters to Demetrianus, Lactantius completely denies the substance of the Holy Spirit and, following the error of the Jews, says that the passages in which he is spoken of refer to the Father or Son." This work, which Lactantius dedicated to his pupil Demetrianus (the same dedicatee of his *De opificio dei*), is now lost.

154. Ps 51.10–12.   155. Cf. Eph 4.24.
156. Cf. Jn 5.22.   157. Ps 72.1.

ly, he calls the Holy Spirit by his familiar name. Although the three spirits are differentiated from one another in name and personhood, they are united in substance and nature, and on account of their shared nature the same Spirit, without distinction, is said to belong now to the Father, now to the Son.

The argument Paul attempts to advance, that we are no longer under the Law but under the grace of the Lord Jesus, concludes as follows. Further up, he had said, "So that we might receive the full rights of [adopted] sons." Now he proves that we are sons of God from the Spirit which we have in us. For, he says, we would never dare to say, "Our Father, who are in heaven, hallowed be your name,"[158] unless we had an awareness of the Spirit dwelling in us and crying out, "Abba, Father," with a loud voice that conveys understanding and teaching (*abba* is a Hebrew word that means "father").[159] In many instances Scripture keeps to this custom of juxtaposing a Hebrew word and its definition: Bartimaeus, "son of Timaeus";[160] Asher, "riches";[161] Tabitha, "Dorcas";[162] in Genesis, Meshech, "household servant";[163] and other comparable examples.

Moreover, seeing that *abba* means "father" in Hebrew and Syriac and that in the Gospel our Lord forbids anyone except God from being called "father,"[164] I am baffled at how loosely in

158. Mt 6.9.

159. The Aramaic-Hebrew word *abba* as an address to God the Father appears three times in the New Testament. Jesus uses it in Mk 14.36 and Paul twice in his epistles, here and in Rom 8.15. There is disagreement among scholars about its precise lexical range. Some understand it as approximating the informal English "daddy," while others, such as James Barr—and Jerome—take it as a solemn, respectful address essentially equivalent to "father." See Barr, "'Abba, Father' and the Familiarity of Jesus' Speech," *ThTo* 91 (1988): 173–79; idem, "*Abba* Isn't Daddy," *JThS*, n.s., 39 (1988): 28–47. For more on this debate, see, among many other things, J. Jeremias, *Abba: Studien zur neutestamentlichen Theologie und Zeitgeschichte* (Göttingen: Vandenhoeck & Ruprecht, 1966); M. R. D'Angelo, "*Abba* and 'Father': Imperial Theology and the Jesus Traditions," *JBL* 111 (1992): 611–30; M. Gnadt, "*Abba* isn't Daddy—Aspekte einer feministische-befreiungstheologische Revision des *Abba* Jesu," in *Von der Wurzel getragen: christlich-feministische Exegese in Auseinandersetzung mit Antijudaismus,* ed. L. Schottroff and M.-T. Wacker (Leiden: E. J. Brill, 1996), 115–31.

160. Mk 10.46. 161. Gn 30.13.
162. Acts 9.36. 163. Gn 15.3.
164. Cf. Mt 23.9.

the monasteries we call others "father" or allow ourselves to be addressed as such.[165] To be sure, the same Lord who issued this prohibition forbade the swearing of oaths.[166] If we refrain from swearing, let us also not call anyone "father." If we adopt another interpretation than this one, we will be forced to think differently also about swearing.

It should be noted that in Scripture "crying out" (*clamor*) refers not to the letting out of a loud sound but to a profundity of knowledge and teaching. The Lord accordingly responded to Moses in Exodus, "Why do you cry out to me?"[167] even though Moses had not made a single sound prior to this. Indeed, in Scriptural parlance a heart that is contrite and weeps for the people is a "crying out." He who has the Spirit of the Son of God is a son of God, and vice versa, he who does not have the Spirit of the Son of God cannot be called a son of God.

4.7. *So he is no longer a slave, but a son; because he is a son, he is also an heir through God.*

Paul says: Having as you do the Spirit of the Son of God crying out in you, "Abba, Father," you have begun to be no longer slaves but sons. Although you were masters by nature, you used to be no different from slaves, yet you lived as children under the care of guardians and trustees. If you are sons, then you are owed an inheritance. Just as you became sons of God by accepting the Spirit of the Son of God, so you who have gone from slavery to freedom are heirs with the heir to the Father, Christ Jesus,[168] who speaks in the Psalm in the *persona* of the man he assumed, "The Lord said to me: 'You are my Son, today I have become your Father. Ask of me, and I will make the nations your inheritance, the ends of the earth your possession.'"[169] What we say here we should observe in other places as well, that the

---

165. In the eastern monastic communities of late antiquity, *abba* (and its Coptic equivalent *apa*) was a title of respect that disciples used for revered spiritual teachers or elders: see L. Regnault, *Abba, dis-moi une parole* (Solesmes: Abbaye St-Pierre, 1984), 7–8. For the use of this form of address in later eastern monasticism, see T. Derda and E. Wipszycka, "L'emploi des titres *abba, apa* et *papas* dans l'Église byzantine," *JJP* 24 (1994): 23–56.

166. Cf. Mt 5.34.   167. Ex 14.15.
168. Cf. Rom 8.17.   169. Ps 2.7–8.

whole human race is being treated under a single term. For all of us believers are one in Christ Jesus and members of his body. Now that we have reached maturity, we have him as our head because the head of a man is Christ.[170]

4.8–9. Formerly, when you did not know God, you were slaves to those things which by nature were not gods. But now that you know God, or rather are known by him, how is it that you are turning back to those basic elements which are weak and miserable? Do you wish to be enslaved to them all over again?

He rebukes the Galatians, whom he had converted from idol worship to faith in the true God, for abandoning their idols, which by nature were not gods, and for knowing God (or rather being known by him) and receiving the spirit of [adopted] sonship, but then desiring again to be children under the care of guardians and a pedagogue and returning to the weak and impoverished elements which had been given in the desert to a people weak and poor in understanding because they were incapable of receiving and holding on to greater things. The same elements he now calls weak and miserable are the ones that he just termed the "basic elements of this world"; the words "weak and miserable" were not added to this latter phrase. Here again, where the basic elements are called "weak," the word "world" is implicit, as I pointed out earlier. Thus, I think that as long as one is a child and has not yet reached the time decreed by the Father to be able to be called a son and heir, he is still subject to the basic principles of this world, that is, to the Mosaic Law. But if, after gaining freedom, the rights of [adopted] sonship, and the inheritance owed to a son, he regresses and wants to be circumcised as the Law prescribes and wants to embrace Jewish superstition to the letter, what had formerly been for him only the basic elements of this world are now also called weak and miserable beginnings. These elements are so worthless to their devotees that they cannot even provide the same benefit to them that they had before the Temple and altar at Jerusalem were demolished.

170. Cf. 1 Cor 11.3.

Someone may respond to this and say: If the Law and the commandments written therein are weak and miserable elements, and if those who know God (or rather are known by him) are not obligated to keep the Law—lest they begin not so much to worship God, by whom they are known, as to turn back to things which by nature are not gods—then either Moses and the prophets kept the Law and neither knew God nor were known by him, or, if they knew God, did not perfectly abide by his commandments. It is perilous to assert either one of these propositions, that they either did not act in accordance with the Law and knew God or did not know God while they kept to the weak and miserable elements of the Law. We can solve this problem by maintaining that those holy men acted in accordance with the Law, though they followed its spirit more than its letter, just as Paul became a Jew to the Jews in order to win them for Christ,[171] cut his hair off in Cenchreae because of a vow,[172] and went barefoot and bald in the Temple at Jerusalem in order to placate the malice of those who had been told that he opposed the Law of Moses and the God of the prophets.[173] They longed, no less than Abraham, to see with an uncovered face[174] the day of Christ's coming; they saw it and rejoiced.[175] They became weak to a weak people in order both to win them and to appear to be under the Law to those who actually were under the Law. Their hope was to rescue them from the idols to which they had become accustomed in Egypt. It is silly to suppose that Moses and the rest of those who conversed with God were in this situation and that the time appointed by the Father did not come for them, that they were not redeemed from their slavery to the Law, that they did not obtain full rights of [adopted] sonship, and that they did not gain an inheritance with Christ. For whatever [blessings] God in his wisdom has conferred on the entire human race as if he were doing so on just one son, these same [blessings] he has always lavished on each one of the saints at times and places appropriate for them.

When we refer to the Mosaic Law as "weak and miserable el-

171. Cf. 1 Cor 9.20.   172. Cf. Acts 18.18.
173. Cf. Acts 21.21–26.   174. Cf. Ex 34.33.
175. Cf. Jn 8.56.

ements," the heretics[176] use this as an opportunity to disparage the Creator who made the world and established the Law. I shall respond to them with the same answer I gave above: They are weak and miserable elements for those who abandon evangelical grace and return to them. Before the time appointed by the Father had come, they were called the basic elements of this world rather than weak and miserable elements. Before the Gospel of Christ had shone throughout the entire world, the commandments of the Law had their own luster. But after the greater light from evangelical grace shone and the sun of righteousness revealed itself to the whole world, the light from the stars was concealed and their rays grew dark, according to what the Apostle says elsewhere: "For what was glorious has no glory now in comparison with the surpassing glory."[177] In the present context he uses different words to express the same thought. The Law of Moses was rich, fulsome, and brightly shining before the Gospel arrived. After Christ's coming, it became weak and miserable by comparison and was eradicated by one greater than Solomon,[178] greater than the Temple,[179] and greater than Jonah.[180] For it is written, "He must become greater; I must become less."[181] It was not so much John, I reckon, as it was the law that said lesser things always give way to greater things and that what is mature has priority over the beginning.

At another time we shall prove that Jewish traditions are weak and miserable elements and worthless things to know, if followed to the letter; they are statutes and laws that are not good.[182] To be sure, spiritual knowledge of the Law is hardy and rich, such that either it must not be called a basic element at all or it is indeed a basic element, but only in comparison with the world to come and with life in Christ Jesus, a life now led by the angels and heavenly principalities. But compared to the Jewish way of understanding, it should be viewed as maturity rather than as a basic element, that is, a beginning.

By saying, "Now that you know God, or rather are known by

176. E.g., Marcion, Valentinus, and Basilides.
177. 2 Cor 3.10.   178. Cf. Mt 12.42.
179. Cf. Mt 12.6.   180. Cf. Mt 12.41.
181. Jn 3.30.   182. Cf. Ezek 20.25.

him," Paul shows that after they had worshiped idols the Galatians had a grasp of God, or rather they were deemed worthy
of being known by him. This does not mean that God, the Creator of everything, is ignorant of anything, but that he is said
to know only those who traded their erring ways for piety. "The
Lord knows those who belong to him."[183] The Savior says in the
Gospel, "I am the good shepherd; I know my [sheep] and my
[sheep] know me."[184] He says the opposite to the impious, "I do
not know you. Depart from me, evildoers."[185] And to the foolish
virgins he says, "I do not know who you are."[186]

4.10–11. *You observe special days, months, seasons, and years. I fear
for you, that somehow I have wasted my efforts on you.*

One who does not love the Father in spirit and in truth[187] is
unaware that the Sabbath rest has been re-appropriated for the
saints,[188] to whom God refers when he says, "If they enter my
rest."[189] He does not recollect the times of which it is written,
"Remember the days of old,"[190] and elsewhere, "I recalled the
former days and thought about the years long ago."[191] He observes Jewish special days, months, seasons, and years.

The special days that are observed include the Sabbath, new
moon celebrations, [Passover,] when a lamb is set aside for sacrifice from the tenth until the fourteenth day of the first month[192]
and from the fourteenth until the twenty-first day of the same
month the Feast of the Unleavened Bread is celebrated,[193] not
in sincerity and truth but in the old yeast of the Pharisees' malice and wickedness. Also, the Jew calculating (according to his
own ritual) seven weeks after the Feast of the Unleavened Bread
observes the Israelites' version of Pentecost.[194] In addition, they
observe other Jewish special days. In the seventh month, on the
first day of that month there are trumpet blasts.[195] On the tenth
day of the same month the people make an offering to the

---

183. 2 Tm 2.19.   184. Jn 10.14.
185. Lk 13.27.   186. Mt 25.12.
187. Cf. Jn 4.23.   188. Cf. Heb 4.9.
189. Ps 95.11.   190. Is 46.9.
191. Ps 77.5.   192. Cf. Ex 12.3–6.
193. Cf. Ex 12.18–20.   194. Cf. Lv 23.15–21; Dt 16.9–12.
195. Cf. Lv 23.23–25.

Lord and they fast,[196] and they set up tents according to their custom.[197] As for those who observe months, they observe the first and seventh months without being aware of the mystery of truth. The observers of seasons think that by going to Jerusalem three times a year they fulfill the commandment of the Lord when he says, "Three times a year you are to celebrate a festival to me: the Feast of the Unleavened Bread; the Feast of First Fruits; the Feast of Ingathering at the end of the year,"[198] and elsewhere, "Three times a year all the men are to appear before the Lord your God."[199]

When Paul says "years," I think he means every seventh year, when debts are canceled,[200] and every fiftieth one, which they call the Jubilee Year. The Apostle elaborates on this in his epistle to the Colossians: "Therefore, do not let anyone judge you by what you eat or drink, or with regard to a part of a religious festival, either a new moon celebration or a Sabbath day, which are a shadow of the things that were to come."[201] Here he wrote "with regard to a part of a religious festival" in contradistinction to never-ending festivity to show that we have the whole duration of our lives for perpetual celebration in Christ, and not some fleeting and minuscule portion of it. If I may link what comes before to what comes after, the sentiment Paul expresses in this same epistle about the Mosaic Law and the superfluous inquisitiveness about foods is followed immediately by, "Since you died with Christ to the basic elements of this world, why, as though you still belonged to it, do you submit to its rules: 'Do not handle, do not taste, do not touch'? These are all destined to perish with use because they are based on human commands and teachings."[202]

Someone may say: If it is not permissible to observe special days, months, seasons, and years, then we run into a similar problem by observing the fourth day of the week, the day before the weekly Sabbath, the Lord's day, Lenten fasting, the Paschal feast,

---

196. Cf. Lv 23.27–32.
197. I.e., the Feast of Tabernacles (Lv 23.34–36).
198. Ex 23.14–16.   199. Ex 23.17.
200. Cf. Dt 31.10.   201. Col 2.16–17.
202. Col 2.20–22.

Pentecost, and feast days established in honor of martyrs that reflect diverse local traditions. A simple answer to this objection is that the days observed by the Jews are not the same as those that we observe. For we do not celebrate Passover but the cross and resurrection. Nor do we do as Israel and keep a tally of the seven weeks in Pentecost. Rather, we stand in awe of the Holy Spirit's coming. Certain days have been designated for all of us to come together as one, to insure that a poorly organized gathering does not compromise the people's faith in Christ. This does not mean that the day on which we congregate is more festive, but instead that a greater joy arises from the fellowship we share with one another, on whatever day we must congregate.

A more pointed answer to the question at hand is that all days are equal and that Christ not only is crucified throughout the day before the Sabbath and raised [from the dead] on the Lord's day, but for the saint every day is the day of Christ's Resurrection and he always feeds on the Lord's flesh. But days for fasting and gathering together for worship were instituted by prudent men for the sake of those who leave more time for the world than for God and are unable, or rather unwilling, to congregate in church every moment of their lives or to put the offering of the sacrifice of their prayers to God ahead of their human activities. For how few people are there who always observe at least these few regulations about the times of prayer or fasting? Thus, while we are allowed to fast always, to pray always, and to celebrate unceasingly and joyfully the Lord's day by receiving his body, the Jews are not allowed perpetually to sacrifice lambs, observe Pentecost, build tents, or fast daily.

Paul walks the fine line between the imperiousness of an apostle and the gentleness of a holy man, saying, "I fear for you, that somehow I have wasted my efforts on you." If he had wanted to issue a swift condemnation, he certainly could have said, "I fear for you because I have wasted my efforts on you." But as things stood, he saw that they were zealous for God but their zeal was not based on knowledge,[203] and he did not completely give up hope for their salvation. They had been deceived by

203. Cf. Rom 10.2.

pious error and he did not let them go unrebuked again, lest by his silence he give them the excuse to persist in their error and give others the excuse of falling into similar reprehensible behavior. Moreover, he wrote "I fear for you" instead of "I fear about you." The teacher wastes his efforts when he exhorts his disciples to reach for greater heights and they lapse and return to lesser things and mediocrity.

4.12a. *Be as I am, for I was as you are.*

Paul is saying something like this: I became weak for you, who are weak,[204] and could not address you as spiritually minded but instead as fleshly minded and as infants in Christ. Because you were not yet capable of taking in solid food, I gave you only the milk of the Gospel[205] because I did not want you to remain infants forever but wanted to guide you gradually to adolescence and then adulthood so that you could receive solid food. Thus, you must be as I am and have a taste for greater things: Do away with milk, move on to hardier foods and better nourishment. He speaks like this in imitation of the Savior, who did not consider equality with God something to be grasped but emptied himself and took on the form of a servant and was found in appearance as a man,[206] so that we might participate in the divine nature[207] and no longer die but be raised with Christ[208] and be called his friends[209] and brothers,[210] with the result that the disciple is just like the teacher and the servant is like his master.

Put another way: Brothers, Paul says, I plead with you to forgo the Jewish custom of observing special days, months, seasons, and years, which are shadows of the things that were to come. Instead, imitate me—I, who was faultless when it came to legalistic righteousness and considered all of it rubbish and refuse that I might gain Christ.[211] So I was as you are now when I was bound by the same obligatory customs and persecuted the church of Christ because it did not practice these things.

204. Cf. 1 Cor 9.22.
206. Cf. Phil 2.6–8.
208. Cf. Col 3.1.
210. Cf. Jn 20.17.

205. Cf. 1 Cor 3.1–2.
207. Cf. 2 Pt 1.4.
209. Cf. Jn 15.15.
211. Cf. Phil 3.6–8.

4.12b–14. *I plead with you, brothers. You have done me no wrong. You know it was on account of fleshly weakness that I first preached the Gospel to you long ago. You neither despised nor disdained the trial which my physical condition caused you. Instead, you welcomed me as if I were an angel of God, as if I were Christ Jesus himself.*

This passage should be connected to the preceding sentence. To illustrate my point, here is the word order I have in mind: "I plead with you, brothers, to be as I am, because I was as you are." This is akin to another verse: "We implore you on Christ's behalf to be reconciled to God."[212] And also: "I plead, first of all, that requests, prayers, intercession, and thanksgiving be made for everyone."[213] And the words of Peter as well: "To the elders among you, I appeal as a fellow elder and witness of Christ's sufferings."[214] These statements exhort us, too, to be humble, and they strike down the haughtiness of bishops, who are situated aloft as if on some lofty watchtower[215] and scarcely deign to look at mere mortals and speak to their fellow servants.[216] Let them realize that the foolish and erring Galatians are called "brothers" by the Apostle, and that after rebuking them he speaks soothing words to them, "I plead with you." Paul pleads that they imitate him just as he imitates Christ. To continue with the theme of this passage, what he asks of them is nothing too ponderous: Just as he went from being greater to lesser for their sake, so should they rise from lesser to greater things.

"You have done me no wrong." The disciple does wrong to his teacher if he wastes the teacher's instruction and effort through his own negligence. Up until now the Galatians had not done

---

212. 2 Cor 5.20.   213. 1 Tm 2.1.

214. 1 Pt 5.1.

215. *Velut in aliqua sublimi specula constituti.* This phrase was borrowed from Lactantius, *Div. inst.* 2.2.18 (ANF 7:42): "It delights me, therefore, as though standing on some lofty watchtower (*velut in aliqua sublimi specula constitutum*), from which all may hear, to proclaim aloud that saying of Persius, 'O souls bent down to the earth, and destitute of heavenly things?' Rather look to the heaven, to the sight of which God your Creator raised you." See A. Cain, *REAug* 55 (2009): 47.

216. Jerome could be notoriously scathing in his criticisms of the clergy of his own day. See D. S. Wiesen, *St. Jerome as a Satirist: A Study in Christian Latin Thought and Letters* (Ithaca: Cornell University Press, 1964), 65–112.

wrong to the Apostle because they had been adhering to his Gospel and his commandments. Or else he means: When I introduced the Gospel to you, I preached to you as if you were infants because you were weak in the flesh and could not apprehend deeper mysteries. I pretended to be weak so that I could win you, who were weak, for Christ. Did you not welcome me as if I were an angel [of God], as if I were Christ Jesus himself? You did me no wrong at that time and regarded me as having become humble and downcast like the Son of God for your sake. So, then, when I exhort you to greater things, how am I wronged by you by wasting my effort and the economy whereby I pretended to be an infant, now mourning over my ineffectual work?

Paul preaches to the Galatians "on account of fleshly weakness"—not his own, but his audience's. They could not submit their flesh to the word of God and were in no position to receive spiritual understanding because they were carnal-minded. To make clearer what Paul means, let us take some examples. When he teaches "on account of an infirmity of the flesh," he says, "If they cannot control themselves, let them marry,"[217] and, "If her husband dies, a woman is free to marry anyone she wishes, but he must belong to the Lord."[218] He does not, however, give instruction on account of fleshly weakness when he reminds his readers, "You are unmarried, do not seek a wife,"[219] and, "The time is short, such that those who have wives should live as if they had none."[220] Some commandments are directed at spiritual people, others at carnal-minded people; in one case, an order is given, in another, an allowance is made.

"You neither despised nor disdained the trial which my physical condition caused you." This is an obscure[221] passage and requires closer attention. I preached to you at first, he says, as if to infants and sucklings on account of the weakness of your flesh,[222] and I began with the basics, almost babbling among

217. 1 Cor 7.9.   218. 1 Cor 7.39.
219. 1 Cor 7.27.   220. 1 Cor 7.29.
221. Modern commentators, too, have struggled with the awkwardness of Paul's Greek here: see, e.g., Matera, *Galatians,* 160. The translation suggested by Matera, which I adopt above, seems best to capture the essence of Paul's meaning.
222. Cf. 1 Cor 3.1–2.

you, so to speak. This economy and pretense of weakness in preaching were according to my plan. Your "trial" consisted in deciding whether you esteemed the things that were by their very nature rather insignificant and were presented by me as if being of little value. You perceived them to be important and significant and you were so in awe of me that you welcomed me, the messenger, as an angel and—to be more emphatic—as the Son of God. Therefore, your trial by which I put you to the test with the fleshly way in which I delivered my message was not worthless but had more value than I imagined.

This passage can be explained another way. When I came to you, I came not in words of wisdom but as a lowly and despised man bringing nothing of consequence with me except Christ and him crucified.[223] When you saw me preaching the kingdom of heaven in a body racked with infirmities, you did not mock me or consider me contemptible. You perceived that the lowliness of my flesh and the plainness of my dress were meant to test you to see whether you would look down on a man whom the unbelieving regarded as pitiable. You, however, welcomed this lowly, contemptible, and despised man as if he were an angel, indeed something more than an angel.

Alternatively, we might suppose that when the Apostle initially arrived among the Galatians he was sick and, although impeded by some bodily ailment, he did not hold his tongue from preaching unceasingly the Gospel message he had begun. They say that Paul often suffered from severe headaches[224] and that his ailment was an angel of Satan sent to be a thorn in his flesh and to keep him from becoming conceited.[225] This bodily infirmity and feebleness were a way to test those to whom the Gospel

223. Cf. 1 Cor 2.1–2. A variant reading has been incorporated here.

224. Tertullian (*De pudic.* 13.16) refers to an early oral tradition according to which Paul's thorn was migraine headaches. Jerome evokes this same tradition and probably does so because of Tertullian's influence: see A. Cain, *REAug* 55 (2009): 35. While Tertullian and Jerome seemed to favor this interpretation of the thorn, other patristic commentators (e.g., Eusebius of Emesa, John Chrysostom, Theodore of Mopsuestia, Augustine) believed it referred to opposition Paul had encountered from his enemies. For a conspectus of ancient opinions about this mysterious thorn, see J. B. Lightfoot, *The Epistle of St. Paul to the Galatians* (Grand Rapids: W. B. Eerdmans; repr., 1967), 186–91.

225. Cf. 2 Cor 12.7.

was preached, to see whether they would look down on a man they saw overwhelmed by physical ailments yet preaching lofty things. It could also be said that when he first came to the Galatians he underwent abuse, persecution, and beatings at the hands of the adversaries of the Gospel, and that it was the worst trial imaginable for the Galatian Christians to witness an apostle of Christ being flogged.

When he says, "You welcomed me as if I were an angel of God, as if I were Christ Jesus himself," he shows that Christ is greater than an angel, whom the Psalmist had celebrated as being lesser as far as the economy of the body was concerned: "You made him a little lower than the angels."[226] He demonstrates that his words carried so much weight at first that they were thought to be the words of an angel and of Christ.

4.15–16. *Where is your happiness? For I bear witness to you that, if possible, you would have torn out your eyes and given them to me. Have I now become your enemy by telling you the truth?*

Happy is he who walks in the way of virtue, provided of course that he reaches perfection in it. There is no point in abstaining from vice unless you embrace moral excellence, because when it comes to noble pursuits, the beginning is not as praiseworthy as the end. A grape goes through many stages between the vine and the winepress. The branch must first be rich in foliage, and its blossoms must show promise. Then, after a blossom is inspected, the appearance of the future crop starts to become apparent, and the gradually swelling grape ripens. Finally, after being crushed in the winepress, it excretes sweet must.[227] Likewise, in the realm of doctrine there are individual steps that lead to

226. Ps 8.5.

227. While it is possible that Jerome picked up the essentials about viticulture (and the technical vocabulary) from agricultural handbooks in Latin such as Columella's *De re rustica* (first century AD) or Palladius's *Opus agriculturae* (fourth century AD), he may instead have learned them during his upbringing on his father Eusebius's sprawling rural estate in Dalmatia. In antiquity this region was indeed known for its wine production: see R. Matijasic, "Oil and Wine Production in Istria and Dalmatia in Classical Antiquity and the Early Middle Ages," in *La production du vin et de l'huile,* ed. M.-C. Amouretti and J.-P. Brun (Paris: École Francaise d'Athènes, 1993), 247–61.

the attainment of happiness. Someone hears the word of God, it takes root in him, and it grows in his soul's uterus up until the point of birth. After it is born, he feeds and nourishes it as it progresses through infancy, childhood, adolescence, and young adulthood, until he becomes a mature man.[228] As I have said, individual stages offer their own incremental happiness, but if the work lacks that final touch, so to speak, the entire effort will be in vain and it will be said, "Where is your happiness?"

[Paul] says: I said you were happy when you had welcomed the gospel according to the flesh because you were full of zeal in the beginning, but now I see no roof on the building and barely any foundation laid, and so I am compelled to ask where that happiness of yours is on account of which I formerly praised you and deemed you blessed. For I frankly confess that at first you loved me so much for preaching an accessible message to you or for weathering persecution that, "if possible, you would have torn out your eyes and given them to me" (we must take this as hyperbole), so that I could see more with all of your eyes. You chose to make yourselves blind out of unspeakable love for me, that the light of the Gospel might arise more in my heart. You wanted me to prosper while you took a loss, and you did this at a time when you were like infants and sucklings—you did so either because I preached a simple and uncomplicated message due to the weakness of your flesh or because I did not seem trustworthy due to the abuse my own flesh had received. But now, because I have begun to exhort you to leave behind childish elements, syllables, and reading habits and to aspire to more advanced things, so that you may hold books in your hands and learn words full of wisdom and meaningfulness, you rebel, you become angry, and the idea of doctrinal enlightenment seems burdensome to you. Your

228. Cf. the agricultural analogy used by Origen (*Hom. Ex.* 1.1) to describe the seed of God's Word taking root in the soul: "I think each word of divine Scripture is like a seed whose nature is to multiply diffusely, reborn into an ear of corn or whatever its species be, when it has been cast into the earth. Its increase is proportionate to the diligent labor of the skillful farmer or the fertility of the earth. . . . Although when first approached [the word] seems small and insignificant, if it find a skillful and diligent farmer, as it begins to be cultivated and handled with spiritual skill, it grows into a tree and puts forth branches and foliage" (trans. Heine, FOTC 71:227).

feelings about me have changed to such an extent that now you regard me—whom you received as if I were an angel and Christ [himself], I to whom you were willing to give your own eyes—as an enemy because I preach to you the truth in its fullness.

He has finished his sentence elegantly, asking, "Have I now become your enemy by telling you the truth?" He says this to show that his initial preaching consisted not so much in truth as in the shadows and image of the truth. That proverb of the poet who is considered noble among the Romans is apt here, "Flattery attracts friends, and truth, hatred."[229] But realize how superior the Apostle is to him. The Apostle has tempered his statement to those he had called fools and infants and has personalized it, targeting individual people and the Galatian Christians. The poet, however, went perilously astray by making a generalized pronouncement about universal behavior. Once truth is taken out of the equation, the flattery by which he thought friends could be made is not so much flattery as it is adulation and obsequiousness, which as we all know should be called covert hostilities rather than friendships.

We should also bear in mind that today, too, we are praised, admired, and held in high regard as long as we explain Scripture according to the letter to infants and sucklings and to people in whose hearts Christ has never reached maturity or grown in stature, wisdom, and favor with God and men.[230] But when we make a modest attempt to nudge them on to greater things, they go from being our panegyrists to being our enemies. They would rather follow the Jews than the apostles, who dissociated themselves from the teaching and traditions of the Pharisees and ad-

---

229. Terence, *Andr.* 68. Among the ancients, this aphorism was cited by Cicero (*Lael.* 89), Quintilian (*Instit. orat.* 8.5.4), Augustine (*Ep.* 82.4), Sulpicius Severus (*Dial.* 1.9.3), and Jerome (*Comm. Gal.* 2.4.15–16; *Dial. Pelag.* 1.27). Terence was Jerome's favorite Roman comedian and the one from whom he quoted the most. See E. Lübeck, *Hieronymus quos noverit scriptores et ex quibus hauserit* (Leipzig, 1872), 110–15; N. Adkin, "Terence's *Eunuchus* and Jerome," *RhM* 137 (1994): 187–95; idem, "Hieronymus Eunuchinus," *GIF* 58 (2006): 327–34. On Terence's reception more generally, see A. Cain, "Terence in Late Antiquity," in *A Companion to Terence*, ed. A. Agoustakis and J. Thorburn (Malden, MA: Wiley-Blackwell, 2012), forthcoming.

230. Cf. Lk 2.52.

vanced towards Christ himself, the sacrifice of atonement[231] and the fulfillment of the Law. They do not consider it worth their while to accept the divine word, which orders the teachers of the church to aspire to ever more profound teachings and to shout these teachings at the top of their lungs and not cringe at the outcry of the children barking, but to say, "Go up on a high mountain, you who bring good tidings to Zion. Lift up your voice with a shout, you who bring good tidings to Jerusalem. Lift it up, do not be afraid."[232]

4.17–18. *They are zealous to win you over, but for no good. What they want is to alienate you [from us], so that you may be zealous for them. Always be zealous for a good cause, and not just when I am with you.*

This is what those do who are zealous to win people over for good. When they see redeeming qualities, gifts, and virtues in certain people, they long to be like them and strive to imitate their faith, their way of life, and the diligence by which they attained those qualities so that they, too, might pursue what is worthy of emulation. About such people the Apostle says, "Eagerly desire spiritual gifts, that you may prophesy more,"[233] and after that, "So it is with you. Since you are eager to have spiritual [gifts], try to excel [in gifts] that build up the church,"[234] and, "Therefore, brothers, be eager to prophesy, and do not forbid speaking in tongues."[235]

This is what those do who are zealous to win people over, but

231. Cf. Rom 3.25.

232. Is 40.9. Jerome's comments in this paragraph about Christians moving "on to greater things" (in their study of the Bible) and about the responsibility of teachers of the Bible "to aspire to ever more profound teachings" have a conspicuously Origenian ring to them. For Origen, Scripture is infinitely rich in mysteries that can never be completely grasped by the human mind (*Comm. Mt.* 14.6). Nevertheless, with the aid of the Holy Spirit the Christian continually progresses to ever more advanced levels of spiritual enlightenment and degrees of perfection (*Hom. Num.* 17.4). See Henri de Lubac's classic study *Histoire et esprit: L'intelligence de l'Écriture d'après Origène* (Paris: Éditions Montaigne, 1950). It has recently been translated by Anne Englund Nash under the title *History and Spirit: The Understanding of Scripture according to Origen* (San Francisco: Ignatius Press, 2007).

233. 1 Cor 14.1.   234. 1 Cor 14.12.
235. 1 Cor 14.39.

for no good. They do not so much hope to become better themselves and imitate those worthy of being copied as they want to make these people worse and pull them back out of spiteful jealousy. Allow me to explain. Anyone who is a Christian reads Moses and the prophets. He knows that their writings led the people's way in shadows and images[236] and that they were written for the sake of us, on whom the fulfillment of the ages has come.[237] He understands that circumcision has to do with the ears and heart and not with the foreskin.[238] He has risen from the dead with Christ and his mind is fixated on heavenly things.[239] He has been freed from the burden and slavery of the Law, which orders, "Do not handle! Do not taste! Do not touch!"[240] If anyone tries to convince him from the words of Scripture not to interpret the Bible metaphorically but according to the letter which kills[241] and to become a Jew outwardly but not inwardly,[242] he is zealous to win him over but not for good, and he moves at full speed to hold him back as he advances towards greater things. The end result is that he is zealous to win himself over instead because he goes backwards or at any rate does not gain much ground.

Paul addresses the Galatians, whom the advocates of the Law had induced to imitate them—although it is they who should have imitated the Galatians instead (for it is natural to go from the lesser to the greater, not the other way around). He says, "Be zealous for a good cause," that is, do not imitate the advocates of Jewish customs, but imitate what is good. The person who imitates the riches, power, and eminence of someone else emulates not what is good but what ought to be shunned. In the same way you should "be zealous for a good cause" and seek things that are spiritual rather than fleshly, so that you might teach them how to be Christians rather than they teach you how to be Jews. Do this always so that you may persevere and actualize the completion of your good work. You were zealous for a good cause when I was with you. After I left, you lost all that

236. Cf. Col 2.17.
237. Cf. 1 Cor 10.11.
238. Cf. Jer 4.4; 6.10.
239. Cf. Col 3.1.
240. Col 2.21.
241. Cf. 2 Cor 3.6.
242. Cf. Rom 2.28–29.

I had passed on to you, and from a safe mooring and secure dock you were carried out again into the high seas by a receding wave.

After the departure of the Apostle, the chosen vessel[243] through whom Christ the Lord spoke,[244] the Galatians were changed. This is not surprising given that even in our own times we see the same thing happening in the churches. For whenever there is a teacher in the church distinguished in his speech and life who spurs his audience to be virtuous, the masses with great urgency, enthusiasm, and diligence busy themselves with almsgiving, fasting, sexual abstinence, relief of the poor, taking care of graves, and other similar tasks.[245] But when he leaves, they gradually waste away and grow thin, pale, and languid from losing their food. Then follows the death of everything that had been thriving before. Therefore, since the harvest is plentiful but the workers are few,[246] let us ask the Lord of the harvest to send workers to harvest the crop among the Christian people which stands in the church ready to be made into wheat, and then to collect the grain and carry it into the storehouse and not let it go to waste.

What Paul says here about this zeal and spiteful emulation, "They are zealous to win you over, but for no good," recalls what is written elsewhere in Scripture, "Do not be envious of evildoers."[247] We find another type of zeal at work in the sons of Jacob, when they were jealous of their brother Joseph,[248] and in Miri-

---

243. Cf. Acts 9.15.

244. Cf. 2 Cor 13.3.

245. Jerome is referring to fiery itinerant preachers who inspired congregations with an ascetic message. Not all, however, would have earned Jerome's approval. In a letter to the church at Vercelli (395/6), Ambrose condemns two itinerant monks named Sarmatio and Barbatianus, perhaps followers of Jovinian, who encouraged its congregation not to put any stock in ascetic virtues like abstinence and virginity (*Ep. ex. coll.* 14.7). David Hunter has recently argued that Ambrose takes allusive shots at Jerome in this letter. This is a significant find because it shows that the bishop of Milan responded in kind to Jerome's numerous allusive attacks on his competence as a theologian and Biblical interpreter. See "The Raven Replies: Ambrose's *Letter to the Church at Vercelli* (*Ep. ex. coll.* 14) and the Criticisms of Jerome," in *Jerome of Stridon,* ed. Cain and Lössl, 175–89.

246. Cf. Mt 9.37.   247. Ps 36.1 (LXX).

248. Cf. Gn 37.11.

am and Aaron, when they were jealous of Moses because he was the friend of God.[249] Neither the sons of Jacob nor Miriam and Aaron were zealous because they wanted to be better than Joseph or Moses; they were aggravated because they were inferior to them. That kind of zeal is akin to envy. It would be tedious to adduce from the treasure-chest of Scripture all the examples of zeal, whether good or bad. We read about the good kind of zeal displayed by Phineas,[250] Elijah,[251] Mattathias,[252] and the Apostle Judas (not the betrayer), who got the name Zealot on account of his remarkable zeal.[253] The evil kind of zeal is what Cain had for Abel[254] and what the rest had for others, such as the man about whom Scripture says, "And should there come upon him a spirit of jealousy."[255] This, though, may be a neutral form of jealousy that is neither good nor evil but hovers between the two extremes and is called rivalry.

The passage in question can be interpreted another way: Those of the circumcision faction saw that the Galatian Gentiles were filled with the power of the Holy Spirit, but they themselves did not speak in tongues and did not have the gift of healing or the ability to prophesy, and so they were zealous to lure them back to the strictures of the Law so that the Galatians might begin to be like them.

4.19. *My dear children, for whom I am again in the pains of childbirth until Christ is formed in you.*

The first curse declares how difficult and painful the process of childbirth is, "You will be in distress when you give birth to children."[256] Paul, wishing to illustrate the concern teachers have for their students and the worry they have about their followers stumbling and losing their salvation, says, "My dear children, for whom I am again in the pains of childbirth." In another place he spoke like a father ("even though you have ten thousand guardians in Christ, you do not have many fathers"),[257] but now he

---

249. Cf. Nm 12.1.
250. Cf. Nm 25.11.
251. Cf. 1 Kgs 19.10.
252. Cf. 1 Mc 2.26–27.
253. Cf. Lk 6.15; Acts 1.13.
254. Cf. Gn 4.8.
255. Nm 5.14 (LXX).
256. Gn 3.16.
257. 1 Cor 4.15.

speaks like a mother in Christ[258] because he wants them to recognize the dutiful anxiety of both parents. Moses speaks in a similar vein about the people of Israel, "Did I give birth to all these people?"[259] Who among us do you think is so concerned about the salvation of his students that he is plagued by worry his entire life—and not just for a few hours or two or three days at a time—until Christ is formed in them?

To get a better idea about what Paul is saying, let us take the example of the pregnant woman conceiving and forming seeds within herself (nature should be the object of reverence and not of blushes).[260] First, an unformed seed is thrust into her womb in such a way as to adhere to its furrow and soil as if by a certain glue; the prophet, mindful of his own conception, refers to insemination when he says, "Your eyes beheld my shapeless body."[261] Then, throughout a period of nine months blood is directed toward the future man, and he takes shape, his body is formed, he is fed and assumes individualized characteristics. After gestating in the womb, he is turned out into the light at the fixed time and is birthed with difficulties as great as those with which afterward he is nourished to keep him alive. Likewise, when the seed of the word of Christ finds its way into the soul of its hearer, it grows incrementally and, to say no more—for we can easily apply a spiritual interpretation to the description of the body's mechanisms—the fate of the seed remains uncertain as long as the one who conceived it is in the process of giving birth to it. The hard work does not end right away at

258. For an analysis of Paul's maternal language in this passage, see B. Gaventa, "The Maternity of Paul: An Exegetical Study of Galatians 4:19," in *The Conversation Continues: Studies in Paul and John in Honor of J. Louis Martyn*, ed. R. Fortna and B. Gaventa (Nashville: Abingdon Press, 1990), 189–201.

259. Nm 11.12.

260. *Natura non erubescenda, sed veneranda est.* Jerome pilfered this pithy line from Tertullian's *De an.* 27.4 (*Natura veneranda est, non erubescenda*): see A. Cain, *REAug* 55 (2009): 37–38. In Tertullian this aphorism prefaces a graphic description of copulation and the reproductive process (in a discussion of how the soul and body are conceived simultaneously). Jerome appropriates this phrase as an apologetic foreword to his own, albeit briefer, description of insemination to visualize for the reader how the seed of the Gospel takes root and is formed in the soul of the Christian.

261. Ps 139.16.

parturition: thereupon another effort commences to support the suckling infant with constant attention and feedings until it reaches maturity in Christ.

In marriage the husband's seed is often to blame for the inability to procreate, sometimes a sterile wife does not retain the seed, and frequently neither the husband nor wife is suited for making children, though in other cases both are fertile. Similarly, there are four scenarios that account for sowers of the word of God. The first: The teacher performs his duty, but the hearer is sterile. The second: The hearer is fertile, but due to the incompetence of the teacher the seed of the word perishes. The third: The one being instructed is as senseless as the one performing the instruction. The fourth: Both teacher and student are perfectly suited for each other, meaning that the teacher dispenses as much as the student can digest or the student absorbs as much as the teacher doles out; this happens rarely. All of us are judges now. We do not know a single Psalm, piece of prophecy, or line from the Law, yet our tongues glide to interpret rashly what we do not understand in the least. It is not in our power to guarantee that Christ is formed in the people, nor that each person returns home with the seed of the word of God and conceives it, saying with the prophet, "From fear of you, O Lord, we have conceived and given birth, and we have brought the sons of salvation upon the earth."[262] Such men turn into apostles and deserve to hear from the Savior, "Whoever does the will of my Father is my brother and sister and mother."[263] Here the various titles by which they are designated indicate how far each has progressed. Furthermore, Christ is formed in the hearts of believers when all the sacred mysteries are revealed to them and the obscure becomes clear. But also consider that when one has stopped living in sin, a teacher gives birth to him by his act of repentance, and he is given the promise of having Christ formed in him again. This fact refutes the Novatianists, who do not believe that those who have repented of their sins once and for all can be reformed.[264]

262. Is 26.17–18.
263. Mt 12.50.
264. Novatianists were followers of the Roman priest Novatian. In 251, No-

4.20. *How I wish I could be with you now and change my tone, because I am perplexed by you.*

Divine Scripture is edifying even when read, but it is much more profitable if it goes from written characters on a page to an audible voice, with the one teaching through an epistle giving instruction to listeners as if he were there in person. The living voice has great power. It resonates from the mouth of its author and is delivered with that characteristic intonation with which it was generated in his heart. The Apostle is aware that speech is more persuasive when addressed to those present, and he longs to turn the epistolary voice, the voice confined within written characters, into actual presence and use live speech (which is more expedient) to lead those who had been seduced into error back to the truth.[265]

Paul takes this approach because he is "perplexed" (*confundatur*) by them. The Greek has it better: ἀπορούμαι does not really denote shame or confusion (*confusionem*)—for these concepts the Greeks used αἰσχύνη or συγχύσις—but rather they denote indigence and want. Therefore, what Paul is saying is this: How I wish I could be with you now and give voice in person to the written characters, for I am in want for you. I do not

---

vatian criticized Pope Cornelius for being too lenient in re-admitting Christians who had renounced their faith under pain of torture during the emperor Decius's persecution of 250. Novatian believed that these lapsed Christians (*lapsi*) should not be allowed back into communion with the church. He and his followers were excommunicated by a Roman synod in the autumn of 251, and he is said to have died a martyr during the reign of the emperor Valerian I (253–260). The Novatianist sect continued to grow over the next century and maintained an active presence in Rome in the late fourth century: see H. O. Maier, "The topography of heresy and dissent in late-fourth-century Rome," *Historia* 44 (1995): 232–49 (234 n. 10). Jerome was certainly aware of their activity there during this time, for in one of his letters to Marcella (*Ep.* 42), dated to 384, he attacks Novatianist teaching about the unpardonable sin against the Holy Spirit. He was most likely responding to the claims of a proselytizer who had tried to recruit Marcella to the Novatianist cause: see A. Cain, *The Letters of Jerome: Asceticism, Biblical Exegesis, and the Construction of Christian Authority in Late Antiquity* (Oxford: Oxford University Press, 2009), 87–88.

265. According to ancient epistolary theory, the letter had an almost mystical ability to unite in virtual presence correspondents who were separated by great distances. See K. Thraede, *Grundzüge griechisch-römischer Brieftopik* (Munich: Beck, 1970), 162–64.

have fruits that other teachers usually have in the form of students, and the seed of my teachings was thrown down in vain, and as a result I suffer so much want for you that I can shout out in the voice of Jeremiah, "I have not helped others, nor has anyone helped me."[266]

This passage can be taken another way. The Apostle Paul had become a Jew to the Jews to win them [for Christ], and to those under the Law he became seemingly under the Law himself, and to the weak he became weak to win them [for Christ]. In order to accommodate the different types of people he hoped to save, he changed his tone, and, like actors (he was indeed on display before the world, angels, and men),[267] he altered his dress and the sound of his voice when he played different characters. This does not mean that he was in reality what he pretended to be but that he only appeared to be what he projected to others. He sees the Galatians to be in need of another teaching and to require salvation by another path, and not the one on which they had first crossed from paganism to faith in Christ. He is forced to say, "I wish I could be with you now and change my tone." He says: I do not see myself as being of any use to you if I say the same things as before. As such, I am uncertain about what to do and am pulled in different directions. I am distressed, perplexed, and torn up. When doctors see that their medical art is inefficacious after the first treatment, they pass on to another remedy, and they keep experimenting and exhausting their options until they find a cure. Hence, the ailment which the gentleness of a poultice could not heal might be healed by the infliction of a more painful powder and a harsher cure. Similarly, since I am perplexed by you and sway back and forth in uncertainty, I wish I could be there to give voice to the written characters and chide you more severely than I usually do. For a letter can neither capture the castigator's tone of voice nor echo the angry man's shouting nor divulge the sorrow of the heart with the point [of a stylus].

A simpler interpretation is possible: I used coaxing words to you just now, saying, "Brothers, I plead with you," and, "My dear

266. Jer 15.10 (LXX).
267. Cf. 1 Cor 4.9.

children, for whom I am again in the pains of childbirth until Christ is formed in you." When I spoke to you as a father, I was coaxing and gentle. But for the sake of that love which prevents me from allowing my sons to perish and stray forever, I wish that the shackles of my ministry did not prevent me from being there in person, and I wish that I could change my coaxing tone to one of castigation. If I am coaxing one time and angry another, it is not because I am fickle. Love and sorrow compel me to speak with diverse emotions. For I do not know what words will burst out first or what treatment I should use to cure you because I am perplexed by you.

4.21. *You who want to be under the Law, tell me, have you not heard what the Law says?*

We should note that the "Law" refers to the narrative in Genesis and not, as is commonly assumed, to commandments and prohibitions.[268] What is called the "Law" comprises everything that is related about Abraham, his wives, and his children. In another place we read that the prophets are also called the "Law." Therefore, according to Paul, he who hears the Law examines it, not its surface but its inmost parts, but he who is like the Galatians and does not hear it, looks only at its outer shell.

4.22–23. *For it is written that Abraham had two sons, one by the slave woman and the other by the free woman. His son by the slave woman was born according to the flesh, the one by the free woman was born according to a promise.*

It is extremely difficult to make the case that only Isaac, born from Sarah, was begotten according to a promise and not also Ishmael, who was born from the Egyptian slave woman Hagar. Scripture of course relates that when Sarah mistreated her, the pregnant Hagar fled, and an angel approached her in the desert and instructed her to submit to the authority of her mistress. The same angel then spoke these words: "I will increase your

268. Jerome's phrase "as is commonly assumed" may be his coy way of correcting (among others) Marius Victorinus, who does assume that the "Law" here refers to the Mosaic Law. See Cooper, *Marius Victorinus' Commentary on Galatians*, 320.

descendants, and they will be too numerous to count."[269] What he subsequently said about Ishmael is indisputably a promise: "He will be a rustic man; his hands will be against all, and the hands of all against him, and he will live in hostility towards all his brothers."[270] But it could be countered that a promise from an angel carries less weight than one from God himself. For just as a star is not resplendent once the sun has arisen, so also an angel's words seem dim, fleeting, and worthless when compared with a promise from God. While this line of reasoning seems plausible enough, it is immediately crushed by the authority of the Scriptural passage that follows the one quoted above. "Abraham said to God, 'Let Ishmael live under your blessing.' Then God replied, 'Your wife Sarah will bear you a son and you will call him Isaac. I will establish my covenant with him as an everlasting covenant and it will include his descendants.' As for Ishmael, God said, 'I have heard you and I have blessed him. I will make him fruitful and greatly increase his numbers. He will be the father of twelve nations, and I will make him into a great nation. But I will establish my covenant with Isaac, whom Sarah will bear to you by this time next year.'"[271]

From the very words of God himself it is clear that Ishmael also was begotten according to a promise. But the answer to the objection raised above is that a promise is truly fulfilled in the giving of a covenant. It is one thing to bless, increase, and multiply greatly, as it is written in Ishmael's case, but another to produce an heir through a covenant, as it is said was the case with Isaac, "I will establish my covenant with him as an everlasting covenant and it will include his descendants,"[272] and in the verse that follows, "But I will establish my covenant with Isaac, whom Sarah will bear to you."[273] There is a difference between gifts, property, legacies, and inheritances—for we read that gifts were given to the sons of Abraham's concubines, but to Sarah's son he left the entirety of his inheritance. There is likewise a difference between legacies and blessings, on the one hand, and a covenant, on the other. It can be said that either an angel

269. Gn 16.10.
270. Gn 16.12 (LXX).
271. Gn 17.18–21.
272. Gn 17.19.
273. Gn 17.21.

or God spoke about Ishmael after he had been conceived but that it was God who had made the promise about Isaac before he was conceived in Sarah's womb. Let this explanation suffice for now, to the extent that our mediocre minds can grasp it. If anyone can come up with a better explanation as to how Isaac, born of a free woman, is the son of the promise instead of Ishmael, born of a slave woman, let him listen to what the Apostle has to say, "If on some point you think differently, that too God will reveal to you."[274]

Now we must briefly venture into deeper matters. Not a single one of us is initially born according to the promise as long as he adheres to the literal words of Scripture and still relishes Jewish expositions. But when he passes on to more ethereal things and understands the spiritual Law, he is begotten according to the promise.[275] And, if I may speak more candidly, every day people are born of Abraham who conduct themselves as he did.[276] Those who have the spirit of slavery are again born of the Egyptian slave woman in fear. Those who have received the spirit of [adopted] sonship are born of Sarah the free woman; we were given this freedom by Christ. To the Jews who still preferred to be the sons of the slave woman the Lord said, "If you hold to my teaching, you will truly be my disciples. Then you will know the truth, and the truth will set you free."[277] Those who do not realize that what is said here is a mystery ask, "We are Abraham's seed and have never been slaves of anyone. How can you say that we will be set free?" "Jesus replied, 'Truly I say

274. Phil 3.15.

275. This notion that the literal interpretation can get one only so far in Scripture, whereas the spiritual or deeper interpretation brings one into the fullness of its mysteries, is of course Origenian. See, e.g., *Peri Archōn* 1, pref. 8 (trans. Butterworth, 5): "Then there is the doctrine that the scriptures were composed through the Spirit of God and that they have not only that meaning which is obvious, but also another which is hidden from the majority of readers. For the contents of scripture are the outward forms of certain mysteries and the images of divine things. On this point the entire Church is unanimous, that while the whole law is spiritual, the inspired meaning is not recognised by all, but only by those who are gifted with the grace of the Holy Spirit in the word of wisdom and knowledge."

276. Cf. Jn 8.39.

277. Jn 8.31–32.

to you, everyone who sins is a slave to sin. Now a slave has no permanent place in the family, but a son belongs to it forever.'"[278] If we are slaves to sin, Hagar the Egyptian has begotten us; if sin does not reign in our mortal body,[279] we truly are the sons of God.

4.24a. *These things are allegorical.*

Allegory is properly part of the art of grammar. As children in school we learn how to differentiate it from metaphor and other figures of speech. It sets out one thing in words and signifies another in sense. The books of the orators and poets are full [of examples of this device]. A good portion of the message of divine Scripture is also expressed through allegory. Aware of this, the Apostle Paul, who knew secular literature to a certain degree, used the name of this figure of speech and called it allegory according to the conventional usage among his contemporaries, employing a Greek word to shed light on the sense of the present passage.

Paul's own words confirm he knew secular literature, even if not to the point of mastery.[280] "One of their own prophets has said, 'Cretans are always liars, evil brutes, lazy gluttons.'"[281] This line was authored by the poet Epimenides, whom Plato and other ancient writers mention. When he was disputing in the Areopagus among the Athenians, Paul added, "As some of your own poets have said, 'We are his offspring.'"[282] This hemistich is attested in the writings of Aratus, who wrote about the constel-

278. Jn 8.33–35.
279. Cf. Rom 6.12.
280. The nature and extent of Paul's rhetorical education has been the subject of two fairly recent monographs: R. D. Anderson, *Ancient Rhetorical Theory and Paul* (Leuven: Peeters, 1999) and B. W. Winter, *Philo and Paul among the Sophists* (Cambridge: Cambridge University Press, 1997). The disparagement of Paul's literary abilities, which Jerome, John Chrysostom, and other patristic commentators on Paul voiced, "served only to enhance the grace of God, which could use so unskilled a writer to so great effect" (Wiles, *The Divine Apostle*, 17).
281. Ti 1.12.
282. Aratus, *Phaen.* 5, quoted by Paul in Acts 17.28. Aratus of Soli was a Hellenistic poet who flourished in the first half of the third century BC. His most famous work was the *Phaenomena*, a Hesiodic-type didactic poem in 1154 Greek hexameters that describes the constellations and weather signs.

lations. There is also this verse in iambic trimeter taken from a comedy by Menander, "Bad company corrupts good character."[283] From these and other citations it is evident that Paul was not ignorant of secular literature. What he has termed allegory here, he elsewhere called spiritual understanding. "We know that the Law is spiritual."[284] He says "spiritual" here instead of "allegorical" or "expressed allegorically." And in another place, "They all ate the same spiritual food and drank the same spiritual drink, for they drank from the spiritual rock that accompanied them, and that rock was Christ."[285] Nobody doubts that the manna, the sudden spouting up of water, and the rock which followed the Israelites are all to be understood allegorically. But there are other passages in which the word "spiritual" means something different than it does in the ones just cited. For example, "Brothers, if someone is caught in a sin, you who are spiritual should restore him in a spirit of gentleness,"[286] and, "The spiritual man makes judgments about all things, but he himself is not subject to any man's judgment."[287] But we hold that the spiritual man, who makes judgments about all things and is himself not subject to any man's judgment, is the one who possesses a profound understanding of all the mysteries of Scripture and who does not allow the traditions of the Jews to have a single foothold in the divine books because he recognizes Christ's presence throughout all of them.

4.24b–26. *These women represent two covenants. One covenant is from Mount Sinai and bears children who are to be slaves; this is Hagar. Now Hagar stands for Mount Sinai in Arabia, which is near the present city of Jerusalem, because she is in slavery with her children. But the Jerusalem that is above is free, and she is the mother of us all.*

Nearly all of the commentators on this passage interpret it to mean that the slave woman Hagar represents the Law and the Jewish people, but that the free woman Sarah symbolizes the church,[288] which has been assembled from the nations and is

---

283. Menander, *Thais*, fr. 147. This line is quoted by Paul in 1 Cor 15.33.
284. Rom 7.14.   285. 1 Cor 10.3–4.
286. Gal 6.1.   287. 1 Cor 2.15.
288. This figurative reading of Hagar as the Jewish Law or the synagogue,

the mother of the saints, according to Paul: "She is the mother of us all." She did not give birth for a long time prior to Christ's being born from a virgin. She was barren, and laughter (that is, of the innocent Isaac)[289] had not yet emanated from the chosen father with the sound of sublime teachings (in Latin Abraham means "chosen father of sound").[290] But Hagar, whose name means παροικία (that is, "wandering" or "sojourning"), gives birth right away to Ishmael. He only hears the commandments of God but does not put them into action. He is an uncouth, bloodthirsty man who inhabits the desert regions and is hostile to all his brothers who were born of the free woman. It is no wonder that the Old Covenant, which is on Mount Sinai in Arabia and near the present city of Jerusalem, was intended to be temporary, seeing that [Hagar's] wandering is different from perpetual possession; that the name Mount Sinai means "tribulation," while Arabia means "death"; and that by contrast the Jerusalem which is above and is free and the mother of the saints[291] shows that the Jerusalem of the present is earthly and submerged in lowliness and baseness.

There are those who have a different understanding of the two covenants (*testamenta*). They identify divine Scripture—both the Old and New [Testaments]—with either the slave woman or the free woman, depending on the hermeneutical orientation of its readers. According to them, those who are still slaves to the literal interpretation and have a spirit of fear are born of the Egyptian Hagar in slavery, while those who aspire to loftier meanings and desire to construe Scripture allegorically are sons of Sarah, whose name means ἄρχουσα, that is, *princeps*[292] in the feminine gender. They assert that they are forced to employ this ap-

---

and Sarah as the Gentile Christian church, was the majority opinion among patristic writers (e.g., Origen, Cyprian, Ambrose, Jerome, John Chrysostom). See E. Clark, "Interpretive Fate amid the Church Fathers," in *Hagar, Sarah, and their Children*, ed. P. Trible and L. Russell (Louisville: John Knox Press, 2006), 127–47.

289. Isaac (*sahaq*) means "laughter" in Hebrew: see Gn 21.1–6.

290. Cf. Philo, *Abr.* 82; Ambrose, *Abr.* 2.10.77.

291. On the patristic development of the theme of the church as the heavenly Jerusalem, see J. Plumpe, *Mater Ecclesia: An Inquiry into the Concept of the Church as Mother in Early Christianity* (Washington, DC: The Catholic University of America Press, 1943), 69–80.

292. *Princeps* = "first" or "foremost."

proach because [they allege] it is unfair to suppose that Moses
and all the prophets had been born of the slave woman and that
any Gentiles whatsoever had their origin in the free woman. They
say that it is preferable to apply this distinction not only to those
in the church—whereby some are deemed slaves and others free
on the basis of their varying degrees of understanding (as I said
above)—but also to the individual man. As long as this man follows the literal meaning, he is a son of the slave woman, but when
his heart catches on fire as Jesus explains Scripture to him,[293] and
when there is a breaking of bread and he gazes at One whom he
did not see before,[294] then he is called the son of Sarah.

Marcion and Mani did not want to omit from their own versions of the Bible Paul's statement "these things are allegorical"
and the subsequent verses because they thought that by letting
them remain they could attack us on the grounds that the Law
should be understood differently than its literal wording.[295] For
even if the Law is to be taken allegorically (as we believe and as
Paul teaches it should be), it was established in deference not to
what the reader wants but to the authority of the one writing it
down. [Marcion and Mani] are defeated by the very thing they
preserved in order to refute us, namely, that Moses, a servant of
God the Creator, wrote down spiritual truths, as was taught by
their Apostle, who they claim is the preacher of another Christ
and a better God.

4.27. *For it is written: "Be glad, O barren woman who bears no children. Cry aloud, you who have no labor pains, because the children of
the desolate woman are greater in number than those of the woman who
has a husband."*

The synagogue has the Law as its husband, and according
to Hannah's prophecy it used to have many children.[296] The
church, however, is barren without her husband Christ, and
for a long time she lingered in the desert deprived of commu-
nication with her spouse. After the synagogue received into her

293. Cf. Lk 24.32.
294. Cf. Lk 24.30–31.
295. For a reconstruction of this portion of Marcion's version of Galatians,
see Harnack, *Marcion: Das Evangelium vom fremden Gott,* pp. 75*–76*.
296. Cf. 1 Sm 2.5.

hands the certificate of divorce[297] and turned over all of her husband's assets for the enrichment of an idol, the husband, because his first belt was ruined,[298] wove another one for his loins, an apron made from the Gentiles. As soon as she was joined to her husband, she conceived and gave birth. In Isaiah the Lord exclaims through the prophet, "If a nation is born at once,"[299] when in the Acts of the Apostles three thousand[300] and five thousand[301] people became believers in a single day. I see no need in us talking about how many Christians there are and how few Jews, since the banner of the cross is resplendent throughout the world and scarcely any noteworthy Jew is found in the cities today.

4.28. *Now we, brothers, like Isaac, are the children of promise.*

It is not hard to fathom that the Apostle and those like him (such as Isaac) are the children of promise. When commenting on this verse, Origen rephrased the Apostle to say, "Now you, brothers, like Isaac, are the children of promise." In view of this, how is it that [Paul] now calls the Galatians children of promise like Isaac, whereas earlier he had addressed them as fools and said that they had begun in the Spirit but were finishing in the flesh?[302] He addresses them as such because he does not completely despair of their salvation and reckons that they can return to the Spirit in whom they had begun and can become children of the free woman. But if they finished in the flesh, they are children of the slave woman.

4.29–31. *At that time the son born by the flesh persecuted the son born by the Spirit. It is the same now. But what does Scripture say? "Get rid of the slave woman and her son, for the slave woman's son will never share in the inheritance with my son Isaac."[303] Therefore, brothers, we are not children of the slave woman, but of the free woman. It is by freedom that Christ has set us free.*

Ishmael's persecution of Isaac refers, I think, to when the Egyptian's son, who was older, was teasing Isaac, and Sarah be-

297. Cf. Is 50.1.
299. Is 66.8.
301. Cf. Acts 4.4.
303. Gn 21.10.

298. Cf. Jer 13.7.
300. Cf. Acts 2.41.
302. Cf. Gal 3.3.

came indignant and said to Abraham, "Get rid of the slave woman and her son, for the slave woman's son will never share in
the inheritance with my son Isaac." A trifling squabble between
children certainly does not warrant expulsion and abdication.
But the Apostle, a Hebrew among Hebrews trained in the Law
under Gamaliel,[304] who with his wise counsel held the Pharisees
in check in their frenzy against the Lord,[305] understood from
Sarah's words "For the slave woman's son will never share in the
inheritance with my son Isaac" that it was not a simple squabble. Scripture has characterized the conflict between the children as a squabble because Ishmael claimed the inheritance of
the firstborn on the grounds that he was the elder brother and
had been circumcised when he was old enough to be cognizant
of the pain. Sarah could not bear to hear these words and refused to acknowledge the slave woman's son's laying claim from
a young age to the firstborn's inheritance. And so she shouted,
"Get rid of the slave woman and her son, for the slave woman's
son will never share in the inheritance with my son Isaac." Since
Abraham would have been distressed not only if Ishmael lost his
position as firstborn but also if he did not even receive an equal
inheritance with his younger brother (for more substantial inheritances are owed to the firstborn), God, who wanted the free
woman to be on the inside and the slave woman to be cast out,
reinforced Sarah's words and said to Abraham, "Do not be so
troubled about the boy and your slave woman. Listen to whatever Sarah tells you, because it is through Isaac that your offspring
will be reckoned."[306]

Ishmael, the older brother, persecuted Isaac when he was
still a nursing infant and claimed for himself the prior right of
circumcision and the inheritance of the firstborn. Likewise, that
which now is Israel according to the flesh is conceived, puffed
up, and incited against her younger brother, the Christian population from among the Gentiles. Let us ponder the madness
of the Jews who killed the Lord, persecuted the prophets and
apostles, and wrestled against God's will, and we shall see that
historical writings report far worse persecutions of Christians by

304. Cf. Acts 22.3.   305. Cf. Acts 5.34–40.
306. Gn 21.12.

the Jews than persecutions of Jews by the Gentiles. Are we surprised at the Jews? Today those who are infants in Christ and live carnally[307] persecute those who have been born of water and the Spirit[308] and have risen again with Christ and set their minds on things above and not on earthly things.[309] Let [the former] do as they please and let them, along with Ishmael, persecute Isaac. They will be cast out with their mother, the Egyptian slave woman, and they will not receive the inheritance to which only the child of promise will lay claim.

Paul puts it elegantly when he says that the one born by the flesh persecutes the one who is spiritual. The latter never persecutes the former, but forgives him as if being an untutored brother, for he knows that he can make progress in time. If he ever lays eyes on the angry son of the slave woman, he recalls that one father created Lucanian oxen[310] and the gnat and that in a spacious house there are articles not only of gold and silver but also of wood and clay.[311] Let us therefore say with the Apostle Paul, "We are not children of the slave woman, but of the free woman." Having been renewed in Christ, let us hearken to the words the Lord spoke to the Jews, "If you hold to my teaching, you will know the truth, and the truth will set you free."[312] The Apostle, himself liberated by this freedom, also said, "Though I am free and belong to no man. Everyone who sins is a slave to sin."[313] Since he knew that he was free from all vice and stood apart from all concupiscence and error, Paul had good reason to rejoice in his freedom in Christ, saying, "We are not children of the slave woman, but of the free woman. It is by freedom that Christ has set us free."

307. Cf. 1 Cor 3.1–2.　　308. Cf. Jn 3.5.
309. Cf. Col 3.1–2.
310. At the Battle of Heraclea (280 BC), in Lucanian territory, King Pyrrhus used war elephants to intimidate the Roman forces. The Roman soldiers had never seen beasts like these before and called them "Lucanian oxen." See H. H. Scullard, *The Elephant in the Greek and Roman World* (Ithaca: Cornell University Press, 1974), 104.
311. Cf. 2 Tm 2.20.　　312. Jn 8.31–32.
313. 1 Cor 9.19; Jn 8.34.

5.1. *Stand firm and do not let yourselves be burdened again by a yoke of slavery.*

By this statement Paul demonstrates that the one who clings to a yoke of slavery does not stand firm and that the one to whom Christ has granted freedom was under a yoke as long as he followed the basic principles of the Law and had a spirit that made him a slave to fear.[314] When he says to stand firm, he is urging the churches in Galatia to have a strong and unshakable faith in Christ and to keep their feet solidly planted in the Savior. The righteous man speaks about this in another place: "He set my feet on a rock."[315] This rock is Christ,[316] who keeps the righteous man's feet from being blown about by every wind of teaching and from being thrown in different directions.[317] Hence it is said to those who stand firm, "And if someone is standing, let him be careful that he does not fall,"[318] and elsewhere, "Stand firm, be courageous, be strong,"[319] so that they may stand firm with the one whom Stephen saw standing at the right hand of the Father when he was being martyred[320] and who said to Moses, "You stand here with me."[321]

He calls the Law a yoke of slavery that is harsh, difficult, and burdensome because it overwhelms those who observe it day and night with a weighty workload. Peter thus says in the Acts of the Apostles, "Now, then, why do you try to put on the necks of the brothers a heavy yoke that neither we nor our fathers have been able to bear?"[322] Paul adds "again" not because the Galatians had previously kept the Law but because the yoke of idolatry is heavy. The Egyptians were weighed down by it as if it were lead, and they drowned in the Red Sea.[323] This is the sense of his statement above: "How is it that you are turning back to those basic elements which are weak and miserable and by which you want to be enslaved all over again, observing special days and months and seasons and years?"[324] After the Apos-

---

314. Cf. Rom 8.15.
315. Ps 40.2.
316. Cf. 1 Cor 10.4.
317. Cf. Eph 4.14.
318. 1 Cor 10.12.
319. 1 Cor 16.13.
320. Cf. Acts 7.55.
321. Dt 5.31.
322. Acts 15.10.
323. Cf. Ex 15.10.
324. Gal 4.9–10.

tle Paul had preached to them, the Galatians forsook their idols
and embraced evangelical grace right away. They did not return
to enslavement to the Jewish Law (a law they had not formerly
known), but in their readiness to observe the [lunar] seasons,
to be circumcised, and to offer animal sacrifices, they were in
a sense returning to the same modes of worship to which they
had previously been enslaved in a state of idolatry. For they say
that the priests of Egypt, the Ishmaelites, and the Midianites are
circumcised. But it is best for us not to know that heathen nations observe special days, months, and years because we do not
want their style of religious celebration to become intermingled
with ours.

*5.2. I, Paul, say to you that if you let yourselves be circumcised, Christ
will be of no value to you.*

In the Gospel the Savior says to his disciples, "Whoever listens to you, listens to me; whoever welcomes you, welcomes
me."[325] The Apostle testifies, "I no longer live, but Christ lives
in me."[326] He says in another place, "Are you demanding proof
that Christ is speaking through me?"[327] His statement "I, Paul,
say to you" implies clearly that the words are to be accepted not
as Paul's alone but as the Lord's. In his first epistle to the Corinthians he said first, "To the married I give this command, not
I, but the Lord,"[328] and then immediately added, "To the rest I
give this instruction."[329] He then said, "I think that I, too, have
the Spirit of God,"[330] in order to ensure that his authority would
not come under fire and that, as long as the Spirit and Christ
were speaking through him, he would not be derided for mim-
icking the prophets in saying, "Thus says the Lord Almighty."
His statement, "I, Paul, say to you that if you let yourselves be
circumcised, Christ will be of no value to you," will have greater import if it is coupled with (among others) what he writes at
the beginning of the epistle, "Paul, an apostle sent not by men
nor through human agency, but through Jesus Christ."[331] Paul's

325. Lk 10.16.   326. Gal 2.20.
327. 2 Cor 13.3.   328. 1 Cor 7.10.
329. 1 Cor 7.12.   330. 1 Cor 7.40.
331. Gal 1.1.

hope is that his audience is persuaded more by the authority of the sender than of the one sent.

Someone may say that this is contrary to what he writes to the Romans, "Circumcision has value if you observe the Law,"[332] and later [in the same epistle], "What advantage, then, is there in being a Jew, or of what use is circumcision? Much in every way. First of all, Jews have been entrusted with the very words of God."[333] If Christ is of no value to the circumcised, how is circumcision of value to those who observe the Law? Here is the answer. The epistle he wrote to the Romans was addressed to believers from both Jewish and Gentile backgrounds, and Paul took this approach to avoid offending either group. He wanted both sets of people to have the same privilege: the Gentiles would not have to be circumcised and the circumcised would not have to be uncircumcised.[334] But when writing to the Galatians he argues differently because they belonged not to the circumcision party but to the believing Gentiles, and because circumcision had no value for those who reverted to the basic elements of the Law after having received evangelical grace.

In the Acts of the Apostles it is told how some from the circumcision party rose up and insisted that Gentile believers be required to undergo circumcision and observe the Law of Moses. The elders at Jerusalem and the apostles who convened there decided unanimously to send a letter [to the Gentile churches] in which they relieved them of the imposition of observing the Law and of doing anything beyond abstaining from food sacrificed to idols, from blood, from sexual immorality, and (as it says in some manuscripts) from the meat of strangled animals.[335] And lest there be any lingering doubt that circumcision has no value but was only granted as a concession to Jew-

---

332. Rom 2.25.

333. Cf. Rom 3.1–2. See Origen, *Comm. Rom.* 2.14.14 (trans. Scheck, FOTC 103:165): "In this letter [Romans] Paul, like an arbiter sitting between the Jews and Greeks, i.e., believing Gentiles, summons and invites both groups to faith in Christ in such a way as not to offend the Jews completely by destroying the Jewish ceremonies nor to cause despair in the Gentiles by affirming the observance of the Law and of the letter."

334. Cf. 1 Cor 7.18.

335. Cf. Acts 15.5–29.

ish believers, Paul tempered his proclamation about circumcision as he came gradually towards the end of the same epistle. He showed that neither circumcision nor uncircumcision is of any avail, saying, "Circumcision is nothing and uncircumcision is nothing; keeping God's commandments is what counts."[336] Circumcision is so useless that it conferred no benefit on the house of Israel, which prided itself on its circumcision, as the prophet says, "All the nations are uncircumcised in the flesh, but the house of Israel is uncircumcised in heart."[337] Furthermore, the uncircumcised Melchisedech blessed Abraham, who was circumcised.[338] When he says, "If you let yourselves be circumcised," what he essentially means is, "If you let yourselves be circumcised in your flesh." Elsewhere he refers to this not as circumcision but as mutilation: "Watch out for the mutilation. For it is we who are the circumcision, we who worship by the Spirit of God, who glory in Christ, and who put no confidence in the flesh."[339] The one who puts no confidence in the flesh looks to Christ for all benefit and does not sow [to please] his sinful nature, only to reap destruction from that nature. He instead sows [to please] the Spirit, from whom eternal life comes.[340]

We should take a closer look at the sentence, "If you let yourselves be circumcised, Christ will be of no value to you." It means that not only circumcision itself is of no value to them if they consent to undergo it, but even if they appear to have the rest of the virtues in Christ without being circumcised, these all vanish as soon as they are circumcised after having believed in Christ. Was circumcision, then, of no value to Timothy?[341] Much in every way. For he was circumcised not because he reckoned that he could derive some benefit from the circumcision itself but because he hoped to win others for Christ. He became a Jew to the Jews, that by virtue of his circumcision he might induce the Jews to believe in Christ.[342] Moreover, circumcision is of no value when it is thought to confer intrinsic benefit.

---

336. 1 Cor 7.19.
338. Cf. Gn 14.18–19.
340. Cf. Gal 6.8.
342. Cf. 1 Cor 9.20–21.

337. Jer 9.26.
339. Phil 3.2–3.
341. Cf. Acts 16.3.

5.3. I declare to every man who lets himself be circumcised that he is obligated to obey the whole Law.

God, who gave the commandment about circumcision first to Abraham and then through Moses in the Law, ordered that not only circumcision but also many other precepts should be observed. These include attending feast days in Jerusalem, offering one sacrificial lamb every morning and one every evening in the same place,[343] a year of rest for the land once every seven years,[344] the year of Jubilee every fifty years,[345] and other examples which any reader can easily compile for himself from Scripture. As for Ebion and his followers, who think that believers in Christ ought to be circumcised after receiving the Gospel, we shall force them either to observe circumcision and everything else prescribed by the Law or, if it is not feasible to observe everything, then to do away with circumcision, which has for all intents and purposes been rendered worthless along with the rest of the requirements of the Law. They might counter that they are obligated to do only what is in their power, arguing that God expects us to do what we can and not what we cannot do. We shall answer them by pointing out that the same God does not wish both for the Law to be kept and to forsake the keepers of the Law. Seeing that the Law has been abolished, on what grounds will he pronounce guilty those who have the will but not the way when it comes to fulfilling all of its commandments? We, however, follow the spiritual Law, which says, "Do not muzzle an ox while it is treading out the grain."[346] And we have the same mindset as the Apostle, "Is it about oxen that God is concerned? Surely he says this for us."[347] We are fastidious about observing Sabbath rests, not so that our ox and ass and lowly animals might enjoy themselves on the Sabbath, but so that these rests might be enjoyed by those men and animals about whom it is written, "O Lord, you will preserve both men and beasts."[348] The "men" refer to all rational and spiritual men, while the "beasts" refer to those of inferior understanding who

343. Cf. Ex 29.38–42.
345. Cf. Lv 25.9–10.
347. 1 Cor 9.9–10.
344. Cf. Lv 25.4.
346. Dt 25.4; 1 Tm 5.18.
348. Ps 36.6.

are taught by the spiritual men to keep the Lord's Sabbath rests. The conclusion drawn here does not contradict what was said above: "If you let yourselves be circumcised, Christ will be of no value to you"; and what comes afterward: "I declare to every man who lets himself be circumcised that he is obligated to obey the whole Law." For the hearers of the Law are not righteous in God's sight, but the doers of the Law will be justified,[349] because the doer of the Law is able to say, "We are the circumcision,"[350] and, "[We are] Jew[s] inwardly,"[351] and, "We know that the Law is spiritual."[352] But whoever abides by mutilation and the murderous letter is not a doer of the Law but an enemy of the true Law. This is especially the case now that the Savior has come and removes the veil from the hearts of us who turn to him,[353] with the result that we all behold the glory of the Lord with uncovered faces and are being transformed from the obsolete letter of the Law into the newness of the Spirit.[354]

5.4. *You who are trying to be justified by the Law have been made void of Christ; you have fallen away from grace.*

Just as no one can serve two masters,[355] so also is it difficult to keep both the shadow and the truth of the Law. The shadow is in the old Law until daytime draws near and the shadows dissipate.[356] The truth is in the Gospel of Christ,[357] "for grace and truth have come through Jesus Christ."[358] If anyone thinks he is justified by observing the Law, he loses the grace of Christ and the Gospel which he possessed. When he loses grace, faith in Christ abandons him, and he stops doing the work of Christ. For κατηργήθητε ἀπὸ τοῦ Χριστοῦ does not mean, "You have been made void of Christ," as it is inaccurately translated in Latin. Closer to the sense of the Greek is, "You have ceased to do

349. Cf. Rom 2.13.
350. Phil 3.3.
351. Rom 2.29.
352. Rom 7.14.
353. Cf. 2 Cor 3.16.
354. Cf. 2 Cor 3.18.
355. Cf. Mt 6.24.
356. Cf. Song 2.17
357. This antithesis between the shadow of the Law and Gospel truth may have been taken from either Origen or Tertullian. See N. Adkin, "The Shadow and the Truth: An Unidentified Antithesis in the Fathers," *GIF* 36 (1984): 245–52.
358. Jn 1.17.

the work of Christ." Hence, what he had said above specifically
about circumcision, "If you let yourselves be circumcised, Christ
will be of no value to you," now applies more generally to the
whole Law, inasmuch as those who believe that they will be justified in keeping some part of the Law derive no benefit when it
comes to doing the work of Christ.

5.5. *By faith we await through the Spirit the righteousness for which
we hope.*

He added "Spirit" in order to distinguish it from the letter.
"The righteousness for which we hope" stands for Christ, because he embodies truth, patience, hope, righteousness, and all
the virtues. We await his second coming,[359] after which he will
judge all things—and he will come no longer with patience, but
with righteousness, to give to each person according to what
he has done.[360] The Apostle and those like him await this day
and say, "Let your kingdom come."[361] When the Son hands the
kingdom over to God the Father and is made subject to him
along with everything else, the head will be placed on the body,
and God will be all in all.[362] For God, who now appears partially
through individuals, will begin to appear in his fullness through
all people.[363]

---

359. Cf. Phil 3.20.   360. Cf. Rom 2.6.
361. Lk 11.2.   362. Cf. 1 Cor 15.24–28.
    363. This is a passing allusion to Origen's eschatological doctrine of ἀποκατά-
στασις (*apokatastasis*), i.e., the restoration of all rational creatures to their original state of spiritual union with God: see H. Crouzel, "L'apocatastase chez
Origène," in *Origeniana quarta. Die Referate des 4. Internationalen Origeneskongresses
(Innsbruck, 2.–6. September 1985)*, ed. L. Lothar (Innsbruck: Tyrolia-Verlag, 1987),
282–90. Rufinus later accused Jerome of embracing this doctrine and its controversial implications (e.g., the salvation of the devil and his fallen angels) in his
Commentary on Ephesians, which he composed immediately after the one on Galatians: see R. Layton, "Recovering Origen's Pauline Exegesis: Exegesis and Eschatology in the *Commentary on Ephesians*," *JECS* 8 (2000): 373–411. Once the Origenist controversy got under way in 393, Jerome began to distance himself from this
and other theological ideas of Origen: see E. Clark, "The Place of Jerome's Commentary on Ephesians in the Origenist Controversy: The *Apokatastasis* and Ascetic
Ideals," *VChr* 41 (1987): 154–71.

5.6. *For in Christ Jesus neither circumcision nor uncircumcision has any value. The only thing that counts is faith expressing itself through love.*

Those who wish to live in Christ Jesus must seek virtue and flee from vice. Circumcision, uncircumcision, and other things which hover between virtue and vice should not be sought after or avoided.[364] Circumcision is of value if you keep the Law. To those who lived under the Law this was beneficial, not because they were circumcised but because the words of God were entrusted to them,[365] and they turned these words into actions and were not excluded from salvation. It should not concern us that Zipporah took a flint knife and circumcised her son to protect her spouse from the angel who was trying to kill him (according to an alternative version of the story told in the Hebrew).[366] Paul argued not so much that circumcision is completely worthless now as he did that it has no value in Christ Jesus. Indeed, as soon as the Gospel began radiating throughout the entire world, the injurious practice of circumcision became superfluous. Like the rest of the commandments of the Law, this one had value at a time when earthly blessings were promised to keepers of the Law. If they abided by it, they would be blessed in the city and in the field. For instance, their grain storehouses would be full and they would receive many other promised blessings.[367] We, however, desire to be worthwhile in Christ Jesus and to find strength in him, that is, in the true circumcision and not in the Jewish mutilation. "A man is not a Jew if he is only one outwardly, nor is circumcision merely outward and physical. A man is a Jew if he is one inwardly, and circumcision is of the heart, by the Spirit, not by the written code."[368] Therefore, physical circumcision has no value in Christ. What counts is circumcision of the heart and of the ears, which eradicates the reason why the Jews were reproached: "Your ears are uncircumcised and you cannot hear."[369] Also of value is circumcision of the lips, which Moses humbly complained that he lacked, as

364. Jerome is referencing the Stoic concept of "indifferent things" (ἀδιά-φορα)—things which the moral law neither commands nor forbids. Circumcision, then, is something morally neutral.

365. Cf. Rom 3.2.   366. Cf. Ex 4.24–26.
367. Cf. Dt 28.3–14.   368. Rom 2.28–29.
369. Jer 6.10.

it is written in the Hebrew, "I am uncircumcised of lips."[370] Circumcision also provides much benefit in terms of lust because impurity is cut off through chastity.

Physical circumcision and uncircumcision are of no value in Christ Jesus because they both loom somewhere between vice and virtue. But faith expressing itself through love *is* of value. For the faith which was credited to Abraham as righteousness[371] is sanctioned, and every work of faith is attributed to love, on which the entire Law and the prophets depend. The Savior affirms that the Law and the prophets hinge on these two commandments: "Love your God and love your neighbor."[372] Paul, too, says, "The commandments, 'Do not commit adultery,' 'Do not steal,' 'Do not covet,' and whatever other commandments there may be, are summed up in this one rule: 'Love your neighbor as yourself.'"[373] So, if all of the commandments are summarized in this one, the faith which expresses itself through love has even more value. It is evident that the expression of faith through love embodies the completeness of all of the commandments. Just as faith without works is dead, as the Apostle James says,[374] so works, even though they be good, are counted as dead without faith. What do unbelievers with good morals have besides the [empty] works of virtue?

An example, taken from the Gospel, of the faith which expresses itself through love is the prostitute who approached the Lord when he was dining at the house of a Pharisee and wet his feet with her tears, wiped them with her hair, and poured perfume on them.[375] When the Pharisee grumbled about this, the Lord told the parable about the two men who owed fifty and five hundred denarii [to a moneylender]. He concluded it by saying, "Therefore, I tell you that her many sins have been forgiven because she loved much."[376] He turned to the woman and said, "Your faith has saved you. Go in peace."[377] It is abundantly clear that this woman had the faith which expresses itself through love, which is of great value in Christ.

370. Ex 6.12.
372. Mt 22.40.
374. Cf. Jas 2.26.
376. Lk 7.47.

371. Cf. Gn 15.6; Gal 3.6.
373. Rom 13.9.
375. Cf. Lk 7.36–39.
377. Lk 7.50.

Someone may say that Paul has succeeded in proving that the circumcision which he knew formerly to be of use is of no value in Christ. But was someone making an issue about uncircumcision, leading him to include the words "nor uncircumcision"? If we consider that most Christians—those of us who were grafted from a wild olive tree into the root of a cultivated olive tree—rejoice at the Jews being the branches that have been broken off[378] and say that uncircumcision, in which Abraham pleased God and had his faith credited to him as righteousness,[379] is better than circumcision, which was given as a sign of faith to a man of faith and was of no profit to Israel, we will see that this arrogant boast has now been excluded with the greatest foresight.

378. Cf. Rom 11.17–19.
379. Cf. Gn 15.6; Gal 3.6.

BOOK THREE (GALATIANS 5.7–6.18)

PREFACE

HAVE FORGED this third installment of the commentary, Paula and Eustochium, bearing in mind my own limitations and recognizing that the little sputtering stream of my meager talent barely makes a sound. Nowadays in churches the purity and simplicity of the Apostle's words are done away with, and other qualities are in demand. We congregate as if we were in the Athenaeum or in lecture halls and we long for the thundering applause of bystanders and a speech that, like a dolled-up harlot strolling in the streets, is decorated in the deceit of rhetorical artifice and aims to win the favor of the masses rather than to instruct them,[1] soothing the ears of the listeners like a sweet-sounding psaltery and flute.[2] Truly applicable to our times is that passage from the prophet Ezekiel in which the Lord says to him, "You have become to them like sound of the lute that is well-

---

1. In this paragraph Jerome borrows some of his concepts and Latin phrases from Cyprian's *Ep. ad Don.* 2 (ANF 5:275): "The poor mediocrity of my shallow understanding produces a very limited harvest, and enriches the soil with no fruitful deposits. . . . In courts of justice, in the public assembly, in political debate, a copious eloquence may be the glory of a voluble ambition; but in speaking of the Lord God, a chaste simplicity of expression strives for the conviction of faith rather with the substance, than with the powers, of eloquence. Therefore accept from me things, not clever but weighty, words, not decked up to charm a popular audience with cultivated rhetoric, but simple and fitted by their unvarnished truthfulness for the proclamation of the divine mercy." See A. Cain, *REAug* 55 (2009): 45–46.

2. Other patristic writers (e.g., John Chrysostom) complained about Christian congregations craving only sermons that were heavy on rhetorical fluff and light on substance. See B. Leyerle, *Theatrical Shows and Ascetic Lives: John Chrysostom's Attack on Spiritual Marriage* (Berkeley: University of California Press, 2001), 63–64 (with references to primary sources).

made and that sings beautifully, for they hear your words but do not act on them."[3]

But what should I do? Should I keep quiet? It is written, however, "You shall not appear empty-handed in the sight of the Lord your God."[4] And Isaiah laments, "Woe to me, a wretch, because I remained silent"[5] (this at any rate is how it translates from the original Hebrew). Shall I speak? I could, but my reading of Hebrew, a harsh and guttural language, has ruined all the elegance of my style and the charm of my Latin prose.[6] You yourselves know that it has been more than fifteen years since Cicero, Virgil, or any writer of secular literature has fallen into my hands.[7] If anyone by chance should call me to question about this,[8] I only vaguely recall the details of my dream.[9] How far I have advanced in my unceasing study of Hebrew, I leave to others to judge; I know what I have lost in my own language.[10] To add to this, I do

3. Ezek 33.32 (LXX).   4. Ex 23.15.

5. Is 6.5.

6. As I noted in the Introduction, Jerome's claim that his Latin was ruined is a conceit meant to imply that he had an extremely advanced knowledge of Hebrew and that consequently his Hebrew philology in the *Commentary* can be trusted. Thus this seemingly benign statement is actually a subtle but potent affirmation of his authority as a Biblical scholar.

7. An allusion to Jerome's famous Ciceronian dream-vision (told at *Ep.* 22.30), in which he was dragged before the throne of God and harshly rebuked for preferring Cicero and the Latin classics to the stylistically uncouth Latin Bible. In the dream he vowed to God never again to read the classics ("Lord, if I ever again possess secular books or read them, I have denied you"). Scholars disagree about exactly when and where the dream took place. Some have placed it in Trier as early as the 360s; others locate it in Antioch in the early or middle 370s. Whatever the case, if taken at face value, Jerome's comment about it happening "more than fifteen years" ago enables us to fix the date to no later than 371. On the dating controversy, see N. Adkin, "The Date of the Dream of Saint Jerome," *SCO* 43 (1993): 263–73.

8. As it turns out, this statement was prophetic. About a decade later, Rufinus (*Apol. c. Hier.* 2.6–7) accused Jerome of hypocrisy and perjury for swearing off the Latin classics in his dream yet continuing to saturate his writings with references to them.

9. Jerome distances himself from his vow perhaps because he invokes the Latin classics so often in the *Commentary* and is aware of the inconsistency. What is more, his supposedly vague recollection is ironic because he had given a vivid account of the dream a mere two years earlier in Rome!

10. For the debate about Jerome's actual proficiency in Hebrew, see New-

not write with my own hand because of the weakness of my eyes and my whole body.[11] I cannot make up for the slowness of my dictation by exerting more effort and diligence, as they say Virgil would do when he cared for the books he wrote in the manner of a bear licking her cubs.[12] I must summon my secretary and either dictate right away whatever comes to me first or, if I wish to ponder a little bit in the hope of producing something better, my secretary, without saying a word, rebukes me; he clenches his fist, wrinkles his brow, and shows by his whole-body fidgeting that he thinks he has come for nothing.[13] A discourse may be the product of an admirable talent, it may be sophisticated in its rhetorical invention, and it may have an ornate word-arrangement, but if it has not been refined and polished by the hand of the author himself, it is unexceptional and lacks a sense of weightiness tempered by elegance. Like wealthy yokels, its riches become grounds for reproach and not distinction.

Where am I heading with all of this? I want you and other read-

---

man, "How should we Measure Jerome's Hebrew Competence?" in Cain and Lössl, eds., *Jerome of Stridon*, 131–40 (with references to all of the relevant scholarly literature).

11. This is one of countless examples of Jerome complaining about physical ailments (for other examples, see Cavallera, *Jérôme*, 1.309–10, 312–13, 319, 334–35). From a rhetorical point of view, such complaints were calculated to glorify Jerome as a scholarly martyr who had prematurely worn out his eyes through excessive study. This is of course not to deny at all that there was reality behind the rhetoric. Jerome's eye troubles can be explained in part by his habit of working late into the night by poor lamplight, and his frequent illnesses may have been related to his ascetic diet (cf. Paula's daughter Blesilla's premature death brought on by too strict a diet, mentioned in Jerome, *Ep.* 39).

12. Cf. Suetonius, *V. Virg.* 22; Aulus Gellius, *Noct. Att.* 17.10.2–3. Jerome told the same story, using almost identical wording, twenty years later (early 407) in the preface to Book 3 of his *Commentary on Zechariah* (CCSL 76A:848).

13. Over-the-shoulder glimpses into the inner workings of his scholarly workshop like this one sprout up everywhere in Jerome's writings. They have been assembled and analyzed topically by Paulo Evaristo Arns in his published dissertation *La technique du livre d'après saint Jérôme* (Paris: Boccard, 1953). No other ancient author was nearly as exhibitionistic as Jerome when it came to documenting his work habits. Indeed, Jerome is our most prolific primary source for the mechanics of stenography in late antiquity: see H. Hagendahl, "Die Bedeutung der Stenographie für die spätlateinische christliche Literatur," *JbAC* 14 (1971): 24–38.

ers to know that I am writing not a panegyric or a declamation but a commentary. Consequently, I hope that my own words receive no praise but that others' sage words may be understood as they originally were written down.[14] The task at hand is to elucidate obscure points, to touch only briefly on what is already clear, and to linger over things that are difficult to figure out. This is why many refer to the work of commentators as "explanation." If anyone is looking for eloquence or enjoys rhetorical declamations, he has Demosthenes and Polemon in Greek and Cicero and Quintilian in Latin. The church of Christ has drawn its members not from the Academy or the Lycaeum but from the common people. The Apostle thus says, "Examine your calling, brothers, and how not many of you are wise, or powerful, or noble according to the flesh. God has chosen the foolish things of this world to shame the wise, the weak things of this world to shame the mighty, and the base and contemptible things of this world, and he chose the things that are not in order to destroy the things that are."[15] Since the world did not have the wisdom to recognize God from the orderliness, diversity, and constancy of his creatures, God saw fit to save those who believed through the foolishness of the Gospel message. He accomplished this neither through the persuasive words of worldly wisdom nor through clever eloquence, lest the cross of Christ be emptied of its potency;[16] where is the wise man, where is the grammarian, where are the natural scientists? [God] accomplished this rather through the display of power and the Spirit,[17] so that the faith of believers might rest in the power of God and not in the wisdom of men.

The Apostle said to the same Corinthians, "When I came to you, brothers, I did not come with excellence of speech or wisdom declaring to you the testimony of the Lord. For I resolved to know nothing among you except Christ Jesus and him cru-

14. Cf. a similar statement in the preface to Book 1: "It is now up to the Lord's mercy to make sure that others' sage sayings are not lost through my incompetence and that they are as commendable somewhere else as they are in their original context."

15. 1 Cor 1.26–28. 16. Cf. 1 Cor 1.17.
17. Cf. 1 Cor 2.4.

cified."[18] He judiciously pre-empted objections to his authority so as not to be thought of as a preacher of foolishness for saying these things. He said further, "We speak the wisdom of God in a mystery, which was hidden and which none of the rulers of this age knew."[19] How few now read Aristotle? How many are familiar with Plato's name and works? Only a few idle old men study them in out-of-the-way places.[20] The entire world, however, speaks of our peasants and fishermen and sings their praises. Their simple words must be presented—and when I say "simple," I mean the words themselves, not the concepts behind them. But if, in answer to your prayers, I could have the same Spirit in expounding their epistles as they had when dictating them,[21] you would see that there were as much majesty and breadth of true wisdom in them as there were arrogance and vanity in the learned men of the world. Let me briefly confess to you a secret of mine: I do not want the person who wishes to understand the Apostle through me to have such a difficult time making sense of my writings that he has to find someone to interpret the interpreter. But now it is time for us to go on to the rest [of the commentary].

BOOK THREE

5.7. *You were running a good race. Who got in your way and kept you from obeying the truth?*

What the Latin translator rendered here as *veritati non oboedire* and what in Greek is τῇ ἀληθείᾳ μὴ πείθεσθαι, he translated

---

18. 1 Cor 2.1–2. 19. 1 Cor 2.7–8.

20. Jerome is probably deliberately downplaying Plato's and Aristotle's influences in his own day because he wants to convey the impression that the Christian church has triumphed over the pagan intellectual past, represented by these two thinkers. On the enormous impact Plato and Aristotle had on late antique philosophy, see, e.g., H. J. Blumenthal, *Aristotle and Neoplatonism in Late Antiquity: Interpretations of the* De Anima (Ithaca: Cornell University Press, 1996), and the relevant essays in *Plato's* Timaeus *and the Foundations of Cosmology in Late Antiquity, the Middle Ages and the Renaissance,* ed. T. Leinkauf and C. Steel (Ithaca: Cornell University Press, 2005).

21. This sounds like an echo of Origen's belief that the same Spirit who inspired the Biblical writers also inspires their commentators (see *Peri archōn* 2.7.2; 4.2.7).

in a previous passage as "not to believe the truth."[22] When commenting on that passage, I noted that this reading was not present in the ancient manuscripts, though even the Greek manuscripts are confused by this mistake. The sense of the verse is as follows. You used to worship the Father in Spirit and in truth,[23] and you have received the fullness of Christ. You knew that the Law had been given through Moses only to the people [of Israel] and that it was not observed [perfectly], whereas grace and truth were not only given through Christ but also brought to pass through him.[24] Given that you were running a good race and were abiding more by the truth than by images [of the truth],[25] what wicked teacher convinced you to follow the shadow of the Law[26] and to relinquish evangelical truth?

The verse continues, "You gave in to no one." It seems best not to comment on this sequence of words since I have not found it either in the Greek manuscripts or in others' commentaries on Galatians.

5.8. *That persuasion of yours does not come from the one who has called you.*

In the Latin manuscripts I have found the reading, "That persuasion of yours comes from God (*ex Deo*) who has called you." I suspect that it originally had been "from the one" (*ex eo*), but due to a misunderstanding and a similarity in spelling it was gradually replaced by "from God" (*ex Deo*). This latter meaning makes no sense because he had just reprimanded them for not obeying the truth, thereby showing that obedience or disobedience lies in their power to choose, yet he now asserts that persuasion and obedience were not so much in the power of the called as in the power of the one doing the calling. Therefore, the reading that is preferable and more faithful [to the Greek] is, "That persuasion of yours does not come from the one who has called you." The work of God is of course one thing, the work of men another. God's work is to call, and men's work is either to believe or not to believe. Elsewhere in Scripture the

22. Gal 3.1b.
23. Cf. Jn 4.23–24.
24. Cf. Jn 1.17.
25. Cf. 1 Thes 1.9.
26. Cf. Heb 10.1.

notion of free will is upheld. "If you are willing and listen to me."[27] "And now, O Israel, what does the Lord your God ask of you?"[28] But it is most forcefully affirmed in the passage under discussion. Some less sophisticated folk have expunged the word "not" and thus have made this verse mean the opposite of what the Apostle intended because they are under the impression that they are giving honor to God by conceding to him absolute control over our will.

Neither God nor the devil is the reason why we incline toward either good or evil. That persuasion comes not from the one who has called us but from us; it is we who choose either to heed or not to heed the one who calls.[29] Put another way: The persuasion you now follow does not come from God, who initially called you, but from those who later caused you trouble.

5.9. *A little yeast works through* [fermentat] *the whole batch of dough.*

A faulty translation is given in the Latin manuscripts: "A little yeast spoils (*corrumpit*) the whole batch of dough." Rather than render the Apostle's words faithfully, the translator has imported his own sense.[30] Paul uses this same sentence in his epistle to the Corinthians when he orders that the man who consorted with his father's wife be removed from the congregation and be handed over for repentance's sake to destruction and bodily tribulation through fasting and infirmity, so that his spirit may be saved on the day of the Lord Jesus Christ. He says, "Your boasting is not good. Do you not know that a little yeast spoils (*corrumpit*) the whole batch of dough?"[31]—or, as I have al-

27. Is 1.19.

28. Dt 10.12.

29. Cf. Origen, *Peri Archōn* 3.2.4 (trans. Butterworth, 217): "We must bear in mind, however, that nothing else happens to us as a result of these good or evil thoughts which are suggested to our heart but a mere agitation and excitement which urges us on to deeds either of good or of evil. It is possible for us, when an evil power has begun to urge us on to a deed of evil, to cast away the wicked suggestions and to resist the low enticements and to do absolutely nothing worthy of blame; and it is possible on the other hand when a divine power has urged us on to better things not to follow its guidance, since our faculty of free will is preserved to us in either case."

30. Jerome's translation better captures Paul's ζυμοῖ ("causes to rise").

31. 1 Cor 5.6.

ready emended it, "works through (*fermentat*) the whole batch of dough?" He immediately adds, "Get rid of the old yeast so that you may be a new batch without yeast. For Christ, our Passover lamb, has been sacrificed. Therefore, let us keep the festival, not with the old yeast, the yeast of malice and wickedness, but with unleavened bread, the bread of sincerity and truth."[32]

Paul now uses this same sentence to show that the spiritual bread of the church, which comes down from heaven,[33] must not be defiled by a Jewish interpretation. The Lord says this very thing to the disciples when he instructs them to stay away from the yeast of the Pharisees.[34] The Evangelist then clarifies this by adding that he was referring to the teaching of the Pharisees.[35]

What else is this teaching of the Pharisees but observance of the Law according to the flesh? This is the sense of the passage: Do not think that the crafty plots of those few men coming from Judea who teach another gospel should be underestimated. An ember is tiny and almost invisible to the eye when you look at it, but if a small flame ignites the tinder, it devours city-walls, cities, vast forests, and whole provinces. Yeast, the parable about which is told in another place in the Gospel,[36] also seems like something small and inconsequential. But when it is mixed in with flour it spoils the entire batch by its vigorous activity, and everything in the mixture gives way to its forcefulness.[37] Similarly, perverse doctrine begins with one person and at first finds a favorable audience of barely two or three people. But the cancer gradually festers in the body and, according to the familiar proverb, one sheep's disease pollutes the entire flock. Therefore, the ember must be extinguished as soon as it appears so that the house does not burn down. Yeast must be kept far from the batch [of flour] so that it does not spoil. Putrid flesh must be amputated so that the body does not rot. And the diseased animal must be sequestered from the sheepfolds so that the flocks

---

32. 1 Cor 5.7–8.   33. Cf. Jn 6.32–33.
34. Cf. Mt 16.6.   35. Cf. Mt 16.12.
36. Cf. Mt 13.33.

37. Cf. Plutarch, *Mor.* 289F: "Yeast is itself also the product of corruption and brings corruption in the dough with which it is mixed; for the dough becomes flabby and inert, and the process of leavening seems to be one of putrefaction . . . if it goes too far, it completely sours and spoils the flour."

do not die. Arius[38] was one ember in Alexandria, but because he was not extinguished at once, his flame destroyed the entire city.

5.10a. *I am confident in the Lord that you will take no other view.*

Paul proclaims, prophetically and not by guesswork (as some claim), that the Galatians will return to the path of truth from which they had deviated. This, after all, is the man who encourages others to desire spiritual gifts eagerly, especially the gift of prophecy,[39] and who, full of the same divine grace, says, "We know in part and we prophesy in part."[40] With spiritual foresight he knew that in the end they would believe nothing but what they had been taught through his epistle. "I am confident in the Lord that you will take no other view." He intensified his tone by mentioning the Lord's name. For if his hope had been a mere conjecture, he could have said simply, "I am confident in you." But by adding "in the Lord," he showed confidence through a certain divine spirit when he prophesied about what he knew would happen.

5.10b. *The one who is throwing you into confusion will assume a penalty, whoever he is.*

Some say that Paul is secretly attacking Peter, whom he says he opposed to his face for not walking uprightly in the truth of the Gospel.[41] Paul, however, would not speak of the head of the

---

38. Arius (c. 256–336) was the most notorious Christian "heretic" of the fourth century. He was a priest in Alexandria around 318, when his troubles with the institutional church began. Arius taught that Jesus was not co-eternal with the Father and that there was a time, before he was "begotten," when he did not exist; this was tantamount to denying Christ's full divinity. In 320, Arius was condemned by a synod of Alexandria and expelled from the city. In 325, his teaching was denounced by the Council of Nicea, which formulated the Creed of Nicea to affirm, in explicit terms, Christ's full divinity and full humanity. Throughout the fourth century and beyond, Arius was vilified by orthodox writers as the archetypical Christian heretic. More recently, though, scholars have taken a more sympathetic approach and have sought to understand Arius on his own terms, as a well-meaning theological conservative, rather than through the polemical filter of his critics. See especially R. Williams, *Arius: Heresy and Tradition* (Grand Rapids: W. B. Eerdmans, 2002).

39. Cf. 1 Cor 14.1.   40. 1 Cor 13.9.

41. Cf. Gal 2.11, 14.

church with such rash imprecation, and Peter does not deserve blame for throwing the church into confusion. We must suppose that he is speaking of someone else who either had been with the apostles or had come from Judea or had been one of the believing Pharisees or at any rate was deemed important enough among the Galatians to "assume a penalty for throwing the church into confusion, whoever he is."[42]

"Assume a penalty" is analogous to what he says in other words in a later verse: "Each one should carry his own load."[43] I find that in Scripture a load can be taken in either a bad sense, to refer to people who are weighed down with heavy sins, or in a good sense, to speak of those who bear the light load of the virtues. In the Psalm the remorseful man speaks of sins: "My iniquities have gone over my head; like a heavy load they have pressed down upon me."[44] The Savior talks about the virtues and how one learns them: "For my yoke is easy and my load is light."[45] That we may take "learning the ropes" of the virtues as a load is made apparent in the Gospel: The Pharisees tie up heavy, immovable loads and put them on men's shoulders, but they themselves are not willing to lift a finger to move them.[46]

The Savior's exhortation to the apostles, "Do not let your heart be troubled and do not be afraid,"[47] throws into relief just how serious an offense it is to agitate, as if with violent waves, the calm hearts of people and to disturb their sense of peace. If anyone disturbs someone in the church or causes him to stumble, it is better for him to have a millstone tied around his neck and to be thrown into the sea with it than for him to cause one of the little ones watched over by the Savior to stumble.[48] Thus

---

42. At the beginning of the epistle (1.7) Paul speaks of the agitators in the plural (οἱ ταράσσοντες ὑμᾶς) but here as one person (ὁ ταράσσων ὑμᾶς); perhaps this individual was the one leading the charge. These agitators were Judaizers, i.e., Christians who insisted that the Mosaic Law is binding on Christians. For a thorough reconstruction (from Paul's counter-arguments and other evidence) of the nature of their demands and the reasons for their apparent success among the Galatian Christians, see J. M. G. Barclay, *Obeying the Truth: A Study of Paul's Ethics in Galatians* (Edinburgh: T & T Clark, 1988), 36–74.

43. Gal 6.5.   44. Ps 38.4.
45. Mt 11.30.   46. Cf. Mt 23.4.
47. Jn 14.27.   48. Cf. Lk 17.1–2.

the Galatians had been thrown into confusion about the distinctions the ignorant were making between the spirit and the letter [of the Law], circumcision and mutilation, and inner Judaism and outer Judaism.

This, in brief, is what he says: If anyone draws you back to the teaching of the Pharisees and wants you to be circumcised in your flesh, though he be eloquent and boast in his knowledge of the Law, I say nothing to you except this—and you cannot brush it aside—that he will assume a penalty for this and will be rewarded according to his labor.[49]

5.11. *Brothers, if I preach circumcision, why am I still being persecuted? In that case the stumbling block of the cross has been made void* (the Greek puts it better as "ceased").[50]

We read in the Acts of the Apostles, and the Apostle Paul himself reminds us often in his epistles, that he very frequently underwent persecution at the hands of the Jews for teaching that Gentile believers in Christ need not be circumcised.[51] In their efforts to deceive the Galatians, those to whom he referred in the previous passage ("The one who is throwing you into confusion will assume a penalty, whoever he is") made this allegation: Peter, James, John, and the rest of the apostles in Judea observe circumcision and other aspects of the Law, but so does Paul, who taught you something other than the truth, who circumcised Timothy,[52] and who often became a Jew to the Jews[53] because that is what he really was. Paul now wishes to expunge this way of thinking from the Galatians' minds. He accordingly says, "Brothers, if I preach circumcision, why am I still being persecuted?" What he means is this: All the hatred of the Jews is directed at me, and they are enraged at me for no other reason than that I teach that the Gentiles do not need to be circumcised or keep the burdensome, superfluous, and obsolete precepts of the Law. The fact that I am persecuted shows that I do not preach circumcision but instead seek to do away with it. For the Jews persecute

49. Cf. 1 Cor 3.8.
50. This parenthetical gloss is Jerome's.
51. Cf. Acts 21.21.   52. Cf. Acts 16.3; 1 Cor 7.18.
53. Cf. 1 Cor 9.20.

me not so much for preaching the Crucifixion, or for preaching that Jesus is the Christ whom the Law and the prophets foretold, as they do for teaching that the Law has been fulfilled.

Our Lord himself, who is called the stone that causes men to trip and a rock that makes them stumble,[54] shows that the Cross is a stumbling block to the Jews and foolishness to the Gentiles.[55] It is a stumbling block for no other reason, I think, than this: The Gospel message sails briskly among its hearers until it comes to the subject of the Cross, whereupon it hits a snag and is unable freely to move ahead any further.[56] But this Cross, which is a stumbling block to Jews and foolishness to Gentiles, is power and wisdom to us believers. "For Christ is the power of God and the wisdom of God."[57] The Cross was called foolishness because God's folly is wiser than men, and it was called weakness and a stumbling block because the weakness of God is stronger than men.[58] Paul says: But since the stumbling block of Christ's Cross still remains and I suffer persecution, which I would not suffer if it were removed, some make a spectacle out of accusing me of preaching circumcision, and the reason I endure persecution is that I attack circumcision.

5.12. *I wish that those causing you trouble would be forcibly castrated.*
The question arises how Paul—a disciple of him who said, "Bless those who curse you,"[59] and who himself said, "Bless and do not curse,"[60] and, "Slanderers will not inherit the kingdom of God"[61]—now curses those who were throwing the churches of Galatia into confusion. He even curses them with an express wish: "I wish that those causing you trouble would be forc-

---

54. Cf. 1 Pt 2.8.   55. Cf. 1 Cor 1.23.

56. Jerome was particularly fond of nautical metaphors, especially when describing the perils of the spiritual life: see, e.g., *Epp.* 14.6; 43.3; 77.6; 125.2; 147.11. Other patristic writers also employed these metaphors: see H. Rondet, "Le symbolisme de la mer chez saint Augustin," in *Augustinus Magister: Congrès International Augustinien, Paris, 21–24 Septembre 1954,* 2 vols. (Paris: Institut d'Études Augustiniennes, 1954), 2.691–711; B. McGinn, "Ocean and Desert as Symbols of Mystical Absorption in the Christian Tradition," *JR* 74 (1994): 155–81.

57. 1 Cor 1.24.   58. Cf. 1 Cor 1.25.
59. Lk 6.28.   60. Rom 12.14.
61. 1 Cor 6.10.

ibly castrated." Castration is so abominable that whoever inflicts this suffering on people against their will is punished as a criminal[62] and whoever castrates himself is held in disrepute. Some say that if Paul is being truthful when he says, "Christ lives in me,"[63] and, "Are you demanding proof that Christ is speaking through me?"[64] then his cursing does not originate from the One who says, "Learn from me, for I am humble, meek, and gentle in heart."[65] The perception is that he was more interested in giving free reign to his anger at the Jews and to a certain unbridled madness than in imitating him who, like a lamb, did not open his mouth before his shearer[66] and did not curse the one cursing him[67] but rather handed himself over to death as a condemned man. Against this charge Paul may be defended by responding that his words are prompted more by love for the churches of God than by anger at his opponents. He watched as the entire province that he had converted from idolatry to faith in Christ (all the while shedding his own blood and undergoing harrowing dangers) was upset by a sudden persuasion, and he could not hold himself in check because of his grief—the grief of an apostle and [the Galatians'] spiritual father. He changed his tone and became irate at the very people whom he had been coaxing, for his aim was at least to restrain with a rebuke those whom he could not restrain by being mild. Since the Apostle was still enclosed in a frail vessel and watched as the law in his own body took him captive and led him into the law of sin,[68] it is no surprise that he should have spoken like this on one occasion, when we find that holy men frequently fall into this trap.

Although it may appear superfluous to some, the point may be made that Paul did not so much curse them as he prayed for them to dispense with the parts of their body that made them go astray. It says in the Gospel that it is better to enter the king-

---

62. For ancient attitudes toward castration, see H. F. J. Horstmanshoff, "La castration dans les textes latins médicaux," in *Maladie et maladies dans les textes latins antiques et médiévaux,* ed. C. Deroux (Brussels: Société d'Études Latines de Bruxelles, 1998), 85–94; C. Serarcangeli and G. Rispoli, "La mutilazione crudele: note storiche su castratori e castrati," *MedSec,* n.s., 13 (2001): 441–54.

63. Gal 2.20.   64. 2 Cor 13.3.
65. Mt 11.29.   66. Cf. Is 53.7.
67. Cf. 1 Pt 2.23.   68. Cf. Rom 7.23.

dom of heaven with only one eye, hand, foot, or any other part of the anatomy than for the whole body to go to hell.[69] Likewise, Paul here wishes for them to lose one part of their body rather than for their entire body to be condemned to eternal fire. In case unbelievers ever take issue with this passage, we have shown how to answer them.

Now it is time to make our advance against the heretics, especially Marcion, Valentinus, and everyone else who undermines the Old Testament. Let us challenge them: On what grounds do they excuse Paul's behavior as an apostle of the good God yet defame the Creator as a savage, bloodthirsty war-monger and unrelenting judge?[70] Without doubt, the old Law does not pronounce a sentence nearly as harsh or cruel as Paul does against certain people when he says, "I wish that those causing you trouble would be forcibly castrated." They cannot claim that the Apostle was praying for the enemies of Christ who upset his churches, nor can they show by their wordiness that a statement full of passion and indignation actually proceeded from love. Therefore, whatever excuse they give for Paul, we shall return in kind with a defense of the old Law.

5.13a. *Brothers, you were called to be free. Just do not use your freedom as an opportunity for the flesh* (The word "use" is implied; the Latin translator supplied it because it is not found in the Greek).

Given the obscurity of this verse, I have thought it best to insert a translated portion from the tenth book of Origen's *Miscellanies*.[71] I have done this not because individual parts [of this verse] cannot be explained according to their proper context and sense, but because, if they are isolated from the preceding passage, they comprise a single, indiscernible mass, and, if they

69. Cf. Mt 18.8–9.

70. Cf. 2.3.13a on how Marcion "maligns [the Creator] as a cruel, bloodthirsty judge."

71. This portion of the *Miscellanies* survives only in Jerome's Latin translation. Origen devoted most of this book to the visions recorded at the end of Daniel. By way of a conclusion he turned to Galatians, perhaps to deal with the ἀλληγορούμενα of Gal 4.24. See R. Grant, "The *Stromateis* of Origen," in *Epektasis: Mélanges patristiques offerts au Cardinal Jean Daniélou*, ed. J. Fontaine and C. Kannengiesser (Paris: Beauchesne, 1972), 285–92 (at 289–90).

are understood literally, they seem internally dissonant and logically inconsistent.

These are Origen's words:

This is a difficult passage and so it requires elucidation. The one who is free and who, in a more elevated sense, pursues the Spirit and truth disdains both the letter and the types which precede [the realities they foreshadow]. He must not look down on lesser [Christians] and give those who cannot grasp spiritual profundities an occasion for despairing completely about their plight. For although they are weak, and although they are called flesh in comparison with the Spirit, they are nevertheless the flesh of Christ. For if he apprehends the mystery of the love which serves the lesser one, let him do what he can for the weak to make sure that a brother for whom Christ died may not perish in deficiency of knowledge. Watch closely to see whether this is the sense that emerges from the discussion below.

"Brothers, you were called to be free." Perhaps he says this because not everyone could understand the calling to freedom. This is why you now hear, "Just do not use your freedom as an opportunity for the flesh." The greater must serve the lesser out of love, and he who aspires to be greater will become the servant of all.[72] Therefore, the spiritual man must not tear to pieces [believers who are] Christ's flesh, nor must he give them an opportunity to bite and devour one another.[73] The one who walks by the Spirit and abides by the words of Scripture in the spirit of Scripture must not gratify the desires of his flesh.

Most take literally the injunction, "Walk by the Spirit and you will not gratify the desires of the flesh."[74] If we do the same, Paul will do a sudden turn-about and contradict the argument and the point of his entire epistle. He continues right after this, "But if you are led by the Spirit, you are not under the Law."[75] The discourse has to some extent been internally consistent up to this point. If we again subscribe to the literal meaning, Paul leads us at once from a discussion about flesh and Spirit to random precepts, that is, "The deeds of the flesh are obvious,"[76] and by contrast, "The fruit of the Spirit is love," and so on.[77] But we must not be dismayed by the implication of these statements. The divine books record deeds of the flesh—a fact that is not edifying for those who take the narrative literally. Who will not be prompted to become a slave to extravagance and regard sexual immorality as something permissible when he reads that Judah propositioned a prostitute[78] and that the patriarchs had many wives at once? How will someone not be inspired to worship idols when he thinks that the blood

72. Cf. Mk 10.44.
73. Cf. Gal 5.15.
74. Gal 5.16.
75. Gal 5.18.
76. Gal 5.19.
77. Gal 5.22.
78. Cf. Gn 38.14–18.

of bulls and the rest of the sacrifices detailed in Leviticus have no further significance attached to them than what the letter of the Law conveys?[79] What Scripture teaches about hostilities is clearly shown in this
passage, "O wretched daughter of Babylon, happy is he who will repay
you for what you have done to us. Happy is he who will seize your infants and dash them against the rocks,"[80] and also in this one, "Every
morning I destroyed all the wicked in the land,"[81] and so on. Comparable passages may be adduced which deal with discord, jealousy, rage,
quarrels, and dissensions. If we do not go with a spiritual interpretation of them, examples from history will stir us toward these [vices]
rather than deter us from them. Heresies, too, have taken rise more
from the literal interpretation of Scripture than from the work of our
flesh, as most people think. We learn envy and drunkenness from the
letter of the Law. After the flood Noah got drunk,[82] and so did the patriarchs when they were in Egypt visiting their brother Joseph.[83] There
are stories in the Book of Kingdoms and elsewhere about revelries. For
instance, David danced in celebration and tambourines made loud
music before God's Ark of the Covenant.[84] One might ask how the literal word of divine Scripture, which is called its flesh, leads us into sorcery and magic, unless we make our way toward the spirit of the same
Scripture. This is what is meant, I believe, when it is said that Moses was
educated in all the wisdom and learning of the Egyptians[85] and that
Daniel and the three boys were found to be ten times wiser than the
magicians, enchanters, sorcerers, and astrologers.[86]

Clinging to the flesh [that is, the literal meaning] of Scripture
opens up the door for many evils. "Those who do these things will not
inherit the kingdom of God."[87] So, then, let us seek the spirit of Scripture and the fruits that are not readily apparent to the eye. For the
fruit of the Spirit is found in Scripture only with great effort, exertion,
and careful study.[88] I reckon that Paul was referring ever so carefully
and cautiously to the literal meaning of Scripture when he said, "The
deeds of the flesh are obvious." As for the spiritual meaning, he did
not say that the fruit of the Spirit is obvious, but he said instead, "The
fruit of the Spirit is love, joy, peace," and so on. Now, if we leave behind types and move towards the Spirit and the truth of Scripture, first
love is spread out before us, and then we move on to joy and peace on

---

79. Cf. *Hom. Lv.* 1.2 (trans. Barkley, FOTC 83:30), where Origen ridicules
a strictly literal interpretation of the Levitical prescriptions because it would
mean that Christians would have "to sacrifice calves and lambs and to offer fine
wheat flour with incense and oil."

80. Ps 137.8–9.   81. Ps 101.8.
82. Cf. Gn 9.21.   83. Cf. Gn 43.34.
84. Cf. 2 Sm 6.5, 14–15.   85. Cf. Acts 7.22.
86. Cf. Dn 1.20; 2.2.   87. Gal 5.21.
88. Cf. Origen, *Peri archōn* 4.2.7.

the way to acquiring patience. Who would not be educated in mercy and goodness when he regards aspects of the Law that seem gloomy to some—I mean penalties, wars, the toppling of nations, and the threats delivered by the prophets to the people—as remedies rather than punishments? For the Lord will not be angry forever.[89] Since these things are evident to us, our faith will be more enlightened by reason and our conduct will be guided by temperance, which continence and chastity follow, and then the Law will begin to be favorable to us.

Here ends the quotation from Origen.

We may add something to Origen's exposition. Those called from slavery to the Law to freedom in the Gospel—those to whom it was said above, "Stand firm and do not let yourselves be burdened again by a yoke of slavery"[90]—are being warned now not to think by any means that they can use this freedom as a license to indulge in the flesh (that is, to live according to the flesh and be circumcised according to the flesh) as they pursue the light yoke of Christ and the Gospel's delectable commandments.[91] They should instead stand firm in the Spirit. By the Spirit they should cut off the foreskin of their fleshly nature and strive towards the higher things of the Spirit, leaving behind the lowliness of the letter.[92]

The passage may be understood another way. Someone may say: So, Paul, if I am no longer under the Law and have been called from slavery to freedom, then I must live in a way that does justice to this freedom and not be bound by any commandments. Whatever tickles my fancy and whatever desire suggests to me, that I must do, that I must fulfill, that I must chase after. The Apostle's response is that we are indeed called to freedom of the Spirit, provided that it does not entail slavery to the flesh. We should not think that everything is expedient just because everything is permissible.[93] Rather, because we have ceased to be slaves to the Law and have been made free, let us serve one another in love more so that the convoluted precepts of the Law may be collected under the one rubric of love.

89. Cf. Is 57.16.   90. Gal 5.1.
91. Cf. 1 Jn 5.3.
92. On figurative circumcision, see Origen, *Comm. Rom.* 2.13.19–26.
93. Cf. 1 Cor 6.12; 10.23.

5.13b–14. *Rather, be slaves to one another in love. The entire Law is summed up in a single command: "Love your neighbor as yourself."*[94]

Even though he was free, Paul nevertheless had made himself the slave of all out of love in order to win the masses to Christ, and he rightly exhorts everyone else to serve one another in love, which seeks not its own interests but those of the neighbor.[95] Whoever wants to be first will be the slave of all.[96] The Savior was in the form of God but did not consider equality with God something to be grasped. He emptied himself, taking the form of a servant, and, being found in appearance as a man, he humbled himself and became obedient unto death, even death on a cross.[97] Likewise, whatever things we seemed to do under compulsion when we were still under the Law, we should know now that we must do them more out of love because we are free.

Love is such a great good that the entire Law is summarized by it. Elsewhere the Apostle compiles a list of the goods that result from love, saying, "Love does not envy, it does not do wrong by another."[98] After enumerating many more attributes of love, he concludes by saying, "Love always hopes, always perseveres, and never fails."[99] In the Gospel the Savior remarks that one is recognized as his disciple if he loves his neighbor.[100] This applies, I think, not only to humans but also to angels. The very same concept is phrased differently in this passage: "Do not do to another what you do not want done to yourself,"[101] and also here: "Do to others what you would have them do to you."[102] I do not want my wife to be defiled, I do not want my property to be stolen, I do not want to be crushed by false testimony, and (to include everything under one heading) I do not tolerate injustice to be committed against me. If, out of the love that expresses itself through me, I do, or intend to do, good to others, I have fulfilled the entire Law.

It is not hard to show how keeping the one commandment to love satisfies all of the commandments ("Do not murder,"

94. Mt 22.39–40.
95. Cf. 1 Cor 13.5.
96. Cf. Mk 10.44.
97. Cf. Phil 2.6–8.
98. 1 Cor 13.4.
99. 1 Cor 13.7–8.
100. Cf. Jn 13.35.
101. Tb 4.16.
102. Mt 7.12; Lk 6.31.

"Do not commit adultery," "Do not steal," "Do not bear false witness")[103] simultaneously. It *is* hard to show, however, how the prescriptions in Leviticus about offerings, the dietary regulations about clean and unclean foods, and the never-ending cycle of annual festivals are summarized by the one command to love, unless perhaps one affirms that the Law is spiritual and that we had been slaves to the images and shadow of heavenly realities before the true high priest arrived.[104] After giving himself once and for all as a sin-offering[105] and having redeemed us by his blood,[106] he put an end to the myriad requirements of the old Law as well as to the difficulty of God's love prevailing over men under these circumstances. For God so loved the world that he gave his precious only-begotten Son for us.[107]

The Law, which was established for the impious, sinners, rogues, and criminals, no longer applies to the one who lives by the Spirit and who has decisively put to death the deeds of the flesh; he is beloved by the Savior and is called not a slave but a friend.[108] Although we do all of the more difficult things (even to a modest degree), the thing that is both easier to do and without which everything we do is in vain—this alone we do not do. Fasting afflicts the body, vigils take their toll on the flesh, begging for alms requires effort, and blood is not shed in martyrdom without some trepidation and pain, no matter how ardent one's faith is. Let people do all of these things; love alone is effortless. Because it alone cleanses the heart, the devil assails it in us to prevent us from apprehending God with a pure mind. When I idly slander my own brother and put a stumbling-block in the way of my mother's son,[109] and when I am tormented by another person's happiness and make someone else's good fortune a cause for my own malcontent,[110] is not the following verse fulfilled in me: "If you keep on biting and devouring each

103. Ex 20.13–16.   104. Cf. Heb 10.1.
105. Cf. Heb 7.27.   106. Cf. Heb 9.12.
107. Cf. Jn 3.16.   108. Cf. Jn 15.15.
109. Cf. Ps 50.20.

110. Cf. Cyprian, *De zel. et liv.* 7 (ANF 5:493): "But what a gnawing worm of the soul is it . . . to be jealous of another . . . [and] to turn the advantages of others into one's own mischief—to be tormented by the prosperity of illustrious men." See A. Cain, *REAug* 55 (2009): 42.

other, watch out that you are not consumed by one another"?[111]
Pure love is a rare find. Who wishes to imitate the Apostle in
being cut off from Christ for the sake of his brothers?[112] Who
mourns with those who mourn, and rejoices with those who rejoice,[113] and is genuinely pained at another's injury? Who is dev-
astated by the death of a brother? For all of us love ourselves
more than we love God. Consider what a truly amazing thing
love is. If we suffer martyrdom in the hope that our mortal remains will be honored by men, and if in pursuit of accolades
from the masses we fearlessly spill our blood and give our mon-
ey and possessions away until we are penniless, we deserve not
so much a reward as a penalty; these acts are the tortures merited by perfidy more than the crown of victory.[114]

5.15. *If you keep on biting and devouring one another, watch out that
you are not consumed by one another.*

This passage can be literally taken as follows: Let us not attack one another, let us not feel compelled to get revenge after
being cursed, let us not harbor a desire to make others sad because we have been made sad, and let us not be like brutes, biting and being bitten in turn and then being killed and eaten.

Paul is not erupting into a sudden rash of unusual precepts

111. Gal 5.15.

112. Cf. Rom 9.3. According to Origen (*Comm. Rom.* 7.13.4–5), Paul's desire
to imitate Christ manifested itself at no time more clearly than when he wished
himself to be accursed for the sake of his fellow Christians. Jerome echoes this
sentiment above.

113. Cf. Rom 12.15.

114. Cf. Cyprian, *De eccl. cath. unit.* 14 (ANF 5:426): "He cannot show himself a martyr who has not maintained brotherly love. Paul the apostle teaches
this, and testifies, saying, 'And though I have faith, so that I can remove mountains, and have not charity, I am nothing. And though I give all my goods to
feed the poor, and though I give my body to be burned, and have not charity, it
profiteth me nothing.' . . . To the rewards of Christ, who said, 'This is my commandment, that ye love one another, even as I have loved you,' he cannot attain
who has violated the love of Christ by faithless dissension. . . . They cannot dwell
with God who would not be of one mind in God's Church. Although they burn,
given up to flames and fires, or lay down their lives, thrown to the wild beasts,
that will not be the crown of faith, but the punishment of perfidy." See A. Cain,
REAug 55 (2009): 42–43.

that run counter to the tenor and sequence of the whole letter. He is still discussing circumcision and the observance of the
Law. If others trouble you, he says, then you are troubled. If you
read the entire Old Testament and understand it according to
the text, "An eye for an eye, a tooth for a tooth,"[115] you will find
that wrath longs for vengeance and that vengeance brings pain.
The Law not only does not prohibit this, but even commands it
in the interest of upholding a sense of like-for-like justice. What
happens is that the despoiled responds by despoiling, the in-
jured seeks to cause harm, and the devoured bites back. What
appears to be justice is consumption: it does not avenge one
thing but consumes everything.[116]

5.16. *So I say, walk by the Spirit and you will not gratify the desires of
the flesh.*

As indicated above [in Origen's exposition], this verse has a
twofold sense. According to the first, some put to death by the
Spirit the deeds of the flesh[117] and sow in the Spirit in order to
reap eternal life from the Spirit.[118] Whenever they feel the tick-
ling sensation of carnal pleasure, they do not gratify its desires (if
they do succumb, it provides only momentary satisfaction), but
rather they suppress these desires by the Spirit and live "more in
obedience to the mind than in servitude to the body," to use Sallust's line.[119] The second sense of the passage is as follows. Giv-
en that the Law is spiritual,[120] and that one is a Jew inwardly and
not outwardly, and that circumcision of the heart is spiritual and

---

115. Dt 19.21.

116. Jerome accentuates the devastating effects of the *lex talionis*, the law of
retribution, but by the same token he defends the fundamentally just nature of
the OT law, which advocated "an eye for an eye" in order to uphold "a sense
of like-for-like justice." Looming somewhere on the horizon of this paragraph is
Marcion, who impugned this law because it condoned mutual injury. See Tertullian's refutation of Marcion on this point in *Adv. Marc.* 2.18.

117. Cf. Rom 8.13.

118. Cf. Gal 6.8.

119. *Bell. Catil.* 1.2: *animi imperio, corporis servitio magis utimur.* This Sallustian
line became proverbial among later Christian writers: see, e.g., Lactantius, *Div.
inst.* 2.12.12; Paulinus of Nola, *Ep.* 5.17; Augustine, *Civ. Dei* 9.9.

120. Cf. Rom 7.14.

not literal, those who leave Egypt in a spiritual manner and get their food and drink from the spiritual rock[121] walk by the Spirit and do not gratify the desires of the flesh. They are not judged on the basis of what they eat or drink or whether they observe a particular festival, new moon celebration, or the Sabbath. They do not gratify the desires of the fleshly Law or of the literal interpretation of Scripture but in every respect they walk by the Spirit and reap the fruits of spiritual understanding.[122]

Some commentators offer a third interpretation that is akin to the second. They assert that the desires of the flesh are found in the children in Christ but that the way of the Spirit is present in mature men. The sense, then, is this: You mature men should walk in the dignity of the Spirit (that is, in the way of the Spirit), and you will not gratify the desires of the children.

5.17. *For the flesh desires what is contrary to the Spirit, and the Spirit what is contrary to the flesh. They are in conflict with each other, so that you do not do what you want.*

The flesh delights in what is present and fleeting, the Spirit in the eternal and in future things. The soul stands in the middle of this struggle. It has in its power to will or not to will good and evil, but is unable to maintain its choice indefinitely. For when the soul gives in to the flesh and performs its deeds, it can strike back at itself through repentance and be joined with the Spirit and perform the Spirit's deeds.[123] This is what Paul means when he says, "They are in conflict with each other," that is, the flesh and the Spirit, "so that you do not do what you want." Paul does not do away with our free will by which we assent either to the flesh or to the Spirit. Rather, he points out that what we do is not our own [work] but that the work itself is attributed to either the flesh or the Spirit.

121. Cf. 1 Cor 10.3–4.
122. Cf. Gal 5.22.
123. Cf. Origen, *Comm. Rom.* 1.18.5 (trans. Scheck, FOTC 103:94): "And when it is said, 'The flesh desires contrary to the spirit, and the spirit desires contrary to the flesh,' the soul is undoubtedly placed in the middle. Either it gives assent to the desires of the spirit or it is inclined toward the lusts of the flesh. If it joins itself to the flesh it becomes one body with it in its lust and sinful desires; but if it should associate itself with the spirit it shall be one spirit with it."

It takes enormous effort and discrimination to scrutinize the deeds of the flesh and the deeds of the Spirit and to pinpoint specific ones that seem to be neither fleshly nor spiritual but somewhere in between. We are said to be carnal when we surrender ourselves to pleasures, and spiritual when we follow the Holy Spirit's lead, that is, when we gain wisdom from his guidance and take him as our teacher. I consider philosophers to be unspiritual men because they fancy that their ruminations amount to wisdom. Paul is right to say about them, "The unspiritual man does not accept the things of the Spirit; they are foolishness to him."[124] Let us consider an example to make this clearer. Suppose that the ground stands for the flesh, gold for the soul, and fire for the Spirit. As long as the gold is in the ground, it relinquishes its name and is designated by the soil with which it has been mixed. But when separated from the soil, it takes on the appearance and name of gold, and indeed it is called gold but it has not yet been tested. If it is heated in the fire and purified, it assumes the luster typical of gold and the value proportional to its decorative appearance. So it is with the soul lingering between soil and fire, that is, between flesh and Spirit. When it succumbs to the flesh it is called flesh, but when it succumbs to the Spirit it is called Spirit. If the soul trusts its own devices and thinks that it can discover the truth without help from the Holy Spirit's grace, then this unrefined gold, as it were, will be designated by the appellation "unspiritual man."

This verse, if explained better, can become an internally cohesive and consistent unit. Brothers, you were called to stop being slaves to the Law and to be free in the Gospel. But I beg you not to use your freedom as an excuse to do whatever you please, not to think that everything which is permissible will be of benefit to you, and not to indulge in debauchery. You should instead recognize that this freedom is a higher form of slavery. The Law used to exact obedience from you against your will, but now you must be slaves to one another in love. The whole weight of the Law and its myriad commandments are not so much eradicated by evangelical grace as they are subsumed under the single heading of love, that we love our neighbor as ourselves. For

124. 1 Cor 2.14.

whoever loves his neighbor and does good to him and not evil fulfills the entire Law. If love is taken out of the equation, villainy prevails in society and people go on the attack and finally are consumed by one another. But you, brothers, must live by the law of the Spirit so that you do not gratify the desires of the flesh.

The flesh fears the cold, despises hunger, is attenuated by vigils, burns white-hot with passion, and pines for what is soothing and succulent.[125] The Spirit, by contrast, seeks the things that are in opposition to the flesh and that can diminish its potency. Do not imagine that you are free just because you are no longer slaves to the Law. The law of nature binds you, more so than the Mosaic Law does. Nature did not instantly cease to be a factor once the former Law stopped being your master. Thus your deeds do not reflect what you in fact want to do. Rather, due to the conflict between the flesh and the Spirit, you are frequently forced to do what you do not want to do. Therefore, brothers, I beg you not to use your freedom as an excuse to indulge in the flesh. Instead, serve one another in the Spirit so that you may begin to do what you want and not be a debtor to the Law and under the dominion of the flesh. You will be able truly to have freedom in the Gospel from the abolished Law when the flesh does not at all force you to do what you do not want to do and when you convince yourselves that you are not under the Law but are slaves to the Spirit.

Since we began to expound this passage according to its twofold sense, let us cover what we left out. The struggle between the flesh and the Spirit symbolizes the antagonism between the literal and surface understanding of Scripture, on the one hand, and allegory and spiritual teaching, on the other. The Spirit's fight against the flesh is symbolic of when the heavenly opposes the earthly, the eternal opposes the temporary, and the truth opposes the shadow. The carnal sense of Scripture, which cannot

---

125. Jerome restates Paul's flesh-Spirit antagonism in explicitly ascetic terms in mentioning fasting and prayer vigils as disciplines useful for subduing corporeal desires. On the central place of fasting in Jerome's ascetic program, see P. Laurence, *Jérôme et le nouveau modèle féminin. La conversion à la vie parfaite* (Paris: Institut d'Études Augustiniennes, 1997), 103–39.

be fulfilled since we cannot do all that is written, shows that we
do not have it in our power to fulfill the Law, for even if we wish
to follow the letter, its unattainability impedes us.

5.18. *If you are led by the Spirit, you are not under the Law.*
    This Spirit is not the one of whom the Apostle speaks else-
where: "The Spirit himself testifies with our spirit that we are
God's children."[126] In other words, Paul does not mean the spirit within man but the Holy Spirit, by following whom we become spiritual and cease to be under the Law. It is noteworthy
that the word "Spirit" here does not have an accompanying article (ἄρθρον) or any qualifier, as it does in the phrases "spirit of
gentleness"[127] and "spirit of faith."[128] He is called simply "Spirit."[129] These details, which apply more to Greek than to Latin
(we do not have articles at all), seem to be of sufficient importance [to be mentioned].
    A threefold question arises in connection with the notion
that the person led by the Spirit is not under the Law. Were
Moses and the prophets led by the Spirit while living under the
Law? The Apostle denies that this could be so. Did they have
the Spirit but were not under the Law? He advocates this in
principle here. Finally, did they not have the Spirit because they
lived under the Law? It is unthinkable to suggest that such great
men were without the Spirit. We will respond to this in brief. Being under the Law is not the same as pretending to be under
the Law, just as being in the likeness of the sinful flesh is not the
same as being in the sinful flesh. Likewise, there is a difference
between a real snake and the bronze snake that Moses raised
up in the desert.[130] Similarly, Moses and the holy prophets, who

126. Rom 8.16.   127. 1 Cor 4.21.
128. 2 Cor 4.13.
129. Jerome is referring to the fact that the Greek text lacks a definite article preceding "Spirit" (εἰ δὲ πνεύματι ἄγεσθε, οὐκ ἐστὲ ὑπὸ νόμον). Cf. Origen, *Peri
archōn* 1.3.4 (trans. Butterworth, 31): "Now some of our predecessors have observed that in the New Testament, whenever the Spirit is mentioned without its
qualifying adjective, the expression should be understood to refer to the Holy
Spirit; as for instance, 'the fruit of the Spirit is love, joy, peace' and the rest."
130. Cf. Nm 21.4–9.

walked by the Spirit and lived by the Spirit, did not live under the Law but pretended to do so in order to win over those who actually were under the Law. They hoped to spur them on from the lowliness of the letter to the loftiness of the Spirit.

Paul likewise became a Jew to the Jews and became all things to all people in order to win them [for Christ]. He did not speak as one under the Law but as one pretending to be under it so that he could give the appearance of upholding the likeness of the Law rather than its substance. It seems to me that this is the solution to the conundrum at hand. But what are we to do with Paul's remark, "When the fullness of time came, God sent his Son, made of a woman and put under the Law to redeem those under the Law"?[131] For if Christ was under the Law really and not just ostensibly, then the entire foregoing discussion becomes pointless. Here is the solution. He was put under the Law to redeem those under the Law. Although he was free from the Law, he willingly made himself subject to it and enjoyed far more freedom than Paul, who testifies that he was not actually under the Law but only pretended to be under it. Just as Christ descended into the filthy abyss of death for the sake of us who pray, "Who will liberate me from this body of death?"[132] so also did he wish to be born of a woman and to be under the Law so as to save those who had been born of a woman and were under the Law. To be precise, he was not born of a married woman but of a virgin. The virgin has inaccurately been referred to as a "woman" on account of people who did not know that she was a virgin. The word "woman," then, was used instead of "virgin" because of those who thought that holy Mary was married. Similarly, Christ is said to have been put under the Law on account of people who did not realize that he pretended to be under the Law for the sake of those who actually were under the Law.

5.19–21. The deeds of the flesh are obvious: sexual immorality, impurity, debauchery, idolatry, witchcraft, hostility, discord, jealousy, rage, quarrels, dissensions, heresies, envy, drunkenness, revelries, and the like.

131. Gal 4.4–5.
132. Rom 7.24.

I warn you, as I did before, that those who live like this will not inherit the kingdom of God.[133]

When I wrote about the flesh and the Spirit earlier, I applied a threefold understanding. First, the fleshly minded are infants in Christ who cannot ingest solid food and the nourishment appropriate for those who are mature. Second, the flesh of the Law stands for those who in the manner of the Jews adhere to the letter and literal interpretation of the Law. Third, according to the simple sense, flesh and Spirit have to do with man's make-up, and deeds are of either the flesh or the Spirit according to the diversity of their substance. Now, then, the deeds of the flesh that are listed (sexual immorality, impurity, debauchery, etc.) seem to me to refer more to the simple understanding of the flesh and the Spirit than to the flesh of the Law and infants in Christ, although another opinion about this matter is expressed in the extract from the tenth book of Origen's *Miscellanies* translated verbatim above.

By saying that the deeds of the flesh are obvious, Paul means that they are known to all; they are so self-evidently evil and abhorrent that even those who do them wish to conceal them. Or else it may mean that these deeds are obvious only to believers in Christ. A great many of the heathens proudly revel in their shameful conduct and imagine that they have achieved a victory in their disgrace if they satisfy a given desire. Paul has put it elegantly by allotting deeds to the flesh and fruits to the Spirit. Vices perish in themselves and pass away, but virtues abound in fruit and multiply. Let us not assume that the soul does nothing if vices are attributed to the flesh and virtues to the Spirit. As I stated above, the soul is positioned in the middle. Because it is joined to the flesh, the following verse applies to it, "My Spirit will not remain among man forever, for he is flesh."[134] Because the soul is united with the Spirit, it assumes the Spirit's name, for "whoever clings to the Lord is one with him in spirit."[135]

133. Paul's list of virtues and the one of vices to follow became the basis for the Seven Virtues and Seven Vices of later church tradition. See W. Meeks, *The Origins of Christian Morality* (New Haven: Yale University Press, 1993), 66–71.

134. Gn 6.3.

135. 1 Cor 6.17.

The first deed of the flesh is sexual immorality. Paul put the word "obvious" up front so that we would not dispute about acts that are not manifestly sins. "Everything else a man does is outside his body, but he who sins sexually sins against his own body."[136] We are not our own, we were bought at a price, so let us honor God with our body and carry him in it.[137] The fornicator is guilty of a more serious offense because he unites the members of Christ with a prostitute, and the two then become one flesh.[138] The unbeliever unites his own members with a prostitute, but the believer who fornicates unites the members of Christ with a prostitute. As for the unbeliever who fornicates, I cannot say whether he violates his bodily temple or builds it in honor of an idol (without doubt, demons are worshiped especially through the vices). The one thing I do know is that a believer in Christ who commits sexual sin defiles the temple of God.[139]

The second deed of the flesh is impurity, and its companion debauchery comes right after it. In the old Law when it came to dealing with offenses committed in secret that were too shameful to name (lest the mouths naming them and the ears hearing them be polluted), Scripture included them under one generic heading, saying, "Keep the modest and reverent sons of Israel away from every impurity."[140] In the same way Paul uses the words "impurity" and "debauchery" to cover every other conceivable lustful desire, including sexual relations within marriage, if these are not performed with a sense of modesty and respectability (as if God was watching), and then only for the purpose of procreation.[141]

Idolatry occupies the fourth position in the catalogue of the deeds of the flesh. Whoever gives in to debauchery or lustful desire even once has no regard at all for the Creator. In general,

136. 1 Cor 6.18.
138. Cf. 1 Cor 6.16.
140. Lv 15.31.
137. Cf. 1 Cor 6.19–20.
139. Cf. 1 Cor 3.17.

141. Cf. Tertullian, *Ad ux.* 2.3 (ANF 4:46): ". . . among the saints, where the duties of the sex are discharged with honour shown to the very necessity which makes them incumbent, with modesty and temperance, as beneath the eyes of God." See A. Cain, *REAug* 55 (2009): 35–36.

all idolatry delights in feasting, gluttony, and the pleasures of both the belly and things that are below the belly.[142]

So that witchcraft and sorcery might not appear to be condoned in the New Testament, they are numbered among the deeds of the flesh because it often happens that wretched people fall in love and are loved in return by the aid of magical arts.[143]

Hostility proves why it deserves to be condemned by being named alongside such an obvious offense as witchcraft. We must try as best we can not to have any enemy but to keep the peace with everyone. If by speaking the truth we make enemies out of some, we are not so much their enemies as they are the enemies of the truth. Understood in this light, what is said to Abraham in Genesis, "I will be an enemy to your enemies, and I will oppose those who oppose you,"[144] means not so much that Abraham was their enemy as it does that they were enemies of his virtues and the pious devotion that empowered him to trample idols underfoot and worship the God he knew personally. In addition, when the people of Israel were told to be enemies with the Midianites and to hate them and have strife with them forever,[145] this command was directed at those who were under the care of a pedagogue[146] and deserved to hear it said to them elsewhere, "Hate your enemy."[147] The conflict was not between the people themselves as much as it was between their morals. Just as God efficaciously put enmity between the serpent and the woman[148] so that their alliance, which caused man to be expelled from paradise, would not prove inefficacious, so also with the Israelites and the Midianites a difference in lifestyle rather than ethnicity is condemned.

In the list of the deeds of the flesh, discord holds the seventh place, as if it held a sacred and esteemed position among

---

142. The phrase *quae infra ventrem sunt* refers to the genitalia. Cf. *Ep.* 147.3, where Jerome uses the same expression also in connection with fornication.

143. Erotic spells were among the most popular form of magic practiced in Greco-Roman antiquity. See C. Faraone, *Ancient Greek Love Magic* (Cambridge: Cambridge University Press, 1999).

144. Ex 23.22. Jerome incorrectly assigns this passage to Genesis.

145. Cf. Nm 31.

146. Cf. Gal 3.25.

147. Mt 5.43.

148. Cf. Gn 3.15.

the vices. The servant of the Lord must not quarrel. Instead, he must be kind to everyone, able to teach, patient, gently instructing even those who disagree with him.[149]

Jealousy (*aemulatio*) comes eighth, after discord. In Greek it goes by the more notable and familiar name ζῆλος (*zelus*). I know of nobody among us who is without this evil. The patriarchs were jealous of their brother Joseph,[150] and Miriam and Aaron, a prophetess and a priest of God, were carried away by such passionate jealousy toward Moses[151] that Miriam, about whom Scripture says, "Then the prophetess Miriam took a tambourine,"[152] and so on, later emerged from the tent fouled with leprosy[153] and sealed her more lengthy repentance by a seven-day quarantine.[154]

Next comes rage, which does not bring about the righteousness that God desires.[155] It is a type of fury. The difference between wrath and anger is this: The wrathful person is always riled, while the angry person is perturbed just for a little while. I have no idea who can inherit the kingdom of God, seeing that anyone who gets riled is kept out of it.

Quarrels (*rixae*) alienate us from the kingdom of God as well. The Greeks call these ἐριθεῖαι; this word has a slightly different connotation than the Latin *rixa* (a "quarrel" is usually designated as μάχη). An ἐριθεία is involved when someone is always ready to contradict, takes joy in irritating others, engages in womanish spats, and provokes the person with whom he is arguing. Among the Greeks this is known by another name, φιλονικία.

Dissensions are also deeds of the flesh. These result when someone who is by no means mature [in faith] says the following and means it, "I follow Paul; I follow Apollo; I follow Cephas; I follow Christ."[156] This same dissension is found in other spheres of life—between households, husband and wife, father and son, brother and brother, servant and servant, soldier and a fellow military companion, and an artisan and another artisan who does the same kind of work.

---

149. Cf. 2 Tm 2.24–25.

150. Cf. Gn 37.4.

151. Cf. Nm 12.1.

152. Ex 15.20.

153. Cf. Nm 12.10.

154. Cf. Nm 12.15.

155. Cf. Jas 1.20.

156. 1 Cor 1.12.

It often happens that dissension arises in the interpretation of Scripture, out of which spring heresies, which are numbered here among the deeds of the flesh. For if the wisdom of the flesh is hostile to God[157] (all false teachings are hostile because they are repugnant to God), then heresies, too, being hostile to God, are consequently included among the deeds of the flesh. "Heresy" comes from the Greek word that means "choice" [αἵρεσις] because each person chooses a [religious] persuasion that he thinks is superior to others. Whoever understands Scripture in a way other than how the Holy Spirit intended, even if he does not actually leave the church, can nevertheless be called a heretic and someone who chooses from among the more egregious of the deeds of the flesh.

Envy follows heresies. We should not imagine that envy is the same as zeal. Zeal can be for a good cause when someone makes a point of emulating better things, but envy is tormented by another person's good fortune and is torn by a twofold passion either when one is in a position in which he does not want another person to be, or when he sees another person better than himself and is pained that he is not like him. A certain Neoteric poet, translating a Greek elegiac couplet, wittily captured the essence of envy, "Nothing is more relentless than envy, which wastes no time in eating away at the envious person and torturing his mind."[158] The blessed Cyprian wrote a truly splendid book *On Jealousy and Envy*, and anyone who reads it will not hesitate to include envy among the deeds of the flesh. Moreover, the difference between the one who envies and the one who is envied is that the former envies someone who is more fortunate than himself, while the latter is the victim of envy.

Drunkenness occupies the fourteenth place in the catalogue of the deeds of the flesh. The drunken will not inherit the king-

157. Cf. Rom 8.7.
158. *Iustius invidia nihil est, quae protinus ipsum / auctorem rodit excruciatque animum* (the Greek original is: Ὁ φθόνος ἐστὶ κάκιστος, ἔχει δέ τι καλὸν ἐν αὐτῷ. / τήκει γὰρ φθονερῶν ὄμματα καὶ κραδίην). This couplet in Latin translation, preserved in the *Anthologia Latina* (485b), was quoted by several authors after Jerome (e.g., Isidore of Seville and John of Salisbury), but its earliest documented appearance in Latin literature is here in the *Commentary on Galatians*.

dom of God. The Lord said to his disciples, "Be careful that your hearts not be weighted down with drunkenness and dissipation."[159] When a man is inebriated, his sensory faculties become debilitated, his feet falter, his mind vacillates, and the fire of lust is ignited within him. This is why the Apostle warns about "wine, which leads to debauchery."[160] Every man has the power to make up his own mind; for my part, I agree with the apostle that wine is the root of drunkenness and debauchery. Not even a person addicted to these vices is able to deny that they should be represented in the list of deeds of the flesh. Although some think that I ought to be chastised for saying in my book *On Preserving Virginity* that young girls should flee from wine as if it were poison [*Ep.* 22.8],[161] I do not regret the opinion I voiced there. For it was not so much a creation of God that I condemned as it was the behavior that stemmed from indulgence in wine. I took away from the virgin inflamed by her own adolescent passions the excuse to drink more wine (when she should be drinking less) and as a result perish. Besides, I was fully aware that wine was consecrated as the blood of Christ[162] and that Timothy was ordered to drink wine.[163] The drinking of not only wine but also other types of variously concocted beverages can lead to drunkenness. This is why it is said about the saints, "He shall not drink wine or *sicera*."[164] *Sicera*[165] means "drunkenness," and, in case anyone who abstains from wine thinks he should drink something else, the excuse is taken away, for everything which can intoxicate is forbidden along with wine.

The fifteenth and final deed of the flesh is revelries. The peo-

---

159. Lk 21.34.

160. Eph 5.18.

161. Some critics of *Ep.* 22 to Eustochium evidently interpreted Jerome's prohibition against wine as a crypto-Manichaean rejection of matter as something intrinsically evil (Jerome was no stranger to allegations of Manichaean sympathies: see Cain, *The Letters of Jerome*, 137–38).

162. Cf. Mt 26.27.   163. Cf. 1 Tm 5.23.

164. Lk 1.15.

165. Many writers in Greco-Roman antiquity used the word *sicera* (Heb. *shekhar*; Gr. σίκερα; Lat. *sicera*) to mean generally any fermented drink other than wine. See M. Nelson, *The Barbarian's Beverage: A History of Beer in Ancient Europe* (London: Routledge, 2005), 118.

ple [of Israel] ate, drank, and rose in the morning to indulge in revelry[166] (debauchery is always linked to drunkenness). The noble orator put it beautifully when he described a drunk man awakened from his sleep as being neither alive nor dead, "He was able neither to sleep while awake nor to stay awake while drunk."[167]

Since it would have been an imposing task to enumerate all of the deeds of the flesh and to compose an exhaustive catalogue of the vices, Paul wrapped up everything in the one phrase "and the like." I wish that we could avoid these vices as easily as we can detect them. Paul says, "I warn you, as I did before, that those who live like this will not inherit the kingdom of God." When he warned them beforehand, he said, "Do not let sin reign in your mortal body so that you obey its desires."[168] Sin takes on all kinds of forms, and we have spent more time perhaps than was necessary making distinctions between them. The kingdom of God cannot reign in the soul where sin reigns. "What do righteousness and wickedness have in common? What fellowship can light have with darkness? What harmony is there between Christ and Belial?"[169] We believe that we attain the kingdom of God if we have nothing to do with sexual immorality, idolatry, and witchcraft. Hostility, discord, rage, quarrels, dissensions, drunkenness, and the rest of the vices that we regard as petty also exclude us from the kingdom of God. And it does not matter whether someone is shut out of blessedness because of one or more than one of these, since all of them in like manner shut him out.

In the Latin manuscripts, adultery, immodesty, and murder are included in this catalogue of vices. But we should be aware that not more than fifteen deeds of the flesh are named [in the Greek manuscripts], and I have already discussed these.

166. Cf. Ex 32.6.

167. This *non ignobilis orator* (I have rendered the litotes simply as "noble") is Cicero's contemporary Marcus Caelius Rufus. Quintilian (*Inst. orat.* 4.2.124) preserves an excerpt from Caelius's speech against Gaius Antonius Hybrida (59 BC), and this is Jerome's source for the quotation. See H. T. Roswell, "A Quotation from Marcus Caelius Rufus in St. Jerome, *In Galatas* III 5, 509," *Eranos* 57 (1959): 59–61.

168. Rom 6.12.

169. 2 Cor 6.14–15.

5.22–23. *But the fruit of the Spirit is love, joy, peace, patience, kindness, goodness, faith, gentleness, and self-control. Against such things there is no law.*

What should hold first place among the fruits of the Spirit besides love? For without it the rest of the virtues are not reckoned virtues; and from love all good things are born. It does, after all, occupy first place in both the Law and the Gospel. "Love the Lord your God with all of your heart and with all of your soul and with all of your strength,"[170] and, "Love your neighbor as yourself."[171] I touched briefly above on how many goods are condensed in love. Now, it is barely enough to have said that love does not seek its own good but the good of others.[172] No matter how hostile (by his own moral failing) someone is to a person who has love, and no matter how much he tries to dash his sense of personal peace against the waves of animosity, the one who loves remains unshaken and never considers a creature of God worthy of hatred. For love covers a multitude of sins.[173] When the Savior said, "A good tree cannot bear bad fruit, and a bad tree cannot bear good fruit,"[174] I reckon that he was talking not so much about people as about the fruit of the flesh and the fruit of the Spirit. For the Spirit cannot commit the vices enumerated among the deeds of the flesh, and likewise the flesh cannot overflow in the fruits arising from the Spirit. Because of a person's negligence it can happen that the spirit which is within man does not have fruits of its own and that the flesh puts to death its evil deeds and stops sinning. Nevertheless, it does not get to the point where the spirit's neglected tree brings forth the deeds of the flesh or the flesh's well-manicured tree sprouts spiritual fruits.

Joy comes second in the list of spiritual fruits. The Stoics, who are meticulous about making distinctions between words, consider it to be something different from gaiety. They say that joy is an elation of mind over things worthy of exultation, whereas gaiety is an undisciplined elation of mind that knows no bounds and takes delight in things associated with vice.[175] Others remove

---

170. Dt 6.5; Mt 22.37.　　171. Lv 19.18; Mt 22.39.
172. Cf. 1 Cor 13.5.　　173. Cf. 1 Pt 4.8.
174. Mt 7.18.　　175. Cf. Cicero, *Tusc.* 4.13.

pleasure from the realm of joy—not the kind of pleasure that incites the body toward lust, titillates the emotions, and coaxes with sweet affection, but another kind similar to it that has no sense of moderation or decorum and raises its voice in raucous laughter.[176] If this is true and if the Stoics' distinction between words is not misleading but rather on the mark, we should wonder whether this was why it was said, "There is no rejoicing for the wicked, says the Lord."[177] Furthermore, it is noteworthy that joy follows love [in the list]. For the one who loves someone else always takes delight in his good fortune. And if he sees that he has been caught up in some foible and has stumbled due to the slippery slope of sin, he will grieve and hasten to lift him back up, but his sadness cannot affect his joy because he knows that no rational creature will ever perish in God's sight.

The third fruit of the Spirit is peace, from which Solomon, who came before as a type of Christ, took his name. The Psalmist sings of the church, "His tabernacle has been established in peace."[178] One of the eight Beatitudes of the Gospel is, "Blessed are the peacemakers, for they shall be called sons of God."[179] In the first of the Psalms of Ascent the Psalmist sings, "I was a peacemaker with those who hated peace."[180] We should not suppose that peace is limited to not quarreling with others. Rather, the peace of Christ (that is, our inheritance) is with us when the mind is at peace and undisturbed by the passions.

After peace comes longsuffering or patience (either word preserves the meaning of μακροθυμία). This is contrary to impetuousness, about which it is written, "A quick-tempered man

---

176. Generally speaking, early Christian writers condemned spontaneous outbursts of laughter because they saw these as a sign that a soul had momentarily lost the ability to regulate itself. Clement of Alexandria, for instance, approved of laughter only insofar as it did not disrupt rational thought and the soul's contemplation of God: see P. Brown, *The Body and Society: Men, Women and Sexual Renunciation in Early Christianity* (London: Columbia University Press, 1989), 122–39. For a brief overview of patristic attitudes toward laughter, see N. Adkin, "The Fathers on Laughter," *Orpheus*, n.s., 6 (1985): 149–52. See also I. M. Resnick, "*Risus Monasticus:* Laughter and Medieval Monastic Culture," *RBén* 97 (1987): 90–100; S. Halliwell, *Greek Laughter: A Study of Cultural Psychology from Homer to Early Christianity* (Cambridge: Cambridge University Press, 2008).

177. Is 57.21 (LXX).   178. Ps 76.2.
179. Mt 5.9.   180. Ps 120.7.

is very foolish, but a man who patiently endures all things is wise."[181] And he is emphatically called exceedingly wise, as it is also written in Proverbs, "The longsuffering man is abundant in prudence."[182]

Kindness, or agreeableness (among the Greeks the word χρησ-τότης covers both of these meanings), is a virtue which is gentle, charming, peaceful, adept at getting along with all good people; it attracts others to close acquaintanceship with itself; it is soft-spoken and well-mannered. Furthermore, the Stoics define it as a virtue whose goal is to do good voluntarily.

Goodness is not much different from kindness because its goal is also to do good voluntarily. But it does differ in that it can be more somber and do good and what is demanded of it with a brow furrowed by austere habits; it is not pleasant company and it does not attract everyone to it by its pleasantness. Zeno's followers define it as a profitable virtue, that is, a virtue out of which usefulness arises, or a self-sufficient virtue or mental disposition that is the source of useful things.[183]

Among the fruits of the Spirit faith holds the sacred seventh place, being elsewhere one of three—faith, hope, and love.[184] It is no wonder that hope is not included in this catalogue, since the object of hope is already included as a part of faith. The Apostle defines it thus when writing to the Hebrews, "Faith is the assurance of things hoped for, the conviction about things not yet seen."[185] How is faith a part of love, seeing that what we hope will come but what has not yet arrived we already possess

181. Prv 14.29 (LXX).

182. Ibid.

183. This paragraph and the previous one were closely adapted and in most places copied verbatim by Aelred of Rievaulx in his treatise *Mirror of Charity* (composed 1142/3). Aelred did not acknowledge his source but passed off the material as his own, a common practice among writers in the Middle Ages. Jerome's *Commentary on Galatians* was used extensively by medieval commentators on Paul, but the Aelredian parallel is the only known appropriation of Jerome's *Commentary* in the non-exegetical literature of the medieval period. See A. Cain, "Aelred of Rievaulx and Jerome's *Commentary on Galatians*," *CSQ* 45 (2010): 3–6.

184. Cf. 1 Cor 13.13.

185. Heb 11.1.

by faith now and hope to hold on to our belief? The one who loves never perceives himself as being attacked, and he never harbors suspicion but only concerns himself with loving and being loved. Moreover, when love is nowhere to be found, faith makes its exit.

Gentleness, which comes after faith in the list, is the enemy of rage, quarrels, and dissensions. It is never attracted to things opposite to itself and it indeed sprouts good fruits from the good tree of the Spirit. On account of his own gentleness Moses, the servant of God, was deemed worthy of having Scripture say about him, "Moses was a gentle man, more so than anyone else on the face of the earth."[186] It says "on the face of the earth" because Moses did not have the same privilege as others who saw God face-to-face;[187] we are often compelled to do many things because of the weakness of the flesh. As for David, although many believe that he prophesied about our Lord (and we do not deny that he did), the Holy Spirit sang about him as a type of the [Messiah] to come, "O Lord, remember David and all his gentleness."[188] It was his gentleness that prevailed so mightily against Saul, Absalom, and Shimei when the first wanted to murder him,[189] when the second plotted a revolution and tried to defraud him of ruling authority,[190] and when the third[191] cried out and said, "Get out, get out, you wicked man,"[192] as he was hurling stones at him and showering him with dirt.[193]

Self-control comes last in the catalogue of the fruits of the Spirit. We must exercise this virtue not only in our chastity but also when we eat and drink and when we are angry or worried or have the inclination to ridicule someone. Moderation differs from self-control in that moderation is present in those who

186. Nm 12.3.
188. Ps 132.1.
190. Cf. 2 Sm 14–18.
192. 2 Sm 16.7.

187. Cf. Gn 32.30.
189. Cf. 1 Sm 24.5–15.
191. Cf. 2 Sm 16.5–14.

193. Raspanti, following the reading in the PL text, punctuates Jerome's prose as follows: *Cuius mansuetudo adversus Saul, Absalon et Semei vel maxime claruit? Cum alius eum vellet occidere* . . . (CCSL 77A:196, lines 104–6). *Cuius* is not interrogative, however, and the passage is better punctuated as the following: *Cuius mansuetudo adversus Saul, Absalon et Semei vel maxime claruit cum alius eum vellet occidere* . . . I have based my translation on this adjusted reading.

are spiritually mature and bountifully virtuous. The Savior says about such people, "Blessed are the meek, for they will inherit the earth,"[194] and he says about himself, "Learn from me, for I am humble, meek, and gentle in heart."[195] The one who has self-control, however, is indeed on his way to becoming virtuous but has not yet arrived at his goal because sinful desires still invade his thoughts and pollute the very core of his mind, though they do not overcome him or entice him to translate thought into action. Self-control is a necessary virtue to have for [regulating] not only longings (*desideria*) and desire (*cupiditas*) but also the remaining three "disorders" (*perturbationes*)—pain (*dolor*), elation (*laetitia*), and fear (*timor*).[196]

"Against such fruits of the Spirit there is no law. The Law was established not for the righteous but for lawbreakers and rebels, the ungodly and sinful, the unholy and irreligious."[197] The Law says to me, "Do not commit adultery, do not murder, do not give false testimony, do not defraud, do not covet others' belongings, do not swear, do not steal."[198] If I do not do all of these things with love as the fruit of the Spirit motivating me to do so, the commandments of the Law are meaningless to me. Finally, the wise men of the world have fancied that philosophy persuades men to do willingly what civic laws force them to do.

5.24. *Those who belong to Christ have crucified the flesh with its vices and sinful desires.*

Origen ties this passage with the preceding ones and reads it as, "Against such things there is no law for those who have cru-

194. Mt 5.4.

195. Mt 11.29.

196. Jerome names the standard Stoic quartet of irrational passions or disorders (*perturbationes*) that upset the equilibrium of the mind: desire (*cupiditas*), elation (*laetitia*), fear (*timor* or *metus*), and pain (*dolor*). The Stoics taught that the wise man must rid himself completely of all passions in order to live a perfectly rational existence in accordance with nature: see M. Nussbaum, "The Stoics on the Extirpation of the Passions," *Apeiron* 20 (1987): 129–77. In the way he conceived of the passions and their adverse effect on the soul, Jerome was influenced by Stoicism but also by other philosophical traditions: see A. Canellis, "Saint Jérôme et les passions: Sur les *quattuor perturbationes* des Tusculanes," *REAug* 54 (2000): 178–203.

197. 1 Tm 1.9.   198. Mk 10.19.

cified the flesh of Christ with its vices and sinful desires." Thus
he does not say, as it says in the Latin, that those who belong to
Christ have crucified their own flesh with its vices and sinful desires, but that they have crucified the flesh of Christ with its vices and sinful desires. Origen then asks how the crucifixion of
the Lord's flesh in those who have the fruits of the Spirit and
over whom the Law no longer has dominion can be something
praiseworthy, given that the Hebrews are scolded for "crucifying
the Son of God all over again and subjecting him to public disgrace."[199] A preferable alternative to "crucifying all over again"
[rursus crucifigentes] is "recrucifying" [recrucifigentes], which corresponds better to the single Greek word ἀνασταυροῦντες.

First of all, we should note that it is one thing to crucify, another to recrucify. Secondly, recrucifying the Son of God is not
the same as crucifying the flesh of Christ with its vices and sinful desires. The "flesh of Christ" is not actually the Son of God
himself. Rather, it is Christ Jesus who, although he was God the
Word, who was with the Father in the beginning,[200] became
flesh and emptied himself, assuming the form of a servant[201] so
that he might crucify the flesh and disarm the principalities and
powers and triumph over them by the Cross,[202] thereby bringing
to pass what the Apostle said: "The death he died, he died to sin
once for all."[203] Thus, if our bodies are the members of Christ,
then our flesh is the flesh of Christ. And while we are on earth
we crucify it and through it we put to death impurity, lust, evil
desire, and avarice. It becomes the reason why we are praised
who have crucified the flesh of Christ Jesus with its vices and sinful desires and who always carry around in our body the death
of Jesus, so that his life may be revealed in our flesh.[204] But it
takes no small effort to live in the present age in such a way that
the life of Jesus is revealed in our flesh right now. For our mortal bodies will accordingly be made alive through the Spirit who
dwells within us.

Where the Latin translator has "vices" (vitia), παθήματα, that
is, "sufferings" (passiones), is found in the Greek. Since the word

199. Heb 6.6.   200. Cf. Jn 1.1.
201. Cf. Phil 2.7.   202. Cf. Col 2.15.
203. Rom 6.10.   204. 2 Cor 4.10.

"suffering" (*passio*) can refer to pain and other hardships of the body, the Apostle has advisedly invoked the concept of desires (*desideria*) because he wants to come across as denying not the nature of the body in spiritually minded people but rather the presence of "vices" (*vitia*) in them. If we follow the common version[205] and accept the reading "Those who belong to Christ have crucified the flesh with its vices and sinful desires," we should bear in mind that we are saying that they have crucified not the flesh of Christ but their own flesh.

I almost forgot the second interpretation. I stated earlier that everything that follows must be taken as referring to the Law and circumcision. The sense is this: Those who have the fruits of the Spirit—love, joy, and so on—have crucified the literal interpretation of Scripture, called here the "flesh of Christ," along with its passions and desires, which provide infants and suckling babes with incitements to vice. He who does not wage war in the way that the flesh of the literal meaning does,[206] but follows the leading of the spirit of allegory, has crucified this very flesh of Christ.

5.25. *If we live by the Spirit, let us also walk by the Spirit.*

Let us use this testimony against those who refuse to understand Scripture in a spiritual way. Who lives by the Spirit but our hidden man[207] who sometimes is in the habit of living according to the flesh? But when he lives by the Spirit, he walks by the Spirit, and when he wants to walk in the flesh, he is dead even though he is alive. The man who is mature in Christ always lives in the Spirit: he obeys the Spirit and never lives in the flesh. By contrast, the one who gives himself over totally to the flesh and surrenders himself to the passions never lives in the Spirit. Somewhere in between these two extremes are those whom we can call neither spiritual nor fleshly. Wavering between virtues and vices, they sometimes are drawn toward better things and are spirit, but at other times they trip on the slipperiness of the flesh and are flesh.

205. I.e., the Old Latin Bible (Vetus Latina).
206. Cf. 2 Cor 10.3.
207. Cf. 1 Pt 3.4.

5.26. *Let us not become desirous of empty glory, provoking and envying one another.*

The Latin translator has rendered the one Greek word κενό- δοξοι with the three-word circumlocution *inanis gloriae cupidi*. The countless books written by the philosophers as well as Cicero's *On Glory* in two volumes[208] attest to the range of definitions and meanings that "glory" has.[209] But since we make an effort to explain the sense of Scripture and not the etymologies of words, we shall connect this passage with the ones that preceded it: If we live by the Spirit,[210] let us obey the Spirit and be slaves to one another not in the Law but in love.[211] We should not quibble about the interpretation of Scripture and say, "Circumcision is better," "No, uncircumcision is," "Literal meaning should be condemned and allegory followed," "No, allegory is empty, obscure, and not held in place by any roots of truth." This is how envy of one another is born. Paul says, "What they want is to alienate you [from us], so that you may be zealous for them,"[212] and they wish not so much to teach you the truth of the Law as to dominate you.

So that we do not completely pass over the word "glory" without touching on it, let us leave to the philosophers their absurdities and review some passages from Scripture. The word "glory" means the regard of the populace and the praise sought by the favor of men in the following verse: "They do everything in order to be glorified by men,"[213] and elsewhere: "How can you believe when you seek glory from one another?"[214] The same verse also speaks of the good kind of glory: "Yet you do not seek the glory that is from God alone?"[215] Hence we understand that

---

208. Cicero mentions his *De gloria* in *Off* 2.31 and in some of his correspondence. It is lost but for a few fragments: see K. Simbeck and O. Plasberg, *M. Tulli Ciceronis scripta quae manserunt omnia, fasc. 47: Cato maior, Laelius, De gloria* (Berlin: Teubner; repr., 1997).

209. On the concept of *gloria*, or renown, in Cicero's philosophical works, see A. D. Leeman, *Gloria. Cicero's waardering van de roem en haar achtergrond in de hellenistische wijsbegeerte en de romeinse samenleving* (Rotterdam: Wyt & Zonen, 1949).

210. Cf. Gal 5.25.
212. Gal 4.17.
214. Jn 5.44.

211. Cf. Gal 5.13.
213. Mt 23.5.
215. Ibid.

the same word sometimes signifies virtue, at other times vice. If I seek glory from men, it is a vice. It is a virtue if I seek glory from God, who exhorts us to true glory, saying, "I shall glorify those who glorify me."[216] Glory has another meaning in divine Scripture, that is, when something more majestic or more divine reveals itself to the gaze of men. The glory of the Lord appeared in the Tabernacle,[217] and glory was in Solomon's Temple[218] as well as in Moses' face when he did not realize that his countenance had been glorified. I reckon that the Apostle is also speaking of this glory of countenance: "We all who with unveiled faces reflect the Lord's glory are being transformed into his likeness with ever-increasing glory."[219] The Savior himself is called the radiance of God's glory and the representation of his substance.[220] Stephen saw the glory of God and Jesus standing at his right hand.[221] Let us exercise our freedom to invent words, for, as a certain one says,[222] new words must be invented for new concepts. When it says, "Let us not become desirous of empty (or vacuous) glory," let us assert that those desirous of abundant glory are people who long for the glory of God, the praise that rightfully comes from virtue, and the beholding of something more divine. This is why our [Latin translators] have put "majesty" instead of "glory" in a good many instances.

I wish in this very instant to erupt into a flurry of words, but I am held back by a fear of speaking. I shall nevertheless speak and shall not be silent about my passion, an almost universal passion—but not for riches, power, or physical beauty and grace (for these are clearly numbered among the deeds of the flesh). If almsgiving is done for the purpose of obtaining praise, it is empty glory, and the same goes for prolonged prayer and the pallor caused by fasting. These words are not mine but the Savior's, who thunderously proclaims them in the Gospel.[223] Chastity in marriage, widowhood, and virginity also often seeks human applause.[224] What I was just now afraid of saying needs to be

---

216. 1 Sm 2.30.   217. Cf. Ex 40.32.
218. Cf. 1 Kgs 8.11.   219. 2 Cor 3.18.
220. Cf. Heb 1.3.   221. Cf. Acts 7.55.
222. Cicero, *Acad.* 1.25.   223. Cf. Mt 6.1–6, 16–18.
224. Cf. Jerome, *Ep.* 22.27: "Do not wish to appear more devout or humble

said: If we undergo martyrdom with the intention of being marveled at and praised by our brothers, then blood has been shed in vain. Let the Apostle, the chosen vessel, speak. "If I hand over my body that I may boast, but I do not have love, I gain nothing."[225] He is the one who had said, "I know a man in Christ who fourteen years ago was caught up to the third heaven. Whether it was in the body or out of the body I do not know; God knows."[226] A little later he said, "After being caught up to paradise, he heard inexpressible words that man is not permitted to tell."[227] This man, I say, worked harder than all others[228] so that his surpassingly great revelations would not puff him up. He was given a thorn in his flesh, a messenger of Satan, to torment him and keep him from becoming conceited. He even pleaded three times with the Lord to have it taken away, but he was told, "My grace is sufficient for you, for my power is made perfect in weakness."[229]

What is the work of God if not to read Scripture, to preach in church, to aspire to the priesthood, and to serve before the altar of the Lord? But even these arise from a longing for praise if one is not very careful about guarding his heart.[230] As even Cicero points out,[231] there are a good many people who write their own books about despising glory and yet attach their names to them out of a desire for glory! We interpret Scripture, we often erase what we have written, and we write what is worthy of being read.[232] If we do this not for the sake of Christ but for the sake of our posthumous reputation and notoriety among the populace, all effort will have been wasted and we will be like a re-

---

than you need to be, lest by shunning glory you actually pursue it. For many who conceal from sight their poverty, charity, and fasting desire to excite admiration by their very disdain of it and oddly seek praise while they profess to avoid it."

225. 1 Cor 13.3. 226. 2 Cor 12.2.
227. 2 Cor 12.4. 228. Cf. 1 Cor 15.10.
229. 2 Cor 12.7–9. 230. Cf. Prv 4.23.
231. Cf. *Tusc.* 1.34.

232. *Interpretamur Scripturas, saepe vertimus stilum, quae digna lectione sunt scribimus.* Jerome is echoing Horace, *Sat.* 1.10.72–73: *Saepe stilum vertas, iterum quae digna legi sint scripturus.* Jerome was extremely fond of this Horatian adage and quoted or paraphrased it on numerous other occasions: see Hagendahl, *The Latin Fathers and the Classics,* 128, 184 n. 1, 211, 228, 282.

sounding tambourine or a clanging cymbal.[233] Take note of how many people quarrel among themselves about Scripture and make an athletic contest out of God's Word. They provoke one another and become envious if they are defeated; these people are desirous of empty glory.

I am aware that in the Latin manuscripts the above-quoted passage, "If I hand over my body that I may boast," has "burn" (*ardeam*) instead of "boast" (*glorier*). But due to the similarity of the word—among the Greeks, the words "burn" and "boast," that is, καυθήσομαι and καυχήσομαι, are distinguished by one letter—the mistake has become entrenched among the Latin translators. Yet even among the Greeks themselves the manuscripts give variant readings.[234]

6.1. *Brothers, if a man is caught up in some sin, you* [plural] *who are spiritual should instruct him in a spirit of gentleness. But watch yourself, that you* [singular] *also are not tempted.*

Paul knows he worships the God who desires not the death of a sinner but his repentance,[235] and he knows that every creature apart from the Trinity is capable of sinning, even if it does not sin. He admonishes the one who is spiritual to make sure that he does not sin as he extends a helping hand to the person who falters. He fittingly calls the person susceptible to death "a man caught up in sin," highlighting by this the fragility of his condition. He does so to demonstrate that a man led astray by error is worthy of pardon and that after having been plunged into an abyss he cannot lift himself up without assistance. The word "man" is not added to "spiritual." Rather, it is as if God is the one ordered to instruct (or, as the Greek puts it better, "perfect"), in a spirit of mildness, the man caught up in sin. He is perfected because he is partially and not completely imperfect. He has gone astray because he has been caught up in a particular vice,

---

233. Cf. 1 Cor 13.1.

234. These two variant readings in the Greek are weighed by B. Metzger, *A Textual Commentary on the Greek New Testament*, 2d ed. (Stuttgart: Deutsche Bibelgesellschaft, 2005), 497–98. Metzger argues that καυχήσομαι is the preferred *lectio*.

235. Cf. Ezek 33.11.

not in a multitude of sins. When he corrects a sinner, the one who is spiritual should have a spirit of mildness and gentleness. He must not be inflexible, angry, or aggrieved in his desire to correct the wayward. He should encourage him with the promise of salvation. He should promise pardon and announce the testimony of Christ, which beckons those oppressed by the heavy burden of the Law and sin to take up his light yoke and pleasant burden so that they may learn that he is humble, meek, and gentle, and may find rest for their souls.

We should use this passage against the heretics who invent tall tales about different natures and claim that he who is spiritual is the good tree that never produces bad fruits.[236] Here the Apostle, whose authority even they follow, says that those who are spiritual are able to sin if their hearts are puffed up in haughtiness and they stumble (we, too, admit this is true), and he says that the earthly become the spiritual if they take a better course. We can be confronted with what is written to the Corinthians: "What do you want? That I come to you with a whip, or in love and a spirit of gentleness?"[237] For if he says in this passage that he comes to sinners not in a spirit of gentleness but with a whip, how is it that he now applies not the rod but a spirit of gentleness to those who had gotten embroiled in some sin? In the passage just quoted, he addresses people who sinned but did not recognize their error and did not want to submit to their elders and be corrected through repentance. But when the sinner is aware of his ailment and commits himself to the care of a physician, a spirit of mildness and not a whip is in order.

But it might be asked: If one must instruct the sinner in a spirit of mildness because he must watch out lest he also be tempted, will the righteous man, who is secure in himself and con-

---

236. Cf. Lk 6.43: "No good tree bears bad fruit, nor again does a bad tree bear good fruit." Mani seized on this verse as Scriptural support for his dualistic doctrine of human natures that were predisposed to be either good or evil (see Augustine, *Serm. Dom. mon.* 2.24.79). Marcion used it to prove the existence of the two deities, the inferior Creator-God and the God of Jesus who was the source of all supreme goodness (see Tertullian, *Adv. Marc.* 1.2). Jerome critiques the Gnostic doctrine of diverse natures earlier in the *Commentary* at 1.1.15–16a.

237. 1 Cor 4.21.

fident that he cannot fall, not instruct the sinner in a spirit of
mildness? To this we reply: Even if he has prevailed, the righteous man knows the effort that went into his triumph and so
he will more readily extend pardon to the sinner. For the Savior
was tempted in every way, just as we are, yet he was without sin.
This was so that, after being shown by his own example how difficult it is to attain victory in the flesh, he would be in a position
to commiserate and empathize with our weaknesses.[238] If anyone
remains a virgin until old age, he should forgive a person once
led astray by adolescent passion, keeping in mind how many difficulties he encountered when passing through his own youth. If
anyone persecuted for confessing the Name [that is, of Christ]
sees another person deny it under pain of torture, he should
empathize with what the denier has suffered and be astonished
not as much because anyone overcame him as because he overcame himself. Notice [Paul's] circumspection. He does not say,
"Watch yourself, that you also do not fall," but, "Watch yourself,
that you also are not tempted." Overcoming or being overcome
is sometimes in our power. But being tempted is in the power of
the tempter. If the Savior was tempted, who can be sure of crossing the seas of this life unscathed by temptation?

Those who think that Paul was being insincere and showing false modesty when he said, "Although I am inelegant in
speech, I am nevertheless not so in knowledge,"[239] must defend
the implication of the present verse. When he says, "You [pl.]
who are spiritual should instruct him in a spirit of gentleness,"
he should have stayed consistent and used the plural instead of
the singular [in the rest of the verse], saying, "Watching yourselves, that you [pl.] also are not tempted." But being a Hebrew
among Hebrews exceptionally proficient in his native tongue,
he could not express deep meanings in a foreign language
[that is, Greek] and he did not care much about the wording as
long as the sense was secure.[240]

238. Cf. Heb 4.15.
239. 2 Cor 2.6.
240. Jerome's comment addresses an apparent discrepancy in Paul's use of
verbs. Paul begins in the plural (καταρτίζετε) but finishes with singular verbs
(σκοπῶν and πειρασθῇς): "Brothers, if a man is caught up in some sin, you who

So much for the literal understanding. Completing the sequence of the second exposition, we must explore a passage from the end of the epistle to the Romans where Paul was writing also about the foods and observances of the Jews. Those who despised the letter of the Law he called strong and mature, but those who still were guided by ancient custom he called weak and infants. He recognized the conflict between spiritual and fleshly believers and admonished the spiritual not to despise the carnal-minded: "Accept him whose faith is weak, without passing judgment on disputable matters. One believes he can eat anything; another, who is weak, eats only vegetables. The man who eats everything must not look down on him who does not, nor judge him, for God has accepted him. Who are you to judge someone else's servant? To his own master he stands or falls. And he will stand, for God is able to make him stand."[241] After speaking in this vein at length in the intervening verses, he added at the end, "Do not destroy the work of God for the sake of food,"[242] and, "We who are strong ought to bear with the failings of the weak and not to please ourselves. Each of you should please his neighbor for his good, to build him up."[243]

6.2. *Carry the burdens of one another, and in this way you will fulfill the Law of Christ.*

The Psalmist also testifies that sin is a burden, saying, "My iniquities have gone over my head; as a heavy burden they weigh too much for me."[244] And Zechariah saw iniquity sitting atop a talent of lead in the guise of a woman.[245] The Savior carried this burden for us, teaching us by his example what we ought to

---

are spiritual should instruct (καταρτίζετε) him in a spirit of gentleness. But watch (σκοπῶν) yourself, that you also are not tempted (πειρασθῆς)." Jerome thinks Paul fumbled his Greek, but modern commentators generally agree that he deliberately switched up the verb forms in order to inculcate the personal responsibility of each individual not to sin: see, e.g., F. F. Bruce, *Commentary on Galatians,* NIGTC (Grand Rapids: W. B. Eerdmans, 1982), 260, and B. Witherington, *Grace in Galatia: A Commentary on St. Paul's Letter to the Galatians* (Grand Rapids: W. B. Eerdmans, 1998), 422.

241. Rom 14.1–4.   242. Rom 14.20.
243. Rom 15.2.   244. Ps 38.4.
245. Zec 5.7–8.

do. He indeed carries our iniquities and grieves for us and invites those who are weighed down by the burden of sin and the Law to take up the light burden of virtue, saying, "My yoke is easy and my burden is light."[246] Therefore, he fulfills the Law of Christ through love who does not despair over a brother's salvation but extends a hand to him when he asks for it, weeps with all his heart with the one who weeps,[247] is weak with the one who is weak,[248] and regards another's sins as his own. What is the Law of Christ? "This is my commandment: that you love one another."[249] What is the Law of the Son of God? "Love one another, just as I have loved you."[250] In what way has the Son of God loved us? "There is no greater love than this, that one would lay his life down for his friends."[251] He has not fulfilled the Law of Christ who, even if he is spiritual, has no clemency and has not put on the bowels of compassion and tears.[252]

But since we are in search of twofold understanding, let us join this passage with what precedes it. If anyone is weak in faith and is still being nourished with infant's milk[253] and cannot quickly pass from observance of the Law to spiritual mysteries, you who are firmly grounded must carry his burdens so that a brother for whom Christ died[254] does not perish on your watch. The one who helps a poor person oppressed by the burden of poverty and uses worldly wealth to gain friends for himself[255] also carries the hardship of his brother.[256] Christ says to such a man after he is resurrected, "Come to me, you who are blessed by my Father. Take your inheritance, the kingdom prepared for you since the creation of the world. For I was hungry and you gave me something to eat; I was thirsty and you gave me something to drink."[257] Along these same lines Paul instructs Timothy in another epistle, saying, "Command those who are rich

246. Mt 11.30.
247. Cf. Rom 12.15.
248. Cf. 1 Cor 9.22.
249. Jn 15.12.
250. Ibid.
251. Jn 13.34.
252. Cf. Col 3.12.
253. Cf. 1 Cor 3.1–2.
254. Cf. 1 Cor 8.11.
255. Cf. Lk 16.9.
256. Cf. J. Stralan, "Burden-bearing and the Law of Christ: A Re-examination of Galatians 6:2," *JBL* 94 (1975): 266–76. Stralan takes Gal 6.2a as referring to the sharing of financial burdens, an interpretation favored also by Jerome.
257. Mt 25.34–35.

in the present world not to be high-minded" (instead of "not to be arrogant")[258] "nor to put their hope in wealth, which is so uncertain, but to put their hope in God, who richly provides us with everything for our enjoyment. Command them to do good, to be rich in good deeds, and to be generous and willing to share. In this way they will lay up treasure for themselves as a firm foundation for the coming age, so that they may take hold of the life that is true."[259] He who takes hold of the life that is true, that is, of the One who says, "I am life,"[260] has fulfilled the Law of Christ, which leads to life.

6.3. *If anyone thinks he is something although he is nothing, he leads himself astray.*

That person deceives himself if he is not interested in carrying another's burdens but is content only with his own work and virtue, and seeks his own good but not the good of others,[261] and (in other words) only loves himself and not God as well. This passage can be punctuated in one of two ways: either, "If anyone thinks he is something although he is nothing," or, "If anyone thinks he is something," and then we add, "although he is nothing, he leads himself astray." This difference is more palpable in the Greek than in the Latin. The sense of the first distinction is this: If anyone thinks he is something and he is nothing, he leads himself astray. The second is deeper and more appealing to me: If anyone thinks he is something, such that he is content with only his own virtue and judges himself according to his own work and effort and not according to kindness shown towards his neighbor, he becomes nothing through this very arrogance and deceives himself. In the Greek this is expressed better with φρεναπατᾷ, which means "he deceives his own mind" (*mentem suam decipit*) though the Latin translator rendered it as "he deceives himself" (*se ipse seducit*). He deceives his own mind who thinks he is wise; in the words of Isaiah, he is wise in his own eyes and clever in his own sight.[262]

258. Jerome corrects the Old Latin Bible rendering of Paul's μὴ ὑψηλοφρονεῖν from *non superbire* to *non sublime sapere*.

259. 1 Tm 6.17–19.   260. Jn 14.6.
261. Cf. 1 Cor 13.5.   262. Cf. Is 5.21.

The meaning of this passage has application also to circumcision and the Law: He who is spiritual yet has no compassion for his neighbor and despises the lowly because of his own lofty sense of self-worth deceives himself because he does not realize that the Law of the Spirit is that we love one another.

6.4. *Each one should test his own actions. Then he can take pride in himself and not in another.*

The sense is this: You who deem yourself spiritual and are firmly grounded by comparison with another's weakness must not take stock of the feebleness of the dejected but only of your own strength. It does not make you a mature Christian if someone else cannot make a smooth transition from Judaism to Christianity. But if your own conscience does not reprimand you,[263] you can take pride in yourself and not in another. The athlete is not strong because he has overcome the weak and outmatched the sluggish limbs of an adversary, but only if he is firmly grounded and boasts in his own strength and not in another's weakness.

Put another way: He who is aware of his own good work and does not find fault with it when he takes stock of himself, must not boast about this to another, nor must he publicize his self-praise and seek others' applause. Rather, let him take pride in himself and say, "God forbid that I boast except in the cross of our Lord Jesus Christ, through whom the world has been crucified to me and I to the world."[264] The world has not been crucified to the person who seeks glory from another, nor has this person been transfixed with Christ, but he has received as his reward what he was seeking from others.

6.5. *For each one will carry his own burden.*

Paul seems to contradict what he said above, "Carry the burdens of one another."[265] For if each will carry his own burden, one person will be unable to carry another's burdens. But observe that in the first passage he instructs us to support one another while we sin in this life, and help one another in the present age. In the second he speaks of the Lord's judgment of us,

263. Cf. 1 Jn 3.21.   264. Gal 6.14.
265. Gal 6.2.

how we are reckoned either sinners or saints not by another's sin nor by comparison with someone in a worse position, but according to what we have done, for this is how each person is rewarded.[266]

This passage shows us, albeit covertly, a new and inconspicuous teaching. While we are in the present age, we are able to be helped by one another's prayers and counsel. When we come before the judgment seat of Christ, however, neither Job nor Daniel nor Noah will be able to intercede on behalf of anyone, but each person will carry his own burden.[267]

6.6. *Anyone who is taught the word should share all good things with the one who teaches him.*

Marcion interpreted this verse to mean that catechumens and the faithful ought to pray at the same time and that the master must share in prayer with his disciples (he got especially carried away by the phrase "all good things").[268] If he had been talking about prayer, however, a directive would not have had to be given to the student but to the teacher, that is, to the master and not the disciple. Furthermore, the rest of what follows— "What a man sows, he will also reap,"[269] and, "Let us not become

---

266. Cf. Rom 2.6.   267. Cf. Ezek 14.14.

268. The "faithful" are those who are baptized. Marcion allowed only virgins, widows, celibates, and eunuchs to be baptized (Tertullian, *Adv. Marc.* 1.29). Married believers, according to him, were "polluted" by the flesh and had to remain perpetual catechumens. Jerome was shocked that the Marcionite congregations made no formal distinction between catechumens and the baptized during their worship (i.e., Eucharistic) services, such that they were allowed to pray together. Along the same lines, Epiphanius (*Pan.* 42.3.3; 4.5) was critical of how Marcion "celebrates the sacraments with the catechumens looking on," though they are not allowed to partake of the Lord's Supper. The presence of catechumens at sacred meals, however, was a typical second-century custom among even orthodox churches: see A. Steward-Sykes, "Bread and Fish, Water and Wine: The Marcionite Menu and the Maintenance of Purity," in *Marcion und seine Kirchengeschichtliche Wirkung: Marcion and His Impact on Church History,* ed. G. May and K. Greschat (Berlin: Walter de Gruyter, 2002), 207–20 (208–9). Thus, what to Epiphanius and Jerome seemed bizarre and irreverent by the standards of the late fourth century was not so in Marcion's day. At any rate, Jerome's comment, which presumably goes back to Origen, indicates that Marcion appealed to Gal 6.6 to justify his liturgical practice.

269. Gal 6.8.

weary in doing good, for at the proper time we will reap a harvest if we do not give up"[270]—does not agree with Marcion's exposition. The sense is as follows. Previously he had told the spiritual to instruct in a spirit of gentleness those caught up in some sin and to carry one another's burdens and thereby fulfill the Law of Christ. But now he speaks to those who are still disciples and rather weak and fleshly minded. He orders them to compensate their masters with material goods in return for spiritual blessings they have reaped from them. For these masters devote themselves completely and wholeheartedly to divine learning and zeal, and are wanting in the basic necessities of this life. He orders that what is written about manna be brought to pass, "He who had much had nothing in excess, and he who had little did not have too little."[271]

According to everyday idiom and common usage, the "good things" in the present passage refer to food, clothing, and other commodities which people classify as good things. "Having food and clothing, we are content with these."[272] It is no wonder that Paul uses the word "good" to signify bodily necessities, when even our Savior said to those who had not yet reached the pinnacle of virtue but were still crawling and asked that their faith be increased, "If you, though you are evil, know how to give good gifts to your children, how much more will your Father in heaven give good gifts to those who ask him!"[273] In addition, when Job addressed his wife as if she were a foolish woman, "If we have received good things from the hand of the Lord,"[274] I imagine he said this because she was thinking of tangible riches. He then said, "Why should we not receive evil things?"[275] because she was thinking of trials, tribulations, and temptation, which afford the opportunity for triumph.[276] Now, the categories of "good" and "evil" do not apply to riches and tribulations but rather to virtues and vices. The righteous man accordingly

270. Gal 6.9.   271. 2 Cor 8.15; cf. Ex 16.18.
272. 1 Tm 6.8.   273. Mt 7.11.
274. Jb 2.10.   275. Ibid.
276. Cf. Jerome, *Ep.* 140.19: "The more we suffer in this world from persecution, poverty, enemy oppression, and the pangs of disease, the greater the reward we will receive after the resurrection."

says in the Psalm, "Who is the man who loves life and desires to see good days? Keep your tongue from evil and your lips from speaking lies. Turn from evil and do good."[277] Thus what must be avoided is appropriately called evil, while what we ought to do is called good. Furthermore, that rich man in the Gospel who had no knowledge of good and evil rightly referred to his bountiful crop as "good things," saying, "[I will say to my soul,] 'Soul, you have plenty of good things laid up for many years. Take life easy; eat, drink, and be merry.'"[278] And another rich man who used to dress in purple and live luxuriously but is now in hell heard Abraham say, "You have received your good things in your lifetime."[279]

We should take careful note that this passage means that disciples are commanded to share the word with their teachers and be obsequious, docile, and compliant, but only with respect to "good things," which are spiritual and not corrupted by heretical or Jewish depravity.

6.7. *Do not be deceived: God is not mocked. A man will reap what he sows.*

With spiritual foresight he anticipates that those who are receiving instruction and thus obligated to provide for their teachers' basic needs and necessities of life can protest that they are poor and say, "My field is dried up this year; hail has obliterated my vineyard; taxes have stolen away whatever profits there could have been; I have no way of contributing what I am ordered to." He therefore added, "Do not be deceived: God is not mocked." He says: God knows your hearts, and he is not unaware of what you are capable of doing; a plausible excuse can satisfy any man you please, but it cannot trick God. In urging them to comply with his command he uses seed-terminology and shows that he does not think that what he will receive back in manifold profits has been lost. When writing to the Corinthians he employed a similar example to inculcate the principle of giving and receiving, "Whoever sows sparingly will also reap sparingly, and whoever sows generously will also reap generously. Each man

277. Ps 34.12–14.   278. Lk 12.19.
279. Lk 16.25.

should give what he has decided in his heart to give, not reluctantly or under compulsion, for God loves a cheerful giver."[280]

6.8. *For the one who sows in his own flesh, from the flesh he will reap destruction. But the one who sows in the Spirit, from the Spirit he will reap eternal life.*

Everything we say, do, or think is sown in two fields, the flesh and the Spirit. If the things proceeding from our hand, mouth, and heart are good, they will overflow with the fruits of eternal life because they were sown in the Spirit. If the field of the flesh welcomes evil, it will sprout up a field of destruction for us. Put another way: The one who understands the Law in a fleshly way also awaits promises that are fleshly and that are destroyed during the present age, but the one who is a spiritual hearer sows in the Spirit, and from the Spirit he will reap eternal life. We should also pay attention to the word order and connect this passage with the preceding one: The one who sows in the Spirit is called a man, but when he begins to reap eternal life, he perhaps will cease to be a man.

Cassianus, the most astute heresiarch among the Encratites, maintained that Christ's flesh was imaginary and considered that every [sexual] union between man and woman is foul.[281] He used the present passage as a pretext for this argument against us: If one sows in the flesh and will reap destruction from the flesh, and if this sower is one who is united to a woman, then he who enjoys his wife and sows in her flesh will reap destruction from the flesh. [Cassianus] can be rebutted in this way. First, Paul did not say "the one who sows in the flesh" but "in his own

280. 2 Cor 9.6–7.
281. The Encratites (Ἐγκρατεῖς, "abstainers") were Gnostic Christians in the second century who abstained from marriage, wine, and animal foods, believing that these things are intrinsically evil (Irenaeus, *Adv. haer.* 1.28; cf. 1 Tm 4.1–5). Julius Cassianus, whom Jerome introduces as an authoritative figure in the Encratite church, taught in Egypt around 170. According to Clement of Alexandria (*Strom.* 3.13.92), he wrote two books, one an exegetical work of some kind and the second entitled *On Abstinence or Eunuchry* (Περὶ ἐγκρατείας ἢ περὶ εὐνουχίας). Two of the short passages Clement quotes from this latter work condemn all sexual intercourse. Cassianus's use of Gal 6.8 as a proof-text for his prohibition against sex is attested only by Jerome, who almost certainly has preserved this detail from Origen's commentary on Galatians.

flesh": nobody has intercourse with himself and sows in his own flesh! Secondly, even if we generously concede to him my observation about the phrase "in his own flesh," the point must also be made that those who eat, drink, sleep, and do something to refresh the body sow in the flesh and reap destruction from it. Now if he reverts to the argument that those who either drink, eat, or sleep act in accordance with reason and do everything in the name of the Lord[282] and sow not in the flesh but in the Spirit, we will respond in kind that those who act in accordance with reason and follow the first command God gave to "be fruitful and multiply and fill the earth"[283] sow not in the flesh but in the Spirit. His syllogism is therefore futile and powerless. He initially deceives his audience by means of a sophism, but upon closer inspection it is easily solved. Moreover, we cannot assert that Abraham, Isaac, Jacob, and the other saintly men born of the promise, not to mention the Lord's very precursor,[284] sprouted from the seed of destruction just because they were born in the flesh.

We should also notice that the words "his own" are added to the phrase "he who sows in the flesh." The word "his," however, is not found in the phrase "he who sows in the Spirit"; it is left simply as "in the Spirit." This is because whoever sows good things does not sow in anything of his own but in the Spirit of God, from whom he will reap eternal life.

6.9. *Let us not give up doing good, for at the proper time we will reap a harvest if we do not give up.*

He exhorts those who await in this life the reward for their good work to persevere. For they do not realize that, just as there is a time for sowing and a time for harvesting, so also in the present life the sowing concerns works which are sown in the Spirit or in the flesh, while the harvest is the future judgment of works. They also do not realize that, depending on the quality and variety of the seeds that are sown, we produce in varying measures, a hundredfold, sixtyfold, and thirtyfold crop.[285] No one can harvest this field if he gives up, "for who-

282. Cf. Col 3.17.   283. Gn 1.22.
284. I.e., John the Baptist.
285. Cf. Mt. 13.1–23; Mk 4.1–20; Lk 8.1–15. Elsewhere Jerome gave this

ever perseveres until the end will be saved."[286] And, "Do not be one who gives up."[287] Moreover, how can we tire out doing good works when sinners rack up more evil works by the day?

6.10. *Therefore, while we still have time, let us do good to all people, especially to those who belong to the household of faith.*

As we have said, there is a time for sowing, and that time is now and the life whose course we are running. While we are in this life, we are allowed to sow whatever we want, but when this life passes away, the time for doing work is taken away. Hence the Savior says, "Work as long as it is day; the night will come, when no one will be able to work."[288] The word of God, the true sun, has arisen for us, and the wild animals have returned to their dens. We should go forth to our work as men and labor until the evening, according to the mystical song in the Psalm, "You appoint darkness and it becomes night, in which the beasts of the forest prowl about, and the young lions roar after their prey and seek their food from God. When the sun rises, they withdraw and lie down in their dens. Man goes forth to his work and to his labor until evening."[289] It matters not if we are sick or healthy, lowly or powerful, poor or rich, undistinguished or renowned, starving or satiated. We should do everything in the name of the Lord[290] patiently and calmly, and that promise will come to pass in us which says, "All things work together for the good for those who love the Lord."[291] Anger, lust, and vengeful insult become an opportunity for me to gain victory, provided that I show self-restraint, stay silent for God's sake, and remember that God is watching over me as I endure each and every agitation of the passions and incitement to vice.

When we give, we should not say, "This person is my friend, but I do not know that person," or, "This person must receive something, but that one must be refused." We should imitate our

---

parable an overtly ascetic reading as a blueprint for the three grades of chastity: the hundredfold crop stands for virginity, the sixtyfold crop for chaste widowhood, and the thirtyfold crop for marriage (see, e.g., *Ep.* 22.15; *Adv. Iov.* 1.3).

286. Mt 10.22; 24.13. 287. Is 5.27.
288. Jn 9.4. 289. Ps 104.20–23.
290. Cf. Col 3.17. 291. Rom 8.28.

Father, who "causes his sun to rise on the evil and the good, and sends rain on the righteous and unrighteous."[292] The fountain of goodness is open to everyone; the slave and the free person, the plebeian and the king, the rich and the poor all drink from it. When a lamp is lit in the house, it gives light to everyone equally.[293] Now if the restraints of generosity are relaxed indiscriminately for everyone, how much more should they be for those who belong to the household of faith, Christians who share the same Father, and are identified by the name of the same master! It seems possible to me that this passage refers back to an earlier statement[294] and that "those who belong to the household of faith" are the teachers who he had said should be supplied with the very best provisions by their students.

This life's race is short. What I say, what I dictate, what is written down, what I correct, and what I proofread is either a gain or a loss to me in terms of my time. It is related that Titus the son of Vespasian, who entered Rome a victor after leveling Jerusalem to avenge the Lord's blood, was so conscientious about doing good that on a certain evening at dinner he recalled that he had done nothing good that day and said, "My friends, today I have squandered the day."[295] Do we imagine that an hour, day, minutes, or any stretch of time or period in life does not go to waste when we utter some idle word for which we will give an account on Judgment Day?[296] Now if [Titus] said and did this by nature, without the aid of the Law, the Gospel, and the teaching of the Savior and apostles, what ought we to do, we who are put to shame by Juno's once-married devotees, Vesta's virgins, and the celibates of other false gods?[297]

292. Mt 5.45. 293. Cf. Mt 5.15.
294. Gal 6.6.
295. This same anecdote is reported by both Suetonius (*V. Tit.* 8.1) and the late antique epitomator Eutropius (*Brev.* 7.21.3). But since Jerome's wording is nearly identical to Eutropius's, it is likely that he was his more immediate source. For an exhaustive inventory of Jerome's borrowings from Eutropius, see R. Helm, "Hieronymus und Eutrop," *RhM* 76 (1927): 138–70 and 254–306.
296. Cf. Mt 12.36.
297. Jerome almost certainly has in mind either one or both of two passages in Tertullian where he attempts to shame lukewarm Christians into being more virtuous by reminding them of examples of outstanding pagan chastity: *De monog.*

The blessed John the Evangelist lived in Ephesus until extreme old age. His disciples could barely carry him to church and he could not muster the voice to speak many words. During individual gatherings he usually said nothing but, "Little children, love one another."[298] The disciples and brothers in attendance, annoyed because they always heard the same words, finally said, "Teacher, why do you always say this?" He replied with a line worthy of John: "Because it is the Lord's commandment and if it alone is kept, it is sufficient."[299] He said this because of the Apostle's present mandate: "Let us do good to all people, especially to those who belong to the household of faith."

6.11. *See with what characters I am writing to you in my own hand.*

Those who wanted the Galatians to be circumcised had spread it around that Paul preached one thing and did another, and that he nullified his words through his deeds inasmuch as he proclaimed that the Law was abolished, yet was found to be living by it. Paul projects himself through a letter since he could not prove this allegation wrong in person for all to see (he was prevented by the chains he bore as a testimony to Christ). So that no one would suspect it was forged, he wrote it in his own hand from here until the end, and thus he demonstrated that the preceding portion had been copied down by someone else.

False teachers were sending epistles in his name to the Thessalonians, as he says, "Concerning the coming of our Lord Jesus Christ and our being gathered to him, we ask you, brothers, not to become easily unsettled or alarmed by some prophecy, report, or epistle supposed to have come from us, saying that

---

17.4 (ANF 4:72): "There are, too, who may judge us on the ground of absolute continence: the virgins of Vesta, and of the Achaian Juno, and of the Scythian Diana, and of the Pythian Apollo. On the ground of continence the priests likewise of the famous Egyptian bull will judge the infirmity of Christians"; *De exhort. cast.* 13.2 (ANF 4:57): "We have heard of Vesta's virgins, and Juno's at the town of Achaia, and Apollo's among the Delphians, and Minerva's and Diana's in some places. We have heard, too, of continent men, and among others the priests of the famous Egyptian bull." See A. Cain, *REAug* 55 (2009): 36–37.

298. Cf. 1 Jn 3.11 and 18.

299. The source for this story was possibly Hegesippus's *Memoirs* via either Clement of Alexandria or Origen.

the day of the Lord has already come. Do not let anyone deceive you in any way."[300] So as to remove suspicion that the entire epistle he sent was a forgery, he wrote in his own hand at the end, saying, "I, Paul, write this greeting in my own hand, which is the distinguishing mark in all of my epistles. This is how I write. The grace of our Lord Jesus Christ be with you all."[301] He similarly signed the letter he had dictated for the Colossians: "I, Paul, write this greeting in my own hand. Remember my chains."[302] Whenever he knew that false teachers were around to spread new teachings under the guise of apostolic authority, he signed his letter in his own hand. Finally, when writing to the Corinthians, among whom there were divisions and factions and different people who said, "I follow Paul, I follow Apollos, I follow Cephas,"[303] he certified his epistle with the following signature: "I, Paul, write this greeting in my own hand. If anyone does not love the Lord Jesus Christ—a curse be upon him. Come, O Lord,"[304] and so on.

He capped his epistle with a signature in his own hand in order to take all leverage away from the false teachers who had seduced the Galatians away from evangelical truth. "See with what characters I am writing to you [in my own hand]." It is not that the characters were large (though in the Greek πηλίκοις has this sense), but that the marks of his handwriting were known to them, meaning that when they recognized the forms of his letters, they would imagine that they were seeing the writer. I am astonished that a man in our time so distinguished for his learning made a ridiculous observation about this very passage. He says, "Paul was a Hebrew and was illiterate in Greek. Since circumstances compelled him to sign his epistle in his own hand, he went against his usual custom and with difficulty traced the contours of the characters. Even in this he demonstrated his love for the Galatians in that he attempted to do something for their sake that did not come easy for him."[305]

---

300. 2 Thes 2.1–3.
301. 2 Thes 3.17–18.
302. Col 4.18.
303. 1 Cor 1.12.
304. 1 Cor 16.21–22.

305. This quotation probably came from Eusebius of Emesa's commentary on Galatians, which is lost but for fewer than two dozen fragments. See A. Cain, "An

Paul wrote his epistle in large characters because their meaning was profound and because they had been transcribed by the Spirit of the living God and not by pen and ink. When he wrote "in my own hand" he was referring to work his hands did. This is why it is frequently said in the prophets, "The word of God which came through the hand of Jeremiah (or of Haggai)."[306] Thus he wanted us to know through this similarity that the word of God had come through his own hand as well. Paul not only wrote in large characters back then to the Galatians, but even today he writes them to all people. And although the forms with which his epistles are signed are small, the characters are nevertheless large because of the profundity contained in them.

6.12. *Those who want to please in the flesh are forcing you to be circumcised. The only reason they do this is to avoid being persecuted for the Cross of Christ.*

In the previous verse he shows that point in the epistle at which he began to write in his own hand, but now he reviews his reason for writing. Gaius [Julius] Caesar, Octavian Augustus, and Augustus's successor Tiberius had published laws that allowed the Jews scattered throughout the whole stretch of the Roman Empire to live by their own rites and to keep their ancestral ceremonies.[307] Therefore, whoever was circumcised, even if he was a Christian, was considered a Jew by outsiders. But anyone who was not circumcised, and by his uncircumcision declared that he was not a Jew, became liable to persecution from Gentile and Jew alike. Those who had led the Galatians astray were hoping to evade persecution and persuaded the disciples to be circumcised for protection. The Apostle now says they put their trust in the flesh because they made circumcision a matter worthy of

---

Unidentified Patristic Quotation in Jerome's *Commentary on Galatians* (3.6.11)," *JThS*, n.s., 61 (2010): 216–25.

306. Cf. Hg 1.1.

307. Jerome's source for this overview of imperial rights conceded to the Jewish people was almost certainly Josephus, *Antiquities* (Julius Caesar: 14.185–215; Augustus: 19.282–310; Tiberius: 15.404–5). For a narrative of Roman accommodation of Jewish special interests under these three leaders, see M. Grant, *The Jews in the Roman World* (London: Orion Books; repr., 1999), 57–103 (*passim*).

persecution for both the Gentiles, whom they feared, and the Jews, whom they wanted to please. For neither the Jews nor the Gentiles could persecute people they saw circumcising new converts and keeping the commandments of the Law.

6.13. *Not even those who are circumcised keep the Law, yet they want you to be circumcised that they may boast about your flesh.*

The Law cannot be fulfilled, he says, on account of the weakness of the flesh. This is why the Jews keep human precepts and teachings rather than God's and observe neither the physical Law (this is impossible) nor the spiritual one, which they do not understand. Therefore, all of their zeal, actions, and aspirations are geared toward enabling them to boast among the Jews about the injury done to your flesh and to flaunt the fact that heathen nations have been circumcised by their authority. They do all of this to please the Jews and make the odious nature of the abrogated Law seem innocuous.

6.14. *God forbid that I boast except in the Cross of our Lord Jesus Christ, through whom the world has been crucified to me and I to the world.*

The only person who can boast in the Cross of Christ is he who takes up his cross and follows the Savior,[308] who has crucified his own flesh with its vices and sinful desires,[309] who has died to the world, and who does not fix his eyes on what is seen but on what is unseen.[310] For he sees the world crucified and its present form passing away.[311] The world, then, is crucified to the righteous man. The Savior speaks of it when he says, "I have overcome the world,"[312] and, "Do not love the world,"[313] and, "You have not received the spirit of the world."[314] The world is crucified to the one to whom it has died. The end of the world has come to him and, having been rendered worthy of the new heaven and new earth and new covenant, he sings a new song and receives a new name written on a stone, a name known only to the one who receives it.[315]

308. Cf. Mt 16.24.
309. Cf. Gal 5.24.
310. Cf. 2 Cor 4.18.
311. Cf. 1 Cor 7.31.
312. Jn 16.33.
313. 1 Jn 2.15.
314. 1 Cor 2.12.
315. Cf. Rv 2.17.

One may ask how it is that Paul here says, "God forbid that I boast except in the Cross of our Lord Jesus Christ," when elsewhere he boasts about other things, "By your glory, which I have in Christ Jesus."[316] And again, "I will boast all the more gladly about my weaknesses, so that Christ's power may dwell in me."[317] And in another place, "I would rather die than have anyone deprive me of this boast."[318] There are other passages to this effect. We should realize that every boast pertaining to the Cross is to its glory and that whatever worthy deed is performed in [the name of] virtue is done for the sake of what the Lord suffered.

6.15. *Neither circumcision nor uncircumcision means anything; what counts is a new creation.*

Even though the believer and unbeliever are one in terms of their substance, they are divided into two groups based upon their difference in understanding. The Apostle thus says, "You have taken off the old self with its works and have put on the new self, which is being renewed in knowledge in the image of its Creator."[319] Likewise, although the world is one in its substance, it becomes one or another thing depending on one's perspective: to the sinner it is old, to the saint it is new. Since the world has been crucified to the saint, neither circumcision nor uncircumcision means anything to him, and neither does being a Jew or Gentile.[320] What counts is a new creation, into which our lowly body is being transformed into the glorious body of Christ.[321] "The old things have passed away, and all things have been made new."[322] "The sun has one kind of splendor, the moon another, and the stars another, and star differs from star in splendor; so it will be with the resurrection of the dead."[323] Daniel agrees with this, saying, "Multitudes who sleep in the dust of the earth will awake, some to everlasting life, others to shame and everlasting contempt,"[324] and, "Those who are wise will shine like the brightness of the firmament, and the many who are righteous, like the

316. 1 Cor 15.31.
317. 2 Cor 12.9.
318. 1 Cor 9.15.
319. Col 3.9–10.
320. Cf. Col 3.11.
321. Cf. Phil 3.21.
322. 2 Cor 5.17.
323. 1 Cor 15.41–42.
324. Dn 12.2.

stars forever."[325] Neither circumcision nor uncircumcision has any value in the sun, moon, firmament, and stars. Rather, it is a new state of being without those parts of bodies which can be divided. So it is with us, who love God and for whom things have been prepared which neither eye has seen nor ear has heard nor which have entered into the heart of man.[326] For we will be transformed from our lowly body into the glorious body of the Lord Jesus Christ,[327] and we will have a body that neither Jew can circumcise nor Gentile can keep uncircumcised. This is not to say that its substance changes; it is just different in glory.[328] "For the perishable must clothe itself with the imperishable, and the mortal with immortality."[329] The blessed evangelist John expressed a similar sentiment: "My beloved, now we are children of God, and what we will be has not yet been made known. But we know that when he appears, we will be like him, for we will see him as he is."[330] Since that glorious body of Jesus Christ which after the resurrection bore the nail marks and passed through closed doors[331] has not yet been made known, we who have already now been raised with Christ in baptism[332] and reborn into a new self should be slaves to neither circumcision nor uncircumcision, and we should believe that we are now already what we will become.

6.16. *As for those who follow this rule—peace be upon them, and mercy, and upon the Israel of God.*

All things are measured by a standard, and when a ruler is set next to them they are revealed to be either wrong or right. In this way the teaching of God is a sort of standard for words that differentiates between what is righteous or unrighteous. Who-

---

325. Dn 12.3.

326. Cf. 1 Cor 2.9.

327. Cf. Phil 3.21.

328. "Same in substance (or nature), different in glory" was the formula Jerome used to describe the resurrected body (see, e.g., *Adv. Iov.* 1.36; *Comm. Mt.* 17.2; *Comm. Is.* 58.14; *Ep.* 108.22). What he meant by this is simply that the risen body will be the same body as it was before, except that its glory will be increased. See further J. P. O'Connell, *The Eschatology of Saint Jerome* (Mundelein: St. Mary of the Lake Seminary Press, 1948), 39–63.

329. 1 Cor 15.53.

330. 1 Jn 3.2.

331. Cf. Jn 20.26.

332. Cf. Col 2.12.

ever follows it will have the inner peace that surpasses all under-standing,[333] and after it mercy, which is the special possession of the Israel of God.

He says "Israel of God" to distinguish it from the Israel that ceased to belong to God.[334] For they call themselves Jews but are not, and they lie since they come from the synagogue of Sa-tan.[335] You should not be surprised that the fleshly Israel mimics the spiritual Israel, but the former lacks both peace and mercy (Paul, writing to the Corinthians, refers to them when he says, "Consider the Israel that is according to the flesh").[336] After all, there are many gods and many lords whether in heaven or on earth who mimic God and the Lord.[337] He uses the single el-egant expression "Israel of God" to summarize the gist of the epistle and to show that everything said up to this point is not extraneous but relevant to the main issue.

6.17a. *Finally, let no one be troublesome to me.*

This does not mean that he seemingly failed as a teacher, but that the farmer experiences hardship because the shrubbery he planted is drying up, and that the shepherd is anxious because the flock he had gathered together is scattered and torn to piec-es. The Greek puts it better: "Finally, let no one bring hardships upon me," so that I am not again forced to be aggrieved among you. He who does not live or think in accordance with what his teacher taught and did causes hardship to him.

[By saying this] Paul is also able to anticipate the argumen-tativeness of those who saw fit to oppose him continually. This is the same strategy he embraced after a long discussion in his epistle to the Corinthians about women covering their heads and men leaving their heads uncovered. He said, "If anyone

333. Cf. Phil 4.7.
334. It is unclear from Paul's Greek syntax whether by "Israel of God" he means exclusively Gentile Christans (i.e., the spiritual Israel) or ethnic Jews. On this ambiguity, see L. E. Keck, "The Jewish Paul among the Gentiles: Two Portrayals," in *Early Christianity and Classical Culture: Comparative Studies in Hon-or of Abraham J. Malherbe,* ed. J. T. Fitzgerald, T. H. Olbricht, and L. M. White (Leiden: E. J. Brill, 2003), 461–81 (474).
335. Cf. Rv 2.9.   336. 1 Cor 10.18.
337. Cf. 1 Cor 8.5.

seems to be argumentative, neither we nor the church of God has any other practice."[338] In other words: What we have told you seems wholesome and right to us, and if anyone is unwilling to give in to the truth and looks instead for counter-arguments, he should know that the person more inclined to argue than to be taught does not deserve an answer.

6.17b. *For I carry on my body the marks of our Lord Jesus Christ.*

Whoever is circumcised in the flesh during the Christian era does not carry the marks of the Lord Jesus, but glories in his own shame. But the one who is severely flogged, frequently jailed, beaten with rods three times, stoned once, and everything else mentioned in [Paul's] list of boast-worthy things[339]—this person carries on his body the marks of the Lord Jesus.[340] It is possible too that he who beats his body and makes it his slave, so that after preaching to others he might not be found to be unqualified,[341] carries the marks of the Lord Jesus on his body. Furthermore, the apostles rejoiced because they had been counted worthy of suffering disgrace for the name of Jesus.[342]

338. 1 Cor 11.16.

339. See 2 Cor 11.23–27.

340. The vast majority of modern commentators take these "marks" (στίγματα, *stigmata*) to be scars or wounds resulting from physical persecution (e.g., flogging) Paul had undergone. Some scholars, however, have put forward some interesting hypotheses. F. J. Dölger suggested that Paul had tattooed Jesus' name on his body: *Sphragis: Eine altchristliche Taufbezeichnung in ihrer Beziehung zur profanen und religiösen Kultur des Altertums* (Paderborn: Schöningh, 1911), 51 n. 1. E. Hirsch thought that the "marks" referred to lasting eye damage Paul had sustained as a result of seeing the blinding light on the road to Damascus: "Zwei Fragen zu Galater 6," *ZNTW* 29 (1930): 192–97 (196–97). F. Fenner hypothesized that Paul literally bore the crucifixion marks of Christ and thus manifested the same stigmata phenomenon attested during the Middle Ages (e.g., St. Francis of Assisi) and down to the twentieth century (e.g., Padre Pio): *Die Krankheit im Neuen Testament: Eine religionsgeschichtliche und medizingeschichtliche Untersuchung* (Leipzig: Hinrichs, 1930), 40. Whatever the case, Jerome and many modern scholars think that Paul mentioned these marks in order to contrast them with the "mark" of circumcision about which his Judaizing opponents boasted: see, e.g., D. Kremendahl, *Die Botschaft der Form: Zum Verhältnis von antiker Epistolographie und Rhetorik im Galaterbrief* (Göttingen: Vandenhoeck & Ruprecht, 2000), 79–80.

341. Cf. 1 Cor 9.27.

342. Cf. Acts 5.41.

6.18. *The grace of our Lord Jesus Christ be with your spirit, brothers. Amen.*

The grace of the Lord Jesus Christ—not dissension, not slavery to the Law, not quarreling, not strife—be with your spirit. He does not say "with your flesh" or "with your soul" either because they had become spiritual and ceased to be flesh and soul or because lesser things are subsumed by the principal one. For the soul and the flesh are subject to the spirit, about which Ecclesiastes speaks, "The spirit will return to him [that is, God] who gave it,"[343] and elsewhere Paul, "The Spirit himself testifies with our spirit."[344]

This grace of the Lord Jesus is not with everyone, but only with those who earn the right to be called "brothers" by the Apostle, both brothers in the faith and blood brothers. *Amen* is a Hebrew word. The Septuagint translators render it as "let it be," while Aquila, Symmachus, and Theodotion translate it as "faithfully" or "truly." In the Old Testament God ratifies his own words with a conventional oath, saying, "As surely as I live, declares the Lord,"[345] and he also swears through his saints, "As surely as your soul lives."[346] Likewise, in the Gospel our Savior uses the word *amen* to confirm that the words he utters are true. *Amen* signifies the hearer's consent and is a sign of truthfulness. Thus Paul teaches us in the first epistle to the Corinthians, "If you praise God with your spirit, how can one who finds himself among those who do not understand say 'amen' to your thanksgiving, since he does not know what you are saying?"[347] He shows by this that a simpleton cannot declare a saying true unless he understands its meaning.

343. Eccl 12.7.
344. Rom 8.16.
345. Nm 14.28.
346. Jdt 12.4.
347. 1 Cor 14.16.

INDICES

GENERAL INDEX

INDEX OF HOLY SCRIPTURE

Entries are referenced by the book number of Jerome's commentary followed by the chapter and verse of Galatians. Psalm numbering is modern unless otherwise noted.

Old Testament

Genesis
1.22: 3.6.8
2.9: 2.3.13b–14
2.17: 2.3.13b–14
3.11: 2.3.13b–14
3.14: 2.3.13b–14
3.15: 3.5.19–21
3.16: 1.3.8–9; 2.4.19
3.17: 2.3.13b–14
4.8: 2.4.17–18
4.10: 1.3.8–9
4.11: 2.3.13b–14
4.26 (LXX): 1.3.8–9
5.24: 1.1.6–7
6.3: 1.1.16b; 3.5.19–21
9.21: 3.5.13a
9.25 (LXX): 2.3.13b–14
12.3: 1.3.8–9
14.18–19: 2.5.2
15.3: 2.4.6
15.5–6: 1.3.8–9
15.6: 2.5.6
15.13: 2.3.15–18
16.10: 2.4.22–23
16.12 (LXX): 2.4.22–23
17.18–21: 2.4.22–23
17.19: 2.4.22–23

17.21: 2.4.22–23
21.1–6: 2.4.24b–26
21.10: 2.4.29–31
21.12: 2.4.29–31
22.18: 1.3.8–9; 2.3.15–18
30.13: 2.4.6
32.30: 3.5.22–23
37.4: 3.5.19–21
37.11: 2.4.17–18
38.14–18: 3.5.13a
38.27–30: 2.3.15–18
43.34: 3.5.13a
47.9: 1.1.4–5
49.7: 2.3.13b–14

Exodus
3.6: 2.3.19–20
3.10: 1.1.1
4.14: 1.1.1
4.24–26: 2.5.6
6.12: 2.5.6
12.2–6: 1.1.18b; 2.4.10–11
12.18–20: 2.4.10–11
14.15: 2.4.6
15.20: 3.5.19–21
15.20–21: pref 1
15.22–25: 2.3.13b–14

16.18: 3.6.6
17.1–7: 2.3.19–20
20.13–16: 3.5.13b–14
21.6: 1.1.4–5
23.14–16: 2.4.10–11
23.15: pref 3
23.17: 2.3.24–26; 2.4.10–11
23.22: 3.5.19–21
29.38–42: 2.5.3
32.5–6: 2.3.19–20
32.6: 3.5.19–21
32.9: 1.3.1a
34.33: 2.4.8–9
34.33–35: 1.1.11–12
40.3: 1.1.11–12
40.32: 3.5.26

Leviticus
15.31: 3.5.19–21
18.5: 2.3.11–12
19.18: 3.5.22–23
23.15–21: 2.4.10–11
23.23–25: 2.4.10–11
23.27–32: 2.4.10–11
23.34–36: 2.4.10–11
25.4: 2.5.3
25.9–10: 2.5.3

New Testament

INDEX OF GREEK AND HEBREW WORDS AND PHRASES

Entries are referenced by the book number of Jerome's commentary followed by the chapter and verse of Galatians.

Greek

ἄδικος, 2.4.4–5
αἵρεσις, 3.5.19–21
αἰσχύνη, 2.4.20
ἀνασταυροῦντες, 3.5.24
ἀνεθέμην, 1.2.1–2
ἄνομος, 2.4.4–5
ἀποκάλυψις, 1.1.11–12
ἀποκατάστασις, 2.5.5
ἀποροῦμαι, 2.4.20
ἀπόστολος, 1.1.1n
ἄρχουσα, 2.4.24b–26
γένοιτο, 1.1.4–5
γυνή, 2.4.4–5
εἰ δὲ πνεύματι ἄγεσθε, οὐκ
    ἐστὲ ὑπὸ νόμον, 3.5.18
ἐριθείαι, 3.5.19–21

ζῆλος, 3.5.19–21
καταρτίζετε, 3.6.1n
κατηργήθητε ἀπὸ τοῦ
    Χριστοῦ, 2.5.4
καυθήσομαι, 3.5.26
καυχήσομαι, 3.5.26
κενόδοξοι, 3.5.26
λοιδορία θεοῦ ὁ
    κρεμάμενος, 2.3.13b–
    14
μακροθυμία, 3.5.22–23
μάχη, 3.5.19–21
ὁ ταράσσων ὑμᾶς,
    3.5.10b
οἱ ταράσσοντες ὑμᾶς,
    3.5.10b

ὁμωνύμως, 1.1.4–5
ὅτι ὕβρις θεοῦ
    κρεμάμενος, 2.3.13b–
    14
παροικία, 2.4.24b–26
πειρασθῇς, 3.6.1n
πεπιστωμένως, 1.1.4–5
πηλίκοις, 3.6.11
σίκερα, 3.5.19–21n
σκοπῶν, 3.6.1n
συγχύσις, 2.4.20
φιλονικία, 3.5.19–21
φρεναπατᾷ, 3.6.3
χρηστότης, 3.5.22–23

Hebrew

abba, 2.4.6; 3.6.18
adama, 2.3.13b–14
amen, 1.1.4–5
cephas, 1.2.11–13

chi klalat eloim talui,
    2.3.13b–14
chol, 2.3.10
galath, 1.1.6–7n

olam, 1.1.4–5
sahaq, 2.4.24b–26n
shaliah, 1.1.1n
shekhar, 3.5.19–21n